Joseph Antony Gillet

The Heavens Above

A Popular Handbook of Astronomy

(

Joseph Antony Gillet

The Heavens Above
A Popular Handbook of Astronomy

ISBN/EAN: 9783744675017

Printed in Europe, USA, Canada, Australia, Japan

Cover: Foto ©Andreas Hilbeck / pixelio.de

More available books at **www.hansebooks.com**

SPECTRA OF VARIOUS SOURCES OF LIGHT.

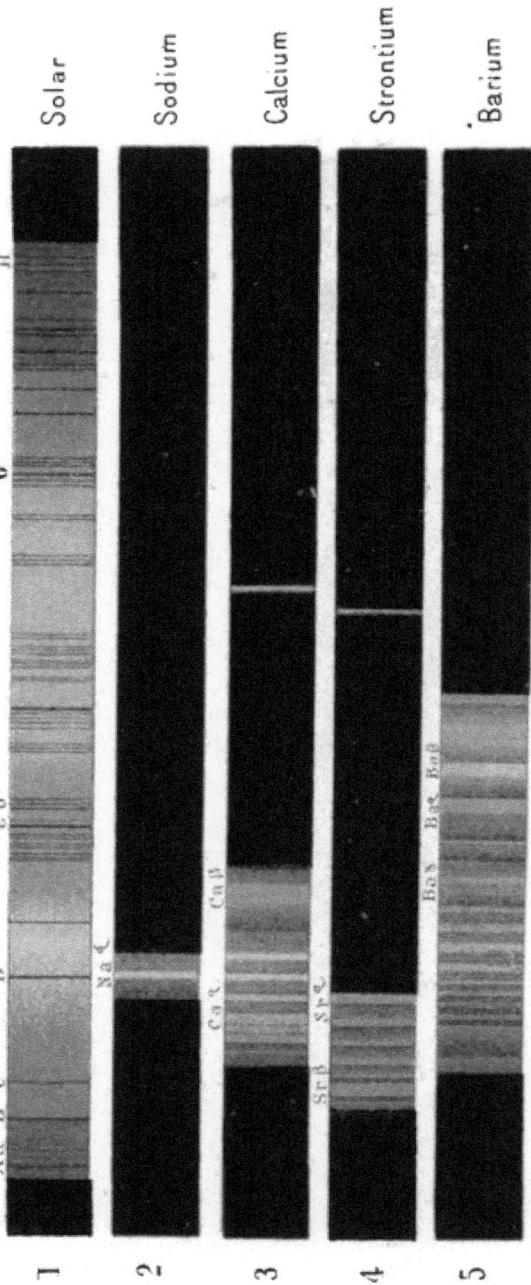

1 — Solar

2 — Sodium

3 — Calcium

4 — Strontium

5 — Barium

THE HEAVENS ABOVE:

A

POPULAR HANDBOOK OF ASTRONOMY.

BY

J. A. GILLET,

PROFESSOR OF PHYSICS IN THE NORMAL COLLEGE OF THE CITY OF NEW YORK,

AND

W. J. ROLFE,

FORMERLY HEAD MASTER OF THE HIGH SCHOOL,
CAMBRIDGE, MASS.

*WITH SIX LITHOGRAPHIC PLATES AND FOUR HUNDRED
AND SIXTY WOOD ENGRAVINGS.*

POTTER, AINSWORTH, & CO.,

NEW YORK AND CHICAGO.

1882.

PREFACE.

IT has been the aim of the authors to give in this little book a brief, simple, and accurate account of the heavens as they are known to astronomers of the present day. It is believed that there is nothing in the book beyond the comprehension of readers of ordinary intelligence, and that it contains all the information on the subject of astronomy that is needful to a person of ordinary culture. The authors have carefully avoided dry and abstruse mathematical calculations, yet they have sought to make clear the methods by which astronomers have gained their knowledge of the heavens. The various kinds of telescopes and spectroscopes have been described, and their use in the study of the heavens has been fully explained.

The cuts with which the book is illustrated have been drawn from all available sources; and it is believed that they excel in number, freshness, beauty, and accuracy those to be found in any similar work. The lithographic plates are, with a single exception, reductions of the plates prepared at the Observatory at Cambridge, Mass. The remaining lithographic plate is a reduced copy of Professor Langley's celebrated sun-spot engraving. Many of the views of the moon are from drawings made from the photographs in Carpenter and Nasmyth's work on the moon. The majority of the cuts illustrating the solar system are copied from the French edition of Guillemin's "Heavens." Most of the remainder are from Lockyer's "Solar Physics," Young's "Sun," and other recent authorities. The cuts illustrating comets, meteors, and nebulæ, are nearly all taken from the French editions of Guillemin's "Comets" and Guillemin's "Heavens."

CONTENTS.

ASTRONOMY.

ASTRONOMY.

I.

THE CELESTIAL SPHERE.

1. *The Sphere.* — A *sphere* is a solid figure bounded by a surface which curves equally in all directions at every point. The rate at which the surface curves is called the *curvature* of the sphere. The smaller the sphere, the greater is its curvature. Every point on the surface of a sphere is equally distant from a point within, called the *centre* of the sphere. The *circumference* of a sphere is the distance around its centre. The *diameter* of a sphere is the distance through its centre. The *radius* of a sphere is the distance from the surface to the centre. The surfaces of two spheres are to each other as the squares of their radii or diameters ; and the volumes of two spheres are to each other as the cubes of their radii or diameters.

Distances on the surface of a sphere are usually denoted in *degrees*. A degree is $\frac{1}{360}$ of the circumference of the sphere. The larger a sphere, the longer are the degrees on it.

A curve described about any point on the surface of a sphere, with a radius of uniform length, will be a circle. As the radius of a circle described on a sphere is a curved line, its length is usually denoted in degrees. The circle described on the surface of a sphere increases with the length of the radius, until the radius becomes 90°, in which case the circle is the largest that can possibly be described on the sphere.   The largest circles that can be described on the surface of a sphere are called *great circles*, and all other circles *small circles*.

Any number of great circles may be described on the surface of a sphere, since any point on the sphere may be used for the centre of the circle.   The plane of every great circle passes through the centre of the sphere, while the planes of all the small circles pass through the sphere away from the centre.   All great circles on the same sphere are of the same size, while the small circles differ in size according to the distance of their planes from the centre of the sphere.   The farther the plane of a circle is from the centre of the sphere, the smaller is the circle.

By a *section* of a sphere we usually mean the figure of the surface formed by the cutting : by a *plane section* we mean one

Fig. 1.

whose surface is plane.   Every plane section of a sphere is a circle.   When the section passes through the centre of the sphere, it is a great circle; in every other case the section is a small circle.   Thus, $A N$ and $S B$ (Fig. 1) are small circles, and $M M'$ and $S N$ are large circles.

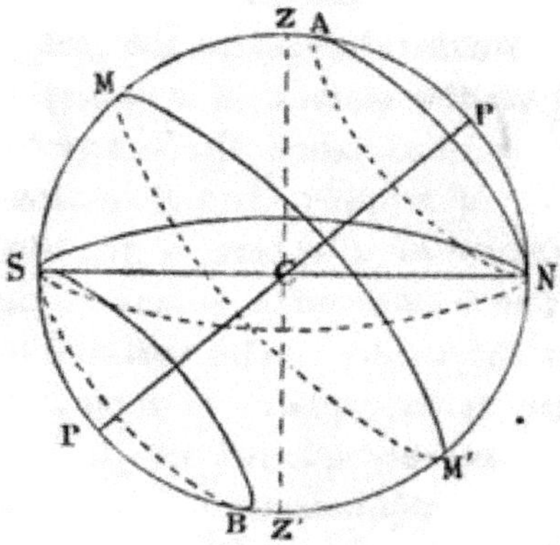

In a diagram representing a sphere in section, all the circles whose planes cut the section are represented by straight lines.   Thus, in Fig. 2. we have a diagram representing in section the sphere of Fig. 1.   The straight lines $A N$, $S B$, $M M'$, and $S N$, represent the corresponding circles of Fig. 1.

The *axis* of a sphere is the diameter on which it rotates. The *poles* of a sphere are the ends of its axis.   Thus, supposing the spheres of Figs. 1 and 2 to rotate on the diameter $P P'$, this line would be called the axis of the sphere, and the points P and P' the poles of the sphere.   A great

circle, *M M'*, situated half way between the poles of a
sphere, is called the *equator* of the sphere.

Every great circle of a sphere has two poles. These are
the two points on the sur-
face of the sphere which lie
90° away from the circle.
The poles of a sphere are
the poles of its equator.

2. *The Celestial Sphere.*
— The heavens appear to
have the form of a sphere,
whose centre is at the eye
of the observer ; and all the
stars seem to lie on the surface of this sphere. This
form of the heavens is a

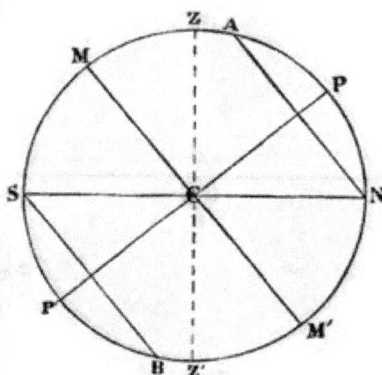
Fig. 2.

mere matter of perspective. The stars are really at very
unequal distances from us ; but they are all seen projected upon the celestial
sphere in the direc-
tion in which they
happen to lie. Thus,
suppose an observer
situated at *C* (Fig. 3).
stars situated at *a*, *b*.
d, *e*, *f*, and *g*, would
be projected upon the
sphere at *A*, *B*, *D*, *E*.
F, and *G*. and would
appear to lie on the
surface of the heav-
ens.

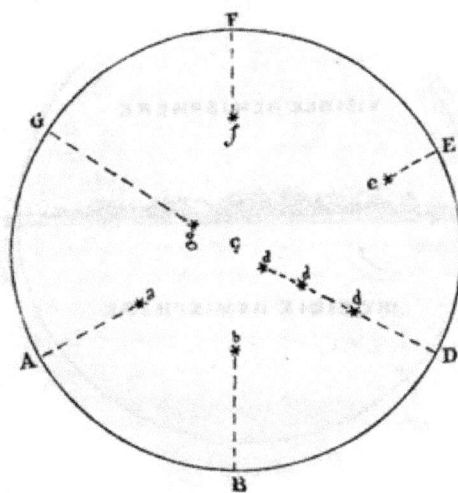
Fig. 3.

3. *The Horizon.* —
Only half of the celestial sphere is visible at a time. The
plane that separates the visible from the invisible portion is

called the *horizon*. This plane is tangent to the earth at the point of observation, and extends indefinitely into space in every direction.   In Fig. 4, *E* represents the earth, *O* the

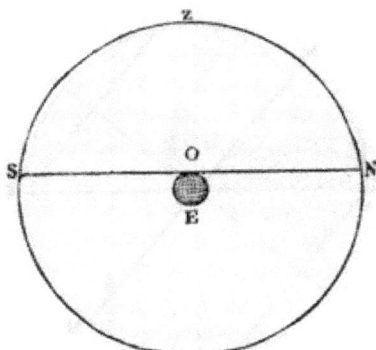

Fig. 4.

point of observation, and *S N* the horizon.   The points on the celestial sphere directly above and below the observer are the poles of the horizon. They are called respectively the *zenith* and the *nadir*.   No two observers in different parts of the earth have the same horizon ; and as a person moves over the earth he carries his horizon with him.

The dome of the heavens appears to rest on the earth, as shown in Fig. 5.   This is because distant objects on

the earth appear projected against the heavens in the direction of the horizon.

The *sensible* horizon is a plane tangent to the earth at the point of observation.   The *rational* horizon is a plane parallel with the sensible horizon, and passing through the centre of the

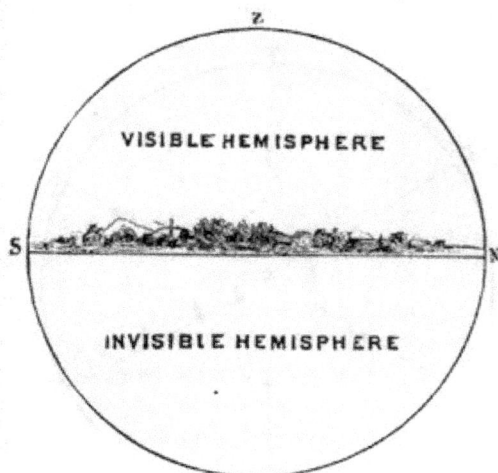

Fig. 5.

earth.   As it cuts the celestial sphere through the centre, it forms a great circle.   *S N* (Fig. 6) represents the sensible horizon, and *S' N'* the rational horizon.

Although these two horizons are really four thousand miles apart, they appear to meet at the distance of the celestial sphere ; a line four thousand miles long at the distance of the celestial sphere becoming a mere point, far too small to be detected with the most powerful telescope.

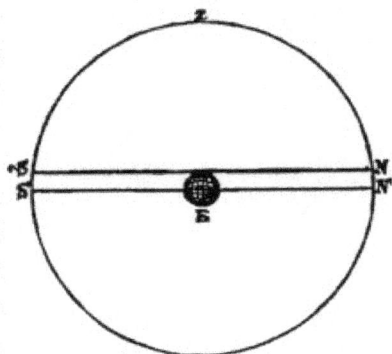

4. *Rotation of the Celestial Sphere.* — It is well known that the sun and the majority of the stars rise in the east, and set in the west. In our latitude there are

Fig. 6.

certain stars in the north which never disappear below the horizon. These stars are called the *circumpolar* stars. A close watch, however, reveals the fact that these all appear to revolve around one of their number called the *pole star*, in the direction indicated by the arrows in Fig. 7. In a word, the whole heavens appear to rotate once a day. from east to west, about an axis, which is the prolongation of the axis of the earth. The ends of this axis are called the *poles* of the heavens ; and the great circle of the

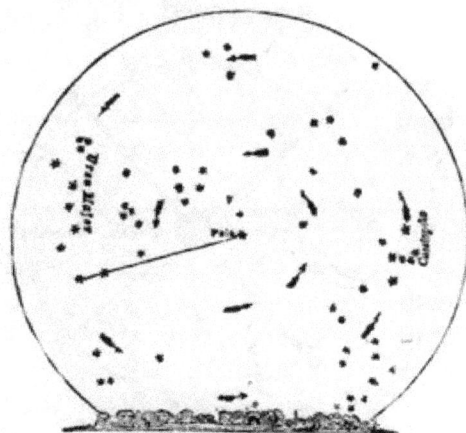

Fig. 7.

heavens, midway between these poles, is called the *celestial equator*, or the *equinoctial*. This rotation of the heavens is apparent only, being due to the rotation of the earth from west to east.

· 5. *Diurnal Circles.* — In this rotation of the heavens, the stars appear to describe circles which are perpendicular to the celestial axis, and parallel with the celestial equator. These circles are called *diurnal circles.* The position of the poles in the heavens and the direction of the diurnal circles with reference to the horizon, change with the position of the observer on the earth. This is owing to the fact that the horizon changes with the position of the observer.

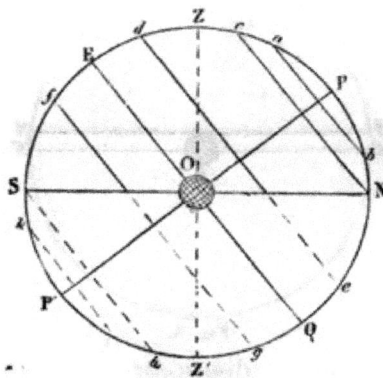

Fig. 8.

When the observer is north of the equator, the north pole of the heavens is *elevated* above the horizon, and the south pole is *depressed* below it, and the diurnal circles are *oblique* to the horizon, leaning to the south. This case is represented in Fig. 8, in which PP' represents the celestial axis, EQ the celestial equator, SN the horizon, and ab, cN, de, fg, Sh, kl, diurnal circles. O is the point of observation, Z the zenith, and Z' the nadir.

When the observer is south of the equator, as at O in Fig. 9, the south pole is *elevated*, the north pole *depressed*, and the diurnal cir-

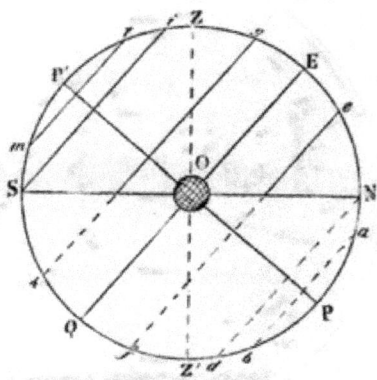

Fig. 9.

cles are *oblique* to the horizon, leaning to the north. When the diurnal circles are oblique to the horizon, as in Figs. 8 and 9. the celestial sphere is called an *oblique sphere.*

When the observer is at the equator, as in Fig. 10, the

poles of the heavens are on the horizon, and the diurnal circles are *perpendicular* to the horizon.

When the observer is at one of the poles, as in Fig. 11. the poles of the heavens are in the zenith and the nadir, and the diurnal circles are *parallel* with the horizon.

6. *Elevation of the Pole and of the Equinoctial.* — At the equator the poles of the heavens lie on the horizon, and the celestial equator passes through the zenith. As a person moves north from the equator, his

Fig. 10.

zenith moves north from the celestial equator, and his horizon moves down from the north pole, and up from the south pole. The distance of the zenith from the equinoctial, and of the horizon from the celestial poles, will always be equal to the distance of the observer from the equator. In other words, the elevation of the pole is equal to the latitude of the place. In Fig. 12, O is the point of observation. Z the zenith, and SN the horizon. NP, the elevation of the pole, is equal to ZE, the distance of the zenith from the equinoctial, and to

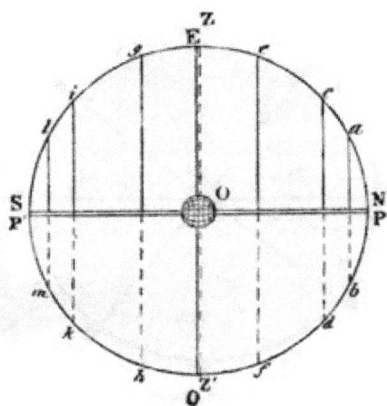

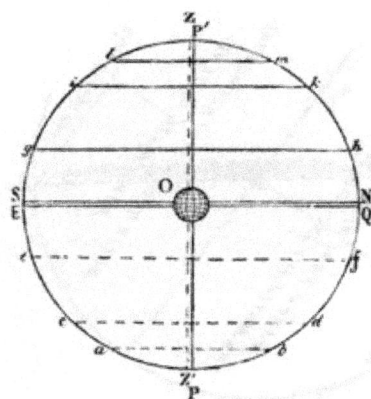

Fig. 11.

the distance of O from the equator, or the latitude of the place.

Two angles, or two arcs, which together equal 90°, are

said to be *complements* of each other. *Z E* and *E S* in
Fig. 12 are together equal to 90° : hence they are complements of each other. *Z E* is equal to the latitude of the

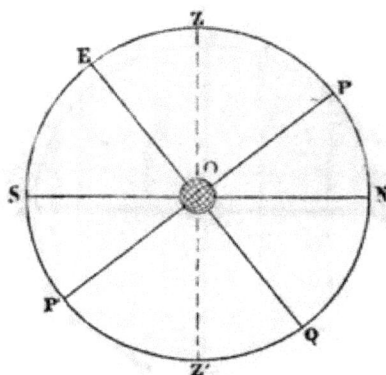

Fig. 12.

place, and *E S* is the *elevation* of the equinoctial above
the horizon : hence the elevation of the equinoctial is
equal to the complement, of
the latitude of the place.

Were the observer south
of the equator, the zenith
would be south of the equinoctial, and the south pole
of the heavens would be the
elevated pole.

7. *Four Sets of Stars.* — At most points of observation
there are four sets of stars. These four sets are shown in
Fig. 13.

(1) The stars in
the neighborhood of
the elevated pole
never set. It will
be seen from Fig.
13, that if the dis-
tance of a star from
the elevated pole
does not exceed the
elevation of the pole,
or the latitude of
the place, its diurnal
circle will be wholly
above the horizon.

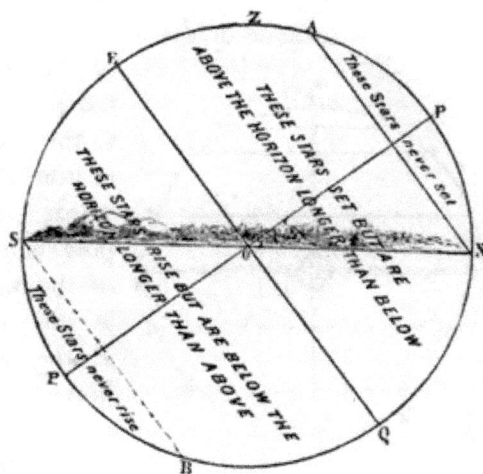

Fig. 13.

As the observer approaches the equator, the elevation of
the pole becomes less and less, and the belt of circumpolar
stars becomes narrower and narrower : at the equator it

disappears entirely.   As the observer approaches the pole.
the elevation of the pole increases, and the belt of circumpolar stars becomes broader and broader, until at the pole
it includes half of the heavens.   At the poles, no stars rise
or set, and only half of the stars are ever seen at all.

(2) The stars in the neighborhood of the depressed pole
never rise. The breadth of this belt also increases as the
observer approaches the pole, and decreases as he approaches
the equator, to vanish entirely when he reaches the equator.
The distance from the depressed pole to the margin of this
belt is always equal to the latitude of the place.

(3) The stars in the neighborhood of the equinoctial, on
the side of the elevated pole, *set, but are above the horizon
longer than they are below it.* This belt of stars extends
from the equinoctial to a point whose distance from the
elevated pole is equal to the latitude of the place : in other
words, the breadth of this third belt of stars is equal to
the complement of the latitude of the place.   Hence this
belt of stars becomes broader and broader as the observer
approaches the equator, and narrower and narrower as he
approaches the pole.   However, as the observer approaches
the equator, the horizon comes nearer and nearer the celestial axis, and the time a star is below the horizon becomes
more nearly equal to the time it is above it.   As the observer approaches the pole. the horizon moves farther and farther from the axis. and the time any star of this belt is
below the horizon becomes more and more unequal to the
time it is above it.   The farther any star of this belt is from
the equinoctial, the longer the time it is above the horizon.
and the shorter the time it is below it.

(4) The stars which are in the neighborhood of the
equinoctial, on the side of the depressed pole, *rise, but are
below the horizon longer than they are above it.* The width
of this belt is also equal to the complement of the latitude
of the place.   The farther any star of this belt is from the

equinoctial; the longer time it is below the horizon, and the shorter time it is above it; and, the farther the place from the equator, the longer every star of this belt is below the horizon, and the shorter the time it is above it.

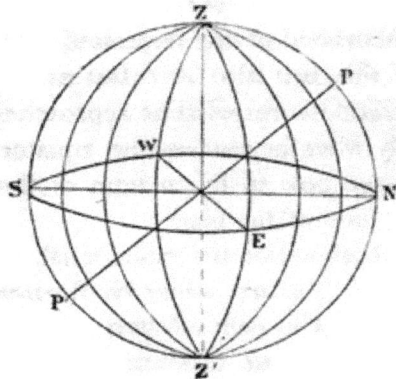

Fig. 14.

At the equator every star is above the horizon just half of the time; and any star on the equinoctial is above the horizon just half of the time in every part of the earth, since the equinoctial and horizon, being great circles, bisect each other.

8. *Vertical Circles.* — Great circles perpendicular to the horizon are called *vertical circles.* All vertical circles pass through the zenith and nadir. A number of these circles are shown in Fig. 14. in which *S E N W* represents the horizon, and *Z* the zenith.

The vertical circle which passes through the north and south points of the horizon is called the *meridian;* and the one which passes through the east and west points. the *prime vertical.* These two circles are shown in Fig. 15 ; *S Z N* being the meridian, and *E Z W* the prime vertical. These two circles are at right angles to each other,

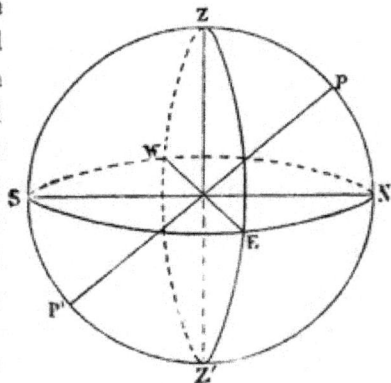

Fig. 15.

or 90° apart ; and consequently they divide the horizon into four quadrants.

9. *Altitude and Zenith Distance.* — The *altitude* of a heavenly body is its distance above the horizon, and its

zenith distance is its distance from the zenith. Both the altitude and the zenith distance of a body are measured on the vertical circle which passes through the body. The altitude and zenith distance of a heavenly body are comple· ments of each other.

10. *Azimuth and Amplitude.* — *Azimuth* is distance measured east or west from the meridian. When a heavenly body lies north of the prime vertical, its azimuth is measured from the meridian on the north; and, when it lies south of the prime vertical, its azimuth is measured from the meridian on the south. The azimuth of a body can, therefore, never exceed 90°. The azimuth of a body is the angle which the plane of the vertical circle passing through it makes with that of the meridian.

The *amplitude* of a body is its distance measured north or south from the prime vertical. The amplitude and azimuth of a body are complements of each other.

11. *Alt-azimuth Instrument.* — An instrument for measuring the altitude and azimuth of a heavenly body is called an *alt-azimuth* instrument. One form of this instrument is shown in Fig. 16. It consists essentially of a telescope mounted on a vertical circle, and capable of turning on a horizontal axis, which, in turn, is mounted on the vertical axis of a horizontal circle. Both the horizontal and the vertical circles are graduated, and the horizontal circle' is placed exactly parallel with the plane of the horizon.

When the instrument is properly adjusted, the axis of the telescope will describe a vertical circle when the telescope is turned on the horizontal axis, no matter to what part of the heavens it has been pointed.

The horizontal and vertical axes carry each a pointer. These pointers move over the graduated circles, and mark how far each axis turns.

To find the *azimuth* of a star, the instrument is turned on its vertical axis till its vertical circle is brought into the plane of the meridian, and the reading of the horizontal circle noted. The telescope is then directed to the star by turning it on both its vertical and horizontal axes. The

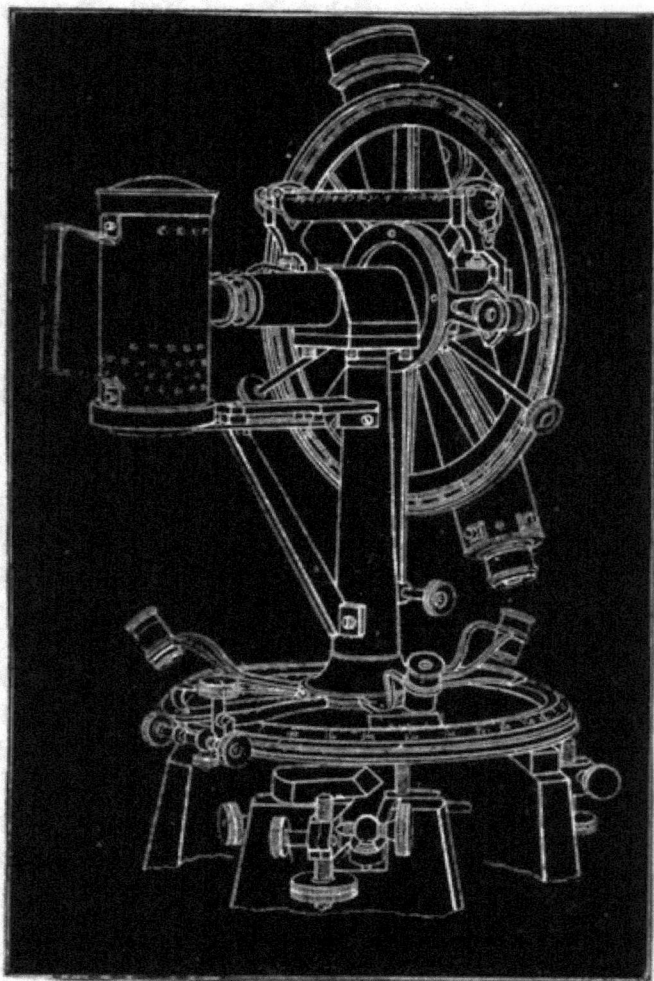

Fig. 16.

reading of the horizontal circle is again noted. The difference between these two readings of the horizontal circle will be the azimuth of the star.

To find the *altitude* of a star, the reading of the vertical circle is first ascertained when the telescope is pointed horizontally, and again when the telescope is pointed at the star. The difference between these two readings of the vertical circle will be the altitude of the star.

12. *The Vernier.*—To enable the observer to read the fractions of the divisions on the circles, a device called a *vernier* is often employed. It consists of a short, graduated arc, attached to the end of an arm c (Fig. 17), which is carried by the axis, and turns with the telescope. This arc is of the length of *nine* divisions on the circle, and it is divided into *ten* equal parts. If o of the vernier coincides with any division, say 6, of the circle, 1 of the vernier will be $\frac{1}{10}$ of a division to the left of 7, 2 will be $\frac{2}{10}$ of a division to the left of 8, 3 will be $\frac{3}{10}$ of a division to the left of 9, etc. Hence, when 1 coincides with 7, o will be at $6\frac{1}{10}$; when 2 coincides with 8, o will

Fig. 17.

be at $6\frac{2}{10}$; when 3 coincides with 9, o will be at $6\frac{3}{10}$, etc.

To ascertain the reading of the circle by means of the vernier, we first notice the zero line. If it exactly coincides with any division of the circle, the number of that division will be the reading of the circle. If there is not an exact coincidence of the zero line with any division of the circle, we run the eye along the vernier, and note which of its divisions does coincide with a division of the circle. The reading of the circle will then be the number of the first division on the circle behind the o of the vernier, and a number of tenths equal to the number of the division of the vernier, which coincides with a division of the circle. For instance, suppose o of the vernier beyond 6 of the circle, and 7 of the vernier to coincide with 13 of the circle. The reading of the circle will then be $6\frac{7}{10}$.

13. *Hour Circles.* — Great circles perpendicular to the celestial equator are called *hour circles.* These circles all pass through the poles of the heavens, as shown in Fig. 18. $E\,Q$ is the celestial equator, and P and P' are the poles of the heavens.

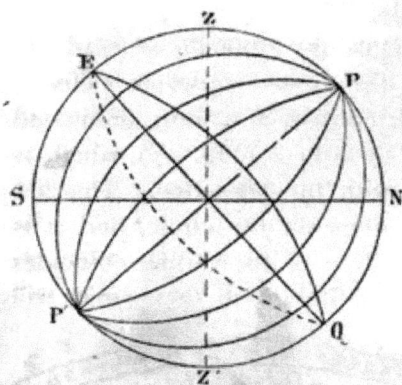

Fig. 18.

The point A on the equinoctial (Fig. 19) is called the *vernal equinox,* or the *first point of Aries.* The hour circle, $A\,P\,P'$, which passes through it, is called the *equinoctial colure.*

14. *Declination and Right Ascension.* — The *declination* of a heavenly body is its distance north or south of the celestial equator. The *polar distance* of a heavenly body is its distance from the nearer pole. Declination and polar distance are measured on hour circles, and for the same heavenly body they are complements of each other.

The *right ascension* of a heavenly body is its distance eastward from the first point of Aries, measured from the

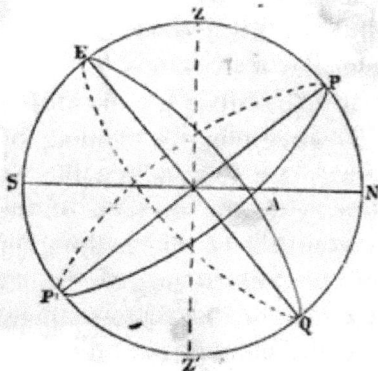

Fig. 19.

equinoctial colure. It is equal to the arc of the celestial equator included between the first point of Aries and the hour circle which passes through the heavenly body. As right ascension is measured eastward entirely around the

celestial sphere, it may have any value from 0° up to 360°.
Right ascension corresponds to longitude on the earth, and
declination to latitude.

15. *The Meridian Circle.* — The right ascension and
declination of a heavenly body are ascertained by means of
an instrument called the *meridian circle*, or *transit instrument.* A side-view of this instrument is shown in Fig. 20.

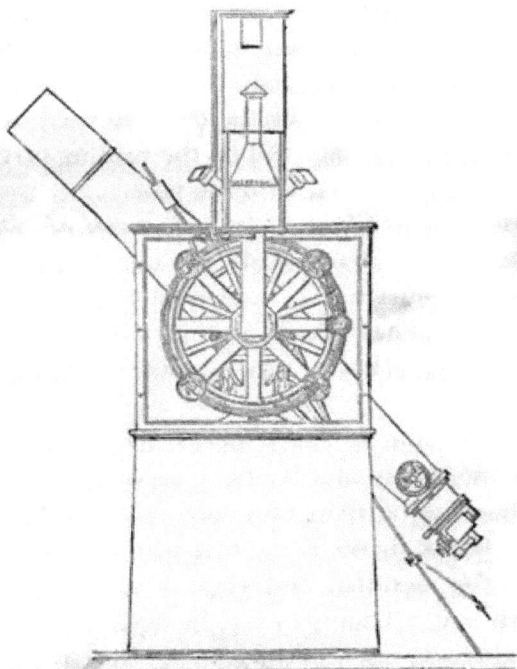

Fig. 20.

It consists essentially of a telescope mounted between two
piers, so as to turn in the plane of the meridian, and carrying a graduated circle. The readings of this circle are
ascertained by means of fixed microscopes, under which it
turns. A heavenly body can be observed with this instrument, only when it is crossing the meridian. For this reason
it is often called the *transit circle*.

To find the declination of a star with this instrument, we

first ascertain the reading of the circle when the telescope is pointed to the pole, and then the reading of the circle when pointed to the star on its passage across the meridian. The difference between these two readings will be the polar distance of the star, and the complement of them the declination of the star.

To ascertain the reading of the circle when the telescope is pointed to the pole, we must select one of the circumpolar stars near the pole, and then point the telescope to it when it crosses the meridian, both above and below the pole, and note the reading of the circle in each case. The mean of these two readings will be the reading of the circle when the telescope is pointed to the pole.

16. *Astronomical Clock.* — An *astronomical clock*, or *sidereal clock* as it is often called, is a clock arranged so as to mark hours from 1 to 24, instead of from 1 to 12, as in the case of an ordinary clock, and so adjusted as to mark o when the vernal equinox, or first point of Aries, is on the meridian.

As the first point of Aries makes a complete circuit of the heavens in twenty-four hours, it must move at the rate of 15° an hour, or of 1° in four minutes : hence, when the astronomical clock marks 1, the first point of Aries must be 15° west of the meridian, and when it marks 2, 30° west of the meridian, etc. That is to say, by observing an accurate astronomical clock, one can always tell how far the meridian at any time is from the first point of Aries.

17. *How to find Right Ascension with the Meridian Circle.* — To find the right ascension of a heavenly body. we have merely to ascertain the exact time, by the astronomical clock, at which the body crosses the meridian. If a star crosses the meridian at 1 hour 20 minutes by the astronomical clock, its right ascension must be 19° ; if at 20 hours, its right ascension must be 300°.

To enable the observer to ascertain with great exactness

the time at which a star crosses the meridian, a number of
equidistant and parallel spider-
lines are stretched across the
focus of the telescope, as shown in
Fig. 21. The observer notes the
time when the star crosses each
spider-line ; and the mean of all
of these times will be the time
when the star crosses the meridian. The mean of several observations is likely to be more nearly
exact than any single observation.

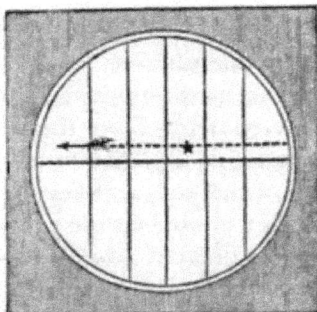

Fig. 21.

18. *The Equatorial Telescope.* — The *equatorial* telescope is mounted on
two axes, — one par-
allel with the axis of
the earth, and the
other at right angles
to this, and therefore
parallel with the plane
of the earth's equator.
The former is called
the *polar axis*, and
the latter the *declina-
tion axis*. Each axis
carries a graduated
circle. These circles
are called respective-
ly the *hour circle* and
the *declination circle*.
The telescope is at-
tached directly to
the declination axis.
When the telescope is

Fig. 22.

fixed in any declination, and then turned on its polar axis.

the line of sight will describe a diurnal circle ; so that, when
the tube is once directed to a star, it can be made to follow the star by simply turning the telescope on its polar axis.

In the case of large instruments of this class, the polar
axis is usually turned by clock-work at the rate at which the
heavens rotate : so that, when the telescope has once been
pointed to a planet or other heavenly body, it will continue to
follow the body and keep it steadily in the field of view without
further trouble on the part of the observer.

The great Washington Equatorial is shown in Fig. 22. Its
object-glass is 26 inches in diameter. and its focal length is
32½ feet. It was constructed by Alvan Clark & Sons of Cambridge, Mass. It is one of the three largest refracting telescopes at present in use. The Newall refractor at Gateshead.
Eng., has an objective 25 inches in diameter, and a focal length
of 29 feet. The great refractor at Vienna has an objective
27 inches in diameter. There are several large refractors now
in process of construction.

19. *The Wire Micrometer.* — Large arcs in the heavens
are measured by means of the graduated circles attached to

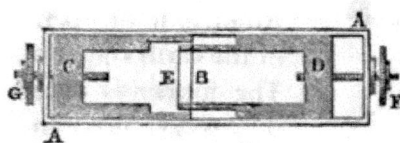

the axes of the
telescopes ; but
small arcs within
the field of view
of the telescope

Fig. 23.

are measured by means of instruments called *micrometers*,
mounted in the focus of the telescope. One of the most
convenient of these micrometers is that known as the *wire
micrometer*, and shown in Fig. 23.

The frame *A A* covers two slides, *C* and *D*. These slides
are moved by the screws *F* and *G*. The wires *E* and *B*
are stretched across the ends of the slides so as to be
parallel to each other. On turning the screws *F* and *G*
one way. these wires are carried apart ; and on turning them
the other way they are brought together again. Sometimes
two parallel wires, *x* and *y*, shown in the diagram at the

right, are stretched across the frame at right angles to the wires *E*, *B*. We may call the wires *x* and *y* the *longitudinal* wires of the micrometer, and *E* and *B* the *transverse* wires. Many instruments have only one longitudinal wire, which is stretched across the middle of the focus. The longitudinal wires are just in front of the transverse wires. but do not touch them.

To find the distance between any two points in the field of view with a micrometer, with a single longitudinal wire, turn the frame till the longitudinal wire passes through the two points ; then set the wires *E* and *B* one on each point, turn one of the screws, known as the *micrometer screw*, till the two wires are brought together. and note the number of times the screw is turned. Having previously ascertained over what arc one turn of the screw will move the wire. the number of turns will enable us to find the length of the arc between the two points.

The threads of the micrometer screw are cut with great accuracy ; and the screw is provided with a large head. which is divided into a hundred or more equal parts.

These divisions, by means of a fixed pointer, enable us to ascertain what fraction of a turn the screw has made over and above its complete revolutions.

20. *Reflecting Telescopes.* — It is possible to construct mirrors of much larger size than lenses : hence reflecting telescopes have an advantage over refracting telescopes as regards size of aperture and of light-gathering power. They are, however, inferior as regards definition ; and. in order to prevent flexure, it is necessary to give the speculum, or mirror, a massiveness which makes the telescope unwieldy. It is also necessary frequently to repolish the speculum ; and this is an operation of great delicacy, as the slightest change in the form of the surface impairs the definition of the image. These defects have been remedied, to a certain extent, by the introduction of silver-on-glass mirrors ; that is,

glass mirrors covered in front with a thin coating of silver. Glass is only one-third as heavy as speculum-metal, and silver is much superior to that metal in reflecting power; and when the silver becomes tarnished, it can be removed and renewed without danger of changing the form of the glass.

The Herschelian Reflector. — In this form of telescope the mirror is slightly tipped, so that the image, instead of being formed in the centre of the tube, is formed near one side of it, as in Fig. 24. The observer can then view it without putting his head inside the tube, and therefore without cutting off any material portion of the light. In observation, he must stand at the upper or outer end of the tube, and look into it, his back being turned towards the object. From his looking directly into the mirror, it is also sometimes called the *front-view* telescope. The great disadvantage of this ar-

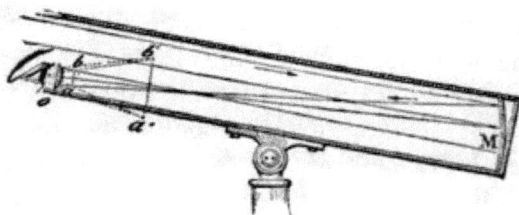

Fig. 24.

rangement is, that the rays cannot be brought to an exact focus when they are thrown so far to one side of the axis, and the injury to the definition is so great that the front-view plan is now entirely abandoned.

The Newtonian Reflector. — The plan proposed by Sir Isaac Newton was to place a small plane mirror just inside the focus, inclined to the telescope at an angle of 45°, so as to throw the rays to the side of the tube, where they come to a focus, and form the image. An opening is made in the side of the tube, just below where the image is formed; and in this opening the eye-piece is inserted. The small mirror cuts off some of the light, but not enough to be a serious defect. An improvement which lessens this defect has been made by Professor Henry Draper. The

inclined mirror is replaced by a small rectangular prism
(Fig. 25), by reflection from which the image is formed
very near the prism. A pair of lenses are then inserted in
the course of the rays, by which a second image is formed
at the opening in the side of the tube; and this second
image is viewed by an ordinary eye-piece.

The Gregorian Reflector. —This is a form proposed by

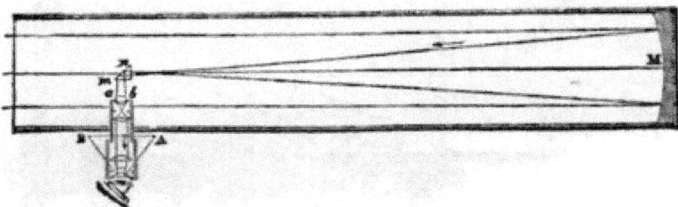

Fig. 25.

James Gregory, who probably preceded Newton as an in-
ventor of the reflecting telescope. Behind the focus, *F*
(Fig. 26), a small concave mirror, *R*, is placed, by which
the light is reflected back again down the tube. The larger
mirror, *M*, has an opening through its centre; and the small
mirror, *R*, is so adjusted as to form a second image of the
object in this opening. This image is then viewed by an
eye-piece which is screwed into the opening.

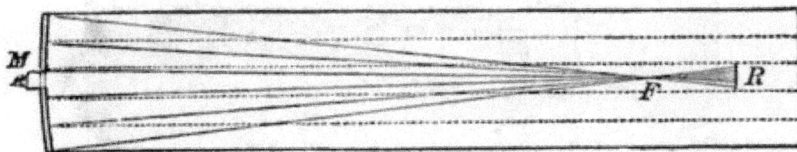

Fig. 26.

The Cassegrainian Reflector. — In principle this is the
same with the Gregorian; but the small mirror, *R*, is convex, and is placed inside the focus, *F*, so that the rays are
reflected from it before reaching the focus, and no image
is formed until they reach the opening in the large mirror.
This form has an advantage over the Gregorian, in that the

telescope may be made shorter, and the small mirror can
be more easily shaped to the required figure.   It has, therefore, entirely superseded the original Gregorian form.

Fig. 27.

Optically these forms of telescope are inferior to the
Newtonian ; but the latter is subject to the inconvenience,
that the observer must be stationed at the upper end of
the telescope, where he looks into an eye-piece screwed
into the tube.

On the other hand, the Cassegrainian Telescope is pointed directly at the object to be viewed, like a refractor ; and the observer stands at the lower end, and looks in at the opening through the large mirror. This is, therefore, the most convenient form of all in management.

Fig. 28.

The largest reflecting telescope yet constructed is that of Lord Rosse, at Parsonstown, Ireland. . Its speculum is 6 feet in diameter, and its focal length 55 feet. It is commonly used as a Newtonian. This telescope is shown in Fig. 27.

The great telescope of the Melbourne Observatory, Australia, is a Cassegranian reflector. Its speculum is 4 feet in diameter, and its focal length is 32 feet. It is shown in Fig. 28.

The great reflector of the Paris Observatory is a Newtonian

Fig. 29.

reflector. Its mirror of silvered glass is 4 feet in diameter, and its focal length is 23 feet. This telescope is shown in Fig. 29.

21. *The Sun's Motion among the Stars.* — If we notice

the stars at the same hour night after night, we shall find
that the constellations are steadily advancing towards the
west. New constellations are continually appearing in the
east, and old ones disappearing in the west. This continual
advancing of the heavens towards the west is due to the fact
that the sun's place among the stars is *continually moving
towards the east.* The sun completes the circuit of the
heavens in a year, and is therefore moving eastward at the
rate of about a degree a day.

This motion of the sun's place among the stars is due
to the revolution of
the earth around the
sun, and not to any
real motion of the
sun. In Fig. 30 sup-
pose the inner circle
to represent the orbit
of the earth around
the sun, and the outer
circle to represent the
celestial sphere. When
the earth is at *E*, the
sun's place on the
celestial sphere is at

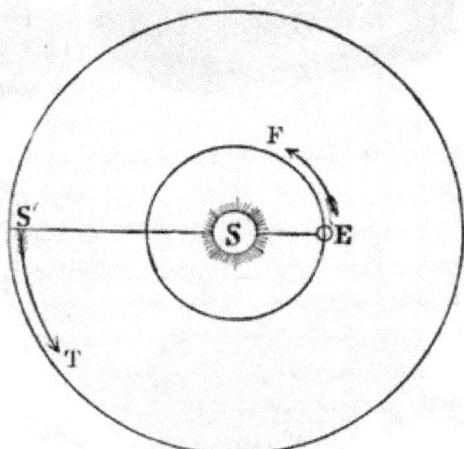

Fig. 30.

S'. As the earth moves in the direction *E F*, the sun's
place on the celestial sphere must move in the direction
S' T: hence the revolution of the earth around the sun
would cause the sun's place among the stars to move around
the heavens in the same direction that the earth is moving
around the sun.

22. *The Ecliptic.* — The circle described by the sun in
its apparent motion around the heavens is called the *ecliptic.*
The plane of this circle passes through the centre of the
earth, and therefore through the centre of the celestial
sphere : the earth being so small, compared with the celes-

tial sphere, that it practically makes no difference whether
we consider a point on its surface, or one at its centre, as
the centre of the celestial sphere. The ecliptic is, therefore,
a great circle.

The earth's orbit lies in the plane of the ecliptic; but it
extends only an inappreciable distance from the sun towards
the celestial sphere.

Fig. 31.

**23. The Obliquity of the
Ecliptic.** — The ecliptic is inclined to the celestial equator
by an angle of about $23\frac{1}{2}°$.
This inclination is called the
obliquity of the ecliptic. The
obliquity of the ecliptic is due
to the deviation of the earth's axis from a perpendicular to
the plane of its orbit. The axis of a rotating body tends
to maintain the same direction; and, as the earth revolves
around the sun, its axis points all the time in nearly the
same direction. The earth's axis deviates about $23\frac{1}{2}°$ from
the perpendicular to its orbit; and, as the earth's equator is
at right angles to its axis, it
will deviate about $23\frac{1}{2}°$ from
the plane of the ecliptic.
The celestial equator has the
same direction as the terrestrial equator, since the axis
of the heavens has the same
direction as the axis of the
earth.

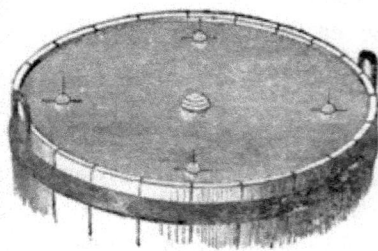

Fig. 32.

Suppose the globe at the centre of the tub (Fig. 31) to
represent the sun, and the smaller globes to represent the
earth in various positions in its orbit. The surface of the
water will then represent the plane of the ecliptic, and
the rod projecting from the top of the earth will represent
the earth's axis, which is seen to point all the time in the

same direction, or to lean the same way. The leaning of the axis from the perpendicular to the surface of the water would cause the earth's equator to be inclined the same amount to the surface of the water, half of the equator being above, and half of it below, the surface. Were the axis of the earth perpendicular to the surface of the water, the earth's equator would coincide with the surface, as is evident from Fig. 32.

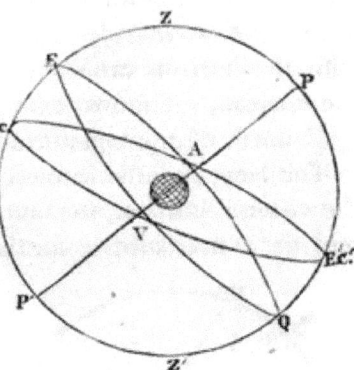

Fig. 33.

24. *The Equinoxes and Solstices.* — The ecliptic and celestial equator, being great circles, bisect each other. Half of the ecliptic is north, and half of it is south, of the equator. The points at which the two circles cross are called the *equinoxes.* The one at which the sun crosses the equator from south to north is called the *vernal* equinox, and the one at which it crosses from north to south the *autumnal* equinox. The points on the ecliptic midway between the equinoxes are called the *solstices.* The one north of the equator is called the *summer* solstice, and the one south of the equator the *winter* solstice. In Fig. 33. F Q is the celestial equator, E c E' c' the ecliptic, V the vernal equinox, A the autumnal equinox, E c the winter solstice, and E' c' the summer solstice.

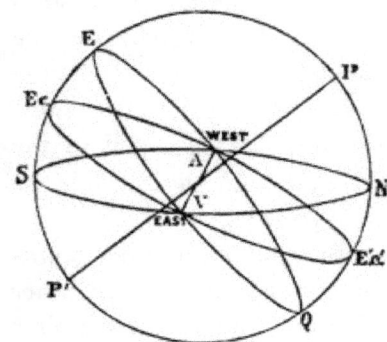

Fig. 34.

25. *The Inclination of the Ecliptic to the Horizon.* — Since the celestial equator is perpendicular to the axis of

the heavens, it makes the same angle with it on every side : hence, at any place, the equator makes always the same angle with the horizon, whatever part of it is above the horizon.   But, as the ecliptic is oblique to the equator, it makes different angles with the celestial axis on different sides ; and hence, at any place, the angle which the ecliptic makes with the horizon varies according to the part which is above the horizon.   The two extreme angles for a place more than $23\frac{1}{2}°$ north of the equator are shown in Figs. 34 and 35.

The least angle is formed when the vernal equinox is on the eastern horizon, the autumnal on the western horizon, and the winter solstice on the meridian, as in Fig. 34.   The angle which the ecliptic then makes with the horizon is equal to the elevation of the equinoctial *minus* $23\frac{1}{2}°$.   In the latitude of New York this angle $= 49° - 23\frac{1}{2}° = 25\frac{1}{2}°$.

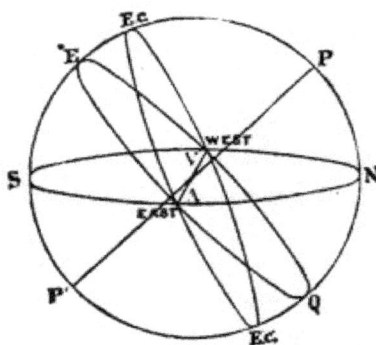

Fig. 35.

The greatest angle is formed when the autumnal equinox is on the eastern horizon, the vernal on the western horizon, and the summer solstice is on the meridian (Fig. 35).   The angle between the ecliptic and the horizon is then equal to the elevation of the equinoctial *plus* $23\frac{1}{2}°$.   In the latitude of New York this angle $= 49° + 23\frac{1}{2}° = 72\frac{1}{2}°$.

Of course the equinoxes, the solstices, and all other points on the ecliptic, describe diurnal circles, like every other point in the heavens ; hence, in our latitude, these points rise and set every day.

26. *Celestial Latitude and Longitude.* — *Celestial latitude* is distance measured north or south from the ecliptic ; and *celestial longitude* is distance measured on the ecliptic eastward from the vernal equinox, or the first point of

Aries. Great circles perpendicular to the ecliptic are called *celestial meridians.* These circles all pass through the poles of the ecliptic, which are some $23\frac{1}{2}°$ from the poles of the equinoctial. The latitude of a heavenly body is measured by the arc of a celestial meridian included between the body and the ecliptic. The longitude of a heavenly body is measured by the arc of the ecliptic included between the first point of Aries and the meridian which passes through the body. There are, of course, always two arcs included between the first point of Aries and the meridian, — one on the east, and the other on the west, of the first point of Aries. The one on the *east* is always taken as the measure of the longitude.

27. *The Precession of the Equinoxes.* — The equinoctial points have a slow westward motion along the ecliptic. This motion is at the rate of about $50''$ a year, and would cause the equinoxes to make a complete circuit of the heavens in a period of about twenty-six thousand

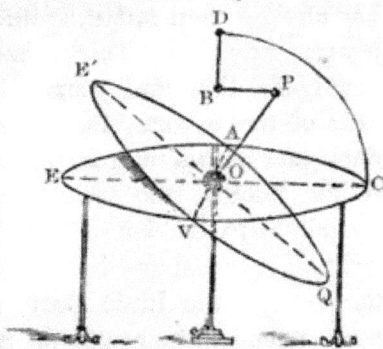

Fig. 36.

years. It is called the *precession of the equinoxes.* This westward motion of the equinoxes is due to the fact that the axis of the earth has a slow gyratory motion, like the handle of a spinning-top which has begun to wabble a little. This gyratory motion causes the axis of the heavens to describe a cone in about twenty-six thousand years, and the pole of the heavens to describe a circle about the pole of the ecliptic in the same time. The radius of this circle is $23\frac{1}{2}°$.

28. *Illustration of Precession.* — The precession of the equinoxes may be illustrated by means of the apparatus shown in Fig. 36. The horizontal and stationary ring $E\,C$ represents

the ecliptic; the oblique ring $E'Q$ represents the equator; V and A represent the equinoctial point, and E and C the solstitial points; B represents the pole of the ecliptic, P the pole of the equator, and PO the celestial axis. The ring $E'Q$ is supported on a pivot at O; and the rod BP, which connects B and P, is jointed at each end so as to admit of the movement of P and B.

On carrying P around B, we shall see that $E'Q$ will always preserve the same obliquity to EC, and that the points V and A will move around the circle EC. The same will also be true of the points E and C.

29. *Effects of Precession.* — One effect of precession, as has already been stated, is the revolution of the pole of the heavens around the pole of the ecliptic in a period of about twenty-six thousand years. The circle described by the pole of the heavens, and the position of the pole at various dates, are shown in Fig. 37, where o indicates the position of the pole at the birth of Christ. The numbers round the circle to the left of o are dates A.D., and those to the right of o are dates B.C. It will be seen that the star at the end of the Little Bear's tail, which is now near the north pole, will be exactly at the pole about the year 2000. It will then recede farther and farther from the pole till the year 15000 A.D., when it will be about forty-seven degrees away from the pole. It will be noticed that one of the stars of the Dragon was the pole star about 2800 years B.C. There are reasons to suppose that this was about the time of the building of the Great Pyramid.

A second effect of precession is the shifting of the signs along the zodiac. The *zodiac* is a belt of the heavens along the ecliptic, extending eight degrees from it on each side. This belt is occupied by twelve constellations, known as the *zodiacal constellations*. They are *Aries, Taurus, Gemini. Cancer, Leo, Virgo, Libra, Scorpio, Sagittarius, Capricornus, Aquarius*, and *Pisces*. The zodiac is also

divided into twelve equal parts of thirty degrees each, called
signs. These signs have the same names as the twelve
zodiacal constellations, and when they were first named,
each sign occupied the same part of the zodiac as the corresponding constellation ; that is to say, the sign Aries was
in the constellation Aries, and the sign Taurus in the con-

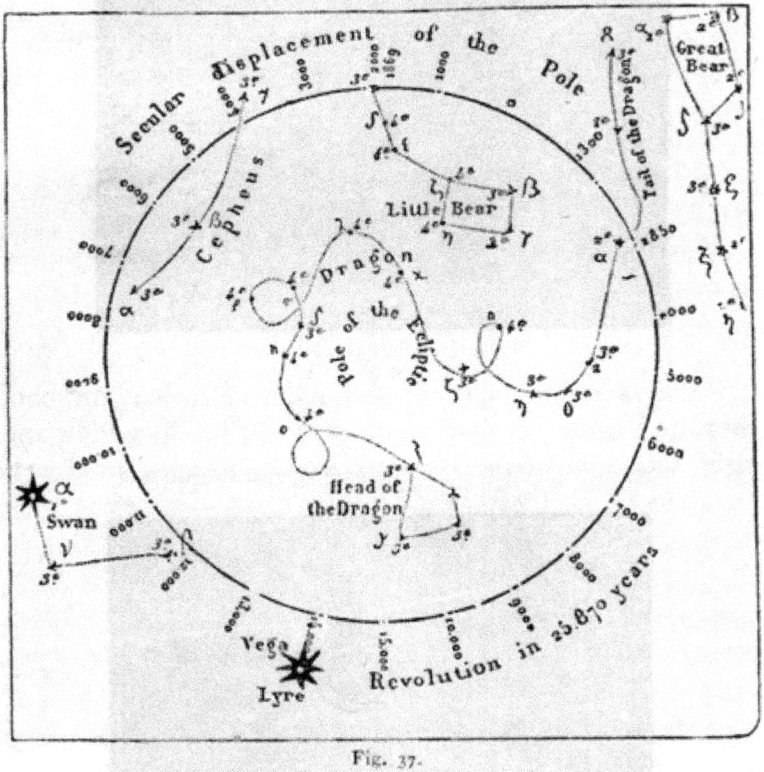

Fig. 37.

stellation Taurus, etc. Now the signs are always reckoned
as beginning at the vernal equinox, which is continually
shifting along the ecliptic ; so that the signs are continually
moving along the zodiac, while the constellations remain
stationary : hence it has come about that the *first point of
Aries* (the *sign*) is no longer in the *constellation* Aries, but
in Pisces.

Fig. 38 shows the position of the vernal equinox 2170 B.C. It was then in Taurus, just south of the Pleiades. It has since moved from Taurus, through Aries, and into Pisces, as shown in Fig. 39.

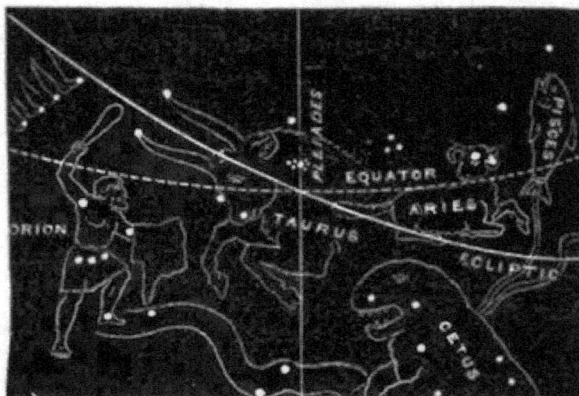

Fig. 38.

Since celestial longitude and right ascension are both measured from the first point of Aries, the longitude and right ascension of the stars are slowly changing from year

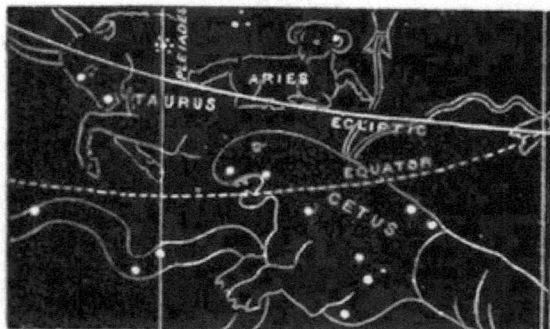

Fig. 39.

to year. It will be seen, from Figs. 38 and 39, that the declination is also slowly changing.

30. *Nutation.* — The gyratory motion of the earth's axis is not perfectly regular and uniform. The earth's axis has

a slight tremulous motion, oscillating to and fro through a short distance once in about nineteen years. This tremulous motion of the axis causes the pole of the heavens to describe an undulating curve, as shown in Fig. 40, and gives a slight unevenness to the motion of the equinoxes along the ecliptic. This nodding motion of the axis is called *nutation*.

31. *Refraction.* — When a ray of light from one of the heavenly bodies enters the earth's atmosphere obliquely, it will be bent towards a perpendicular to the surface of the atmosphere, since it will be entering a denser medium. As the ray traverses the

Fig. 40.

atmosphere, it will be continually passing into denser and denser layers, and will therefore be bent more and more towards the perpendicular. This bending of the ray is shown in Fig. 41. A ray which started from *A* would enter the eye at *C*, as if it came from *I*: hence a star at *A* would appear to be at *I*.

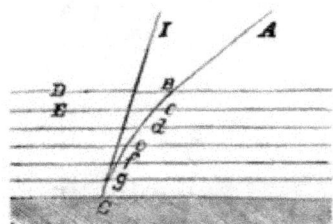

Atmospheric refraction displaces all the heavenly bodies from the horizon towards the zenith. This is evident from Fig. 42. *O D* is the horizon. and *Z* the zenith, of an observer at *O*. Refraction would make a star at *Q* appear at *P*: in other words, it would displace it towards the zenith. A star in the zenith is not displaced by the zenith is not displaced by

Fig. 41.

refraction, since the rays which reach the eye from it traverse the atmosphere vertically. The farther a star is from the zenith, the more it is displaced by refraction, since the greater is the obliquity with which the rays from it enter the atmosphere.

At the horizon the displacement by refraction is about

half a degree ; but it varies considerably with the state of
the atmosphere. Refraction causes a heavenly body to

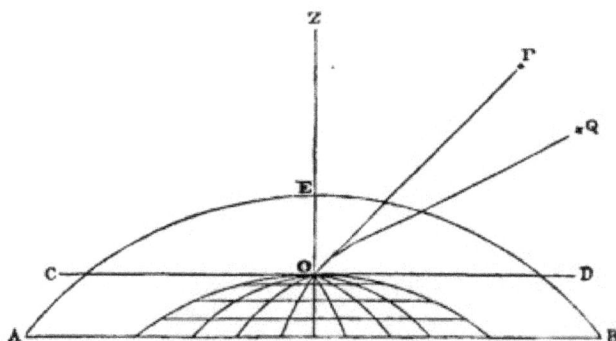

Fig. 42.

appear above the horizon longer than it really is above it.
since it makes it appear to be on the horizon when it is
really half a degree below it.

Fig. 43.

The increase of refraction towards the horizon often
makes the sun, when near the horizon, appear distorted,

the lower limb of the sun being raised more than the upper limb. This distortion is shown in Fig. 43. The vertical diameter of the sun appears to be considerably less than the horizontal diameter.

32. *Parallax.* — *Parallax* is the displacement of an object caused by a change in the point of view from which it is seen. Thus in Fig. 44, the top of the tower S would be seen projected against the sky at a by an observer at A, and at b by an observer at B. In passing from A to B, the top of the tower is displaced from a to b, or by the

Fig. 44.

angle $a\,S\,b$. This angle is called the parallax of S, as seen from B instead of A.

The *geocentric parallax* of a heavenly body is its displacement caused by its being seen from the surface of the earth, instead of from the centre of the earth. In Fig. 45, R is the centre of the earth, and O the point of observation on the surface of the earth. Stars at S, S', and S'', would, from the centre of the earth, appear at Q, Q', and Q''; while from the point O on the surface of the earth, these same stars would appear at P, P', and P'', being displaced from their position, as seen from the centre of the earth, by the angles QSP, $Q'S'P'$, and $Q''S''P''$. It will be seen that parallax displaces a body from the zenith towards the horizon, and that the parallax of a body is greatest when it is on the horizon. The parallax of a heavenly body when on the horizon is called its *horizontal parallax*. A body in the zenith is not displaced by parallax, since it would be seen in the same direction from both the centre and the surface of the earth.

The parallax of a body at S''' is $Q'''S'''P$, which is seen to be greater than QSP; that is to say, the parallax of a heavenly body increases with its nearness to the earth. The

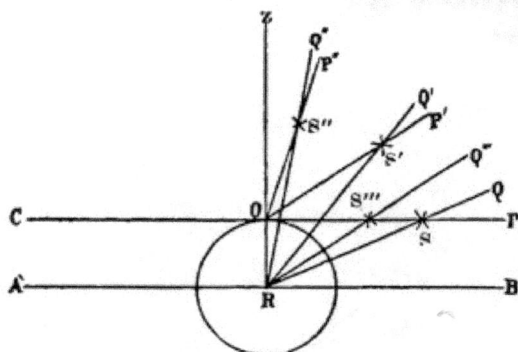

Fig. 45.

distance and parallax of a body are so related, that, either being known, the other may be computed.

33. *Aberration.* — *Aberration* is a slight displacement of a star, owing to an apparent change in the direction of the rays of light which proceed from it, caused by the motion of the earth in its orbit. If we walk rapidly in any direction in the rain, when the drops are falling vertically, they will appear to come into our faces from the direction in which we are walking. Our own motion has apparently changed the direction in which the drops are falling.

In Fig. 46 let A be a gun of a battery, from which a shot is fired at a ship, DE, that is passing. Let ABC be the course of the shot. The shot enters the ship's side at B, and passes out at the other side at C; but in the mean time the ship has moved from E to e, and the part B, where the shot entered, has been carried to b. If a person on board the ship could see the ball as it crossed the ship, he would see it cross in the diagonal line *bC;* and he would at once say that the cannon was in the direction of *Cb*. If the ship were moving in the opposite direction, he would say that the cannon was just as far the other side of its true position.

Now, we see a star in the direction in which the light coming from the star appears to be moving. When we examine a star with a telescope, we are in the same condition as the person who on shipboard saw the cannon-ball cross the ship. The telescope is carried along by the earth

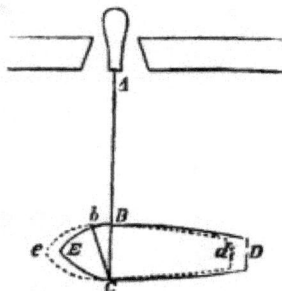

Fig. 46.

at the rate of eighteen miles a second; hence the light will appear to pass through the tube in a slightly different direction from that in which it is really moving: just as the cannon-ball appears to pass through the ship in a different direction from that in which it is really moving. Thus in Fig. 47. a ray of light coming in the direction *S O T* would appear to traverse the tube *O T* of a telescope, moving in the direction of the arrow, as if it were coming in the direction *S' O*.

As light moves with enormous velocity, it passes through the tube so quickly, that it is apparently changed from its true direction only by a very slight angle; but it is sufficient to displace the star. This apparent change in the direction of light caused by the motion of the earth is called *aberration of light*.

Fig. 47.

34. *The Planets.* — On watching the stars attentively night after night, it will be found, that while the majority of them appear *fixed* on the surface of the celestial sphere, so as to maintain their relative positions, there are a few that *wander* about among the stars, alternately advancing towards the east, halting, and retrograding towards the west. These wandering stars are called *planets*.

Their motions appear quite irregular; but, on the whole,

their eastward motion is in excess of their westward. and in
a longer or shorter time they all complete the circuit of the
heavens.   In almost every instance, their paths are found to
lie wholly in the belt of the zodiac.

Fig. 48.

Fig. 48 shows a portion of the apparent path of one of
the planets.

II.

THE SOLAR SYSTEM.

I. THEORY OF THE SOLAR SYSTEM.

35. *Members of the Solar System.* — The solar system is composed of the *sun, planets, moons, comets,* and *meteors.* Five planets, besides the earth, are readily distinguished by the naked eye, and were known to the ancients: these are *Mercury, Venus, Mars, Jupiter,* and *Saturn.* These, with the *sun* and *moon,* made up the *seven planets* of the ancients, from which the seven days of the week were named.

THE PTOLEMAIC SYSTEM.

36. *The Crystalline Spheres.* — We have seen that all the heavenly bodies appear to be situated on the surface of the celestial sphere. The ancients assumed that the stars were really fixed on the surface of a crystalline sphere, and that they were carried around the earth daily by the rotation of this sphere. They had, however, learned to distinguish the planets from the stars, and they had come to the conclusion that some of the planets were nearer the earth than others, and that all of them were nearer the earth than the stars are. This led them to imagine that the heavens were composed of a number of crystalline spheres, one above another, each carrying one of the planets, and all revolving around the earth from east to west, but at different rates. This structure of the heavens is shown in section in Fig. 49.

41

37. *Cycles and Epicycles.* — The ancients had also noticed that, while all the planets move around the heavens from west to east, their motion is not one of uniform advancement. Mercury and Venus appear to oscillate to and fro across the sun, while Jupiter and Saturn appear to oscillate to and fro across a centre which is moving around the earth, so as to describe a series of loops, as shown in Fig. 50.

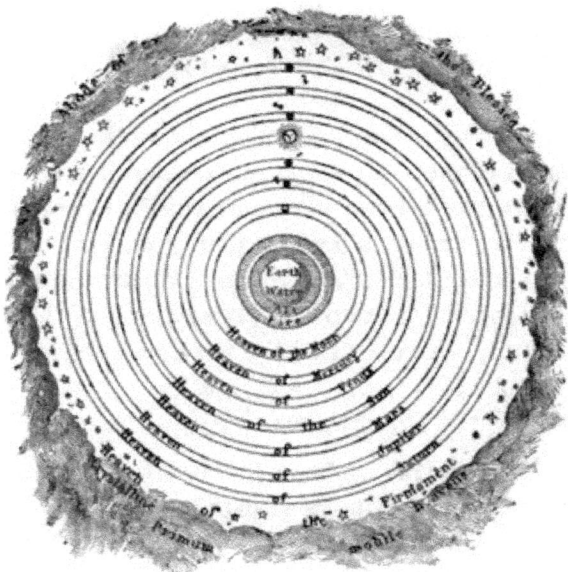

Fig. 49.

The ancients assumed that the planets moved in exact circles, and, in fact. that all motion in the heavens was circular, the circle being the simplest and most perfect curve. To account for the loops described by the planets, they imagined that each planet revolved in a circle around a centre, which, in turn, revolved in a circle around the earth. The circle described by this centre around the earth they called the *cycle*, and the circle described by the planet around this centre they called the *epicycle*.

38. *The Eccentric.* — The ancients assumed that the planets moved at a uniform rate in describing the epicycle, and also the centre in describing the cycle. They had, however, discovered that the planets advance eastward more rapidly in some parts of their orbits than in others. To

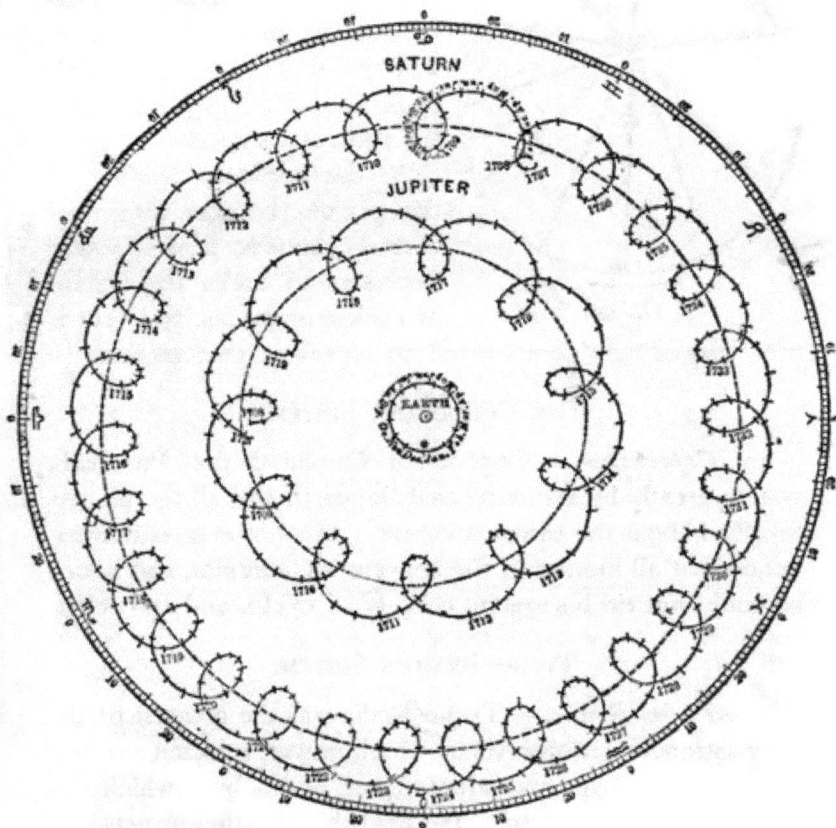

Fig. 50.

account for this they assumed that the cycles described by the centre, around which the planets revolved, were *eccentric;* that is to say, that the earth was not at the centre of the cycle, but some distance away from it, as shown in Fig. 51. *E* is the position of the earth, and *C* is the centre of the cycle. The lines from E are drawn so as to intercept equal arcs of the cycle. It will be seen at once that the angle between any pair of lines is greatest at P, and

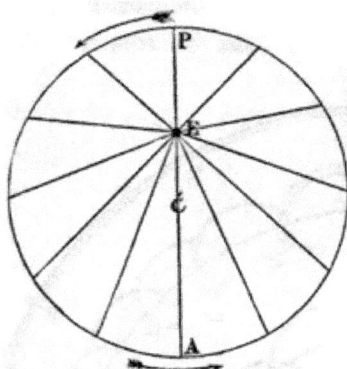

Fig. 51.

least at A; so that, were a planet moving at the same rate at P and A, it would seem to be moving much faster at P. The point P of the planet's cycle was called its *perigee*, and the point A its *apogee*.

As the apparent motion of the planets became more accurately known, it was found necessary to make the system of cycles, epicycles, and eccentrics exceedingly complicated to represent that motion.

THE COPERNICAN SYSTEM.

39. *Copernicus.* — Copernicus simplified the Ptolemaic system greatly by assuming that the earth and all the planets revolved about the sun as a centre. He, however, still maintained that all motion in the heavens was circular, and hence he could not rid his system entirely of cycles and epicycles.

TYCHO BRAHE'S SYSTEM.

40. *Tycho Brahe.* — Tycho Brahe was the greatest of the early astronomical observers. He, however, rejected the system of Copernicus, and adopted one of his own, which was much more complicated. He held that all the planets but the earth revolved around the sun, while the sun and moon revolved around the earth. This system is shown in Fig. 52.

KEPLER'S SYSTEM.

41. *Kepler.* — While Tycho Brahe devoted his life to the observation of the planets, Kepler gave his to the study

of Tycho's observations, for the purpose of discovering the true laws of planetary motion. He banished the complicated system of cycles, epicycles, and eccentrics forever from the heavens, and discovered the three laws of planetary motion which have rendered his name immortal.

42. *The Ellipse.* — An *ellipse* is a closed curve which has two points within it, the sum of whose distances from every point on the curve is the same. These two points are called the *foci* of the ellipse.

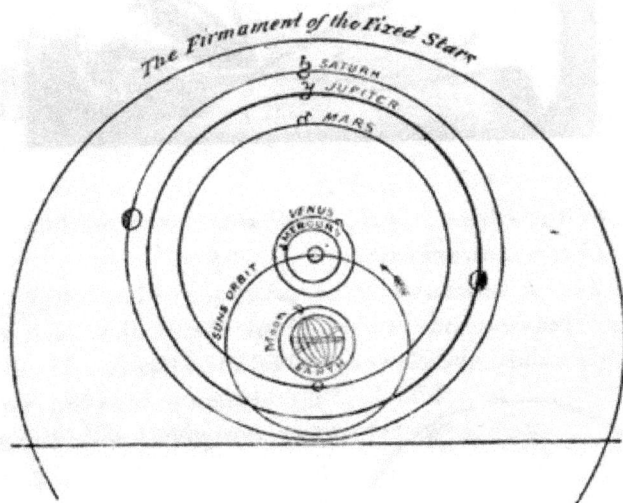

Fig. 52.

One method of describing an ellipse is shown in Fig. 53. Two tacks, F and F', are stuck into a piece of paper, and to these are fastened the two ends of a string which is longer than the distance between the tacks. A pencil is then placed against the string, and carried around, as shown in the figure. The curve described by the pencil is an ellipse. The two points F and F' are the foci of the ellipse: the sum of the distances of these two points from every point on the curve is equal to the length of the string. When half of the ellipse has been described, the pencil must be held against the other side of the string in the same way, and carried around as before.

The point *O*, half way between *F* and *F'*, is called the

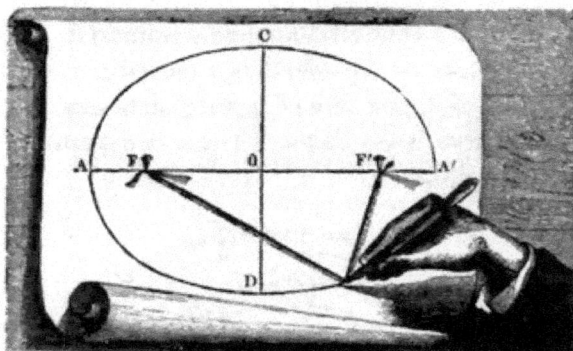

Fig. 53.

centre of the ellipse ; *A A'* is the *major axis* of the ellipse, and *C D* is the *minor axis*.

43. *The Eccentricity of the Ellipse.* — The ratio of the distance between the two foci to the major axis of the ellipse is called the *eccentricity* of the ellipse. The greater

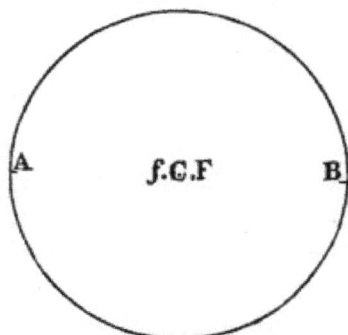

Fig. 54.

the distance between the two foci, compared with the major axis of the ellipse, the greater is the eccentricity of the ellipse ; and the less the distance between the foci, compared with the length of the major axis, the less the eccentricity of the ellipse. The ellipse of Fig. 54 has an eccentricity of $\frac{1}{8}$. This ellipse scarcely differs in appearance from a circle. The ellipse of Fig. 55 has an eccentricity of $\frac{1}{2}$, and that of Fig. 56 an eccentricity of $\frac{7}{8}$.

44. *Kepler's First Law.* — Kepler first discovered that *all the planets move from west to east in ellipses which have*

the sun as a common focus. This law of planetary motion is known as *Kepler's First Law.* The planets appear to describe loops, because we view them from a moving point.

The ellipses described by the planets differ in eccentricity ; and, though they all have one focus at the sun, their major axes have different directions. The eccentricity of the planetary orbits is comparatively small. The ellipse of Fig. 54 has seven times the eccentricity of the earth's orbit, and twice that of the orbit of any of the larger planets except Mercury ; and its eccentricity is more than half of that of the orbit of Mercury. Owing to their small eccentricity, the orbits of

Fig. 55.

the planets are usually represented by circles in astronomical diagrams.

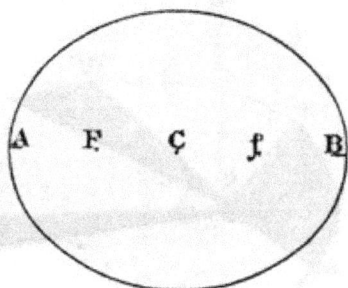

45. *Kepler's Second Law.* — Kepler next discovered that a planet's rate of motion in the various parts of its orbit is such that *a line drawn from the planet to the sun would always sweep over equal areas in equal times.* Thus, in Fig. 57, suppose the planet would move from *P* to *P*¹ in the same time that it would move from *P*² to *P*³, or from *P*⁴ to *P*⁵; then the dark spaces, which would be swept over by a line joining the sun and the planet, in these equal times. would all be equal.

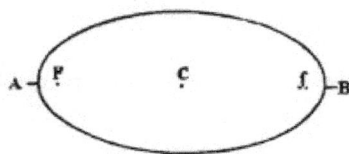

Fig. 56.

A line drawn from the sun to a planet is called the *radius vector* of the planet. The radius vector of a planet is shortest when the planet is nearest the sun, or at *perihelion*, and longest when the planet is farthest from the sun, or at *aphelion :* hence, in order to have the areas equal, it follows that a planet must move fastest when at perihelion. and slowest at aphelion.

Kepler's Second Law of planetary motion is usually stated as follows : *The radius vector of a planet describes equal areas in equal times in every part of the planet's orbit.*

46. *Kepler's Third Law.* — Kepler finally discovered that the periodic times of the planets bear the following relation to the distances of the planets from the sun : *The squares of the periodic times of the planets are to each other as the cubes of their mean distances from the sun.* This is known as *Kepler's Third Law* of planetary motion. By *periodic time* is meant the time it takes a planet to revolve around the sun.

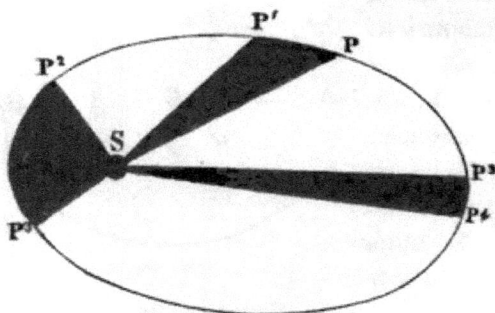

Fig. 57.

These three laws of Kepler's are the foundation of modern physical astronomy.

THE NEWTONIAN SYSTEM.

47. *Newton's Discovery.* — Newton followed Kepler, and by means of his three laws of planetary motion made his own immortal discovery of the *law of gravitation.* This law is as follows : *Every portion of matter in the universe attracts every other portion with a force varying directly as the product of the masses acted upon, and inversely as the square of the distances between them.*

48. *The Conic Sections.* — The *conic sections* are the figures formed by the various plane sections of a right cone. There are four classes of figures formed by these sections,

according to the angle which the plane of the section makes with the axis of the cone.

OPQ, Fig. 58, is a right cone, and ON is its axis. Any section, AB, of this cone, whose plane is perpendicular to the axis of the cone, is a *circle*.

Any section, CD, of this cone, whose plane is oblique to the axis, but forms with it an angle greater than NOP, is an *ellipse*. The less the angle which the plane of the section makes with the axis, the more elongated is the ellipse.

Any section, EF, of this cone, whose plane makes with the axis an angle equal to NOP, is a *parabola*. It will be seen, that, by changing the obliquity of the plane CD to the axis NO, we may pass uninterruptedly from the circle through ellipses of greater and greater elongation to the parabola.

Any section, GH, of this cone, whose plane makes with the axis ON an angle less than NOP, is a *hyperbola*.

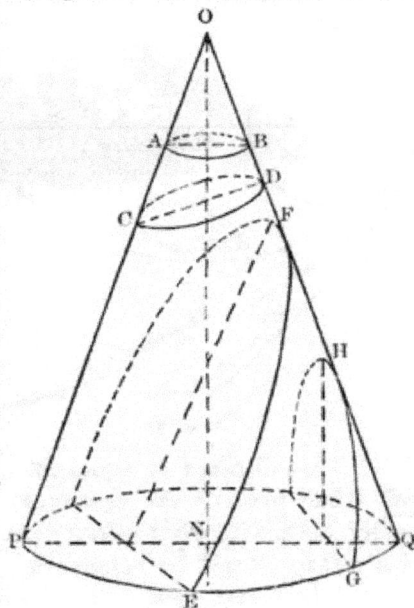

Fig. 58.

It will be seen from Fig. 59, in which comparative views of the four conic sections are given, that the circle and the ellipse are *closed* curves, or curves which return into themselves. The parabola and the hyperbola are, on the contrary, *open* curves, or curves which do not return into themselves.

49. *A Revolving Body is continually Falling towards its Centre of Revolution.* — In Fig. 60 let M represent the moon,

and E the earth around which the moon is revolving in the direction MN. It will be seen that the moon, in moving from M to N, falls towards the earth a distance equal to mN. It is kept from falling into the earth by its orbital motion.

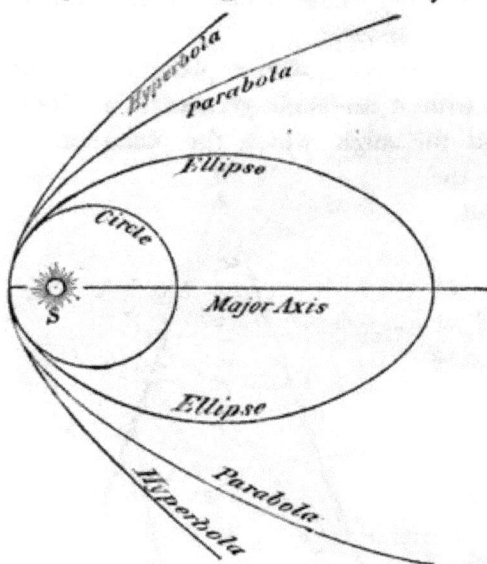

The fact that a body might be projected forward fast enough to keep it from falling into the earth is evident from Fig. 61. AB represents the level surface of the ocean, C a mountain from the summit of which a cannon-ball is supposed to be fired in the direction CE. AD is a line parallel with CE; DB is a line equal to the distance between the two parallel lines AD and CE. This distance is equal to that over which gravity would pull a ball towards the centre of the earth in a minute. No matter, then, with what velocity the ball C is fired, at the end of a minute it will be somewhere on the line AD. Suppose it were fired fast enough to reach the point D in a minute: it would be on the line AD at the end of the minute, but still just as far from the surface of the water as when it started. It will be seen, that, although it has all the while been falling towards the earth, it has all the while kept at exactly the same distance from the surface. The same thing would of course be true during each succeeding minute, till the ball came round to C again, and the ball would continue to revolve in a circle around the earth.

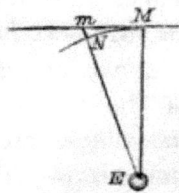

50. *The Form of a Body's Orbit depends upon the Rate of*

its Forward Motion. — If the ball *C* were fired fast enough to reach the line *A D* beyond the point *D*, it would be farther from the surface at the end of the second than when it started. Its orbit would no longer be circular, but *ellipti-*

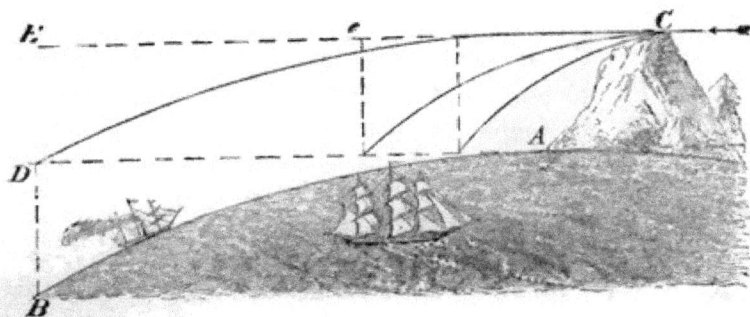

Fig. 61.

cal. If the speed of projection were gradually augmented, the orbit would become a more and more elongated ellipse. At a certain rate of projection, the orbit would become a *parabola;* at a still greater rate, a *hyperbola.*

51. *The Moon held in her Orbit by Gravity.* — Newton compared the distance *m N* that the moon is drawn to the earth in a given time, with the distance a body near the surface of the earth would be pulled toward the earth in the same time: and he found that these distances are to each other inversely as the squares of the distances of the two bodies from the centre of the earth. He therefore concluded that *the moon is drawn*

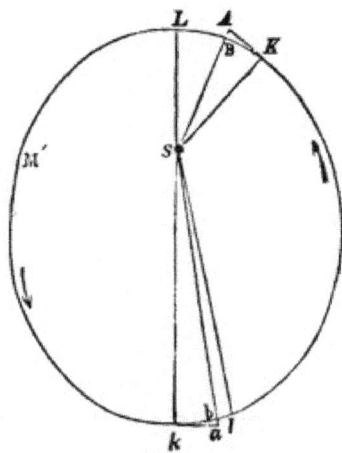

Fig. 62.

to the earth by gravity, and that *the intensity of gravity decreases as the square of the distance increases.*

52. *Any Body whose Orbit is a Conic Section, and which moves according to Kepler's Second Law, is acted upon by a*

Force varying inversely as the Square of the Distance. — New-ton compared the distance which any body, moving in an ellipse, according to Kepler's Second Law, is drawn towards the sun in the same time in different parts of its orbit. He found these distances in all cases to vary inversely as the square of the distance of the planet from the sun. Thus, in Fig. 62, suppose a planet would move from K to B in the same time that it would move from k to b in another part of its orbit. In the first instance the planet would be drawn towards the sun the distance AB, and in the second instance the distance ab. Newton found that $AB : ab = SK^2 : Sk^2$. He also found that the same would be true when the body moved in a parabola or a hyperbola: hence he concluded that *every body that moves around the sun in an ellipse, a parabola, or a hyperbola, is moving under the influence of gravity.*

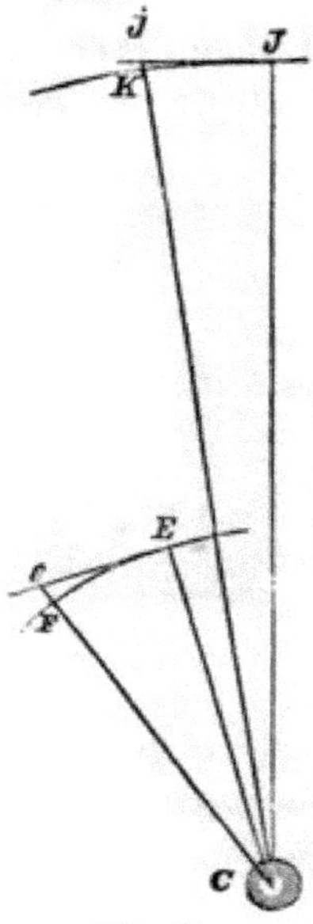

Fig. 63.

53. *The Force that draws the Different Planets to the Sun Varies inversely as the Squares of the Distances of the Planets from the Sun.* — Newton compared the distances jK and eF, over which two planets are drawn towards the sun in the same time, and found these distances to vary inversely as the squares of the distances of the planets from the sun: hence he concluded that *all the planets are held in their orbits by gravity.* He also showed that this would be true of any two bodies that were revolving around the sun's centre, according to Kepler's Third Law.

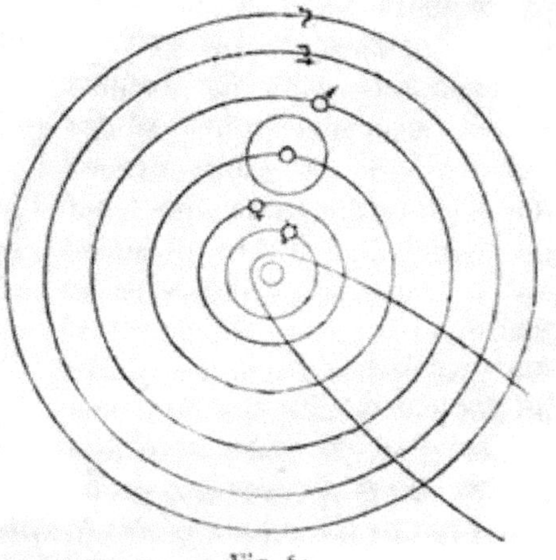

Fig. 64.

54. *The Copernican System.* — The theory of the solar system which originated with Copernicus, and which was developed and completed by Kepler and Newton, is commonly known as the *Copernican System.* This system is shown in Fig. 64.

II. THE SUN AND PLANETS.

I. THE EARTH.

FORM AND SIZE.

55. *Form of the Earth.* — In ordinary language the term *horizon* denotes the line that bounds the portion of the earth's surface that is visible at any point.

(1) It is well known that the horizon of a plain presents the form of a circle surrounding the observer. If the latter moves, the circle moves also; but its form remains the same, and is modified only when mountains or other obstacles limit the view. Out at sea, the circular form of the horizon is still more decided, and changes only near the coasts, the outline of which breaks the regularity.

Here, then, we obtain a first notion of the rotundity of the earth, since a sphere is the only body which is presented always to us under the form of a circle, from whatever point on its surface it is viewed.

(2) Moreover, it cannot be maintained that the horizon is the vanishing point of distinct vision, and that it is this which causes the appearance of a circular boundary, because the horizon is enlarged when we mount above the surface of the plain. This will be evident from Fig. 65, in which a mountain is depicted in the middle of a plain, whose uniform curvature is that of a sphere. From the foot of the mountain the spectator will have but a very limited horizon. Let him ascend half way, his visual radius extends, is inclined below the first horizon, and reveals a more extended circu-

lar area.   At the summit of the mountain the horizon still
increases ; and, if the atmosphere is pure, the spectator will

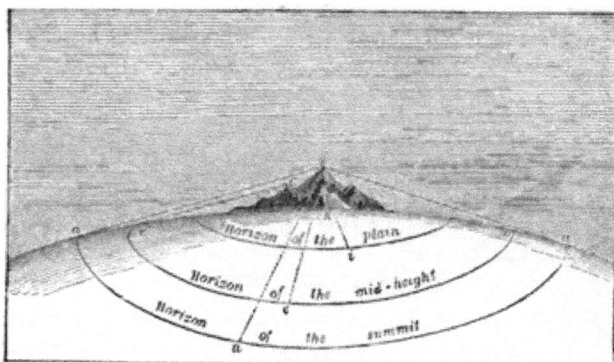

Fig. 65.

see numerous objects where from the lower stations the sky
alone was visible.

Fig. 66.

This extension of the horizon would be inexplicable if
the earth had the form of an extended plane.

(3) The curvature of the surface of the sea manifests itself in a still more striking manner. If we are on the coast at the summit of a hill, and a vessel appears on the horizon (Fig. 66), we see only the tops of the masts and the highest sails; the lower sails and the hull are invisible. As the vessel approaches, its lower part comes into view above the horizon, and soon it appears entire.

In the same manner the sailors from the ship see the different parts of objects on the land appear successively, beginning with the highest. The reason of this will be evident from Fig. 67, where the course of a vessel, seen in profile, is figured on the convex surface of the sea.

As the curvature of the ocean is the same in every direction, it follows that the surface of the ocean is *spherical.*

Fig. 67.

The same is true of the surface of the land, allowance being made for the various inequalities of the surface. From these and various other indications, we conclude that *the earth is a sphere.*

56. *Size of the Earth.* — The size of the earth is ascertained by measuring the length of a degree of a meridian, and multiplying this by three hundred and sixty. This gives the circumference of the earth as about twenty-five thousand miles, and its diameter as about eight thousand miles. We know that the two stations between which we measure are one degree apart when the elevation of the pole at one station is one degree greater than at the other.

57. *The Earth Flattened at the Poles.* — Degrees on the meridian have been measured in various parts of the earth, and it has been found that they invariably increase in length

as we proceed from the equator towards the pole : hence
the earth must curve less and less rapidly as we approach the
poles ; for the less the curvature of a circle, the larger the
degrees on it.

58. *The Earth in Space.* — In Fig. 68 we have a view
of the earth suspended in space. The side of the earth

Fig. 68.

turned towards the sun is illumined, and the other side is in
darkness. As the planet rotates on its axis, successive portions of it will be turned towards the sun. As viewed from
a point in space between it and the sun, it will present
light and dark portions, which will assume different forms
according to the portion which is illumined. These different appearances are shown in Fig. 69.

DAY AND NIGHT.

59. *Day and Night.* — The succession of day and night

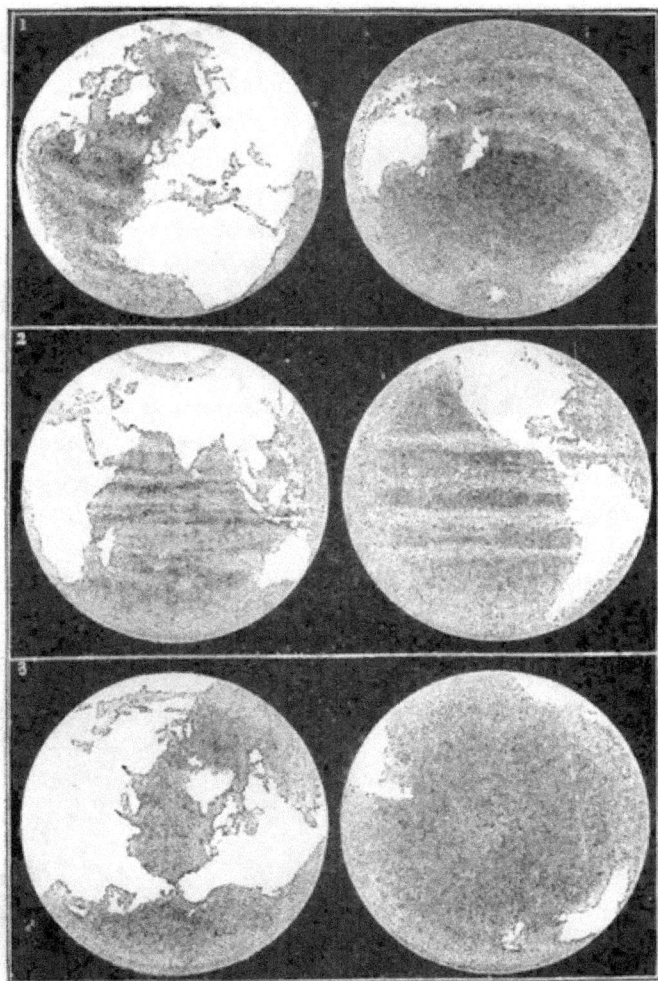

Fig. 69.

is due to *the rotation of the earth on its axis,* by which a place on the surface of the earth is carried alternately into the sunshine and out of it. As the sun moves around the heavens on the ecliptic, it will be on the celestial equator when at the equinoxes, and $23\frac{1}{2}°$ north of the equator when at the summer solstice, and $23\frac{1}{2}°$ south of the equator when at the winter solstice.

60. *Day and Night when the Sun is at the Equinoxes.* — When the sun is at either equinox. the diurnal circle described by the sun will coincide with the celestial equator ; and therefore half of this diurnal circle will be above the horizon at every point on the surface of the globe.

Fig. 70.

At these times *day and night will be equal in every part of the earth.*

The equality of days and nights when the sun is on the celestial equator is also evident from the following considerations : one-half of the earth is in sunshine all of the time ; when the sun is on the celestial equator, it is directly over the equator of the earth, and the illumination extends from pole to pole. as is evident from Figs. 70 and 71. in the former of which the sun is represented as on the eastern horizon at a place along the central line

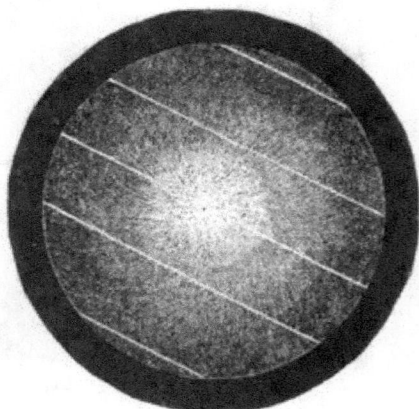

Fig. 71.

of the figure. and in the latter as on the meridian along the same line. In each diagram it is seen that the illumination extends from pole to pole : hence, as the earth rotates on its axis, every place on the surface will be in the sunshine and out of it just half of the time.

61. *Day and Night when the Sun is at the Summer Solstice.* — When the sun is at the summer solstice, it will be $23\frac{1}{2}°$ north of the celestial equator. The diurnal circle described by the sun will then be $23\frac{1}{2}°$ north of the celestial equator ; and more than half of this diurnal circle will be above the horizon at all places north of the equator, and less than half of it at places

Fig. 72.

south of the equator : hence *the days will be longer than the nights at places north of the equator, and shorter than the nights at places south of the equator.* At places within $23\frac{1}{2}°$ of the north pole, the entire diurnal circle described by the sun will be above the horizon, so that the sun will not set. At places within $23\frac{1}{2}°$ of the south pole of the earth, the entire diurnal circle will be below the horizon, so that the sun will not rise.

Fig. 73.

The illumination of the earth at this time is shown in Figs. 72 and 73. In Fig. 72 the sun is represented as on the western horizon along the middle line of the figure, and in Fig. 73 as on the meridian. It is seen at once that the illumination extends $23\frac{1}{2}°$ beyond the north pole, and falls $23\frac{1}{2}°$ short of the south pole. As the earth rotates on its axis, places near the north pole will be in the sunshine all the time, while places near the south pole will be out of the sunshine all the time. All places north of the equator will be in the sunshine longer than they are out of it, while all places south of the equator will be out of the sunshine longer than they are in it.

62. *Day and Night when the Sun is at the Winter Solstice.* — When the sun is at the winter solstice, it is $23\frac{1}{2}°$ south of the celestial equator. The diurnal circle described by the sun is then $23\frac{1}{2}°$ south of the celestial equator. More than half of this diurnal circle will therefore be above the horizon at all places south of the equator, and less than half of it at all places north of the equator : hence *the days will be longer than the nights south of the equator, and shorter than the nights at places north of the equator.* At places within $23\frac{1}{2}°$ of the south pole, the diurnal circle described by the sun will be entirely above the horizon, and the sun will therefore not set. At places within $23\frac{1}{2}°$ of the north pole, the diurnal circle described by the sun will be wholly below the horizon, and therefore the sun will not rise.

The illumination of the earth at this time is shown in Figs. 74 and 75, and is seen to be the reverse of that shown in Figs. 72 and 73.

63. *Variation in the Length of Day and Night.* — As long as the sun is north of the equinoctial, the nights will be longer than the days south of the equator, and shorter than the days north of the equator. It is just the reverse when the sun is south of the equator.

The farther the sun is from the equator, the greater is the inequality of the days and nights.

The farther the place is from the equator, the greater the inequality of its days and nights.

When the distance of a place from the *north* pole is less

than the distance of the sun north of the equinoctial, it will have *continuous day without night*, since the whole of the sun's diurnal circle will be above the horizon. A place within the same distance of the *south* pole will have *continuous night.*

When the distance of a place from the *north* pole is less than the distance of the sun south of the equinoctial, it will have *continuous night*, since the whole of the sun's diurnal circle will then be below the horizon. A place within the same

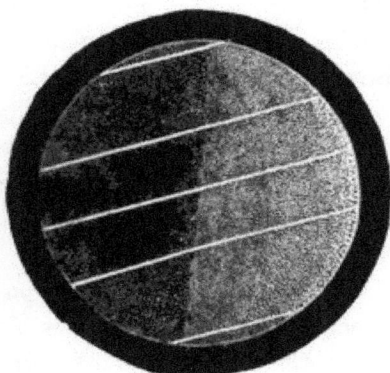

Fig. 74.

distance of the *south* pole will then have *continuous day.*

At the *equator* the *days and nights are always equal;* since, no matter where the sun is in the heavens, half of all the diurnal circles described by it will be above the horizon, and half of them below it.

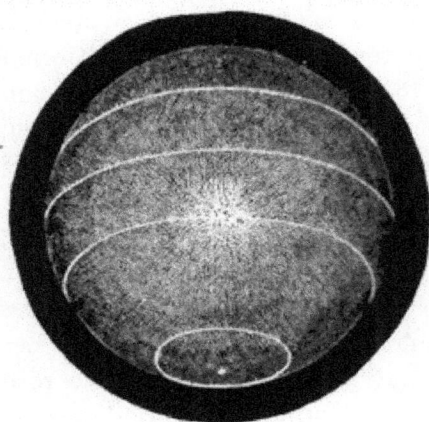

Fig. 75.

64. *The Zones.* — It will be seen, from what has been stated above, that the sun will at some time during the year be directly overhead at every place within $23\frac{1}{2}°$ of the equator on either side. This belt of the earth is called the *torrid zone.* The torrid zone is bounded by circles called the *tropics;* that of *Cancer* on the north, and that of *Capricorn* on the south.

It will also be seen, that, at every place within $23\frac{1}{2}°$ of either pole, there will be, some time during the year, a day during which the sun will not rise, or on which it will not set. These two belts of the earth's surface are called the *frigid zones.* These zones are bounded by the *arctic* circles. The nearer a place is to the poles, the greater the number of days on which the sun does not rise or set.

Between the frigid zones and the torrid zones, there are two belts on the earth which are called the *temperate zones.* The sun is never overhead at any place in these two zones, but it rises and sets every day at every place within their limits.

65. *The Width of the Zones.* — The distance the frigid zones extend from the poles, and the torrid zones from the equator, is exactly equal to *the obliquity of the ecliptic,* or the deviation of the axis of the earth from the perpendicular to the plane of its orbit. Were this deviation forty-five degrees, the obliquity of the ecliptic would be forty-five degrees, the torrid zone would extend forty-five degrees from the equator, and the frigid zones forty-five degrees from the poles. In this case there would be no temperate zones. Were this deviation fifty degrees, the torrid and frigid zones would overlap ten degrees, and there would be two belts of ten degrees on the earth, which would experience alternately during the year a torrid and a frigid climate.

Were the axis of the earth perpendicular to the plane of the earth's orbit, there would be no zones on the earth, and no variation in the length of day and night.

66. *Twilight.* — Were it not for the atmosphere, the darkness of midnight would begin the moment the sun sank below the horizon, and would continue till he rose again above the horizon in the east, when the darkness of the night would be suddenly succeeded by the full light of day. The gradual transition from the light of day to the darkness of the night, and from the darkness of the night to the light of day, is called *twilight,* and is due to

the *diffusion of light from the upper layers of the atmosphere* after the sun has ceased to shine on the lower layers at night, or before it has begun to shine on them in the morning.

Let *A B C D* (Fig. 76) represent a portion of the earth, *A* a point on its surface where the sun *S* is setting; and let *S A H* be a ray of light just grazing the earth at *A*, and leaving the atmosphere at the point *H*. The point *A* is illuminated by the whole reflective atmosphere *H G F E*. The point *B*, to which the sun has set, receives no direct

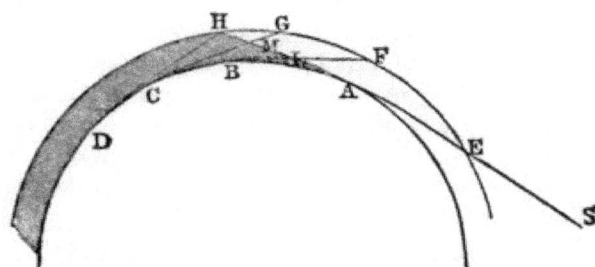

Fig. 76.

solar light, nor any reflected from that part of the atmosphere which is below *A L H;* but it receives a twilight from the portion *H L F*, which lies above the visible horizon *B F*. The point *C* receives a twilight only from the small portion of the atmosphere *H M G;* while at *D* the twilight has ceased altogether.

67. *Duration of Twilight.* — The astronomical limit of twilight is generally understood to be the instant when stars of the sixth magnitude begin to be visible in the zenith at evening, or disappear in the morning.

Twilight is usually reckoned to last until the sun's depression below the horizon amounts to eighteen degrees: this, however, varies; in the tropics a depression of sixteen or seventeen degrees being sufficient to put an end to the phenomenon, while in England a depression of seventeen to twenty-one degrees is required. The duration of twilight differs in differ-

ent latitudes; it varies also in the same latitude at different
seasons of the year, and depends, in some measure, on the
meteorological condition of the atmosphere. When the sky
is of a pale color, indicating the presence of an unusual
amount of condensed vapor, twilight is of longer duration.
This happens habitually in the polar regions. On the contrary,
within the tropics, where the air is pure and dry, twilight sometimes lasts only fifteen minutes. Strictly speaking, in the latitude of Greenwich there is no true night from May 22 to
July 21, but constant twilight from sunset to sunrise. Twilight
reaches its minimum three weeks before the vernal equinox,
and three weeks after the autumnal equinox, when its duration
is an hour and fifty minutes. At midwinter it is longer by
about seventeen minutes; but the augmentation is frequently
not perceptible, owing to the greater prevalence of clouds and
haze at that season of the year, which intercept the light, and
hinder it from reaching the earth. The duration is least at
the equator (an hour and twelve minutes), and increases as
we approach the poles; for at the former there are two twi-
lights every twenty-four hours, but at the latter only two in a
year, each lasting about fifty days. At the north pole the sun
is below the horizon for six months, but from Jan. 29 to the
vernal equinox, and from the autumnal equinox to Nov. 12,
the sun is less than eighteen degrees below the horizon; so
that there is twilight during the whole of these intervals, and
thus the length of the actual night is reduced to two months
and a half. The length of the day in these regions is about
six months, during the whole of which time the sun is constantly above the horizon. The general rule is, *that to the
inhabitants of an oblique sphere the twilight is longer in proportion as the place is nearer the elevated pole, and the sun is
farther from the equator on the side of the elevated pole.*

THE SEASONS.

68. *The Seasons.* — While the sun is north of the celestial equator, places north of the equator are receiving heat
from the sun by day longer than they are losing it by radiation at night, while places south of the equator are losing

heat by radiation at night longer than they are receiving it from the sun by day. When, therefore, the sun passes north of the equator, the temperature begins to rise at places north of the equator, and to fall at places south of it. The rise of temperature is most rapid north of the equator when the sun is at the summer solstice; but, for some time after this, the earth continues to receive more heat by day than it loses by night, and therefore the temperature continues to rise. For this reason, the heat is more excessive after the sun passes the summer solstice than before it reaches it.

69. *The Duration of the Seasons.* — Summer is counted as beginning in June, when the sun is at the summer solstice, and as continuing until the sun reaches the autumnal equinox, in September. Autumn then begins, and continues until the sun is at the winter solstice, in December. Winter follows, continuing until the sun comes to the vernal equinox, in March, when spring begins, and continues to the summer solstice. In popular reckoning the seasons begin with the first day of June, September, December, and March.

The reason why winter is counted as occurring after the winter solstice is similar to the reason why the summer is placed

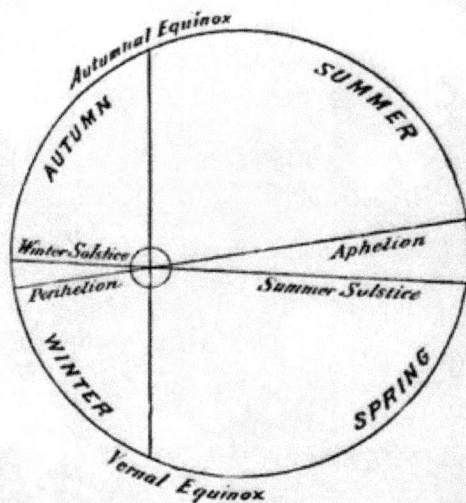

Fig. 77.

after the summer solstice. The earth north of the equator is losing heat most rapidly at the time of the winter solstice; but for some time after this it loses more heat by night than it receives by day: hence for some time the temperature

continues to fall, and the cold is more intense after the
winter solstice than before it.

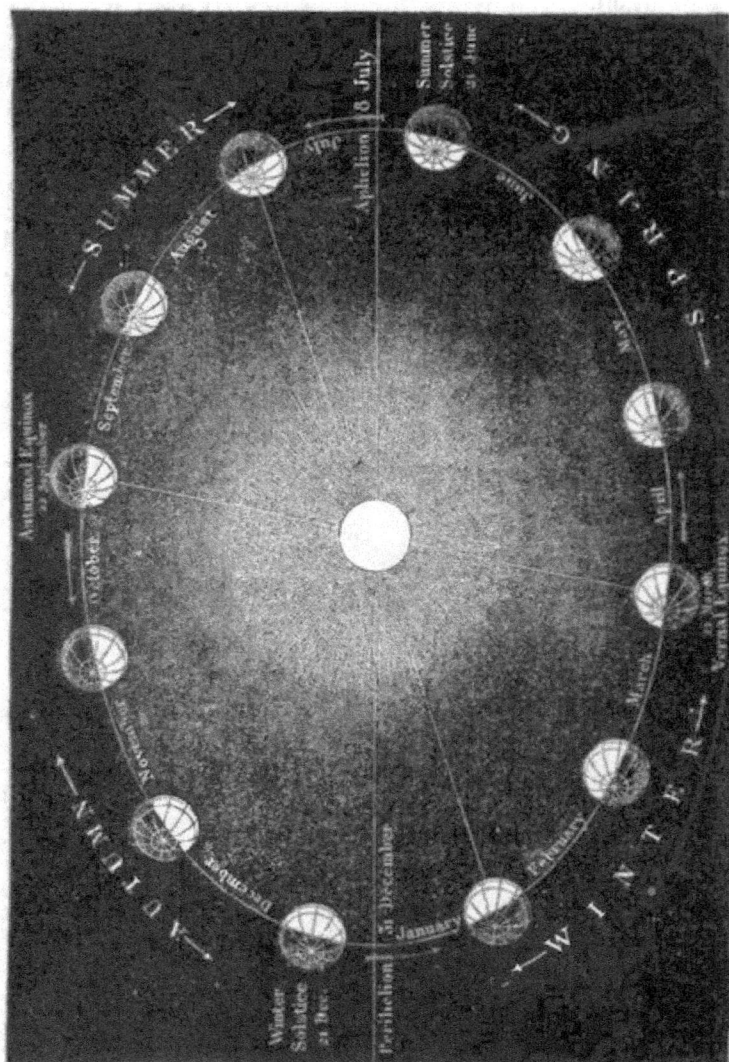

Fig. 78.

Of course, when it is summer in the northern hemisphere,
it is winter in the southern hemisphere, and the reverse.

Fig. 77 shows the portion of the earth's orbit included in each season. It will be seen that the earth is at perihelion in the winter season for places north of the equator, and at aphelion in the summer season. This tends to mitigate somewhat the extreme temperatures of our winters and summers.

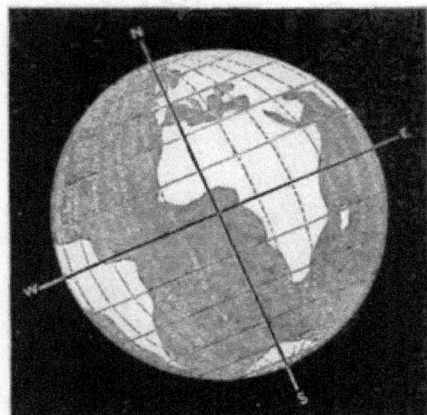

Fig. 79.

70. *The Illumination of the Earth at the different Seasons.* — Fig. 78 shows the earth as it would appear to an observer at the sun during each of the four seasons; that is to say, the portion of the earth that is receiving the sun's rays. Figs. 79, 80, 81, and 82 are enlarged views of the earth, as seen from the sun at the time of the summer solstice, of the autumnal equinox, of the winter solstice, and of the vernal equinox.

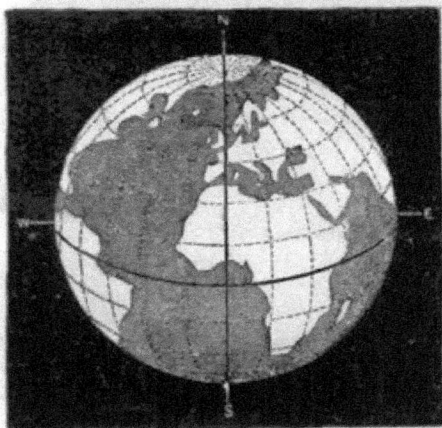

Fig. 80.

Fig. 83 is, so to speak, a side view of the earth, showing the limit of sunshine on the earth when the sun is at the summer solstice; and Fig. 84. showing the limit of sunshine when the sun is at the autumnal equinox.

71. *Cause of the Change of Seasons.* — Variety in the length of day and night, and diversity in the seasons, depend

upon *the obliquity of the ecliptic.* Were there no obliquity of the ecliptic, there would be no inequality in the length of day and night, and but slight diversity of seasons. The greater the obliquity of the ecliptic, the greater would be the variation in the length of the days and nights, and the more extreme the changes of the seasons.

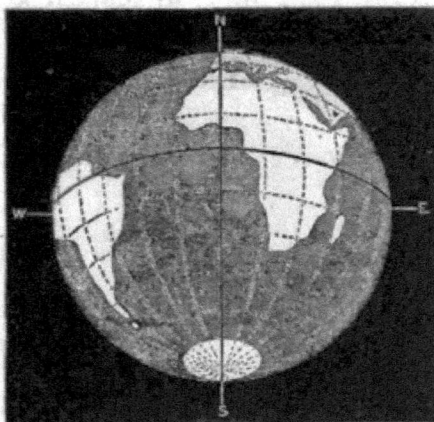

Fig. 81.

TIDES.

72. *Tides.* — The alternate rise and fall of the surface of the sea twice in the course of a lunar day, or of twenty-four hours and fifty-one minutes, is known as the *tides.* When the water is rising, it is said to be *flood* tide; and when it is falling, *ebb* tide. When the water is at its greatest height, it is said to be *high* water; and when at its least height, *low* water.

73. *Cause of the Tides.* — It has been known to seafaring nations from a remote antiquity that there is a singular connection between the ebb and flow of the tides and the diurnal motion of the moon.

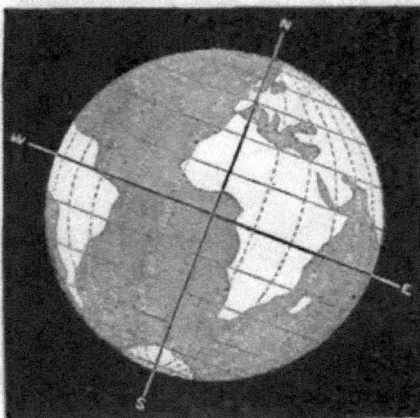

Fig. 82.

This tidal movement in seeming obedience to the moon was a mystery until the study of the law of gravitation showed it to be due to *the attraction of the moon on the waters of the ocean.* The reason why there are two tides a day will appear

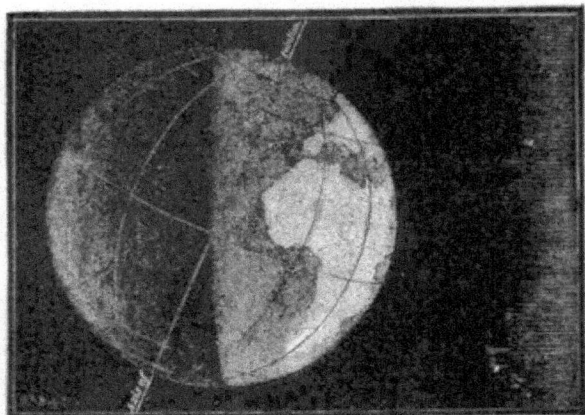

Fig. 83.

from Fig. 85. Let M be the moon, E the earth, and EM the line joining their centres. Now, strictly speaking, the moon does not revolve around the earth any more than the earth

Fig. 84.

around the moon : but the centre of each body moves around the common centre of gravity of the two bodies. The earth

being eighty times as heavy as the moon, this centre is situated
within the former, about three-quarters of the way from its
centre to its surface, at the point *G*. The body of the earth
itself being solid, every part of it, in consequence of the
moon's attraction, may be considered as describing a circle
once in a month, with a radius equal to *E G*. The centrifugal
force caused by this rotation is just balanced by the mean
attraction of the moon upon the earth. If this attraction were
the same on every part of the earth, there would be everywhere an exact balance between it and the centrifugal force.
But as we pass from *E* to *D* the attraction of the moon diminishes, owing to the increased distance: hence at *D* the centrifugal force predominates, and the water therefore tends to move
away from the centre *E*. As we pass from *E* towards *C*, the
attraction of the moon increases, and therefore exceeds the cen-

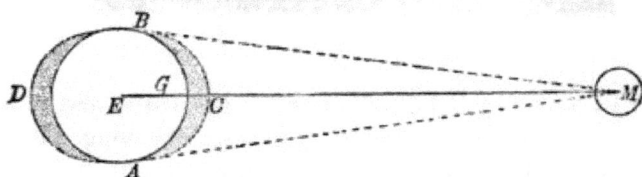

Fig. 85.

trifugal force: consequently at *C* there is a tendency to draw
the water towards the moon, but still away from the centre *E*.
At *A* and *B* the attraction of the moon increases the gravity
of the water, owing to the convergence of the lines *B M* and
A M, along which it acts: hence the action of the moon tends
to make the waters rise at *D* and *C*, and to fall at *A* and *B*,
causing two tides to each apparent diurnal revolution of the
moon.

74. *The Lagging of the Tides.* — If the waters everywhere
yielded immediately to the attractive force of the moon, it would
always be high water when the moon was on the meridian, low
water when she was rising or setting, and high water again
when she was on the meridian below the horizon. But, owing
to the inertia of the water, some time is necessary for so slight
a force to set it in motion; and, once in motion, it continues
so after the force has ceased, and until it has acted some time
in the opposite direction. Therefore, if the motion of the

water were unimpeded. it would not be high water until some hours after the moon had passed the meridian. The free motion of the water is also impeded by the islands and continents. These deflect the tidal wave from its course in such a

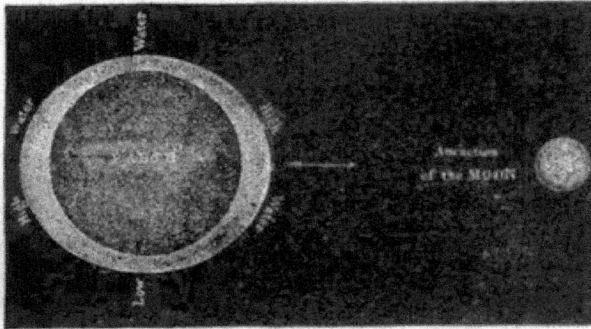

Fig. 86.

way that it may, in some cases, be many hours, or even a whole day, behind its time. Sometimes two waves meet each other, and raise a very high tide. In some places the tides

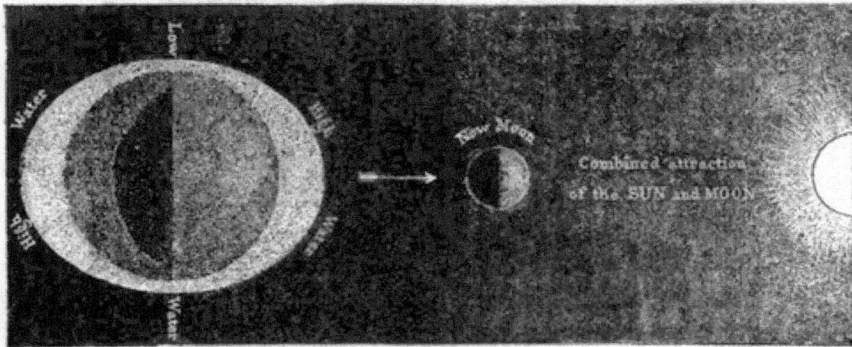

Fig. 87.

run up a long bay, where the motion of a large mass of water will cause an enormous tide to be raised. In the Bay of Fundy both of these causes are combined. A tidal wave coming up the Atlantic coast meets the ocean wave from the east, and, entering the bay with their combined force, they

raise the water at the head of it to the height of sixty or
seventy feet.

75. *Spring-Tides and Neap-Tides.* — The sun produces
a tide as well as the moon; but the tide-producing force
of the sun is only about four-tenths of that of the moon.
At new and full moon the two bodies unite their forces,
the ebb and flow become greater than the average, and
we have the *spring-tides.* When the moon is in her first

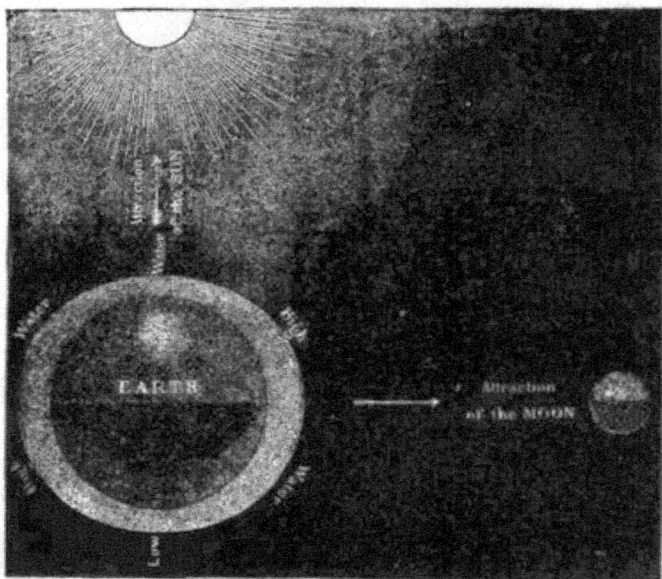

Fig. 88.

or third quarter, the two forces act against each other;
the tide-producing force is the difference of the two; the
ebb and flow are less than the average; and we have the
neap-tides.

Fig. 86 shows the tide that would be produced by the
moon alone; Fig. 87, the tide produced by the combined
action of the sun and moon; and Fig. 88, by the sun and
moon acting at right angles to each other.

The tide is affected by the distance of the moon from

the earth, being highest near the time when the moon is in
perigee, and lowest near the time when she is in apogee.
When the moon is in perigee, at or near the time of a new
or full moon, unusually high tides occur.

76. *Diurnal Inequality of Tides.* — The height of the tide
at a given place is influenced by the declination of the moon.
When the moon has no declination, the highest tides should
occur along the equator, and the heights should diminish from
thence toward the north and south; but the two daily tides at
any place should have the same height. When the moon has
north declination, as shown in Fig. 89, the highest tides on
the side of the earth next the moon will be at places having
a corresponding
north latitude,
as at *B*, and on
the opposite
side at those
which have an
equal south lati-
tude. Of the
two daily tides
at any place, that
which occurs
when the moon
is nearest the

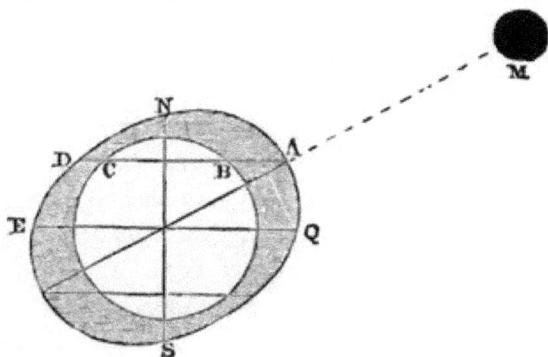

Fig. 89.

zenith should be the greatest: hence, when the moon's declination is north, the height of the tide at a place in north latitude
should be greater when the moon is above the horizon than
when she is below it. At the same time, places south of the
equator have the highest tides when the moon is below the
horizon, and the least when she is above it. This is called
the *diurnal inequality*, because its cycle is one day; but it
varies greatly in amount at different places.

77. *Height of Tides.* — At small islands in mid-ocean
the tides never rise to a great height, sometimes even less
than one foot; and the average height of the tides for the
islands of the Atlantic and Pacific Oceans is only three feet

and a half. Upon approaching an extensive coast where the water is shallow, the height of the tide is increased ; so that, while in mid-ocean the average height does not exceed three feet and a half, the average in the neighborhood of continents is not less than four or five feet.

THE DAY AND TIME.

78. *The Day.* — By the term *day* we sometimes denote the period of sunshine as contrasted with that of the absence of sunshine, which we call *night*, and sometimes the period of the earth's rotation on its axis. It is with the latter signification that the term is used in this section. As the earth rotates on its axis, it carries the meridian of a place with it ; so that, during each complete rotation of the earth, the portion of the meridian which passes overhead from pole to pole sweeps past every star in the heavens from west to east. The *interval between two successive passages of this portion of the meridian across the same star* is the exact period of the complete rotation of the earth. This period is called a *sidereal day*. The sidereal day may also be defined as *the interval between two successive passages of the same star across the meridian;* the passage of the meridian across the star, and the passage or *transit* of the star across the meridian, being the same thing looked at from a different point of view. The interval *between two successive passages of the meridian across the sun*, or *of the sun across the meridian*, is called a *solar day*.

79. *Length of the Solar Day.* — The solar day is a little longer than the sidereal day. This is owing to the sun's eastward motion among the stars. We have already seen that the sun's apparent position among the stars is continually shifting towards the east at a rate which causes it to make a complete circuit of the heavens in a year, or three hundred and sixty-five days. This is at the rate of about one degree a day : hence, were the sun and a star on the

meridian together to-day, when the meridian again came around to the star, the sun would appear about one degree to the eastward : hence the meridian must be carried about one degree farther in order to come up to the sun. The solar day must therefore be *about four minutes longer* than the sidereal day.

The fact that the earth must make more than a complete rotation is also evident from Figs. 90 and 91. In Fig. 90, *b a* represents the plane of the meridian, and the small arrows indicate the direction the earth is rotating on its axis, and revolving in its orbit. When

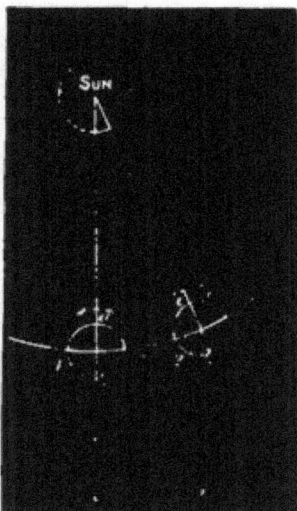

Fig. 90.

the earth is at 1, the sun is on the meridian at *a*. When

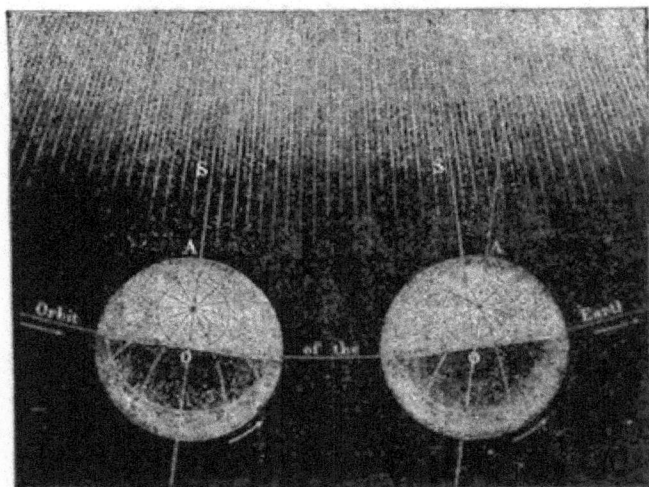

Fig. 91

the earth has moved to 2, it has made a complete rotation, as is shown by the fact that the plane of the meridian is parallel with its position at 1; but it is evident that the meridian has not yet come up with the sun. In Fig. 91, *OA* represents the plane of the meridian, and *OS* the direction of the sun. The small arrows indicate the direc-

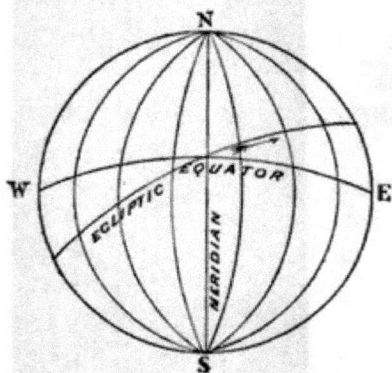

Fig. 92.

tion of the rotation and revolution of the earth. In passing from the first position to the second the earth makes a complete rotation, but the meridian is not brought up to the sun.

80. *Inequality in the Length of Solar Days.* — The sidereal days are all of the same length; but the solar days differ somewhat in length. This difference is due to the fact that the sun's apparent position moves eastward, or *away from the meridian*, at a variable rate.

There are three reasons why this rate is variable : —

(1) The sun's eastward motion is due to the revolution of the earth in its orbit. Now, the earth's orbital motion is *not uniform*, being fastest when the earth is at perihelion, and slowest when the earth is at aphelion : hence, other things being equal, solar days will be longest when the earth is at perihelion, and shortest when the earth is at aphelion.

(2) The sun's eastward motion

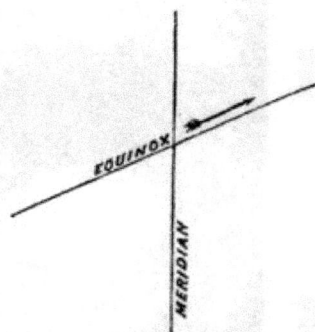

Fig. 93.

is along the ecliptic. Now, from Figs. 92 and 93, it will be seen, that, when the sun is at one of the equinoxes, it will be moving away from the meridian *obliquely;* and, from Figs. 94 and 95, that, when the sun is at one of the solstices, it will be moving away from the meridian *perpendicularly:* hence, other things being equal, the sun would move away from the meridian *fastest,* and the days be *longest,* when the sun is at the *solstices;* while it would move away from the meridian *slowest,* and the days be *shortest,* when the sun is at the *equinoxes.* - That a body moving along the ecliptic must be moving at a variable angle to the meridian becomes very evident on turning a celestial globe so as to bring each portion of the ecliptic under the meridian in turn.

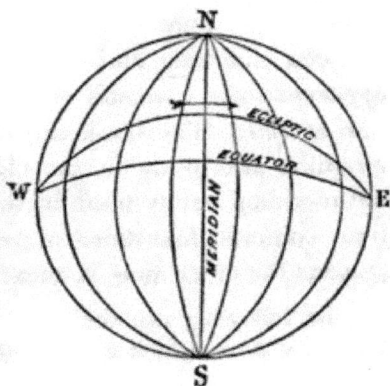

Fig. 94.

(3) The sun, moving along the ecliptic, always moves *in a great circle,* while the point of the meridian which is to overtake the sun moves in a diurnal circle, which is *sometimes a great circle* and *sometimes a small circle.* When the sun is at the equinoxes, the point of the meridian which is to overtake it moves in a great circle. As the sun passes from the equinoxes to the solstices, the point of the meridian which is to overtake it moves on a smaller and smaller circle : hence, as we pass away from the celestial equator, the points of the meridian move slower and slower. Therefore, other things being equal, the meridian will gain upon the sun *most rapidly,* and the days be *shortest,* when the sun is at the *equinoxes;* while it will gain on the sun *least rapidly,* and the days will be *longest,* when the sun is at the *solstices.*

Fig. 95.

The ordinary or *civil day* is the mean of all the solar days in a year.

81. *Sun Time and Clock Time*. — It is noon by the sun when the sun is on the meridian, and by the clock at the middle of the civil day. Now, as the civil days are all of the same length, while solar days are of variable length, it seldom happens that the middles of these two days coincide, or that sun time and clock time agree. The difference between sun time and clock time, or what is often called *apparent solar time* and *mean solar time*, is called the *equation of time*. The sun is said to be *slow* when it crosses the meridian after noon by the clock, and *fast* when it crosses the meridian before noon by the clock. Sun time and clock time coincide four times a year; during two intermediate seasons the clock time is ahead, and during two it is behind.

The following are the dates of coincidence and of maximum deviation, which vary but slightly from year to year: —

February 10 . . .	True sun fifteen minutes slow.
April 15	True sun correct.
May 14	True sun four minutes fast.
June 14	True sun correct.
July 25	True sun six minutes slow.
August 31	True sun correct.
November 2 . . .	True sun sixteen minutes fast.
December 24 . . .	True sun correct.

One of the effects of the equation of time which is frequently misunderstood is, that the interval from sunrise until noon, as given in the almanacs, is not the same as that between noon and sunset. The forenoon could not be longer or shorter than the afternoon, if by "noon" we meant the passage of the sun across the meridian; but the noon of our clocks being sometimes fifteen minutes before or after noon by the sun, the former may be half an hour nearer to sunrise than to sunset, or *vice versa*.

THE YEAR.

82. *The Year*. — The *year* is the time it takes the earth to revolve around the sun, or, what amounts to the same thing, *the time it takes the sun to pass around the ecliptic.*

(1) The time it takes the sun to pass from a star around to the same star again is called a *sidereal year*. This is, of course, the exact time it takes the earth to make a complete revolution around the sun.

(2) The time it takes the sun to pass around from the vernal equinox, or the *first point of Aries*, to the vernal equinox again, is called the *tropical* year. This is a little shorter than the sidereal year, owing to the precession of the equinoxes. This will be evident from Fig. 96. The circle represents the ecliptic, *S* the sun, and *E* the vernal equinox. The sun moves

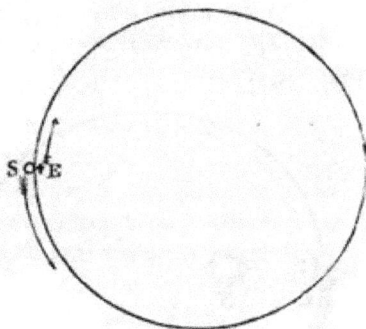

Fig. 96.

around the eliptic *eastward*, as indicated by the long arrow, while the equinox moves slowly *westward*, as indicated by the short arrow. The sun will therefore meet the equinox before it has quite completed the circuit of the heavens. The exact lengths of these respective years are : —

	DAYS.	HOURS.	MIN.	SEC.
Sidereal year . .	365.25636=365	6	9	9
Tropical year . .	365.24220=365	5	48	46

Since the recurrence of the seasons depends on the tropical year, the latter is the one to be used in forming the calendar and for the purposes of civil life generally. Its true length is eleven minutes and fourteen seconds less than three hundred and sixty-five days and a fourth.

It will be seen that the tropical year is about twenty minutes shorter than the sidereal year.

(3) The time it takes the earth to pass from its perihelion point around to the perihelion point again is called the *anomalistic year*. This year is about four minutes longer than the sidereal year. This is owing to the fact that the major axis of

the earth's orbit is slowly moving around to the east at the rate of about ten seconds a year. This causes the perihelion point *P* (Fig. 97) to move *eastward* at that rate, as indicated by the short arrow. The earth *E* is also moving eastward, as indicated by the long arrow. Hence the earth, on starting at the perihelion, has to make a little more than a complete circuit to reach the perihelion point again.

83. *The Calendar.* — The *solar year*, or the interval between two successive passages of the same equinox by the sun,

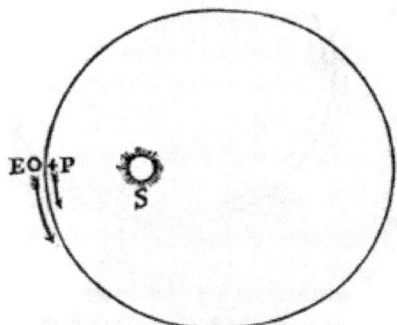

Fig. 97.

is 365 days, 5 hours, 48 minutes, 46 seconds. If, then, we reckon only 365 days to a common or *civil year*, the sun will come to the equinox 5 hours, 48 minutes, 46 seconds, or nearly a quarter of a day, later each year; so that, if the sun entered Aries on the 20th of March one year, he would enter it on the 21st four years after, on the 22d eight years after, and so on. Thus in a comparatively short time the spring months would come in the winter, and the summer months in the spring.

Among different ancient nations different methods of computing the year were in use. Some reckoned it by the revolution of the moon, some by that of the sun; but none, so far as we know, made proper allowances for deficiencies and excesses. Twelve moons fell short of the true year, thirteen exceeded it; 365 days were not enough, 366 were too many. To prevent the confusion resulting from these errors. Julius Cæsar reformed the calendar by making the year consist of 365 days, 6 hours (which is hence called a *Julian* year), and made every fourth year consist of 366 days. This method of reckoning is called *Old Style.*

But as this made the year somewhat too long, and the error in 1582 amounted to ten days, Pope Gregory XIII., in order to bring the vernal equinox back to the 21st of March again, ordered ten days to be struck out of that year, calling the next day after the 4th of October the 15th; and, to prevent similar confusion in the future, he decreed that three leap-years should be omitted in the course of every four hundred years. This way of reckoning time is called *New Style*. It was immediately adopted by most of the European nations, but was not accepted by the English until the year 1752. The error then amounted to eleven days, which were taken from the month of September by calling the 3d of that month the 14th. The Old Style is still retained by Russia.

According to the Gregorian calendar, *every year whose number is divisible by four* is a *leap-year*, except, that, *in the case of the years whose numbers are exact hundreds, those only are leap-years which are divisible by four after cutting off the last two figures.* Thus the years 1600, 2000, 2400, etc., are leap-years; 1700, 1800, 1900, 2100, 2200, etc., are not. The error will not amount to a day in over three thousand years.

84. *The Dominical Letter.* — The *dominical letter* for any year is that which we often see placed against Sunday in the almanacs, and is always one of the first seven in the alphabet. Since a common year consists of 365 days, if this number is divided by seven (the number of days in a week), there will be a remainder of one: hence a year commonly begins one day later in the week than the preceding one did. If a year of 365 days begins on Sunday, the next will begin on Monday; if it begins on Thursday, the next will begin on Friday; and so on. If Sunday falls on the 1st of January, the *first* letter of the alphabet, or *A*, is the *dominical letter.* If Sunday falls on the 7th of January (as it will the next year, unless the first is leap-year), the *seventh* letter, *G*, is the dominical letter. If Sunday falls on the 6th of January (as it will the third year, unless the first or second is leap-year), the *sixth* letter, *F*, will be the dominical letter. Thus, if there were no leap-years, the dominical letters would regularly follow a retrograde order, *G, F, E, D, C, B, A.*

But *leap*-years have 366 days, which, divided by seven, leaves two remainder: hence the years following leap-years will begin two days later in the week than the leap-years did. To prevent the interruption which would hence occur in the order of the dominical letters, leap-years have *two* dominical letters, one indicating Sunday till the 29th of February, and the other for the rest of the year.

By *Table I.* below, the dominical letter for any year (New

TABLE I.

				Centuries.			
				100	200	300	400
				500	600	700	800
				900	1000	1100	1200
				1300	1400	1500	1600
Years less than				1700	1800	1900	2000
One Hundred.				2100	2200	2300	2400
				2500	2600	2700	2800
				2900	3000	3100	3200
				3300	3400	3500	3600
				3700	3800	3900	4000
				C	E	G	BA
1	29	57	85	B	D	F	G
2	30	58	86	A	C	E	F
3	31	59	87	G	B	D	E
4	32	60	88	FE	AG	CB	DC
5	33	61	89	D	F	A	B
6	34	62	90	C	E	G	A
7	35	63	91	B	D	F	G
8	36	64	92	AG	CB	ED	FE
9	37	65	93	F	A	C	D
10	38	66	94	E	G	B	C
11	39	67	95	D	F	A	B
12	40	68	96	CB	ED	GF	AG
13	41	69	97	A	C	E	F
14	42	70	98	G	B	D	E
15	43	71	99	F	A	C	D
16	44	72	..	ED	GF	BA	CB
17	45	73	..	C	E	G	A
18	46	74	..	B	D	F	G
19	47	75	..	A	C	E	F
20	48	76	..	GF	BA	DC	ED
21	49	77	..	E	G	B	C
22	50	78	..	D	F	A	B
23	51	79	..	C	E	G	A
24	52	80	..	BA	DC	FE	GF
25	53	81	..	G	B	D	E
26	54	82	..	F	A	C	D
27	55	83	..	E	G	B	C
28	56	84	..	DC	FE	AG	BA

TABLE II.

	A	B	C	D	E	F	G
Jan. 31.	1	2	3	4	5	6	7
	8	9	10	11	12	13	14
	15	16	17	18	19	20	21
Oct. 31.	22	23	24	25	26	27	28
	29	30	31	..	..	..	..
Feb. 28–29.	..	..	..	1	2	3	4
	5	6	7	8	9	10	11
March 31.	12	13	14	15	16	17	18
	19	20	21	22	23	24	25
Nov. 30.	26	27	28	29	30	31	..
	..	..	..	..	..	..	1
April 30.	2	3	4	5	6	7	8
	9	10	11	12	13	14	15
July 31	16	17	18	19	20	21	22
	23	24	25	26	27	28	29
	30	31	..	..	..	..	..
	..	..	1	2	3	4	5
	6	7	8	9	10	11	12
Aug. 31.	13	14	15	16	17	18	19
	20	21	22	23	24	25	26
	27	28	29	30	31	..	..
	..	..	..	..	..	1	2
Sept. 30.	3	4	5	6	7	8	9
	10	11	12	13	14	15	16
Dec. 31.	17	18	19	20	21	22	23
	24	25	26	27	28	29	30
	31	..	..	..	..	..	..
	..	1	2	3	4	5	6
	7	8	9	10	11	12	13
May 31.	14	15	16	17	18	19	20
	21	22	23	24	25	26	27
	28	29	30	31	..	..	..
	..	..	..	..	1	2	3
	4	5	6	7	8	9	10
June 30.	11	12	13	14	15	16	17
	18	19	20	21	22	23	24
	25	26	27	28	29	30	..

Style) for four thousand years from the beginning of the Christian Era may be found; and it will be readily seen how the

Table could be extended indefinitely by continuing the centuries at the top in the same order.

To find the dominical letter by this table, *look for the hundreds of years at the top, and for the years below a hundred, at the left hand.*

Thus the letter for 1882 will be opposite the number 82, and in the column having 1800 at the top; that is, it will be *A.* In the same way, the letters for 1884, which is a leap-year, will be found to be *FE.*

Having the dominical letter of any year, *Table II.* shows what days of every month of the year will be *Sundays.*

To find the Sundays of any month in the year by this table, *look in the column, under the dominical letter, opposite the name of the month given at the left.*

From the Sundays the date of any other day of the week can be readily found.

Thus, if we wish to know on what day of the week Christmas falls in 1889, we look opposite December, under the letter *F* (which we have found to be the dominical letter for the year), and find that the 22d of the month is a Sunday; the 25th, or Christmas, will then be Wednesday.

In the same way we may find the day of the week corresponding to any date (New Style) in history. For instance, the 17th of June, 1775, the day of the fight at Bunker Hill, is found to have been a *Saturday.*

These two tables then serve as a *perpetual almanac.*

WEIGHT OF THE EARTH AND PRECESSION.

85. *The Weight of the Earth.* — There are several methods of ascertaining the weight and mass of the earth The simplest, and perhaps the most trustworthy method is to compare the pull of the earth upon a ball of lead with that of a known mass of lead upon it. The pull of a known mass of lead upon the ball may be measured by means of a torsion balance. One form of the balance employed for this purpose is shown in Figs. 98 and 99. Two small balls of lead, *b* and *b*, are fastened to the ends of a light rod *e*, which is suspended from the point *F* by means of the thread *FE.* Two large balls of lead, *W* and *W*, are placed on a turn-table, so that one of them shall

be just in front of one of the small balls, and the other just
behind the other small ball. The pull of the large balls turns
the rod around a little so as to bring the small balls nearer the
large ones. The small balls move towards the large ones till

Fig. 98.

they are stopped by the torsion of the thread, which is then
equal to the pull of the large balls. The deflection of the rod
is carefully measured. The table is then turned into the position indicated by the dotted lines in Fig. 99, so as to reverse
the position of the large balls with reference to the small ones.

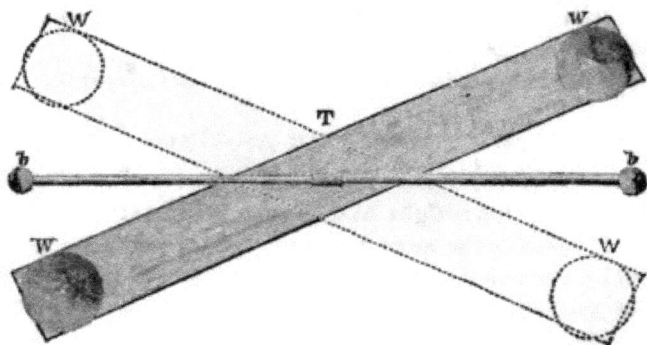

Fig. 99.

The rod is now deflected in the opposite direction, and the
amount of deflection is again carefully measured. The second
measurement is made as a check upon the accuracy of the first.
The force required to twist the thread as much as it was

twisted by the deflection of the rod is ascertained by measurement. This gives the pull of the two large balls upon the two
small ones. We next calculate what this pull would be were
the balls as far apart as the small balls are from the centre of
the earth. We can then form the following proportion: the
pull of the large balls upon the small ones is to the pull of the
earth upon the small ones as the mass of the large balls is to
the mass of the earth, or as the weight of the large balls is
to the weight of the earth. Of course, the pull of the earth
upon the small balls is the weight of the small balls. In this
way it has been ascertained that the mass of the earth is about
5.6 times that of a globe of water of the same size. In other
words, the *mean density* of the earth is about 5.6.

The weight of the earth in pounds may be found by multiplying the number of cubic feet in it by 62½ (the weight, in
pounds, of one cubic foot of water), and this product by 5.6.

86. *Cause of Precession.* — We have seen that the earth is

Fig. 100.

flattened at the poles: in other words, the earth has the form
of a sphere, with a protuberant ring around its equator. This
equatorial ring is inclined to the plane of the ecliptic at an angle
of about 23½°. In Fig. 100 this ring is represented as detached
from the enclosed sphere. *S* represents the sun, and *Sc* the
ecliptic. As the point *A* of the ring is nearer the sun than the
point *B* is, the sun's pull upon *A* is greater than upon *B*:
hence the sun tends to pull the ring over into the plane of the
ecliptic; but the rotation of the earth tends to keep the ring in
the same plane. The struggle between these two tendencies
causes the earth, to which the ring is attached, to wabble like
a spinning-top, whose rotation tends to keep it erect, while
gravity tends to pull it over. The handle of the top has a
gyratory motion, which causes it to describe a curve. The axis
of the heavens corresponds to the handle of the top.

II. THE MOON.

DISTANCE, SIZE, AND MOTIONS.

87. *The Distance of the Moon.* — The moon is the nearest of the heavenly bodies. Its distance from the centre of
the earth is only about sixty times the radius of the earth,
or, in round numbers, two hundred and forty thousand miles.

The ordinary method of finding the distance of one of the
nearer heavenly bodies is first to ascertain its horizontal parallax. This enables us to form a right-angled triangle, the
lengths of whose sides are easily computed, and the length of
whose hypothenuse is the distance of the body from the centre
of the earth. ·

Horizontal parallax has already been defined (32) as the displacement of a heavenly
body when on the horizon,
caused by its being seen
from the surface, instead of
the centre, of the earth.
This displacement is due

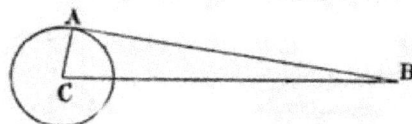

Fig. 101.

to the fact that the body is seen in a different direction from
the surface of the earth from that in which it would be seen
from the centre. Horizontal parallax might be defined as the
difference in the directions in which a body on the horizon
would be seen from the surface and from the centre of the
earth. Thus, in Fig. 101, C is the centre of the earth, A a
point on the surface, and B a body on the horizon of A. $A B$
is the direction in which the body would be seen from A, and
$C B$ the direction in which it would be seen from C. The difference of these directions, or the angle $A B C$, is the parallax
of the body.

The triangle $B A C$ is right-angled at A; the side $A C$ is the
radius of the earth, and the hypothenuse is the distance of the
body from the centre of the earth. When the parallax $A B C$
is known, the length of $C B$ can easily by found by trigonometrical computation.

We have seen (32) that the parallax of a heavenly body

grows less and less as the body passes from the horizon towards the zenith. The parallax of a body and its altitude are, however, so related, that, when we know the parallax at any altitude, we can readily compute the horizontal parallax.

The usual method of finding the parallax of one of the nearer heavenly bodies is first to find its parallax when on the meridian, as seen from two places on the earth which differ considerably in latitude: then to calculate what would be the parallax of the body as seen from one of these places and the centre of the earth: and then finally to calculate what would be the parallax were the body on the horizon.

Thus, we should ascertain the parallax of the body B (Fig. 102) as seen from A and D, or the angle ABD. We should then calculate its parallax as seen from A and C, or the angle ABC. Finally we should calculate what its parallax would be were the body on the horizon, or the angle $AB'C$.

The simplest method of finding the parallax of a body B (Fig. 102) as seen from the two points A and D is to compare its direction at each point with that of the same fixed star near the body. The star is so distant, that it will be seen in the same direction from both points: hence, if the

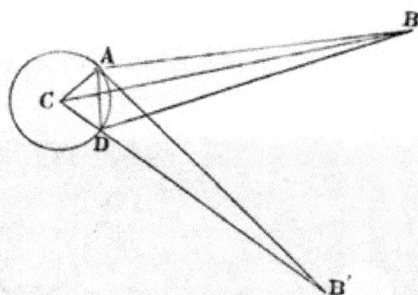

Fig. 102.

direction of the body differs from that of the star 2° as seen from one point, and 2° 6' as seen from the other point, the two lines AB and DB must differ in direction by 6'; in other words, the angle ABD would be 6'.

The method just described is the usual method of finding the parallax of the moon.

88. *The Apparent Size of the Moon.*—The *apparent size* of a body is the visual angle subtended by it: that is, the angle formed by two lines drawn from the eye to two opposite points on the outline of the body. The apparent size of a body depends upon both its *magnitude* and its *distance*.

The apparent size, or *angular diameter*, of the moon is about thirty-one minutes. This is ascertained by means of the wire micrometer already described (19). The instrument is adjusted so that its longitudinal wire shall pass through the centre of the moon, and its transverse wires

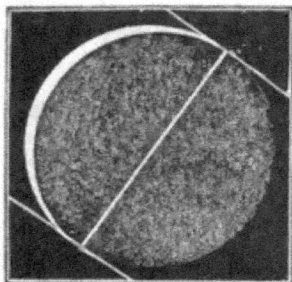

Fig. 103.

shall be tangent to the limbs of the moon on each side, at the point where they are cut by the longitudinal wire. The micrometer screw is then turned till the wires are brought together. The number of turns of the screw needed to accomplish this will indicate the arc between the wires, or the angular diameter of the moon.

In order to be certain that the longitudinal wire shall pass through the centre of the moon, it is best to take the moon when its disc is in the form of a crescent, and to place the

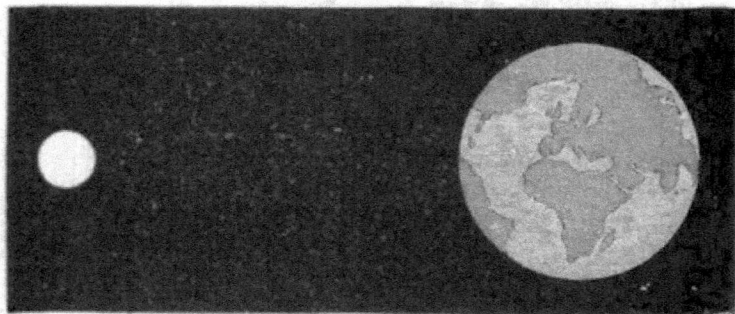

Fig. 104.

longitudinal wire against the points, or *cusps*, of the crescent, as shown in Fig. 103.

89. *The Real Size of the Moon.* — The real diameter of the moon is a little over one-fourth of that of the earth, or a little more than two thousand miles. The comparative sizes of the earth and moon are shown in Fig. 104.

The distance and apparent size of the moon being known. her real diameter is found by means of a triangle formed as shown in Fig. 105. *C* represents the centre of the moon, *CB* the distance of the moon from the earth, and *CA* the radius of the moon. *BAC* is a triangle, right-angled at *A*. The angle *ABC* is half the apparent diameter of the moon. With the angles *A* and *B*, and the side *CB* known, it is easy to find the length of *AC* by trigonometrical computation. Twice *AC* will be the diameter of the moon.

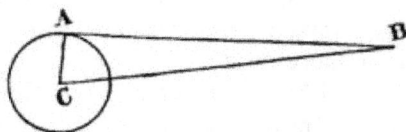

Fig. 105.

The volume of the moon is about one-fiftieth of that of the earth.

90. *Apparent Size of the Moon on the Horizon and in the Zenith.* — The moon is nearly four thousand miles farther from the observer when she is on the horizon than when she is in the zenith. This is evident from Fig. 106. *C* is the centre of the earth, *M* the moon on the horizon, *M'* the moon in the zenith, and *O* the point of observation. *OM* is the distance of the moon when she is on the horizon, and *OM'* the distance of the moon from the observer when she is in the zenith. *CM* is equal to *CM'*, and *OM* is about the length of *CM*; but *OM'* is about four thousand miles shorter than *CM'*: hence *OM'* is about four thousand miles shorter than *OM*.

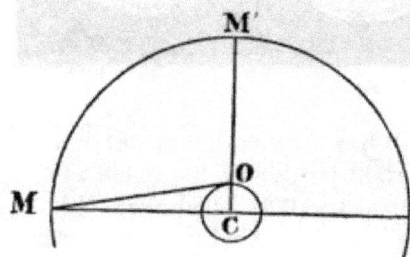

Fig. 106.

Notwithstanding the moon is much nearer when at the zenith than at the horizon, it seems to us much larger at the horizon.

This is a pure illusion, as we become convinced when we measure the disc with accurate instruments, so as to make the

result independent of our ordinary way of judging. When the
moon is near the horizon, it seems placed beyond all the objects
on the surface of the earth in that direction, and therefore farther off than at the zenith, where no intervening objects enable
us to judge of its distance. In any case, an object which keeps
the same apparent magnitude seems to us, through the instinc-
tive habits of the eye, the larger in proportion as we judge it
to be more distant.

91. *The Apparent Size of the Moon increased by Irradiation.* — In the case of the moon, the word *apparent* means much
more than it does in the case of other celestial bodies. Indeed,
its brightness causes our eyes to play us false. As is well
known, the crescent of the new moon seems part of a much

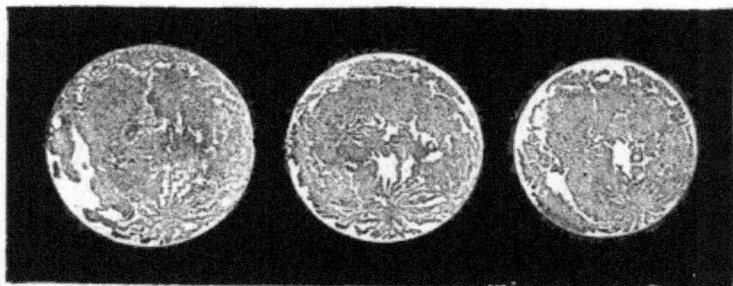

Fig. 107.

larger sphere than that which it has been said, time out of mind,
to "hold in its arms." The bright portion of the moon as seen
with our measuring instruments, as well as when seen with the
naked eye, covers a larger space in the field of the telescope
than it would if it were not so bright. This effect of *irradiation*, as it is called, must be allowed for in exact measurements
of the diameter of the moon.

92. *Apparent Size of the Moon in Different Parts of
her Orbit.* — Owing to the eccentricity of the moon's orbit,
her distance from the earth varies somewhat from time to
time. This variation causes a corresponding variation in
her apparent size, which is illustrated in Fig. 107.

93. *The Mass of the Moon.* — The moon is considerably

less dense than the earth, its mass being only about one-eightieth of that of the earth; that is, while it would take only about fifty moons to make the bulk of the earth, it would take about eighty to make the mass of the earth.

One method of finding the mass of the moon is to compare her effect in producing the *tides* with that of the sun. We first calculate what would be the moon's effect in producing the tides, were she as far off as the sun. We then form the following proportion: as the sun's effect in producing the tides is to the moon's effect at the same distance, so is the mass of the sun to the mass of the moon.

The method of finding the mass of the sun will be given farther on.

94. *The Orbital Motion of the Moon.* — If we watch the moon from night to night, we see that she moves eastward quite rapidly among the stars. When the new moon is first visible, it appears near the horizon in the west, just after sunset. A week later the moon will be on the meridian at the same hour, and about a week later still on the eastern horizon. The moon completes the circuit of the heavens in a period of about thirty days, moving eastward at the rate of about twelve degrees a day. This eastward motion of the moon is due to the fact that she is revolving around the earth from west to east.

95. *The Aspects of the Moon.* — As the moon revolves around the earth, she comes into different positions with reference to the earth and sun. These different positions of the moon are called the *aspects* of the moon. The four chief aspects of the moon are shown in Fig. 108. When the moon is at M, she appears in the opposite part of the heavens to the sun, and is said to be in *opposition;* when at M' and at M''', she appears ninety degrees away from the sun, and is said to be in *quadrature;* when at M'', she appears in the same part of the heavens as the sun, and is said to be in *conjunction.*

96. *The Sidereal and Synodical Periods of the Moon.* —
The *sidereal period* of the moon is the time it takes her to
pass around from a star to that star again, or the time it

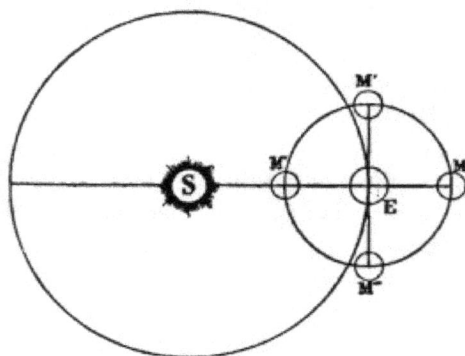

takes her to *make
a complete revolution
around the earth.*
This is a period
of about twenty-seven
days and a third. It
is sometimes called
the *sidereal month.*

The *synodical peri-
od* of the moon is the
time that it takes the
moon to *pass from*

Fig. 108.

one aspect around to the same aspect again. This is a
period of about twenty-nine days and a half, and it is sometimes called the *synodical month.*

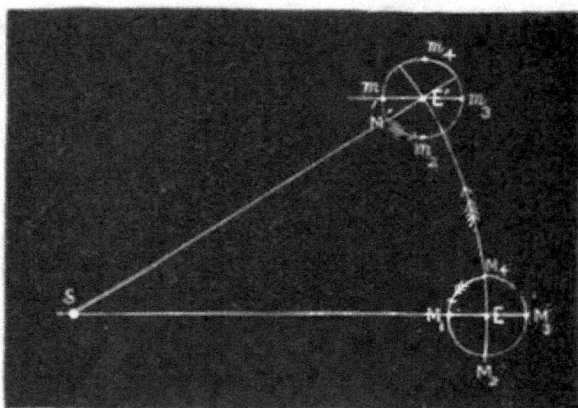

Fig. 109.

The reason why the synodical period is longer than the
sidereal period will appear from Fig. 109. *S* represents the
position of the sun, *E* that of the earth, and the small

circle the orbit of the moon around the earth. The arrow in the small circle represents the direction the moon is revolving around the earth, and the arrow in the arc between E and E' indicates the direction of the earth's motion in its orbit. When the moon is at M_1, she is in conjunction. As the moon revolves around the earth, the earth moves forward in its orbit. When the moon has come round to m_1, so that $m_3 m_1$ is parallel with $M_3 M_1$, she will have made a complete or *sidereal* revolution around the earth ; but she will not be in conjunction again till she has come round to M, so as again to be between the earth and sun. That

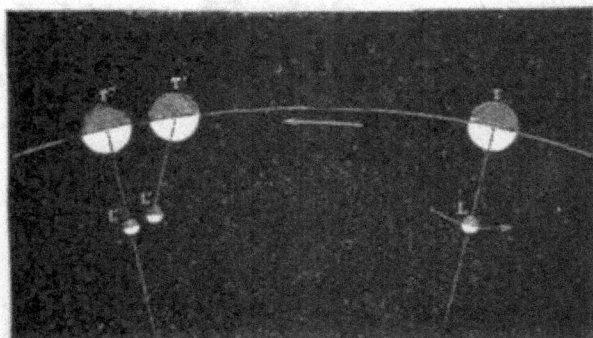

Fig. 110.

is to say, the moon must make more than a complete revolution in a synodical period.

The greater length of the synodical period is also evident from Fig. 110. T represents the earth, and L the moon. The arrows indicate the direction in which each is moving. When the earth is at T, and the moon at L, the latter is in conjunction. When the earth has reached T', and the moon L', the latter has made a sidereal revolution ; but she will not be in conjunction again till the earth has reached T'', and the moon L''.

97. *The Phases of the Moon.* — When the new moon appears in the west, it has the form of a *crescent*, with its

convex side towards the sun, and its horns towards the east.

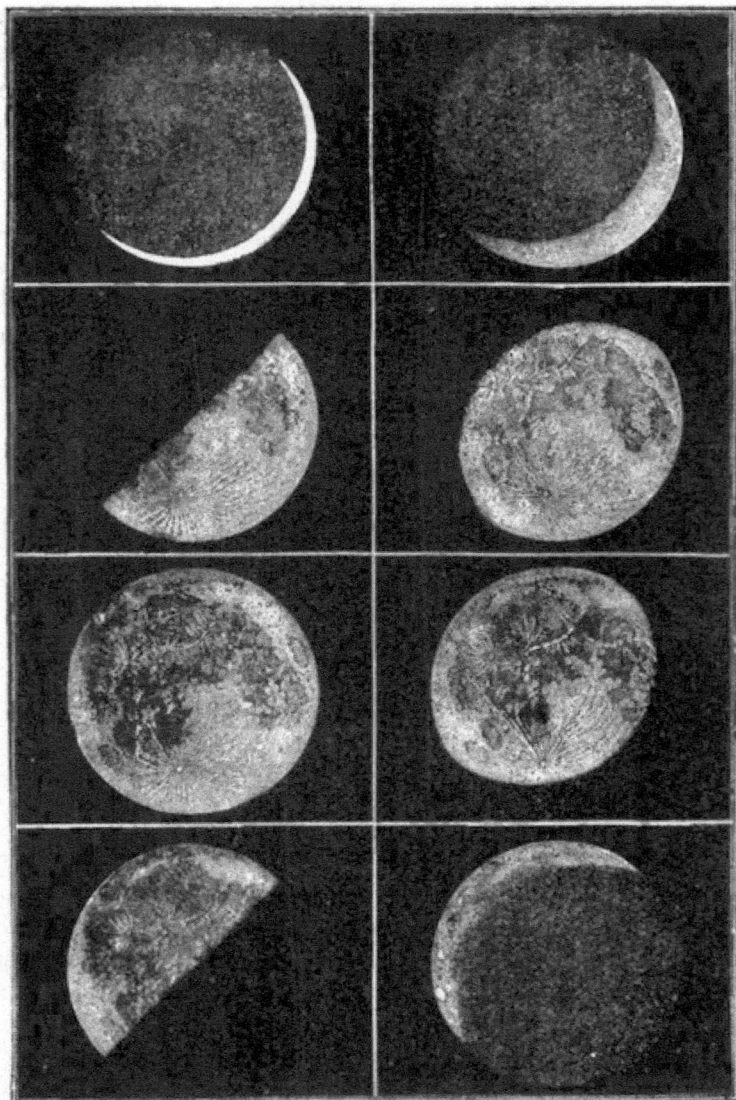

Fig 111.

As the moon advances towards quadrature, the crescent grows thicker and thicker, till it becomes a *half-circle* at first quarter. When it passes quadrature, it begins to become convex also on the side away from the sun, or *gibbous* in form. As it approaches opposition, it becomes more and more nearly circular, until at opposition it is a *full* circle. From full moon to last quarter it is again gibbous, and at last quarter a half-circle. From last quarter to new moon it is again crescent; but the horns of the crescent are now turned towards the west. The successive phases of the moon are shown in Fig. 111.

98. *Cause of the Phases of the Moon.* — Take a globe, half of which is colored white and the other half black in such a way that the line which separates the white and black portions shall be a great circle which passes through the poles of the globe, and rotate the globe slowly, so as to bring the white half gradually into view. When the white part first comes into view, the line of separation between it and the black part, which we may call the *terminator*, appears concave, and its projection on a plane perpendicular to the line of vision is a concave line. As more and more of the white portion comes into view, the projection of the terminator becomes less and less concave. When half of the white portion comes into view, the terminator is projected as a straight line. When more than half of the white portion comes into view, the terminator begins to appear as a convex line, and this line becomes more and more convex till the whole of the white half comes into view, when the terminator becomes circular.

The moon is of itself a dark, opaque globe; but the half that is towards the sun is always bright, as shown in Fig. 112. This bright half of the moon corresponds to the white half of the globe in the preceding illustration. As the moon revolves around the earth, different portions of this illumined half are turned towards the earth. At new moon, when the moon is in conjunction, the bright half is turned entirely away from the earth, and the disc of the moon is black and invisible. Between new moon and first quarter, less than half of the illumined side is turned towards the earth, and we see this illumined portion projected as a crescent. At first quarter, just half of the illumined side is turned towards the earth, and we see this half projected as a half-circle.

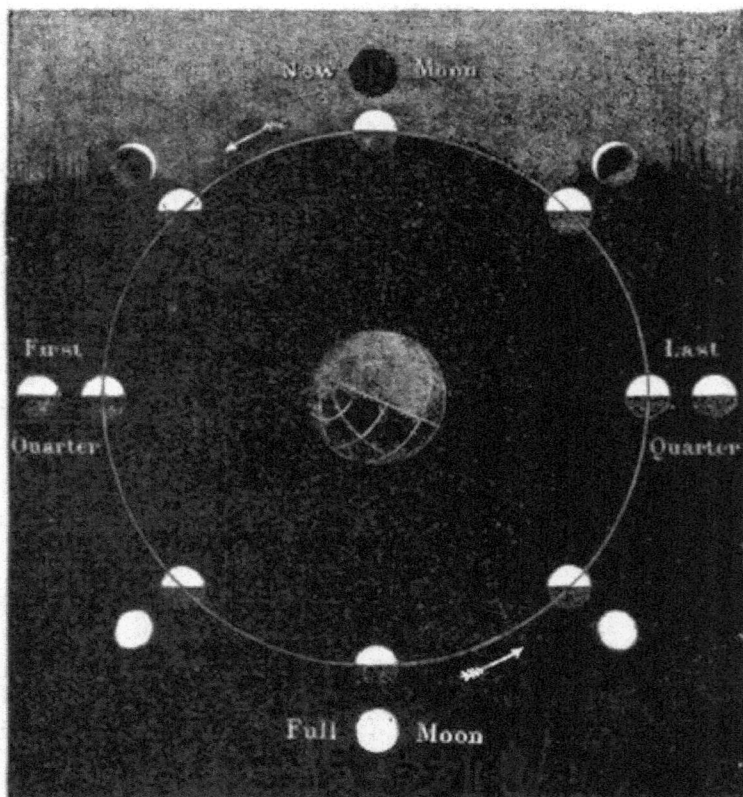

Fig. 112.

Between first quarter and full, more than half of the illumined side is turned towards the earth, and we see it as gibbous. At full, the whole of the illumined side is turned towards us, and we see it as a full circle. From full to new moon again, the phases occur in the reverse order.

99. *The Form of the Moon's Orbit.* — The orbit of the moon around the earth is an ellipse of slight eccentricity. The form of this ellipse is shown in Fig. 113. *C* is the centre of the ellipse, and *E* the position of the earth at one of its foci. The eccentricity of the ellipse is only about one-eighteenth. It is impossible for the eye to distinguish such an ellipse from a circle.

100. *The Inclination of the Moon's Orbit.* — The plane

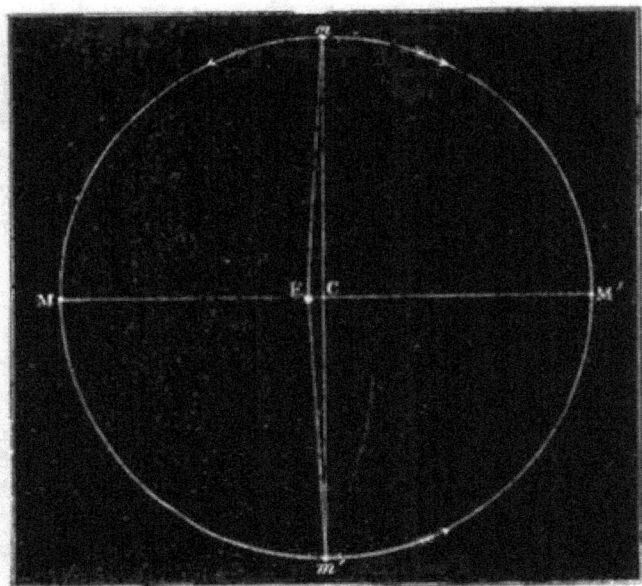

Fig. 113.

of the moon's orbit is inclined to the ecliptic by an angle of about five degrees. The two points where the moon's orbit cuts the ecliptic are called her *nodes*. The moon's nodes have a westward motion corresponding to that of the equinoxes, but much more rapid. They complete the circuit of the ecliptic in about nineteen years.

The moon's latitude ranges from 5° north to 5° south; and since, owing to the motion of her nodes, the moon is, during a period of nineteen years, $5°$ north and $5°$ south of every part of the ecliptic, her declination will range from $23\frac{1}{2}° + 5° = 28\frac{1}{2}°$ north to $23\frac{1}{2}° + 5° = 28\frac{1}{2}°$ south.

101. *The Meridian Altitude of the Moon.*—The *meridian altitude* of any body is its altitude when on the meridian. In our latitude, the meridian altitude of any point on the equinoctial is forty-nine degrees. The meridian altitude of the summer solstice is $49° + 23\frac{1}{2}° = 72\frac{1}{2}°$, and that of the winter solstice is $49° - 23\frac{1}{2}° = 25\frac{1}{2}°$. The greatest meridian altitude of the moon is $72\frac{1}{2}° + 5° = 77\frac{1}{2}°$, and its least meridian altitude, $25\frac{1}{2}° - 5° = 20\frac{1}{2}°$.

When the moon's meridian altitude is greater than the elevation of the equinoctial, it is said to run *high*, and when less, to run *low*. The full moon runs high when the sun is south of the equinoctial, and low when the sun is north of the equinoctial. This is because the full moon is always in the opposite part of the heavens to the sun.

102. *Wet and Dry Moon.*—At the time of new moon, the cusps of the crescent sometimes lie in a line which is nearly perpendicular with the horizon, and sometimes in a line which is nearly parallel with the horizon. In the former case the moon is popularly described as a *wet* moon, and in the latter case as a *dry* moon.

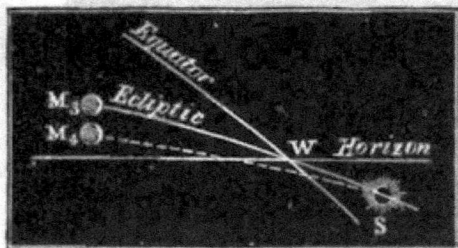

Fig. 114.

The great circle which passes through the centre of the sun and moon will pass through the centre of the crescent, and be perpendicular to the line joining the cusps. Now the ecliptic makes the least angle with the horizon when the vernal equinox is on the eastern horizon and the autumnal equinox is on the western. In our latitude, as we have seen, this angle is $25\frac{1}{2}°$: hence in our latitude, if the moon were at new on the ecliptic when the sun is at the autumnal equinox, as shown at M_3 (Fig. 114), the great circle passing through the centre of the sun and moon would be the ecliptic, and at New York would be inclined to the horizon at an angle of $25\frac{1}{2}°$. If the moon happened to be $5°$ south of the ecliptic at this time, as at M_4, the great circle pass-ing through the centre of the sun and moon would make an angle of only $20\frac{1}{2}°$ with the horizon. In either of these cases the line joining the cusps would be nearly perpen-dicular to the horizon.

If the moon were at new on the ecliptic when the sun is near the vernal equinox, as shown at M_1 (Fig. 115), the great circle

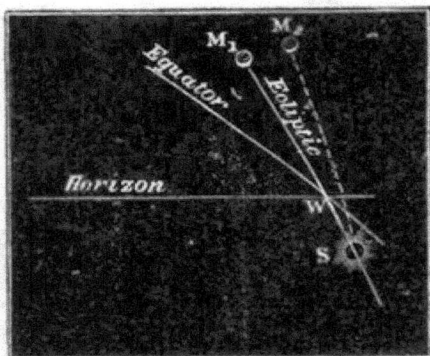

Fig. 115.

passing through the centres of the sun and moon would make an angle of $72\frac{1}{2}°$ with the horizon at New York; and were the moon $5°$ north of the ecliptic at that time, as shown at M_2, this great circle would make an angle of $77\frac{1}{2}°$ with the horizon. In either of these cases, the line joining the cusps would be nearly parallel with the horizon.

At different times, the line joining the cusps may have every possible inclination to the horizon between the extreme cases shown in Figs. 114 and 115.

103. *Daily Retardation of the Moon's Rising.* — The moon rises, on the average, about fifty minutes later each day. This is owing to her eastward motion. As the moon makes a complete revolution around the earth in about twenty-seven days, she moves eastward at the rate of about thirteen degrees a day, or about twelve degrees a day faster than the sun. Were the moon, therefore, on the horizon at any hour to-day, she would be some twelve degrees below the horizon at the same hour to-morrow. Now, as the hori-

zon moves at the rate of one degree in four minutes, it
would take it some fifty minutes to come up to the moon so
as to bring her upon the horizon. Hence the daily retardation of the moon's rising is about fifty minutes ; but it
varies considerably in differ-
ent parts of her orbit.

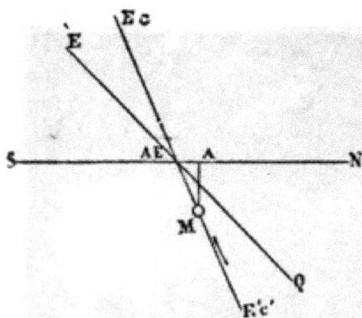

Fig. 116.

There are two reasons for
this variation in the daily
retardation : —

(1) The moon moves at a
varying rate in her orbit; her
speed being greatest at perigee,
and least at apogee : hence,
other things being equal, the
retardation is greatest when
the moon is at perigee, and least when she is at apogee.

(2) The moon moves at a *varying angle to the horizon.*
The moon moves nearly in the plane of the ecliptic, and of
course she passes both equinoxes every lunation. When she
is near the autumnal equinox, her path makes the greatest
angle with the eastern horizon, and when she is near the
vernal equinox, the least angle:
hence the moon moves away
from the horizon fastest when
she is near the autumnal equinox, and slowest when she is
near the vernal equinox. This
will be evident from Figs. 116
and 117. In each figure, *SN*
represents a portion of the
eastern horizon, and *Ec, E'c',*
a portion of the ecliptic. *AE,*

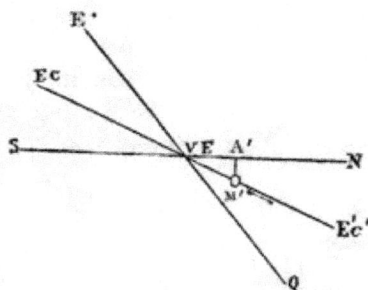

Fig. 117.

in Fig. 116, represents the autumnal equinox, and *A E M* the
daily motion of the moon. *VE,* in Fig. 117, represents the
vernal equinox, and *VE M'* the motion of the moon for one
day. In the first case this motion would carry the moon away
from the horizon the distance *A M,* and in the second case the

distance $A'M'$. Now, it is evident that AM is greater than $A'M'$; hence, other things being equal, the greatest retardation of the moon's rising will be when the moon is near the autumnal equinox, and the least retardation when the moon is near the vernal equinox.

The least retardation at New York is twenty-three minutes, and the greatest an hour and seventeen minutes. The greatest and least retardations vary somewhat from month to month; since they depend not only upon the position of the moon in her orbit with reference to the equinoxes, but also

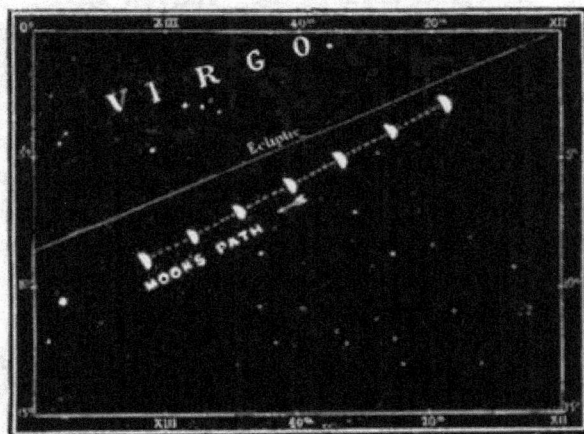

Fig. 118.

upon the latitude of the moon, and upon her nearness to the earth.

The direction of the moon's motion with reference to the ecliptic is shown in Fig. 118, which shows the moon's motion for one day in July, 1876.

104. *The Harvest Moon.* — The long and short retardations in the rising of the moon, though they occur every month, are not likely to attract attention unless they occur at the time of full moon. The long retardations for full moon occur when the moon is near the autumnal equinox at full. As the full moon is always opposite to the sun, the

sun must in this case be near the vernal equinox : hence the long retardations for full moon occur in the spring, the greatest retardation being in March.

The least retardations for full moon occur when the moon is near the vernal equinox at full : the sun must then be near the autumnal equinox. Hence the least retardations for full moon occur in the months of August, September, and October. The retardation is, of course, least for September ; and the full moon of this month rises night after night less than half an hour later than the previous night. The full moon of September is called the " Harvest Moon," and that of October the " Hunter's Moon."

105. *The Rotation of the Moon.* — A careful examination of the spots on the disc of the moon reveals the fact that she always presents the same side to the earth. In order to do this, she must rotate on her axis while making a revolution around the earth, or in about twenty-seven days.

106. *Librations of the Moon.* — The moon appears to rock slowly to and fro, so as to allow us to see alternately a little farther around to the right and the left, or above and below, than we otherwise could. This apparent rocking of the moon is called *libration*. The moon has three librations : —

(1) *Libration in Latitude.* — This libration enables us to see alternately a little way around on the northern and southern limbs of the moon.

This libration is due to the fact that the axis of the moon is not quite perpendicular to the plane of her orbit. The deviation from the perpendicular is six degrees and a half. As the axis of the moon, like that of the earth, maintains the same direction, the poles of the moon will be turned alternately six degrees and a half toward and from the earth.

(2) *Libration in Longitude.* — This libration enables us to see alternately a little farther around on the eastern and western limbs of the moon.

It is due to the fact that the moon's axial motion is **uniform**, while her orbital motion is not. At perigee her orbital motion will be in advance of her axial motion, while at apogee the axial motion will be in advance of the orbital. In Fig. 119, *E* represents the earth. *M* the moon, the, large arrow the direction of the moon's motion in her orbit, and the small arrow the direction of her motion of rotation. When the moon is at *M*, the line *A B*, drawn perpendicular to *E M*, represents the circle which divides the visible from the invisible portion of the moon. While the moon is passing from *M* to *M'*, the moon performs less than a quarter of a rotation, so that *A B* is no longer perpendicular to *E M'*. An observer on the earth can now see somewhat beyond *A* on the western limb of the moon, and not quite up to *B* on the eastern limb. While the moon is passing from *M'* to *M"*, her axial motion again overtakes her orbital motion, so that the line *A B* again becomes perpendicular to the line joining the centre of the moon to the centre of the earth. Exactly the same side is now turned

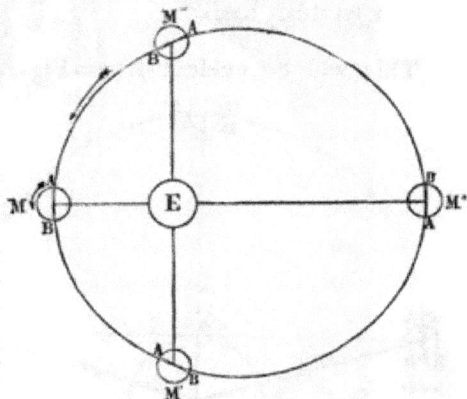

Fig. 119.

towards the earth as when the moon was at *M*. While the moon passes from *M"* to *M'''*, her axial motion gets in advance of her orbital motion, so that *A B* is again inclined to the line joining the centres of the earth and moon. A portion of the eastern limb of the moon beyond *B* is now brought into view to the earth, and a portion of the western limb at *A* is carried out of view. While the moon is passing from *M'''* to *M*, the orbital motion again overtakes the axial motion, and *A B* is again perpendicular to *M E*.

(3) *Parallactic Libration.* — While an observer at the centre of the earth would get the same view of the moon,

whether she were on the eastern horizon, in the zenith, or on the western horizon, an observer on the surface of the earth does not get exactly the same view in these three cases. When the moon is on the eastern horizon, an observer on the surface of the earth would see a little farther around on the western limb of the moon than when she is in the zenith, and not quite so far around on the eastern limb. On the contrary, when the moon is on the western horizon, an observer on the surface of the earth sees a little farther around on the eastern limb of the moon than when she is in the zenith, and not quite so far around ,on her western limb.

This will be evident from Fig. 120.

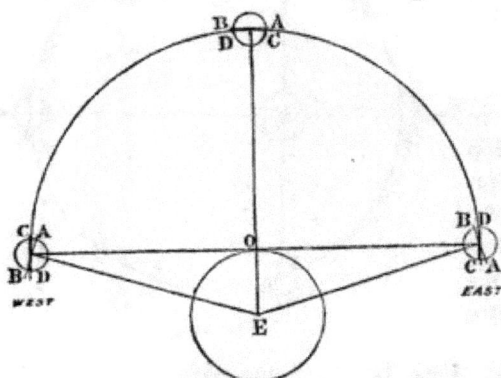

Fig. 120.

E is the centre of the earth, and O a point on its surface. AB is a line drawn through the centre of the moon, perpendicular to a line joining the centres of the moon and the earth. This line marks off the part of the moon turned towards the centre of the earth, and remains essentially the same during the day. CD is a line drawn through the centre of the moon perpendicular to a line joining the centre of the moon and the point of observation. This line marks off the part of the moon turned towards O. When the moon is in the zenith, CD coincides with AB; but, when the moon is on the horizon, CD is inclined to AB. When the moon is on the eastern horizon, an observer at O sees a little beyond B, and not quite to A; and, when she is on the western horizon, he sees a little beyond A, and not quite to B. B is on the western limb of the moon, and A on her eastern limb.

Since this libration is due to the point from which the moon is viewed, it is called *parallactic* libration; and, since it occurs daily, it is called *diurnal* libration.

107. *Portion of the Lunar Surface brought into View by Libration.* — The area brought into view by the first two librations is between one-twelfth and one-thirteenth of the whole lunar surface, or nearly one-sixth of the hemisphere of the moon which is turned away from the earth when the moon is at her state of mean libration. Of course a precisely equal portion

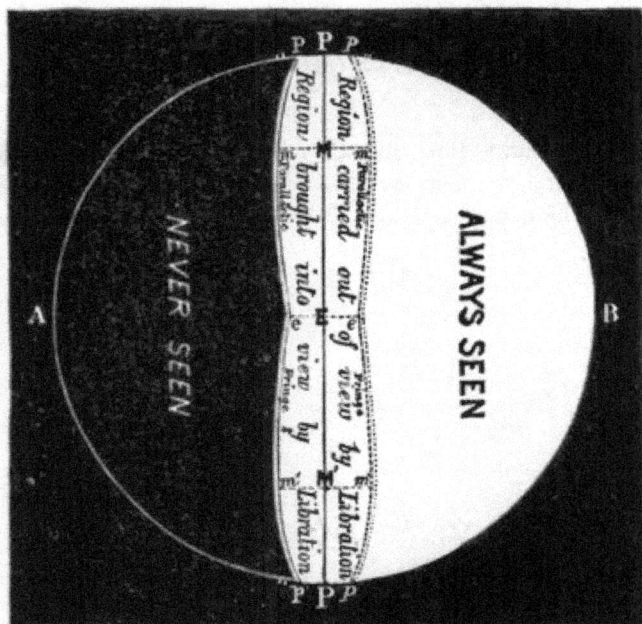

Fig. 121.

of the hemisphere turned towards us during mean libration is carried out of view by the lunar librations.

If we add to each of these areas a fringe about one degree wide, due to the diurnal libration, and which we may call the *parallactic* fringe, we shall find that the total area brought into view is almost exactly one-eleventh part of the whole surface of the moon. A similar area is carried out of view; so that the whole region thus swayed out of and into view amounts to two-elevenths of the moon's surface. This area is shown in Fig. 121, which is a side view of the moon.

108. *The Moon's Path through Space.* — Were the earth stationary, the moon would describe an ellipse around it similar to that of Fig. 113; but, as the earth moves forward in her

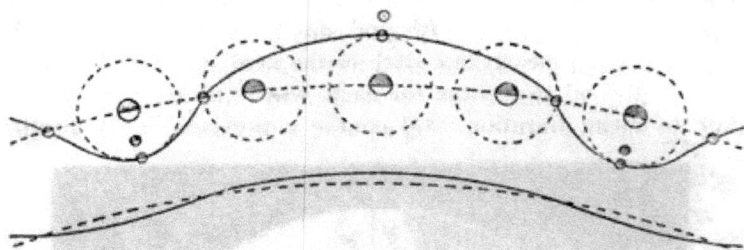

Fig. 122.

orbit at the same time that the moon revolves around it, the moon is made to describe a sinuous path, as shown by the continuous line in Fig. 122.   This feature of the moon's path is

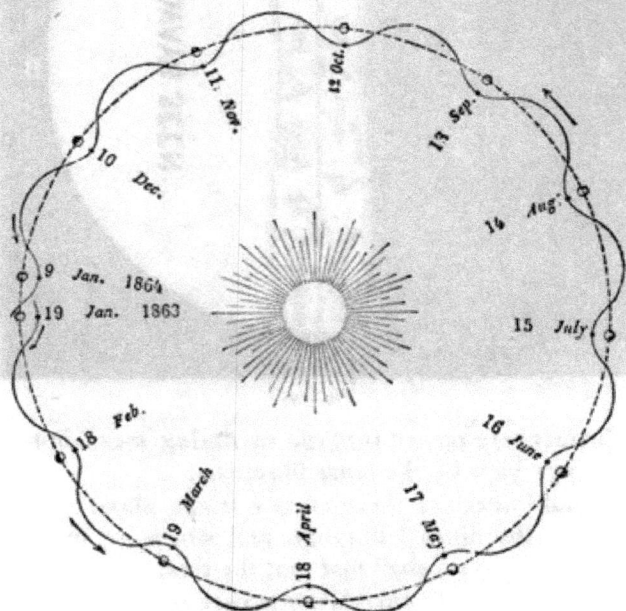

Fig. 123.

greatly exaggerated in the upper portion of the diagram.   The form of her path is given with a greater degree of accuracy in the lower part of the figure (the broken line represents the path, of the earth); but even here there is considerable exaggeration. The complete serpentine path of the moon around the sun is shown, greatly exaggerated, in Fig. 123, the broken line being the path of the earth.

The path described by the moon through space is much the same as that described by a point on the circumference of a wheel which is rolled over another wheel. If we place a circular disk against the wall, and carefully roll along its edge another circular disk (to which a piece of lead pencil has been

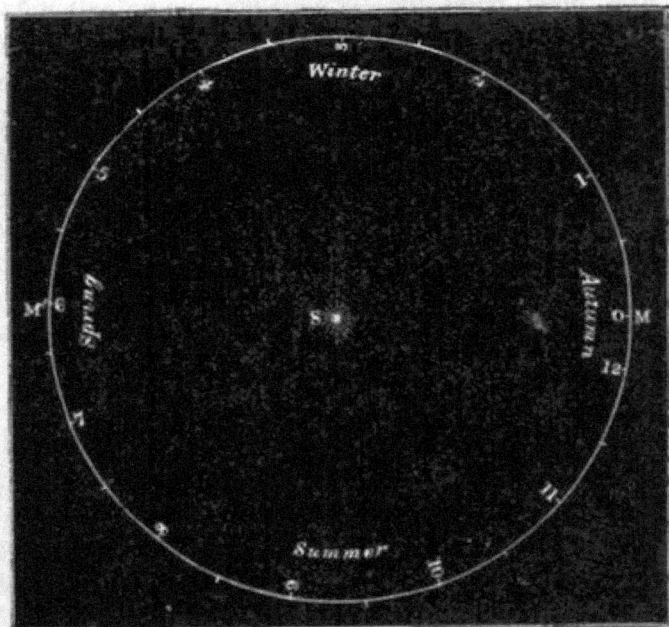

Fig. 124.

fastened so as to mark upon the wall), the curve described will somewhat resemble that described by the moon. This curve is called an *epicycloid*, and it will be seen that at every point it is concave towards the centre of the larger disk. In the same way the moon's orbit is *at every point concave towards the sun*.

The exaggeration of the sinuosity in Fig. 123 will be more evident when it is stated, that, on the scale of Fig. 124, the whole of the serpentine curve would lie *within the breadth* of the fine circular line MM'.

109. *The Lunar Day.* — The lunar day is twenty-nine times and a half as long as the terrestrial day. Near the moon's equator the sun shines without intermission nearly fifteen of our days, and is absent for the same length of time. Consequently, the vicissitudes of temperature to which the surface is exposed must be very great. During the long lunar night the temperature of a body on the moon's surface would probably fall lower than is ever known on the earth, while during the day it must rise higher than anywhere on our planet.

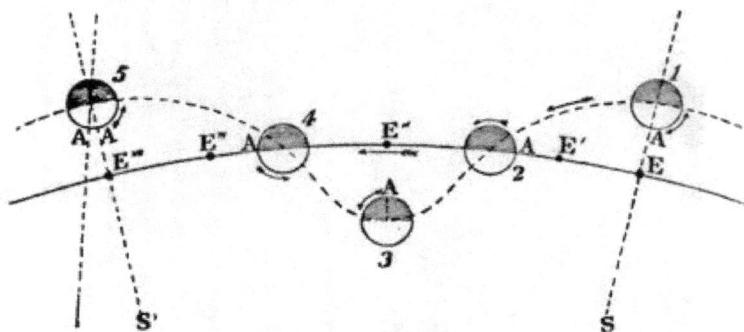

Fig. 125.

It might seem, that, since the moon rotates on her axis in about twenty-seven days, the lunar day ought to be twenty-seven days long, instead of twenty-nine. There is, however, a solar, as well as a sidereal, day at the moon, as on the earth; and the solar day at the moon is longer than the sidereal day, for the same reason as on the earth. During the solar day the moon must make both a *synodical rotation* and a *synodical revolution.* This will be evident from Fig. 125, in which is shown the path of the moon during one complete lunation. E, E', E'', etc., are the successive positions of the earth; and 1, 2, 3, 4, 5, the successive positions of the moon. The small arrows indicate the direction of the moon's rotation. The moon is full at 1 and 5. At 1, A, at the centre of the moon's disk, will have the sun, which lies in the direction *A S*, upon the meridian. Before *A* will again have the sun on the meridian, the moon must have made a synodical revolution; and, as will be seen by the dotted lines, she must have made more than a complete rotation. The rotation which brings the point *A* into the same relation to the earth and sun is called a *synodical* rotation.

It will also be evident from this diagram that the moon must make a synodical rotation during a synodical revolution, in order always to present the same side to the earth.

110. *The Earth as seen from the Moon.* — To an observer on the moon, the earth would be an immense moon, going through the same phases that the moon does to us; but, instead of rising and setting, it would only oscillate to and fro through a few degrees. On the other side of the moon it would never be seen at all. The peculiarities of the moon's motions which cause the librations, and make a spot on the moon's disk seem to an observer on the earth to oscillate to and fro, would cause the earth as a whole to appear to a lunar observer to oscillate to and fro in the heavens in a similar manner.

It is a well-known fact, that, at the time of new moon, the dark part of the moon's surface is partially illumined, so that it becomes visible to the naked eye. This must be due to the light reflected to the moon from the earth. Since at new moon the moon is between the earth and sun, it follows, that, when it is new moon at the earth, it must be *full earth* at the moon : hence, while the bright crescent is enjoying full sunlight, the dark part of its surface is enjoying the light of the full *earth*. Fig. 126 represents the full earth as seen from the moon.

THE ATMOSPHERE OF THE MOON.

111. *The Moon has no Appreciable Atmosphere.* — There are several reasons for believing that the moon has little or no atmosphere.

(1) Had the moon an atmosphere, it would be indicated

Fig. 126.

at the time of a solar eclipse, when the moon passes over
the disk of the sun. If the atmosphere were of any con-

siderable density, it would absorb a part of the sun's rays, so as to produce a dusky border in front of the moon's disk, as shown in Fig. 127. In reality no such dusky border is ever seen; but the limb of the moon appears sharp, and clearly defined, as in Fig. 128.

If the atmosphere were not dense enough to produce this dusky border, its refraction would be sufficient to distort the delicate cusps of the sun's crescent in the manner shown at the top of Fig. 125;

Fig. 127.

but no such distortion is ever observed. The cusps always appear clear and sharp, as shown at the bottom of the figure : hence it would seem that there can be no atmosphere of appreciable density at the moon.

Fig. 128.

(2) The absence of an atmosphere from the moon is also shown by the absence of twilight and of diffused daylight.

Upon the earth, twilight continues until the sun is eighteen degrees below the horizon; that is, day and night are separated by a belt twelve hundred miles in breadth, in which the transition from light to darkness is gradual. We have seen (66) that this twilight results from the refraction and reflection of light by our atmosphere; and, if the moon had an atmos-

phere, we should notice a similar gradual transition from
the bright to the dark portions of her surface. Such, however, is not the case. The boundary between the light and
darkness, though irregular, is sharply defined. Close to this
boundary the unillumined portion of the moon appears just
as dark as at any distance from it.

The shadows on the moon are also pitchy black, without
a trace of diffused daylight.

(3) The absence of an atmosphere is also proved by the
absence of refraction when the moon passes between us and
the stars. Let AB (Fig. 129) represent the disk of the moon,
and CD an atmosphere supposed to surround it. Let SAE
represent a straight line from the earth, touching the moon at
A, and let S be a star situated in the direction of this line. If

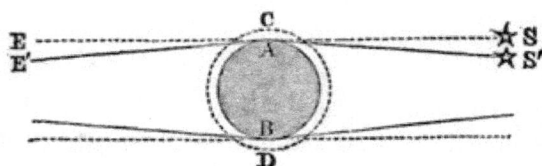

the moon had no
atmosphere, this
star would appear
to touch the edge
of the moon at
A; but, if the
moon had an at-

Fig. 129.

mosphere, a star behind the edge of the moon, at S', would
be visible at the earth; for the ray $S'A$ would be bent by the
atmosphere into the direction AE'. So, also, on the opposite
side of the moon, a star might be seen at the earth, although
really behind the edge of the moon : hence, if the moon had an
atmosphere, the time during which a star would be concealed
by the moon would be less than if it had no atmosphere, and
the amount of this effect must be proportional to the density
of the atmosphere.

The moon, in her orbital course across the heavens, is continually passing before, or *occulting*, some of the stars that so
thickly stud her apparent path; and when we see a star thus
pass behind the lunar disk on one side, and come out again on
the other side, we are virtually observing the setting and rising
of that star upon the moon. The moon's apparent diameter
has been measured over and over again, and is known with

great accuracy; the rate of her motion across the sky is also known with perfect accuracy: hence it is easy to calculate how long the moon will take to travel across a part of the sky exactly equal in length to her own diameter. Supposing, then, that we observe a star pass behind the moon, and out again, it is clear, that, if there is no atmosphere, the interval of time during which it remains occulted ought to be exactly equal to the computed time which the moon would take to pass over the star. If, however, from the existence of a lunar atmosphere, the star disappears too late, and re-appears too soon, as we have seen it would, these two intervals will not agree; the computed time will be greater than the observed time, and the difference will represent the amount of refraction the star's light has sustained or suffered, and hence the extent of atmosphere it has had to pass through.

Comparisons of these two intervals of time have been repeatedly made, the most extensive being executed under the direction of the Astronomer Royal of England, several years ago, and based upon no less than two hundred and ninety-six occultation observations. In this determination the measured or telescopic diameter of the moon was compared with the diameter deduced from the occultations; and it was found that the telescopic diameter was greater than the occultation diameter by two seconds of angular measurement, or by about a thousandth part of the whole diameter of the moon. This discrepancy is probably due, in part at least, to *irradiation* (91), which augments the apparent size of the moon, as seen in the telescope as well as with the naked eye; but, if the whole two seconds were caused by atmospheric refraction, this would imply a horizontal refraction of one second, which is only one two-thousandth of the earth's horizontal refraction. It is possible that an atmosphere competent to produce this refraction would not make itself visible in any other way.

But an atmosphere two thousand times rarer than our air can scarcely be regarded as an atmosphere at all. The contents of an air-pump receiver can seldom be rarefied to a greater extent than to about a thousandth of the density of air at the earth's surface; and the lunar atmosphere, if it exists at all, is thus proved to be twice as attenuated as what we commonly call a vacuum.

THE SURFACE OF THE MOON.

112. *Dusky Patches on the Disk of the Moon.* — With the naked eye, large dusky patches are seen on the moon, in which popular fancy has detected a resemblance to a human face. With a telescope of low power, these dark patches appear as smooth as water, and they were once

Fig. 130.

supposed to be seas. This theory was the origin of the name *mare* (Latin for *sea*), which is still applied to the larger of these plains; but, if there were water on the surface of the moon, it could not fail to manifest its presence by its vapor, which would form an appreciable atmosphere. Moreover, with a high telescopic power, these plains present a more or less uneven surface; and, as the elevations and depressions are found to be permanent, they cannot, of course, belong to the surface of water.

The chief of these plains are shown in Fig. 130. They are *Mare Crisium*, *Mare Fœcunditatis*, *Mare Nectaris*, *Mare Tranquillitatis*, *Mare Serenitatis*, *Mare Imbrium*, *Mare Frigoris*, and *Oceanus Procellarum*. All these plains can easily be recognized on the surface of the full moon with the unaided eye.

113. *The Terminator of the Moon.* — The *terminator* of the moon is the line which separates the bright and dark portions of its disk. When viewed with a telescope of even moderate power, the terminator is seen to be very irregular and uneven. Many bright points are seen just outside of the terminator in the dark portion of the disk, while all along in the neighborhood of the terminator are bright patches

Fig. 131.

and dense shadows. These appearances are shown in Figs. 131 and 132, which represent the moon near the first and last quarters. They indicate that the surface of the moon is very rough and uneven.

As it is always either sunrise or sunset along the terminator, the bright spots outside of it are clearly the tops of mountains, which catch the rays of the sun while their bases

are in the shade.   The bright patches in the neighborhood
of the terminator are the sides of hills and mountains which
are receiving the full light of the sun, while the dense
shadows near by are cast by these elevations.

114. *Height of the Lunar Mountains.* — There are two
methods of finding the height of lunar mountains : —

Fig. 132.

(1) We may measure the length of the shadows, and
then calculate the height of the mountains that would cast
such shadows with the sun at the required height above the
horizon.

The length of a shadow may be obtained by the following
method : the longitudinal wire of the micrometer (19) is adjusted
so as to pass through the shadow whose length is to be meas-

ured, and the transverse wires are placed one at each end of the shadow, as shown in Fig. 133. The micrometer screw is then turned till the wires are brought together, so as to ascertain the length of the arc between them. We may then form the proportion: the number of seconds in the semi-diameter of the moon is to the number of seconds in the length of the shadow, as the length of the moon's radius in miles to the length of the shadow in miles.

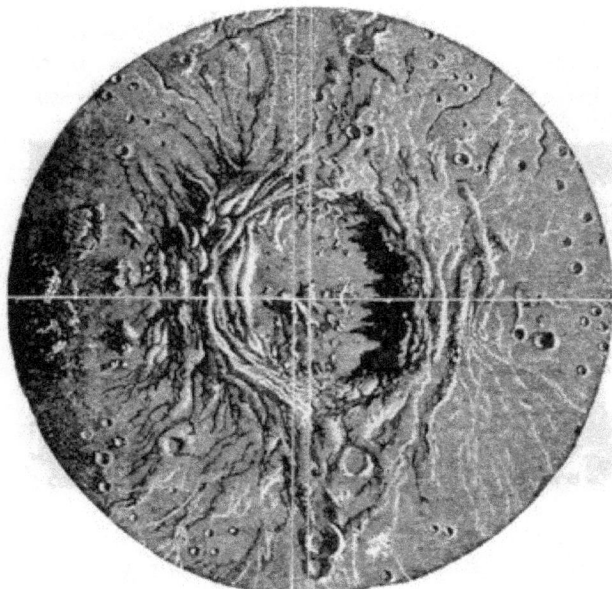

Fig. 133.

The height of the sun above the horizon is ascertained by measuring the angular distance of the mountain from the terminator.

(2) We may measure the distance of a bright point from the terminator, and then construct a right-angled triangle, as shown in Fig. 134. A solution of this triangle will enable us to ascertain the height of the mountain whose top is just catching the level rays of the sun.

B is the centre of the moon, M the top of the mountain,

and SAM a ray of sunlight which just grazes the terminator
at A, and then strikes the top of the mountain at M. The
triangle BAM is right-angled at A. BA is the radius of the
moon, and AM is known by measurement; BM, the hypothenuse, may then be found by computation. BM is evidently
equal to the radius of the moon *plus* the height of the mountain.

By one or the other of these methods, the heights of
the lunar mountains have been found with a great degree
of accuracy. It is claimed that the heights of the lunar
mountains are more accurately known than those of the

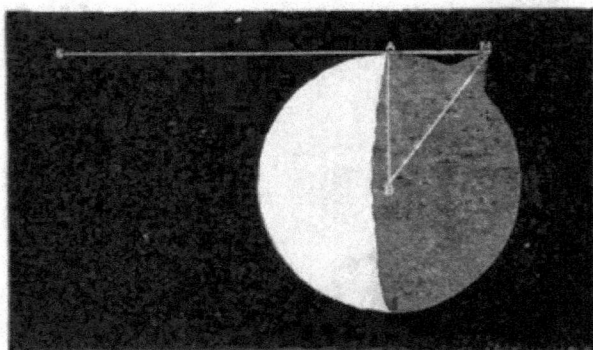

Fig. 134.

mountains on the earth. Compared with the size of the
moon, lunar mountains attain a greater height than those
on the earth.

115. *General Aspect of the Lunar Surface.* — A cursory
examination of the moon with a low power is sufficient to
show the prevalence of crater-like inequalities and the general tendency to *circular* shape which is apparent in nearly
all the surface markings ; for even the large "seas" and
the smaller patches of the same character repeat in their
outlines the round form of the craters. It is along the
terminator that we see these crater-like spots to the best
advantage ; as it is there that the rising or setting sun casts

long shadows over the lunar landscape, and brings elevations into bold relief. They vary greatly in size ; some being
so large as to bear a sensible proportion to the moon's
diameter, while the smallest are so minute as to need the
most powerful telescopes and the finest conditions of atmosphere to perceive them.

The prevalence of ring-shaped mountains and plains will

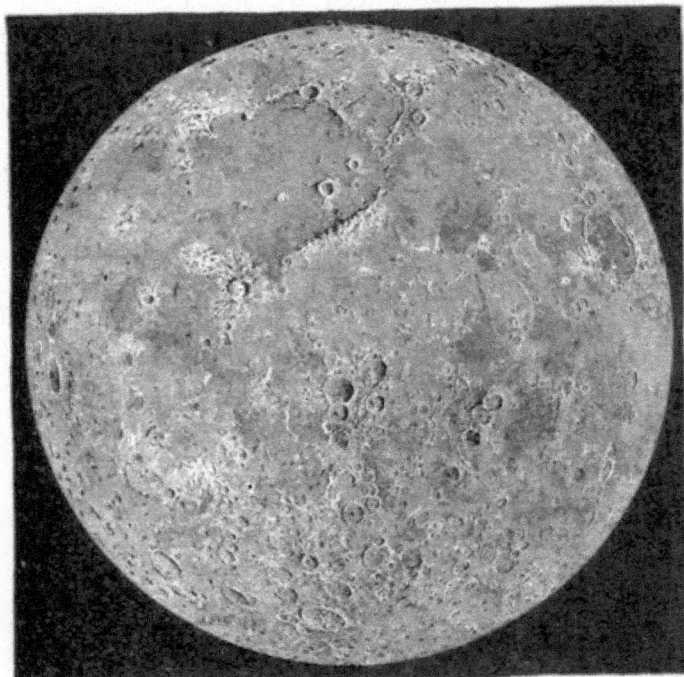

Fig. 135.

be evident from Fig. 135, which is from a photograph of a
model of the moon constructed by Nasmyth.

This same feature is nearly as marked in Figs. 131 and
132, which are copies of Rutherfurd's photographs of the
moon.

116. *Lunar Craters.* — The smaller saucer-shaped formations on the surface of the moon are called *craters.* They

are of all sizes, from a mile to a hundred and fifty miles in diameter; and they are supposed to be of volcanic origin. A high telescopic power shows that these craters vary remarkably, not only in size, but also in structure and arrangement. Some are considerably elevated above the surrounding surface, others are basins hollowed out of that surface, and with low surrounding ramparts; some are like walled plains, while the majority have their lowest depression considerably below the surrounding surface; some are isolated upon the plains, others are thickly crowded together, overlapping and intruding upon each other; some have elevated peaks or cones in their centres, and some are without these central cones, while others, again, contain several minute craters instead; some have their ramparts whole and perfect, others have them broken or deformed, and many have them divided into terraces, especially on their inner sides.

A typical lunar crater is shown in Fig. 136.

It is not generally believed that any active volcanoes exist on the moon at the present time, though some observers have thought they discerned indications of such volcanoes.

117. *Copernicus.* — This is one of the grandest of lunar craters (Fig. 137). Although its diameter (forty-six miles) is exceeded by others, yet, taken as a whole, it forms one of the most impressive and interesting objects of its class. Its situation, near the centre of the lunar disk, renders all its wonderful details conspicuous, as well as those of objects immediately surrounding it. Its vast rampart rises to upwards of twelve thousand feet above the level of the plateau, nearly in the centre of which stands a magnificent group of cones, three of which attain a height of more than twenty-four hundred feet.

Many ridges, or spurs, may be observed leading away from the outer banks of the great rampart. Around the crater, extending to a distance of more than a hundred miles on every side, there is a complex network of bright streaks, which diverge in all directions. These streaks do not

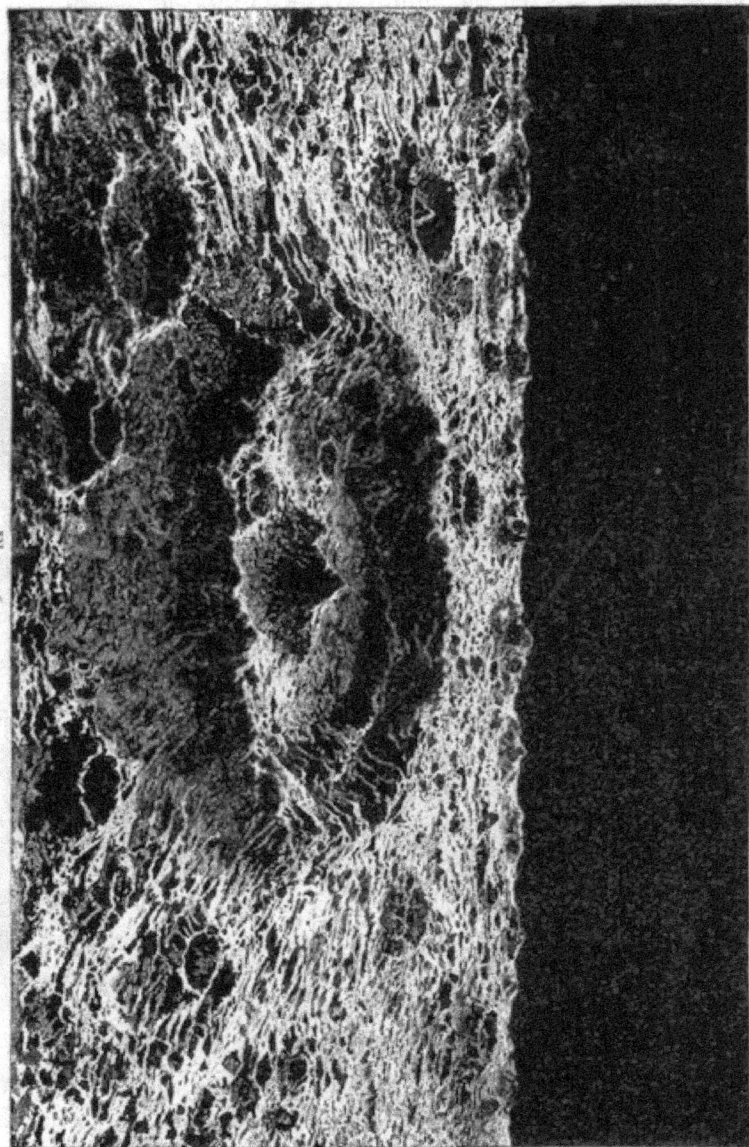

Fig. 136.

appear in the figure, nor are they seen upon the moon,

except at and near the full phase. They show conspicu-
ously, however, by their united lustre on the full moon.

This crater is seen just to the south-west of the large
dusky plain in the upper part of Fig. 132. This plain is
Mare Imbrium, and the mountain-chain seen a little to the
right of Copernicus is named the *Apennines.* Copernicus

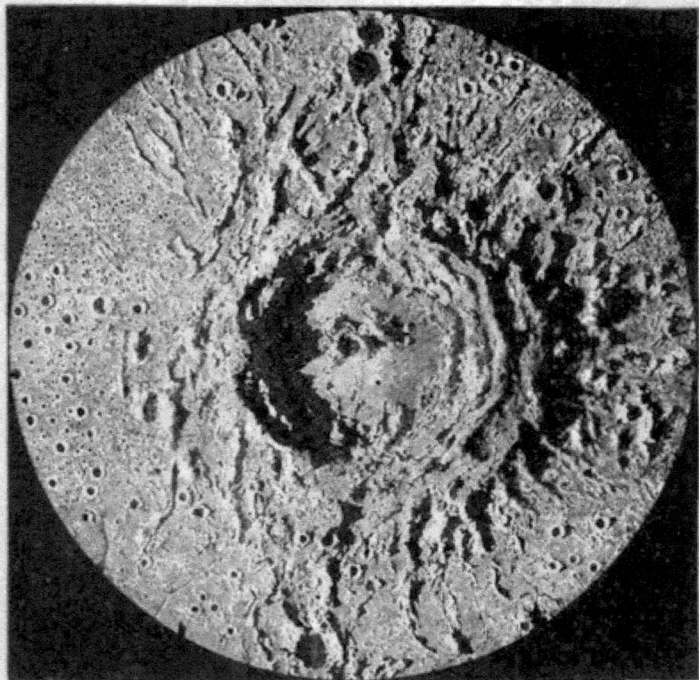

Fig. 137.

is also seen in Fig. 135, a little to the left of the same
range.

Under circumstances specially favorable, myriads of comparatively minute but perfectly formed craters may be observed for more than seventy miles on all sides around
Copernicus. The district on the south-east side is specially
rich in these thickly scattered craters, which we have reason
to suppose stand over or upon the bright streaks.

118. *Dark Chasms.* — Dark cracks, or chasms, have been observed on various parts of the moon's surface. They sometimes occur singly, and sometimes in groups. They are often seen to radiate from some central cone, and they appear to be of volcanic origin. They have been called *canals* and *rills.*

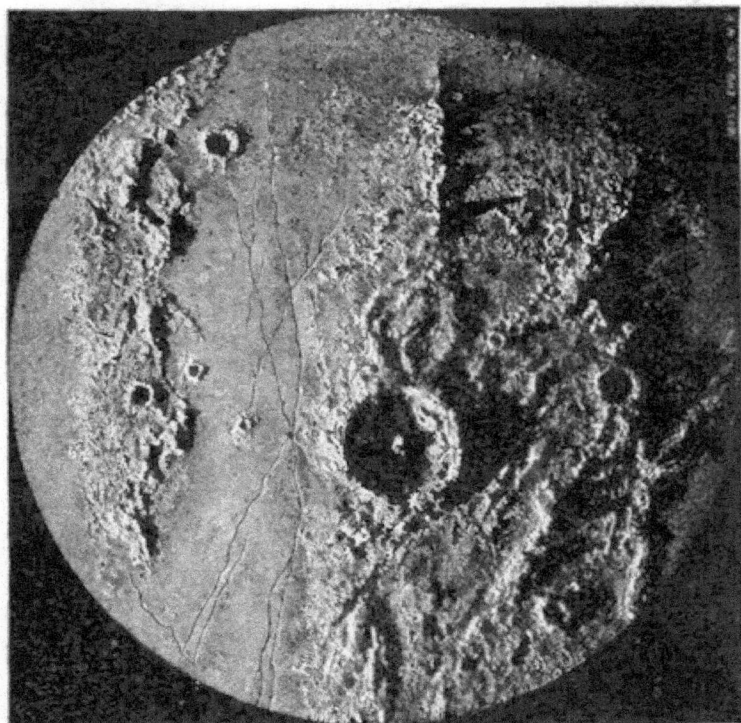

Fig. 138.

One of the most remarkable groups of these chasms is that to the west of the crater named *Triesneker.* The crater and the chasms are shown in Fig. 138. Several of these great cracks obviously diverge from a small crater near the west bank of the great one, and they subdivide as they extend from the apparent point of divergence, while they are crossed by others. These cracks, or chasms, are nearly a mile broad at the widest part, and, after extending full a hundred miles, taper away till they become invisible.

119. *Mountain-Ranges.* — There are comparatively few mountain-ranges on the moon. The three most conspicuous

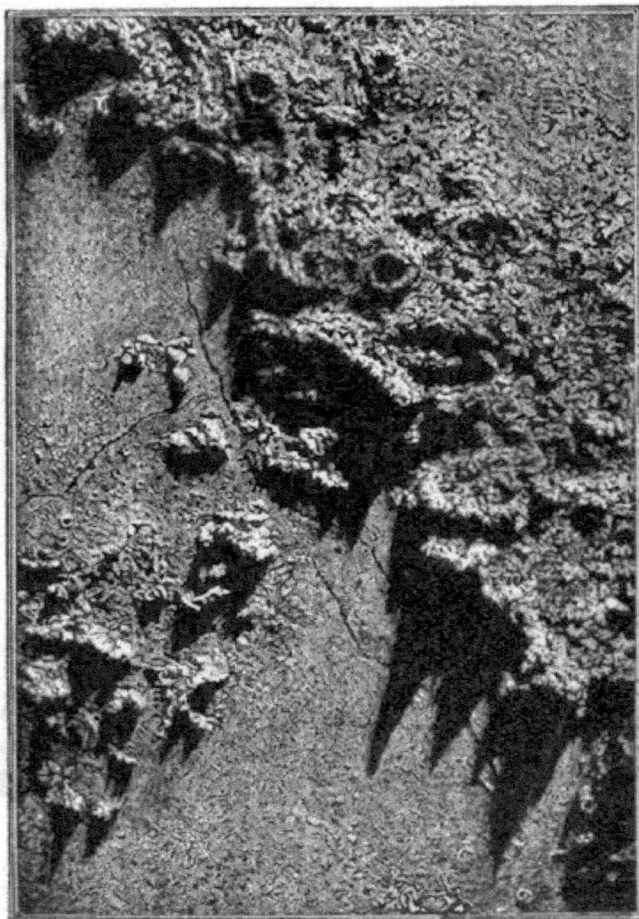

Fig. 139.

are those which partially enclose Mare Imbrium; namely, the *Apennines* on the south, and the *Caucasus* and the *Alps* on the east and north-east. The Apennines are the most extended of these, having a length of about four hun-

dred and fifty miles. They rise gradually, from a comparatively level surface towards the south-west, in the form of
innumerable small elevations, which increase in number and

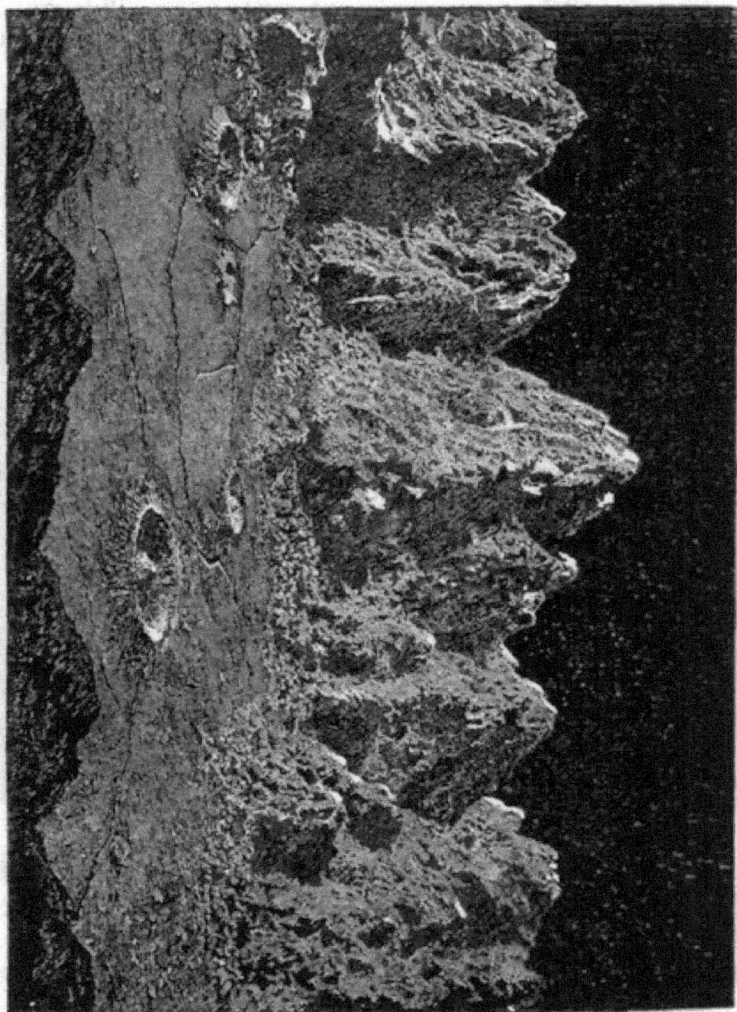

Fig. 140.

height towards the north-east, where they culminate in a
range of peaks whose altitude and rugged aspect must form
one of the most terribly grand and romantic scenes which

imagination can conceive.   The north-east face of the range
terminates abruptly in an almost vertical precipice ; while
over the plain beneath, intensely black spire-like shadows
are cast, some of which at sunrise extend full ninety miles,
till they lose themselves in the general shading due to the
curvature of the lunar surface.   Many of the peaks rise to

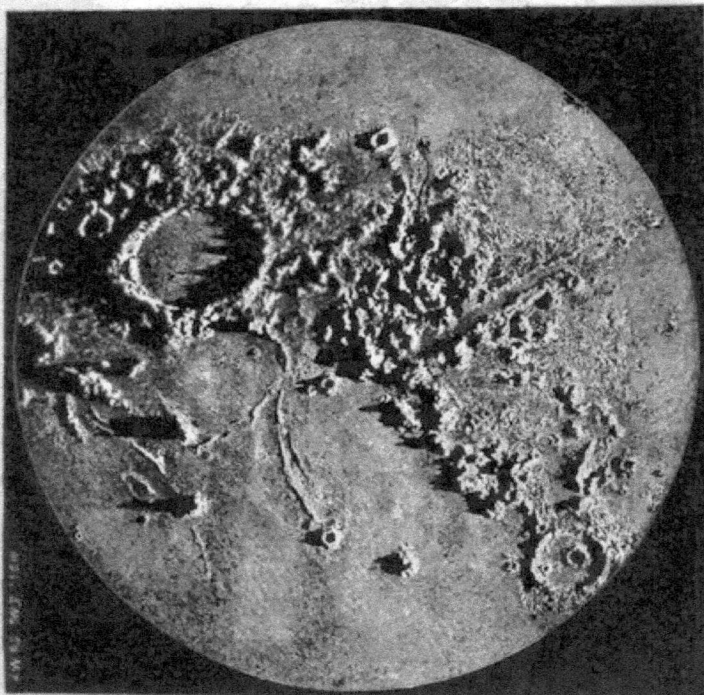

Fig. 141.

heights of from eighteen thousand to twenty thousand feet
above the plain at their north-east base (Fig. 139).

Fig. 140 represents an ideal lunar landscape near the base
of such a lunar range.   Owing to the absence of an atmosphere, the stars will be visible in full daylight.

120. *The Valley of the Alps.* — The range of the *Alps*
is shown in Fig. 141.   The great crater at the north end of
this range is named *Plato*.   It is seventy miles in diameter.

The most remarkable feature of the Alps is the valley near the centre of the range. It is more than seventy-five miles long, and about six miles wide at the broadest part. When examined under favorable circumstances, with a high magnifying power, it is seen to be a vast flat-bottomed valley, bordered by gigantic mountains, some of which attain heights of ten thousand feet or more.

121. *Isolated Peaks.* — There are comparatively few isolated peaks to be found on the surface of the moon. One of the most remarkable of these is that known as *Pico*,

Fig. 142.

and shown in Fig. 142. Its height exceeds eight thousand feet, and it is about three times as long at the base as it is broad. The summit is cleft into three peaks, as is shown by the three-peaked shadow it casts on the plain.

122. *Bright Rays.* — About the time of full moon, with a telescope of moderate power, a number of bright lines may be seen radiating from several of the lunar craters, extending often to the distance of hundreds of miles. These streaks do not arise from any perceptible difference of level of the surface, they have no very definite outline,

and they do not present any sloping sides to catch more sunlight, and thus shine brighter, than the general surface. Indeed, one great peculiarity of them is, that they come out most forcibly when the sun is shining perpendicularly upon them : hence they are best seen when the moon is at full,

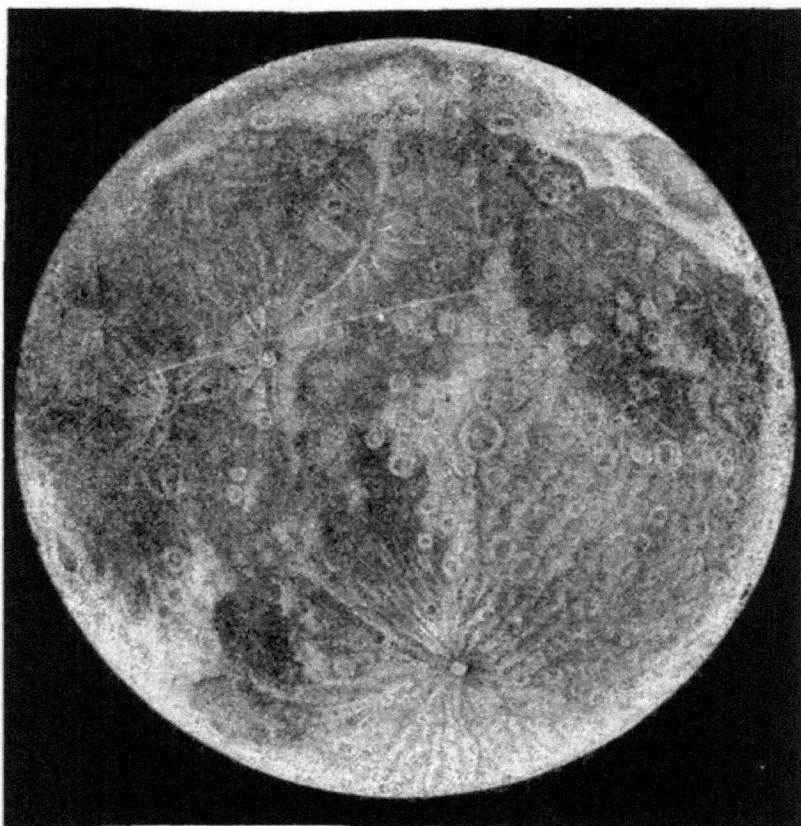

Fig. 143.

and they are not visible at all at those regions upon which the sun is rising or setting. They are not diverted by elevations in their path, but traverse in their course craters, mountains, and plains alike, giving a slight additional brightness to all objects over which they pass, but producing no other effect upon them. " They look as if, after the whole surface of the moon had assumed its final configuration, a vast brush charged with a whitish pigment had been drawn over the globe in straight lines, radiating from a central point, leaving its trail upon every thing it touched, but obscuring nothing."

The three most conspicuous craters from which these lines radiate are *Tycho*, *Copernicus*, and *Kepler*. Tycho is seen at the bottom of Figs. 143 and 130. Kepler is a little to the left of Copernicus in the same figures.

It has been thought that these bright streaks are chasms which have been filled with molten lava, which, on cooling, would afford a smooth reflecting surface on the top.

123. *Tycho.* — This crater is fifty-four miles in diameter, and about sixteen thousand feet deep, from the highest ridge of the rampart to the surface of the plateau, whence rises a central cone five thousand feet high. It is one of the most conspicuous of all the lunar craters ; not so much on account of its dimensions as from its being the centre from whence diverge those remarkable bright streaks, many of which may be traced over a thousand miles of the moon's surface (Fig. 143). Tycho appears to be an instance of a vast disruptive action which rent the solid crust of the moon into radiating fissures, which were subsequently filled with molten matter, whose superior luminosity marks the course of the cracks in all directions from the crater as their common centre. So numerous are these bright streaks when examined by the aid of the telescope, and they give to this region of the moon's surface such increased luminosity, that, when viewed as a whole, the locality can be distinctly seen at full moon by the unassisted eye, as a bright patch of light on the southern portion of the disk.

III. INFERIOR AND SUPERIOR PLANETS.

INFERIOR PLANETS.

124. *The Inferior Planets.* — The *inferior planets* are those which lie between the earth and the sun, and whose orbits are included by that of the earth. They are *Mercury* and *Venus*.

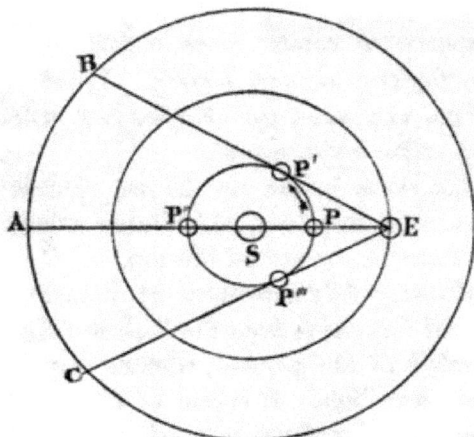

Fig. 144.

125. *Aspects of an Inferior Planet.* — The four chief *aspects* of an inferior planet as seen from the earth are shown in Fig. 144, in which *S* represents the sun, *P* the planet, and *E* the earth.

When the planet is between the earth and the sun, as at *P*, it is said to be in *inferior conjunction.*

When it is in the same direction as the sun, but beyond it, as at *P''*, it is said to be in *superior conjunction.*

When the planet is at such a point in its orbit that a line

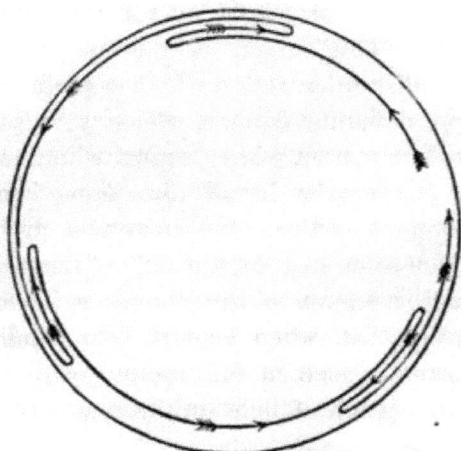

Fig. 145.

drawn from the earth to it would be tangent to the orbit, as at *P'* and *P'''*, it is said to be at its *greatest elongation.*

126. *Apparent Motion of an Inferior Planet.*— When the planet is at P, if it could be seen at all, it would appear in the heavens at A. As it moves from P to P', it will appear to move in the heavens from A to B. Then, as it moves from P' to P'', it will appear to move back again from B to A. While it moves from P'' to P''', it will appear to move from A to C; and, while moving from P''' to P,

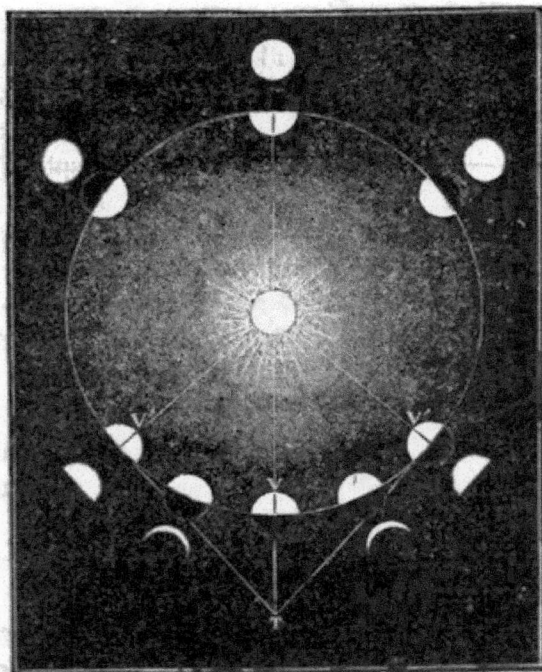

Fig. 146.

it will appear to move back again from C to A. Thus the planet will appear to oscillate to and fro across the sun from B to C, never getting farther from the sun than B on the west, or C on the east : hence, when at these points, it is said to be at its *greatest western* and *eastern elongations*. This oscillating motion of an inferior planet across the sun, combined with the sun's motion among the stars. causes the planet to describe a path among the stars similar to that shown in Fig. 145.

127. *Phases of an Inferior Planet.* — An inferior planet, when viewed with a telescope, is found to present a succession of phases similar to those of the moon. The reason of this is evident from Fig. 146. As an inferior planet passes around the sun, it presents sometimes more and sometimes less of its bright hemisphere to the earth. When the earth is at T, and Venus at superior conjunction, the planet turns the whole of its bright hemisphere towards the earth, and appears *full;* it then becomes *gibbous, half,* and *crescent.* When it comes into *inferior conjunction,* it turns its dark hemisphere towards the earth: it then becomes *crescent, half, gibbous,* and *full* again.

128. *The Sidereal and Synodical Periods of an Inferior Planet.* — The time it takes a planet to make a complete revolution around the sun is called the *sidereal period* of the planet;

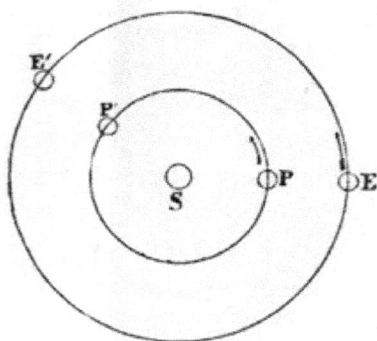

Fig. 147.

and the time it takes it to pass from one aspect around to the same aspect again, its *synodical period.*

The synodical period of an inferior planet is longer than its sidereal period. This will be evident from an examination of Fig. 147. S is the position of the sun, E that of the earth, and P that of the planet at inferior conjunction. Before the planet can be in inferior conjunction again, it must pass entirely around its orbit, and overtake the earth, which has in the mean time passed on in its orbit to E'.

While the earth is passing from E to E', the planet passes entirely around its orbit, and from P to P' in addition.

Now the arc PP' is just equal to the arc EE': hence the planet has to pass over the same arc that the earth does, and 360° more. In other words, the planet has to gain 360° on the earth.

The synodical period of the planet is found by direct observation.

129. *The Length of the Sidereal Period.* — The length of the sidereal period of an inferior planet may be found by the following computation : —

> Let a denote the synodical period of the planet,
> Let b denote the sidereal period of the earth,
> Let x denote the sidereal period of the planet.

Then $\dfrac{360°}{b}$ = the daily motion of the earth,

And $\dfrac{360°}{x}$ = the daily motion of the planet.

And $\dfrac{360°}{x} - \dfrac{360°}{b}$ = the daily gain of the planet :

Also $\dfrac{360°}{a}$ = the daily gain of the planet :

Hence $\dfrac{360°}{x} - \dfrac{360°}{b} = \dfrac{360°}{a}$.

Dividing by 360°, we have $\dfrac{1}{x} - \dfrac{1}{b} = \dfrac{1}{a}$;

Clearing of fractions, we have $ab - ax = bx$:

Transposing and collecting, we have $(a + b)x = ab$:

$$\text{Therefore } x = \frac{ab}{a + b}$$

130. *The Relative Distance of an Inferior Planet.* — By the *relative distance* of a planet, we mean its distance from the sun compared with the earth's distance from the sun. The relative distance of an inferior planet may be found by the following method : —

Let V, in Fig. 148. represent the position of Venus at its greatest elongation from the sun, S the position of the sun, and E that of the earth. The line EV will evidently be tangent to a circle described about the sun with a radius equal to the distance of Venus from the sun at the time of this greatest elongation. Draw the radius SV and the line SE. Since SV is a radius, the angle at V is a right angle. The angle at E is known by measurement, and the angle at S is equal to $90°$ — the angle E. In the right-angled triangle EVS, we then know the three angles, and we wish to find the ratio of the side SV to the side SE.

The ratio of these lines may be found by trigonometrical computation as follows : —

$$VS : ES = \sin SEV : 1.$$

Substitute the value of the sine of SEV, and we have

$$VS : ES = .723 : 1.$$

Hence the relative distances of Venus and of the earth from the sun are .723 and 1.

SUPERIOR PLANETS.

131. *The Superior Planets.* — The *superior planets* are those which lie beyond the earth. They are *Mars*, the *Asteroids, Jupiter, Saturn, Uranus*, and *Neptune*.

132. *Apparent Motion of a Superior Planet.* — In order to deduce the apparent motion of a superior planet from the real motions of the earth and planet, let S (Fig. 149) be 'the place of the sun; 1, 2, 3. etc., the orbit of the earth; a, b, c, etc., the orbit of Mars; and CGL a part of the starry firmament. Let the orbit of the earth be divided into twelve equal parts, each described in one month; and let ab, bc, cd, etc., be the spaces described by Mars in the same time. Suppose the earth to be at the point 1 when Mars is at the point a, Mars will then appear in the heavens in the direction of 1 a. When the earth is at 3, and Mars at c. he will appear in the heavens at C. When the earth arrives

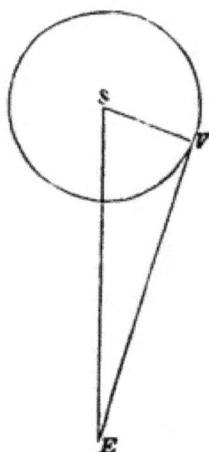
Fig. 148.

at 4, Mars will arrive at d, and will appear in the heavens at D. While the earth moves from 4 to 5 and from 5 to 6, Mars will appear to have advanced among the stars from *D* to *E* and

from *E* to *F*,
in the direction
from west to
east. During
the motion of
the earth from 6
to 7 and from 7
to 8, Mars will
appear to go
backward from
F to *G* and
from *G* to *H*,
in the direction
from east to
west. During
the motion of
the earth from 8
to 9 and from 9
to 10, Mars will

Fig. 149.

appear to advance from *H* to *I* and from *I* to *K*, in the direction

Fig. 150.

from west to east,
and the motion will
continue in the
same direction until
near the succeeding
opposition.

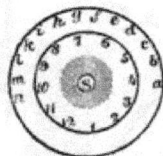

The apparent motion of a superior
planet projected on
the heavens is thus
seen to be similar
to that of an inferior planet, except
that, in the latter
case, the retrogression takes place near

inferior conjunction, and in the former it takes place near
opposition.

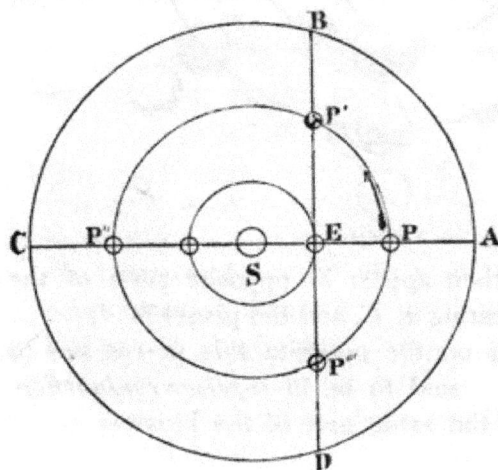

133. *Aspects of a Superior Planet.* — The four aspects of
a superior planet are shown in Fig. 150, in which *S* is the
position of the sun, *E* that of the earth, and *P* that of the
planet.

When the planet is on the opposite side of the earth to
the sun, as at *P*, it is said to be in *opposition.* The sun

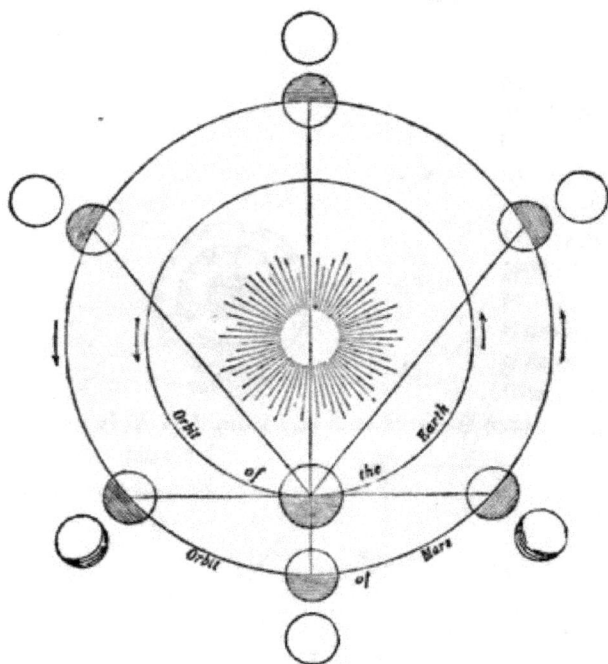

Fig. 151.

and the planet will then appear in opposite parts of the
heavens, the sun appearing at *C*, and the planet at *A*.

When the planet is on the opposite side of the sun to
the earth, as at *P''*, it is said to be in *superior conjunction.*
It will then appear in the same part of the heavens as the
sun, both appearing at *C*.

When the planet is at *P'* and *P'''*, so that a line drawn
from the earth through the planet will make a right angle
with a line drawn from the earth to the sun, it is said to be

in *quadrature*. At P' it is in its western quadrature, and at P''' in its eastern quadrature.

134. *Phases of a Superior Planet.* — Mars is the only one of the superior planets that has appreciable phases. At quadrature, as will appear from Fig. 151, Mars does not present quite the same side to the earth as to the sun : hence, near these parts of its orbit, the planet appears slightly gibbous. Elsewhere in its orbit, the planet appears full.

All the other superior planets are so far away from the sun and earth, that the sides which they turn towards the sun and the earth in every part of their orbit are so nearly the same, that no change in the form of their disks can be detected.

135. *The Synodical Period of a Superior Planet.* — During a synodical period of a superior planet the earth must gain one revolution, or 360°, on the planet, as will be evident from an examination of Fig. 152, in which S represents the sun, E the earth, and P the planet at opposi-

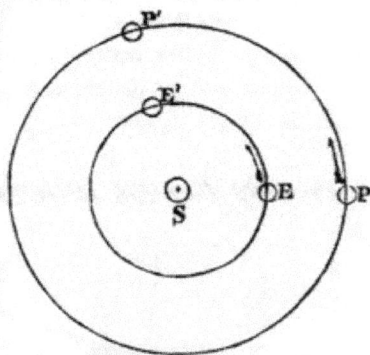

Fig. 152.

tion. Before the planet can be in opposition again, the earth must make a complete revolution, and overtake the planet, which has in the mean time passed on from P to P'.

In the case of most of the superior planets the synodical period is shorter than the sidereal period ; but in the case of Mars it is longer, since Mars makes more than a complete revolution before the earth overtakes it.

The synodical period of a superior planet is found by direct observation.

136. *The Sidereal Period of a Superior Planet.* — The sidereal period of a superior planet is found by a method of computation similar to that for finding the sidereal period of an inferior planet : —

Let a denote the synodical period of the planet,
Let b denote the sidereal period of the earth,
Let x denote the sidereal period of the planet.

Then will $\dfrac{360°}{b}$ = daily motion of the earth,

And $\dfrac{360°}{x}$ = daily motion of the planet;

Also $\dfrac{360°}{b} - \dfrac{360°}{x}$ = daily gain of the earth.

But $\dfrac{360°}{a}$ = daily gain of the earth:

Hence $\dfrac{360°}{b} - \dfrac{360°}{x} = \dfrac{360°}{a}$

$$\frac{1}{b} - \frac{1}{x} = \frac{1}{a}$$
$$ax - ab = bx$$
$$(a - b)x = ab$$
$$x = \frac{ab}{a - b}$$

137. *The Relative Distance of a Superior Planet.* — Let

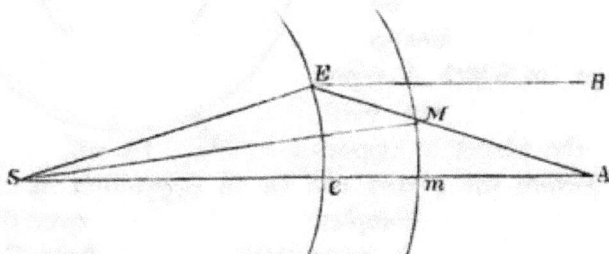

Fig. 153.

S, e, and m, in Fig. 153, represent the relative positions of the sun, the earth, and Mars, when the latter planet is in opposition. Let E and M represent the relative positions of the earth and Mars the day after opposition. At the first observation Mars will be seen in the direction emA, and at the second observation in the direction EMA.

But the fixed stars are so distant, that if a line, eA, were drawn to a fixed star at the first observation, and a line, EB, drawn from the earth to the same fixed star at the second observation, these two lines would be sensibly parallel; that is, the fixed star would be seen in the direction of the line eA at the first observation, and in the direction of the line EB, parallel to eA, at the second observation. But if Mars were seen in the direction of the fixed star at the first observation, it would appear back, or west, of that star at the second observation by the angular distance $BEA;$ that is, the planet would have retrograded that angular distance. Now, this retrogression of Mars during one day, at the time of opposition, can be measured directly by observation. This measurement gives us the value of the angle $BEA;$ but we know the rate at which both the earth and Mars are moving in their orbits, and from this we can easily find the angular distance passed over by each in one day. This gives us the angles ESA and MSA. We can now find the relative length of the lines MS and ES (which represent the distances of Mars and of the earth from the sun), both by construction and by trigonometrical computation.

Since EB and eA are parallel, the angle EAS is equal to BEA.

$$SEA = 180° - (ESA + EAS)$$
$$ESM = ESA - MSA$$
$$EMS = 180° - (SEA + ESM).$$

We have then

$$MS : ES = \sin SEA : \sin EMS.$$

Substituting the values of the sines, and reducing the ratio to its lowest terms, we have

$$MS : ES = 1.524 : 1.$$

Thus we find that the relative distances of Mars and the earth from the sun are 1.524 and 1. By the simple observation of its greatest elongation, we are able to determine the relative distances of an inferior planet and the earth from the sun; and, by the equally simple observation of the daily retrogression of a superior planet, we can find the relative distances of such a planet and the earth from the sun.

IV. THE SUN.

I. MAGNITUDE AND DISTANCE OF THE SUN.

138. *The Volume of the Sun.* — The apparent diameter of the sun is about 32′, being a little greater than that of the moon. The real diameter of the sun is 866,400 miles, or about a hundred and nine times that of the earth.

As the diameter of the moon's orbit is only about 480,000

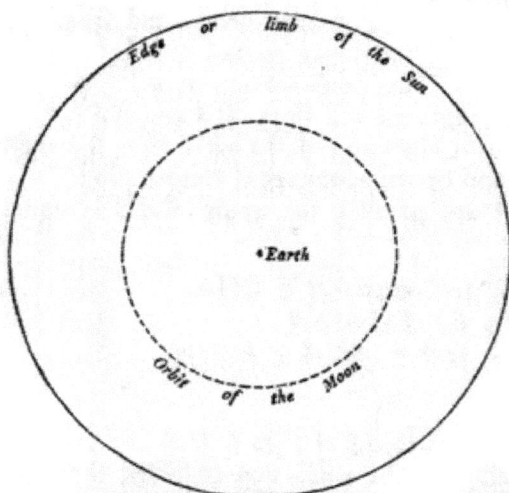

Fig. 154.

miles, or some sixty times the diameter of the earth, it follows that the diameter of the sun is nearly double that of the moon's orbit : hence, were the centre of the sun placed at the centre of the earth, the sun would completely fill the moon's orbit, and reach nearly as far beyond it in every direction as it is from the earth to the moon. The circumference of the sun as compared with the moon's orbit is shown in Fig. 154.

The volume of the sun is 1,305,000 times that of the earth.

139. *The Mass of the Sun.* — The sun is much less dense than the earth. The mass of the sun is only 330,000 times that of the earth, and its density only about a fourth that of the earth.

To find the mass of the sun, we first ascertain the distance the earth would draw the moon towards itself in a given time, were the moon at the distance of the sun, and then form the proportion: as the distance the earth would draw the moon towards itself is to the distance that the sun draws the earth towards itself in the same time, so is the mass of the earth to the mass of the sun.

Although the mass of the sun is over three hundred thou-

Fig. 155.

sand times that of the earth, the pull of gravity at the surface of the sun is only about twenty-eight times as great as at the surface of the earth. This is because the distance from the surface of the sun to its centre is much greater than from the surface to the centre of the earth.

140. *Size of the Sun Compared with that of the Planets.* —The size of the sun compared with that of the larger

planets is shown in Fig. 155. The mass of the sun is more than seven hundred and fifty times that of all of the planets and moons in the solar system. In Fig. 156 is shown the

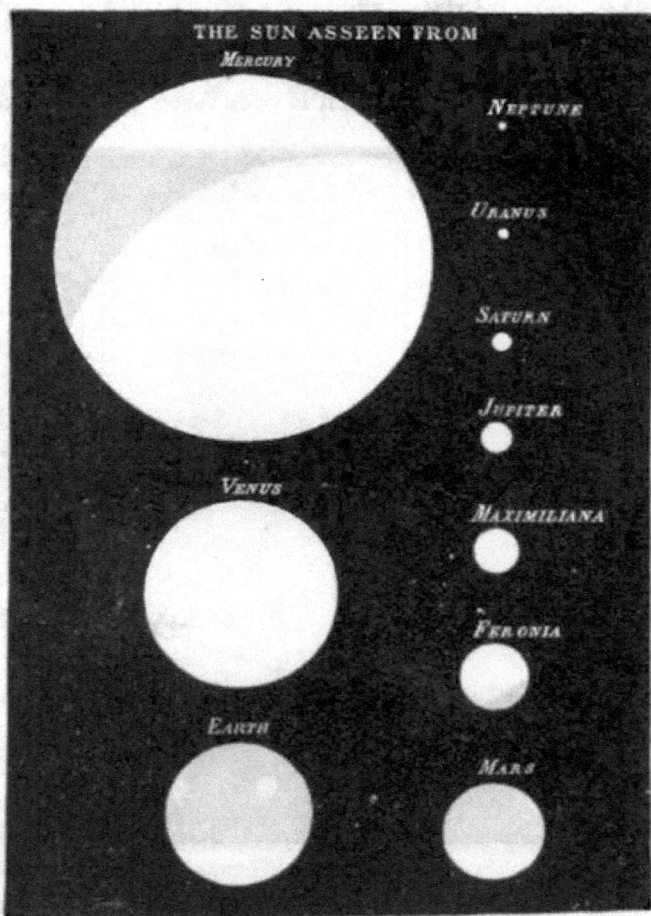

Fig. 156.

apparent size of the sun as seen from the different planets. The apparent diameter of the sun decreases as the distance from it increases, and the disk of the sun decreases as the square of the distance from it increases.

141. *The Distance of the Sun.* — The mean distance

of the sun from the earth is about 92,800,000 miles. Owing to the eccentricity of the earth's orbit, the distance of the sun varies somewhat ; being about 3,000,000 miles less in January, when the earth is at perihelion, than in June, when the earth is at aphelion.

" But, though the distance of the sun can easily be stated in figures, it is not possible to give any real idea of a space so enormous : it is quite beyond our power of conception. If one were to try to walk such a distance, supposing that he could walk four miles an hour, and keep it up for ten hours every day, it would take sixty-eight years and a half to make a single million of miles, and more than sixty-three hundred years to traverse the whole.

" If some celestial railway could be imagined, the journey to the sun, even if our trains ran sixty miles an hour day and night and without a stop, would require over a hundred and seventy-five years. Sensation, even, would not travel so far in a human lifetime. To borrow the curious illustration of Professor Mendenhall, if we could imagine an infant with an arm long enough to enable him to touch the sun and burn himself, he would die of old age before the pain could reach him; since, according to the experiments of Helmholtz and others, a nervous shock is communicated only at the rate of about a hundred feet per second, or 1,637 miles a day, and would need more than a hundred and fifty years to make the journey. Sound would do it in about fourteen years, if it could be transmitted through celestial space ; and a cannon-ball in about nine, if it were to move uniformly with the same speed as when it left the muzzle of the gun. If the earth could be suddenly stopped in her orbit, and allowed to fall unobstructed toward the sun, under the accelerating influence of his attraction, she would reach the centre in about four months. I have said if she could be stopped ; but such is the compass of her orbit, that, to make its circuit in a year, she has to move nearly nineteen miles a second, or more than fifty times faster than the swiftest rifle-ball ; and, in moving twenty miles, her path deviates from perfect straightness by less than an eighth of an inch. And yet, over all the circumference of this tremendous orbit, the sun exercises his dominion, and every pulsation of his surface receives its response from the subject earth." [1]

142. *Method of Finding the Sun's Distance.* — There are several methods of finding the sun's distance. The simplest method is that of finding the actual distance of one of the nearer planets by observing its displacement in the sky as seen from widely separated points on the earth. As the *relative* distances of the planets from each other and from the sun are well known, we can easily deduce the actual distance of the sun if we can find that of any of the planets. The two planets usually chosen for this method are Mars and Venus.

(1) The displacement of Mars in the sky, as seen from two observatories which differ considerably in latitude, is, of course, greatest when Mars is nearest the earth. Now, it is evident than Mars will be nearer the earth when in opposition than

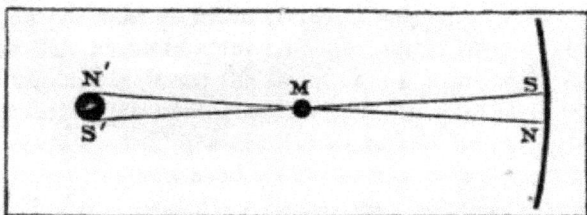

Fig. 157.

when in any other part of its orbit; and the planet will be least distant from the earth when it is at its perihelion point, and the earth is at its aphelion point, at the time of opposition. This method, then, can be used to the best advantage, when, at the time of opposition, Mars is near its perihelion, and the earth near its aphelion. These favorable oppositions occur about once in fifteen years, and the last one was in 1877.

Suppose two observers situated at N'' and S' (Fig. 157), near the poles of the earth. The one at N'' would see Mars in the sky at N, and the one at S' would see it at S. The displacement would be the angle NMS. Each observer measures carefully the distance of Mars from the same fixed star near it. The difference of these distances gives the displacement of the planet, or the angle NMS. These observations were made with the greatest care in 1877.

---

[1] Professor C. A. Young: The Sun.

(2) Venus is nearest the earth at the time of inferior conjunction; but it can then be seen only in the daytime. It is, therefore, impossible to ascertain the displacement of Venus, as seen from different stations, by comparing her distances from a fixed star. Occasionally, at the time of inferior conjunction, Venus passes directly across the sun's disk. The last of these *transits* of Venus occurred in 1874, and the next will occur in 1882. It will then be over a hundred years before another will occur.

Suppose two observers, A and B (Fig. 158), near the poles of the earth at the time of a transit of Venus. The observer at A would see Venus crossing the sun at V_2, and the one at B would see it crossing at V_1. Any observation made upon

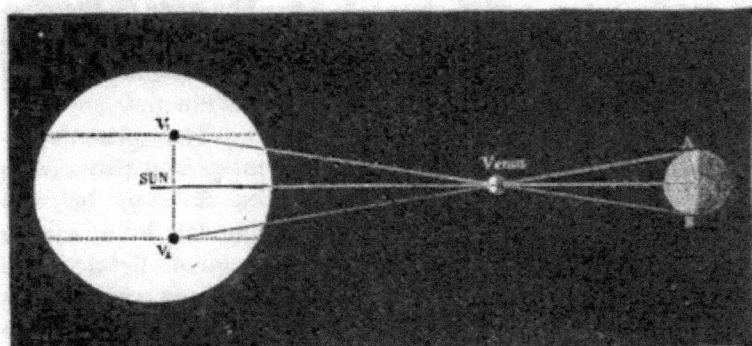

Fig. 158.

Venus, which would give the distance and direction of Venus from the centre of the sun, as seen from each station, would enable us to calculate the angular distance between the two chords described across the sun. This, of course, would give the displacement of Venus on the sun's disk. This method was first employed at the last transits of Venus which occurred before 1874; namely, those of 1761 and 1769.

There are three methods of observation employed to ascertain the apparent direction and distance of Venus from the centre of the sun, called respectively the *contact method*, the *micrometric method*, and the *photographic method*.

(a) In the *contact* method, the observation consists in noting the exact time when Venus crosses the sun's limb. To ascertain this it is necessary to observe the exact time of external and internal contact. This observation, though apparently simple, is really very difficult. With reference to this method Professor Young says, —

"The difficulties depend in part upon the imperfections of optical instruments and the human eye, partly upon the essential nature of light leading to what is known as diffraction, and partly upon the action of the planet's atmosphere. The two first-named causes produce what is called irradiation, and operate to make the apparent diameter of the planet, as seen on the solar disk, smaller than it really is ; smaller, too, by an amount which varies with the size of the telescope, the perfection of its lenses, and the tint and brightness of the sun's image. The edge of the planet's image is also rendered slightly hazy and indistinct.

Fig. 159.

"The planet's atmosphere also causes its disk to be surrounded by a narrow ring of light, which becomes visible long before the planet touches the sun, and, at the moment of internal contact, produces an appearance, of which the accompanying figure is intended to give an idea, though on an exaggerated scale. The planet moves so slowly as to occupy more than twenty minutes in crossing the sun's limb; so that even if the planet's edge were perfectly sharp and definite, and the sun's limb undistorted, it would be very difficult to determine the precise second at which contact occurs. But, as things are, observers with precisely similar telescopes, and side by side, often differ from each other five or six seconds : and, where the telescopes are not similar, the differences and uncertainties are much greater. . . . Astronomers, therefore, at present are pretty much agreed that such observations can be of little value in removing the remaining uncertainty of the parallax, and are disposed to put more reliance upon the micrometric and photographic methods, which are free from these peculiar difficulties, though, of course, beset with others, which, however, it is hoped will prove less formidable."

(*b*) Of the *micrometric* method, as employed at the last transit, Professor Young speaks as follows : —

"The micrometric method requires the use of a heliometer, — an instrument common only in Germany, and requiring much skill and practice in its use in order to obtain with it accurate measures. At the late transit, a single English party, two or three of the Russian parties, and all five of the German, were equipped with these instruments; and at some of the stations extensive series of measures were made. None of the results, however, have appeared as yet; so that it is impossible to say how greatly, if at all, this method will have the advantage in precision over the contact observations."

(*c*) The following observations, with reference to the *photographic* method, are also taken from Professor Young : —

"The Americans and French placed their main reliance upon the photographic method, while the English and Germans also provided for its use to a certain extent. The great advantage of this method is, that it makes it possible to perform the necessary measurements (upon whose accuracy every thing depends) at leisure after the transit, without hurry, and with all possible precautions. The field-work consists merely in obtaining as many and as good pictures as possible. A principal objection to the method lies in the difficulty of obtaining good pictures, i.e., pictures free from distortion, and so distinct and sharp as to bear high magnifying power in the microscopic apparatus used for their measurement. The most serious difficulty, however, is involved in the accurate determination of the scale of the picture ; that is, of the number of seconds of arc corresponding to a linear inch upon the plate. Besides this, we must know the exact Greenwich time at which each picture is taken, and it is also extremely desirable that the *orientation* of the picture should be accurately determined ; that is, the north and south, the east and west points of the solar image on the finished plate. There has been a good deal of anxiety lest the image, however accurate and sharp when first produced, should alter, in course of time, through the contraction of the collodion film on the glass plate ; but the experiments of

Rutherfurd, Huggins. and Paschen, seem to show that this danger is imaginary. . . . The Americans placed the photographic telescope exactly in line with a meridian instrument. and so determined, with the extremest precision, the direction in which it was pointed. Knowing this and the time at which any picture was taken, it becomes possible, with the help of the plumb-line image, to determine precisely the orientation of the picture,— an advantage possessed by the American pictures alone, and making their value nearly twice as great as otherwise it would have been.

"The figure below is a representation of one of the American photographs reduced about one-half. V is the image of Venus, which, on the actual plate, is about a seventh of an inch in diameter; $a a'$ is the image of the plumb-line. The centre of the reticle is marked with a cross."

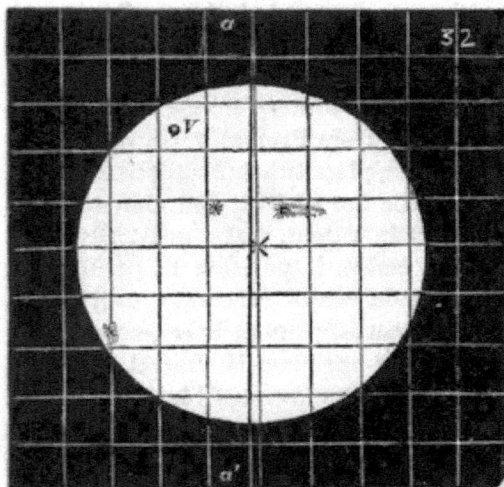

Fig. 160.

The English photographs proved to be of little value, and the results of the measurements and calculations upon the American pictures have not yet been published. There is a growing apprehension that no photographic method can be relied upon.

The most recent determinations by various methods indicate that the sun's distance is such that his parallax is about eighty-eight seconds. This would make the linear value of a second at the surface of the sun about four hundred and fifty miles.

PLATE I.

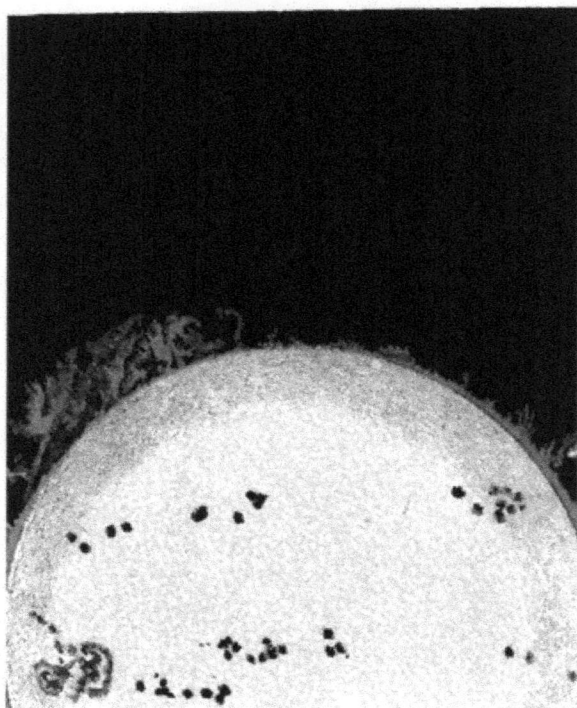

II. PHYSICAL AND CHEMICAL CONDITION OF THE SUN.

PHYSICAL CONDITION OF THE SUN.

143. *The Sun Composed mainly of Gases.* — It is now generally believed that the sun is mainly a ball of gas, or vapor, powerfully condensed at the centre by the weight of the superincumbent mass, but kept from liquefying by its exceedingly high temperature.

The gaseous interior of the sun is surrounded by a layer of luminous clouds, which constitutes its visible surface, and which is called its *photosphere.* Here and there in the photosphere are seen dark *spots*, which often attain an immense magnitude.

These clouds float in the *solar atmosphere*, which extends some distance beyond them.

The luminous surface of the sun is surrounded by a *rose-colored* stratum of gaseous matter, called the *chromosphere.* Here and there great masses of this chromospheric matter rise high above the general level. These masses are called *prominences.*

Outside of the chromosphere is the *corona*, an irregular halo of faint, pearly light, mainly composed of filaments and streamers, which radiate from the sun to enormous distances, often more than a million of miles.

In Fig. 161 is shown a section of the sun, according to Professor Young.

The accompanying lithographic plate gives a general view of the photosphere with its spots, and of the chromosphere and its prominences.

144. *The Temperature of the Sun.* — Those who have investigated the subject of the temperature of the sun have come to very different conclusions; some placing it as high as four million degrees Fahrenheit, and others as low as ten thousand degrees. Professor Young thinks that Rosetti's

estimate of eighteen thousand degrees as the *effective temperature* of the sun's surface is probably not far from correct. By this is meant the temperature that a uniform surface of lampblack of the size of the sun must have in order to radiate as much heat as the sun does. The most intense artificial heat does not exceed four thousand degrees Fahrenheit.

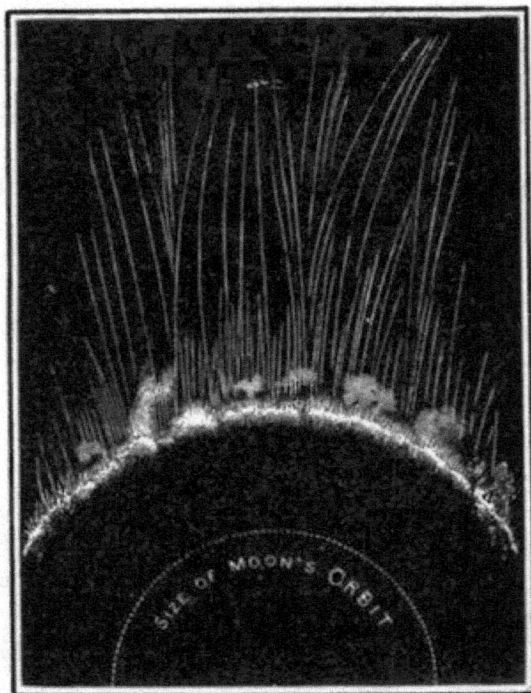

Fig. 161.

145. *The Amount of Heat Radiated by the Sun.* — A *unit* of heat is the amount of heat required to raise a pound of water one degree in temperature. It takes about a hundred and forty-three units of heat to melt a pound of ice without changing its temperature. A cubic foot of ice weighs about fifty-seven pounds. According to Sir William Herschel, were all the heat radiated by the sun concentrated

on a cylinder of ice forty-five miles in diameter, it would melt it off at the rate of about a hundred and ninety thousand miles a second.

Professor Young gives the following illustration of the energy of solar radiation : " If we could build up a solid column of ice from the earth to the sun, two miles and a quarter in diameter, spanning the inconceivable abyss of ninety-three million miles, and if then the sun should concentrate his power upon it, it would dissolve and melt, not in an hour, nor a minute, but in a single second. One swing of the pendulum, and it would be water ; seven more, and it would be dissipated in vapor."

This heat would be sufficient to melt a layer of ice nearly fifty feet thick all around the sun in a minute. To develop this heat would require the hourly consumption of a layer of anthracite coal, more than sixteen feet thick, over the entire

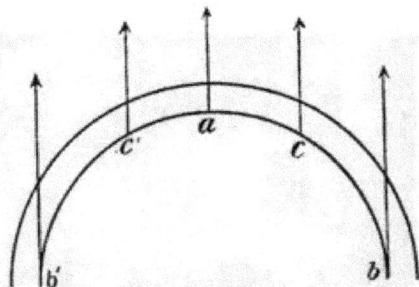

Fig. 162.

surface of the sun ; and the *mechanical equivalent* of this heat is about ten thousand horse-power on every square foot of the sun's surface.

146. *The Brightness of the Sun's Surface.* — The sun's surface is a hundred and ninety thousand times as bright as a candle-flame, a hundred and forty-six times as bright as the calcium-light, and about three times and a half as bright as the voltaic arc.

The sun's disk is much less bright near the margin than near the centre, a point on the limb of the sun being only about a fourth as bright as one near the centre of the disk. This diminution of brightness towards the margin of the disk is due to the increase in the absorption of the solar

atmosphere as we pass from the centre towards the margin
of the sun's disk ; and this increased absorption is due to
the fact, that the rays which reach us from near the margin
have to traverse a much greater thickness of the solar
atmosphere than those which reach us from the centre of
the disk. This will be evident from Fig. 162, in which the
arrows mark the paths of rays from different parts of the
solar disk.

THE SPECTROSCOPE.

147. *The Spectroscope as an Astronomical Instrument.*
—The *spectroscope* is now continually employed in the
study of the physical condition and chemical constitution

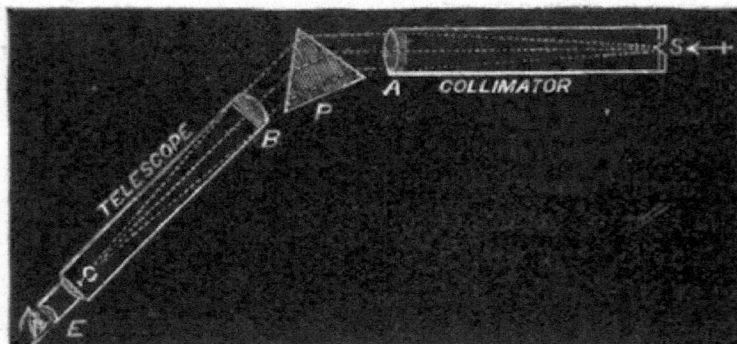

Fig. 163.

of the sun and of the other heavenly bodies. It has
become almost as indispensable to the astronomer as the
telescope.

148. *The Dispersion Spectroscope.*—The essential parts
of the *dispersion* spectroscope are shown in Fig. 163.
These are the *collimator tube*, the *prism*, and the *telescope*.
The collimator tube has a narrow slit at one end, through
which the light to be examined is admitted, and somewhere within the tube a lens for condensing the light. The
light is dispersed on passing through the prism : it then
passes through the objective of the telescope, and forms

within the tube an image of the spectrum. which is examined by means of the eye-piece. The power of the spectroscope is increased by increasing the number of prisms, which are arranged so that the light shall pass through one after another in succession. Such an arrangement of prisms is shown in Fig. 164. One end of the collimator tube is seen at the left, and one end of the telescope at the right. Sometimes the prisms are made long, and the light is sent twice through the same train of prisms, once through the lower, and once

Fig. 164.

through the upper, half of the prisms. This is accomplished by placing a rectangular prism against the last

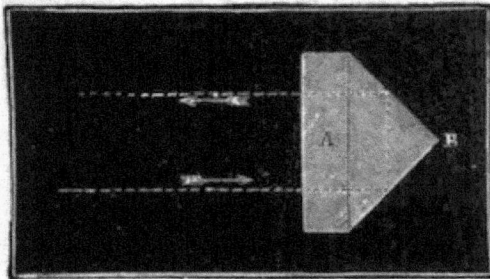

Fig. 165.

prism of the train, as shown in Fig. 165.

149. *The Micrometer Scale.* — Various devices are employed to obtain an image of a micrometer scale in the tube of the telescope beside that of the spectrum.

One of the simplest of these methods is shown in Fig. 166. *A* is the telescope, *B* the collimator, and *C* the micrometer tube. The opening at the outer end of C contains a piece of glass which has a micrometer scale marked upon it. The light from the candle shines through this

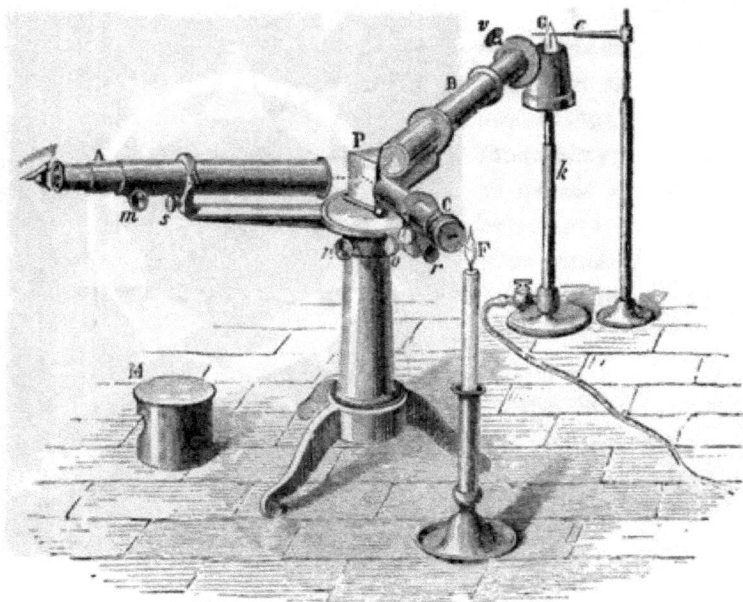

Fig. 166.

glass, falls upon the surface of the prism P, and is thence reflected into the telescope, where it forms an enlarged

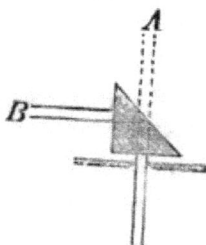

Fig. 167.

image of the micrometer scale alongside the image of the spectrum.

150. *The Comparison of Spectra.* — In order to com-

pare two spectra, it is desirable to be able to see them
side by side in the telescope. The images of two spectra
may be obtained side by side in the telescope tube by the
use of a little rectangular prism, which covers one-half
of the slit of the collimator tube, as shown in Fig. 167.
The light from one source is admitted directly through
the uncovered half of the slit, while the light from the
other source is sent
through the covered
portion of the slit
by reflection from
the surface of the
rectangular prism.

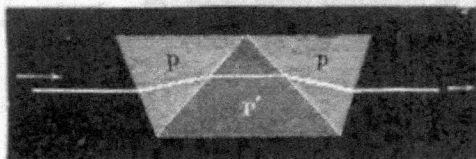

Fig. 168.

This arrangement and its action will be readily understood
from Fig. 167.

151. *Direct-Vision Spectroscope.* — A beam of light may
be dispersed, without any ultimate deflection from its
course, by combining prisms of crown and flint glass with
equal refractive, but unequal dispersive powers. Such a
combination of prisms is called a *direct-vision* combination.

Fig. 169.

One of three prisms is shown in Fig. 168, and one of five
prisms in Fig. 169.

A *direct-vision spectroscope* (Fig. 170) is one in which
a direct-vision combination of prisms is employed. *C* is
the collimator tube, *P* the train of prisms, *F* the telescope,
and *r* the comparison prism.

152. *The Telespectroscope.* — The spectroscope, when
used for astronomical work, is usually combined with a

telescope.   The compound instrument is called a *telespec-troscope.*   The spectroscope is mounted at the end of the telescope in such a way that the image formed by the

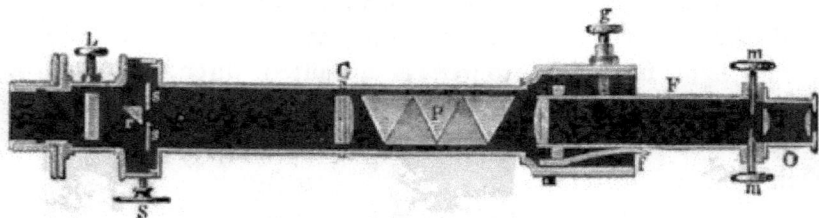

Fig. 170.

object-glass of the telescope falls upon the slit at the end of the collimator tube.   A telespectroscope of small dis-persive power is shown in Fig. 171 : *a* being the object-glass of the telescope, *cc* the tube of the telescope, and

Fig. 171.

e the comparison prism at the end of the collimator tube. A more powerful instrument is shown in Fig. 172.   *A* is the telescope, *C* the collimator tube of the spectroscope,

P the train of prisms, and E the telescope tube. Fig. 173 shows a still more powerful spectroscope attached to the great Newall refractor (18).

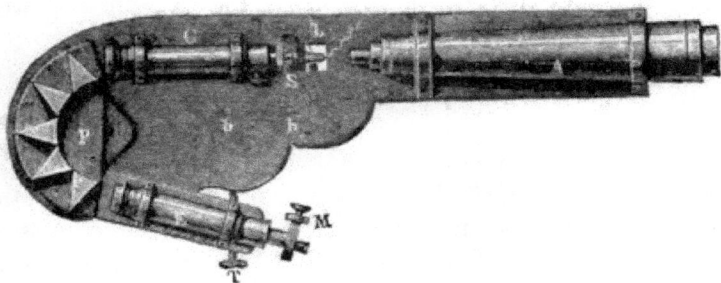

Fig. 172.

153. *The Diffraction Spectroscope.* — A *diffraction* spectroscope is one in which the spectrum is produced by

Fig. 173.

reflection of the light from a finely ruled surface, or *grating*, as it is called, instead of by dispersion in passing through a

prism. The essential parts of this instrument are shown
in Fig 174. This spectroscope may be attached to the
telescope in the same manner as the dispersion spectroscope.
When the spectroscope is thus used, the eye-piece of the
telescope is removed.

SPECTRA.

154. *Continuous Spectra.* — Light from an incandescent
solid or liquid which has suffered no absorption in the
medium which it has traversed gives a spectrum consisting
of a continuous colored band, in which the colors, from
the red to the violet, pass gradually and imperceptibly into

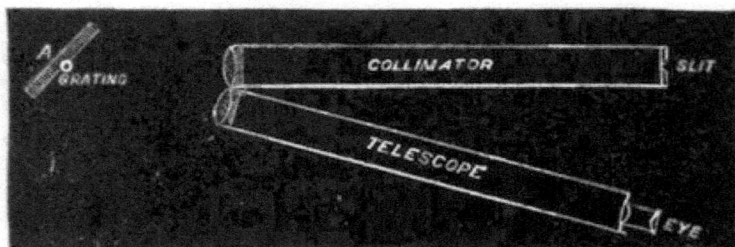

Fig. 174.

one another. The spectrum is entirely free from either light
or dark lines, and is called a *continuous spectrum.*

155. *Bright-Lined Spectra.* — Light from a luminous gas
or vapor gives a spectrum composed of bright lines separated by dark spaces, and known as a *bright-lined spectrum.* It has been found that the lines in the spectrum of
a substance in the state of a gas or vapor are the most
characteristic thing about the substance, since no two vapors
give exactly the same lines : hence, when we have once
become acquainted with the bright-lined spectrum of any
substance, we can ever after recognize that substance by
the spectrum of its luminous vapor. Even when several
substances are mixed, they may all be recognized by the
bright-lined spectrum of the mixture, since the lines of

all the substances will be present in the spectrum of the mixture. This method of identifying substances by their spectra is called *spectrum analysis*.

The bright-lined spectra of several substances are given in the frontispiece. The number of lines in the spectra of the elements varies greatly. The spectrum of sodium is one of the simplest, while that of iron is one of the most complex. The latter contains over six hundred lines. Though no two vapors give identical spectra, there are many cases in which one or more of the spectral lines of one element coincide in position with lines of other elements.

156. *Methods of rendering Gases and Vapors Luminous.*— In order to study the spectra of vapors and gases it is necessary to have some means of converting solids and liquids into vapor, and also of rendering the vapors and gases luminous. There are four methods of obtaining luminous vapors and gases in common use.

(1) *By means of the Bunsen Flame.*— This is a very hot but an almost non-luminous flame. If any readily volatilized substance, such as the compounds of sodium, calcium, strontium, etc., is introduced into this flame on a fine platinum wire, it is volatilized in the flame, and its vapor is rendered

Fig. 175.

luminous, giving the flame its own peculiar color. The flame thus colored may be examined by the spectroscope. The arrangement of the flame is shown in Fig. 175.

(2) *By means of the Voltaic Arc.*— An electric lamp is shown in Fig. 176. When this lamp is to be used for obtaining luminous vapors, the lower carbon is made larger than the

upper one, and hollowed out at the top into a little cup. The substance to be volatilized is placed in this cup, and the current is allowed to pass. The heat of the voltaic arc is much more intense than that of the Bunsen flame: hence substances that cannot be volatilized in the flame are readily volatilized in the arc, and the vapor formed is raised to a very high temperature.

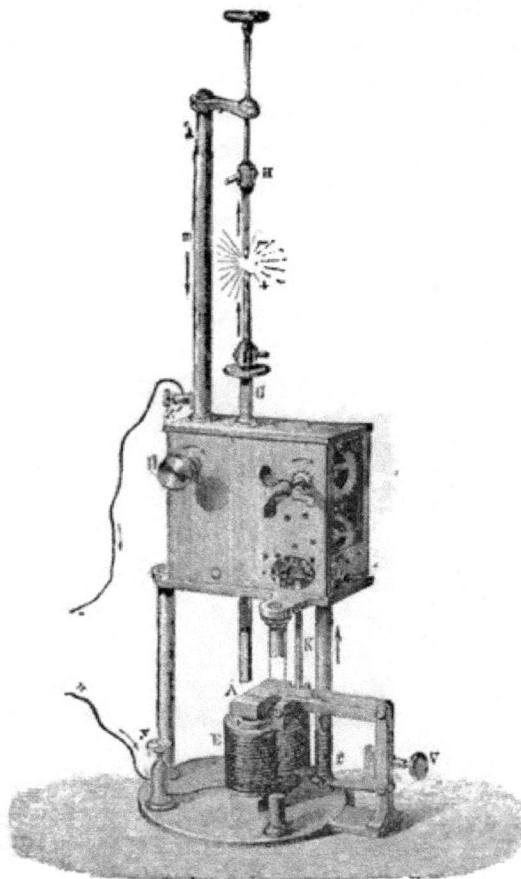

Fig. 176.

(3) *By means of the Spark from an Induction Coil.* — The arrangement of the coil for obtaining luminous vapors is shown in Fig. 177.

The terminals of the coil between which the spark is to pass are brought quite close together. When we wish to vaporize any metal, as iron, the terminals are made of iron. On the passage of the spark, a little of the iron at the ends of the terminals is evaporated; and the vapor is rendered luminous in the space traversed by the spark. A condenser is usually placed in the circuit. With the coil, the temperature may be varied at pleasure; and the vapor may be raised even to a higher temperature than with the electric lamp. To obtain a low temperature, the coil is used without the condenser. By using a larger and larger condenser, the temperature may be raised higher and higher.

By means of the induction coil we may also heat gases to incandescence. It is only necessary to allow the spark to pass through a space filled with the gas.

(4) *By means of a Vacuum Tube.* — The form of the vacuum tube commonly used for this purpose is shown in Fig. 178. The gas to be examined, and which is contained in the tube, has very slight density; but upon the passage of the discharge from an induction coil or a Holtz machine, through the tube, the gas in the capillary part of the tube becomes heated to a high temperature, and is then quite brilliant.

157. *Reversed Spectra.* — If the light from an incandescent cylinder of lime, or from the incandescent point of an electric lamp, is allowed to pass through luminous sodium vapor, and is then examined with a spectroscope, the spectrum will be found to be a bright spectrum crossed by a single *dark* line in the position of the yellow line of the sodium vapor. The spectrum of sodium vapor is *reversed*, its bright lines becoming dark and its dark spaces bright. With a spectroscope of any considerable power, the yellow line of sodium vapor is resolved into a double line. With a spectroscope of the same power, the dark sodium line of the reversed spectrum is seen to be a double line.

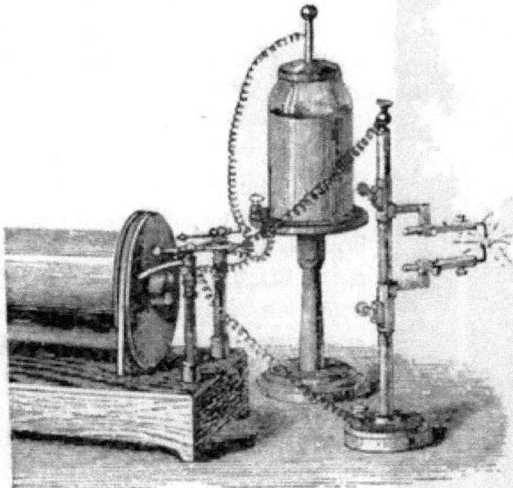

Fig. 177.

It is found to be generally true, that the spectrum of the light from an incandescent solid or liquid which has passed *through a luminous vapor* on its way to the spectroscope is made up of a bright ground crossed by dark lines; there being a dark line for every bright line that the vapor alone would give.

Fig. 178.

158. *Explanation of Reversed Spectra.* — It has been found that gases absorb and quench rays of the same degree of refrangibility as those which they themselves emit, and no others. When a solid is shining through a luminous vapor, this absorbs and quenches those rays from the solid which have the same degrees of refrangibility as those which it is itself emitting: hence the lines of the spectrum receive light from the vapor alone, while the spaces between the lines receive light from the solid. Now, solids and liquids, when heated to incandescence, give a very much brighter light than vapors and gases at the same temperature: hence the lines of a reversed spectrum, though receiving light. from the vapor or gas, appear dark by contrast.

159. *Effect of Increasing the Power of the Spectroscope upon the Brilliancy of a Spectrum.* —An increase in the power of a spectroscope diminishes the brilliancy of a *continuous* spectrum, since it makes the colored band longer, and therefore spreads the light out over a greater extent of surface; but, in the case of a *bright-lined* spectrum, an increase of power in the spectroscope produces scarcely any alteration in the brilliancy of the lines, since it merely separates the lines farther without making the lines themselves any wider. In the case of a *reversed* spectrum, an increase of power in the spectroscope dilutes the light in the spaces between the lines without diluting that of the lines: hence lines which appear dark in a spectroscope of slight dispersive power may appear bright in an instrument of great dispersive power.

160. *Change of the Spectrum with the Density of the Luminous Vapor.* — It has been found, that, as the density of a luminous vapor is diminished, the lines in its spectrum become fewer and fewer, till they are finally reduced to one. On the other hand, an increase of density causes new lines to appear in the spectrum, and the old lines to become thicker.

161. *Change of the Spectrum with the Temperature of the Luminous Vapor.* — It has also been found that the appearance of a bright-lined spectrum changes considerably with the temperature of the luminous vapor. In some cases, an increase of temperature changes the relative intensities of the lines; in other cases, it causes new lines to appear, and old lines to disappear.

In the case of a compound vapor, an increase of temperature causes the colored bands (which are peculiar to the spectrum of the compound) to disappear, and to be replaced by the spectral lines of the elements of which the compound is made up. The heat appears to *dissociate*

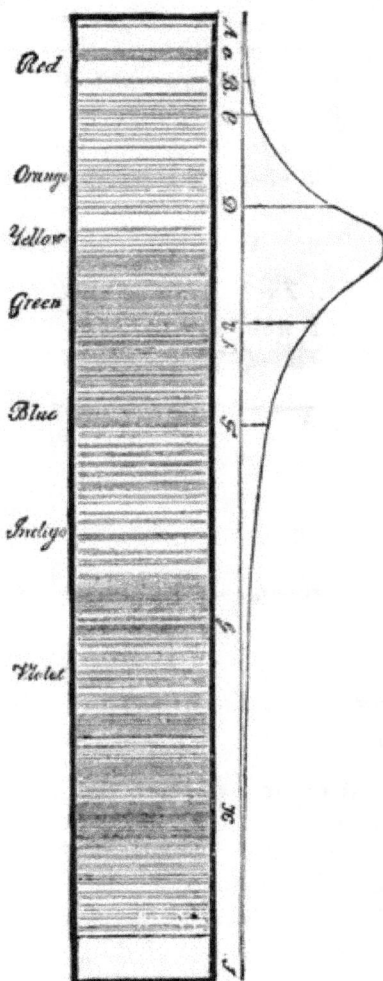

Fig. 179.

the compound; that is, to resolve it into its constituent elements. In this case, each elementary vapor would give its own spectral lines. As the compound is not completely dissociated at once, it is possible, of course, for one or more of the spectral lines of the elementary vapors to co-exist in the spectrum with the bands of the compound.

It has been found, that, in some cases, the spectra of the elementary gases change with the temperature of the gas; and Lockyer thinks he has discovered conclusive evidence, in the spectra of the sun and stars, that many of the substances regarded as elementary are really resolved into simpler substances by the intense heat of the sun; in other words, that our so-called elements are really compounds.

CHEMICAL CONSTITUTION OF THE SUN.

162. *The Solar Spectrum.* — The solar spectrum is crossed transversely by a great number of fine dark lines, and hence it belongs to the class of *reversed* spectra.

Fig. 180.

These lines were first studied and mapped by Fraunhofer, and from him they have been called *Fraunhofer's lines*.

A reduced copy of Fraunhofer's map is shown in Fig. 179. A few of the most prominent of the dark solar lines are designated by the letters of the alphabet. The other lines are usually designated by the numbers at which they are found on the scale which accompanies the map. This scale is usually drawn at the top of the map, as will be seen in some of the following diagrams. The two most elaborate maps of the solar spectrum are those of Kirchhoff and Angström. The scale on Kirchhoff's map is an arbitrary one, while that of Angström is based upon the wave-lengths of the rays of light which would fall upon the lines in the spectrum.

The appearance of the spectrum varies greatly with the

power of the spectroscope employed. Fig. 180 shows a portion of the spectrum as it appears in a spectroscope of a single prism: while Fig. 181 shows the *b* group of lines alone, as they appear in a powerful diffraction spectroscope.

163. *The Telluric Lines.* — There are many lines of the solar spectrum which vary considerably in intensity as the sun passes from the horizon to the meridian, being most intense when the sun is nearest the horizon, and when his rays are obliged to pass through the greatest depth of the earth's atmosphere. These lines are of atmospheric origin, and are due to the absorption of the aqueous vapor in our atmosphere. They are the same lines that are obtained

Fig. 181.

when a candle or other artificial light is examined with a spectroscope through a long tube filled with steam. Since these lines are due to the absorption of our own atmosphere, they are called *telluric lines*. A map of these lines is shown in Fig. 182.

164. *The Solar Lines.* — After deducting the telluric lines, the remaining lines of the solar spectrum are of solar origin. They must be due to absorption which takes place in the sun's atmosphere. They are, in fact, the reversed spectra of the elements which exist in the solar atmosphere in the state of vapor: hence we conclude that the luminous surface of the sun is surrounded with an atmosphere of luminous vapors. The temperature of this atmosphere, at

least near the surface of the sun, must be sufficient to enable all the elements known on the earth to exist in it as vapors.

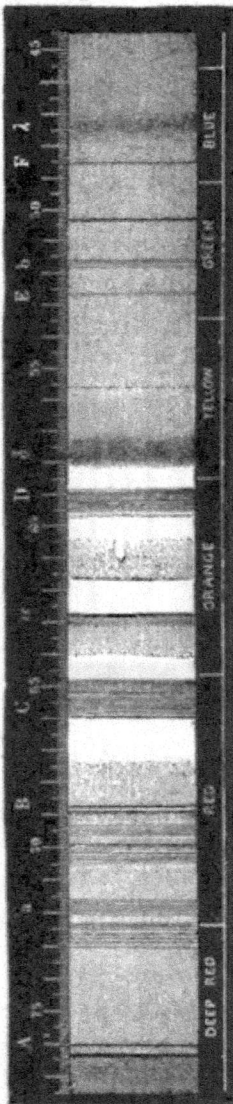

Fig. 182.

165. *Chemical Constitution of the Sun's Atmosphere.* — To find whether any element which exists on the earth is present in the solar atmosphere, we have merely to ascertain whether the bright lines of its gaseous spectrum are matched by dark lines in the solar spectrum when the two spectra are placed side by side. In Fig. 183, we have in No. 1 a portion of the red end of the solar spectra, and in No. 2 the spectrum of sodium vapor, both as obtained in the same spectroscope by means of the comparison prism. It will be seen that the double sodium line is exactly matched by a double dark line of the solar spectrum : hence we conclude that sodium vapor is present in the sun's atmosphere. Fig. 184 shows the matching of a great number of the bright lines of iron vapor by dark lines in the solar spectrum. This matching of the iron lines establishes the fact that iron vapor is present in the solar atmosphere.

The following table (given by Professor Young) contains a list of all the elements which have, up to the present time, been detected with certainty in the sun's atmosphere. It also gives the number of bright lines in the spectrum of each element, and the number of those

lines which have been matched by dark lines in the solar
spectrum : —

ELEMENTS.	Bright Lines in Spectrum.	Lines Reversed in Solar Spectrum.	Observer.
1. Iron	600	460	Kirchhoff.
2. Titanium . . .	206	118	Thalen.
3. Calcium . . .	89	75	Kirchhoff.
4. Manganese . .	75	57	Angström.
5. Nickel	51	33	Kirchhoff.
6. Cobalt	86	19	Thalen.
7. Chromium . .	71	18	Kirchhoff.
8. Barium	26	11	Kirchhoff.
9. Sodium . . .	9	9	Kirchhoff.
10. Magnesium . .	7	7	Kirchhoff.
11. Copper? . . .	15	7?	Kirchhoff.
12. Hydrogen . . .	5	5	Angström.
13. Palladium . . .	29	5	Lockyer.
14. Vanadium . . .	54	4	Lockyer.
15. Molybdenum . .	27	4	Lockyer.
16. Strontium . . .	74	4	Lockyer.
17. Lead	41	3	Lockyer.
18. Uranium . . .	21	3	Lockyer.
19. Aluminium . .	14	2	Angström.
20. Cerium	64	2	Lockyer.
21. Cadmium . . .	20	2	Lockyer.
22. Oxygen a } . .	42	12 $\pm$ bright	H. Draper.
Oxygen β } . .	4	4?	Schuster.

In addition to the above elements, it is probable that several
other elements are present in the sun's atmosphere; since at
least one of their bright lines has been found to coincide with
dark lines of the solar spectrum. There are, however, a large
number of elements, no traces of which have yet been detected;
and, in the cases of the elements whose presence in the solar
atmosphere has been established, the matching of the lines is
far from complete in the majority of the cases, as will be seen
from the above table. This want of complete coincidence of
the lines is undoubtedly due to the very high temperature of

the solar atmosphere. We have already seen that the lines of the spectrum change with the temperature; and, as the temperature of the sun is far higher than any that we can produce by artificial means, we might reasonably expect that it would cause the disappearance from the spectrum of many lines which we find to be present at our highest temperature.

Lockyer maintains that the reason why no trace of the spectral lines of certain of our so-called elements is found in the solar atmosphere is, that these substances are not really elementary, and that the intense heat of the sun resolves them into simpler constituents.

MOTION AT THE SURFACE OF THE SUN.

166. *Change of Pitch caused by Motion of Sounding Body.* — When a sounding body is moving rapidly towards

Fig. 183.

us, the pitch of its note becomes somewhat higher than when the body is stationary; and, when such a body is moving rapidly from us, the pitch of its note is lowered somewhat. We have a good illustration of this change of pitch at a country railway station on the passage of an express-train. The pitch of the locomotive whistle is considerably higher when the train is approaching the station than when it is leaving it.

167. *Explanation of the Change of Pitch produced by Motion.* — The pitch of sound depends upon the rapidity with which the pulsations of sound beat upon the drum of

the ear. The more rapidly the pulsations follow each other, the higher is the pitch : hence the shorter the sound-waves (provided the sound is all the while travelling at the same rate), the higher the pitch of the sound. Any thing, then, which tends to shorten the waves of sound tends also to raise its pitch, and any thing which tends to lengthen these waves tends to lower its pitch.

When a sounding body is moving rapidly forward, the sound-waves are crowded together a little, and therefore shortened ; when it is moving backward, the sound-waves are drawn out, or lengthened a little.

The effect of the motion of a sounding body upon the length of its sonorous waves will be readily seen from the following illustration : Suppose a number of persons stationed at equal intervals in a line on a long platform capable of moving backward and forward. Suppose the men are four feet apart, and all walking forward at the same rate, and that the platform is stationary, and that, as the men leave the platform, they keep on walking at the same rate : the men

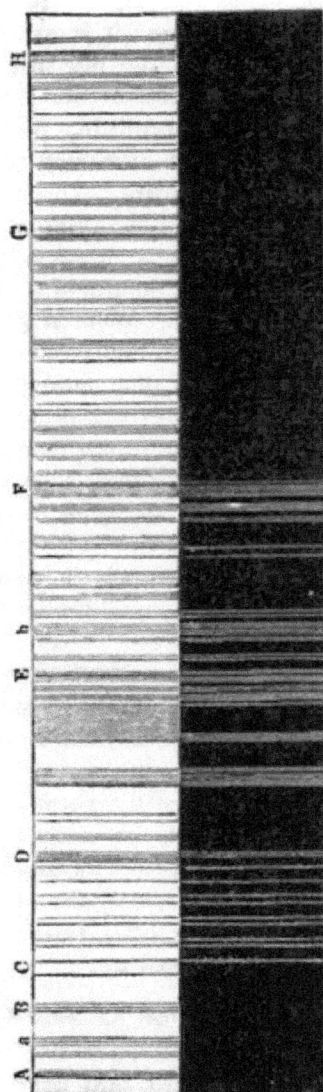

Fig. 184.

will evidently be four feet apart in the line in front of the platform, as well as on it. Suppose next, that the platform is moving forward at the rate of one foot in the interval between two men's leaving the platform, and that the men continue to walk as before: it is evident that the men will then be three feet apart in the line after they have left the platform. The forward motion of the platform has the effect of crowding the men together a little. Were the platform moving backward at the same rate, the men would be five feet apart after they had left the platform. The backward motion of the platform has the effect of separating the men from one another.

The distance between the men in this illustration corresponds to the length of the sound-wave, or the distance between its two ends. Were a person to stand beside the line, and count the men that passed him in the three cases given above, he would find that more persons would pass him in the same time when the platform is moving forward than when it is stationary, and fewer persons would pass him in the same time when the platform is moving backward than when it is stationary. In the same way, when a sounding body is moving rapidly forward, the sound-waves beat more rapidly upon the ear of a person who is standing still than when the body is at rest, and less rapidly when the sounding body is moving rapidly backward.

Were the platform stationary, and were the person who is counting the men to be walking along the line, either towards or away from the platform, the effect upon the number of men passing him in a given time would be precisely the same as it would be were the person stationary, and the platform moving either towards or away from him at the same rate. So the change in the rapidity with which pulsations of sound beat upon the ear is precisely the same whether the ear is stationary and the sounding body moving, or the sounding body is stationary and the ear moving.

168. *Change of Refrangibility due to the Motion of a Luminous Body.* — Refrangibility in light corresponds to pitch in sound, and depends upon the length of the luminous waves. The shorter the luminous waves, the greater the refrangibility of the waves. Very rapid motion of a luminous body has the same effect upon the length of the

luminous waves that motion of a sounding body has upon the length of the sonorous waves. When a luminous body is moving very rapidly towards us, its luminous waves are shortened a little, and its light becomes a little more refrangible; when the luminous body is moving rapidly from us, its luminous waves are lengthened a little, and its light becomes a little less refrangible.

169. *Displacement of Spectral Lines.* — In examining the spectra of the stars, we often find that certain of the dark lines are *displaced* somewhat, either towards the red or the violet end of the spectrum. As the dark lines are in the same position as the bright lines of the absorbing vapor would be, a displacement of the lines towards the red end of the spectrum indicates a lowering of the refrangibility of the rays, due to a motion of the luminous vapor away from us; and a displacement of the lines towards the violet end of the spectrum indicates an increase of refrangibility, due to a motion of the luminous vapor

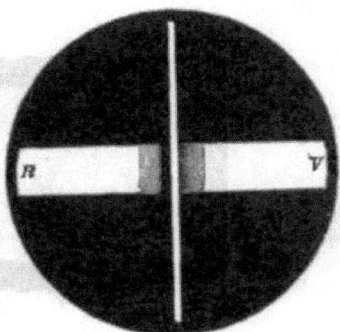

Fig. 185.

towards us. From the amount of the displacement of the lines, it is possible to calculate the velocity at which the luminous gas is moving. In Fig. 185 is shown the displacement of the F line in the spectrum of Sirius. This is one of the hydrogen lines. RV is the spectrum, R being the red, and V the violet end. The long vertical line is the bright F line of hydrogen, and the short dark line to the left of it is the position of the F line in the spectrum of Sirius. It is seen that this line is displaced somewhat towards the red end of the spectrum. This indicates that Sirius must be moving from us; and the amount of the displacement indicates that the star must be moving at the rate of some twenty-five or thirty miles a second.

170. *Contortion of Lines on the Disk of the Sun.* — Certain of the dark lines seen on the centre of the sun's disk often appear more or less distorted, as shown in Fig. 186, which represents the contortion of the hydrogen line as seen at various times. 1 and 2 indicate a rapid motion of hydrogen away from us, or a *down-rush* at the sun; 3 and 4 (in which the line at the centre is dark on one side, and bent towards the red end of the spectrum, and bright on the other side with a distortion towards the violet end of the spectrum) indicate a *down-rush* of *cool* hydrogen side by side with an *up-rush* of *hot and bright*

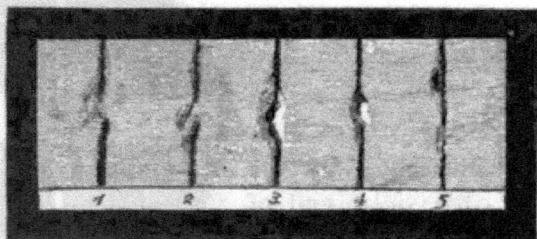

Fig. 186.

hydrogen; 5 indicates local *down-rushes* associated with *quiescent* hydrogen.

The contorted lines, which indicate a violently agitated state of the sun's atmosphere, appear in the midst of other lines which indicate a quiescent state. This is owing to the fact that the absorption which produces the dark lines takes place at various depths in the solar atmosphere. There may be violent commotion in the lower layers of the sun's atmosphere, and comparative quiet in the upper layers. In this case, the lines which are due to absorption in the lower layers would indicate this disturbance by their contortions; while the lines produced by absorption in the upper layers would be free from contortion.

It often happens, too, that the contortions are confined to one set of lines of an element, while other lines of the same element are entirely free from contortions. This is undoubtedly due to the fact that different layers of the solar atmosphere differ greatly in temperature ; so that the same element would give one set of lines at one depth, and another set at another depth : hence commotion in the solar atmosphere at any particular depth would be indicated by the contortion of those lines of the element only which are produced by the temperature at that particular depth.

A remarkable case of contortion witnessed by Professor Young is shown in Fig. 187. Three successive appearances of the C line are shown. The second view was taken three minutes after the first, and the third five minutes after the second. The contortion in this case indicated a velocity ranging

Fig. 187.

from two hundred to three hundred miles a second.

171. *Contortion of Lines on the Sun's Limb.* — When the spectroscope is directed to the centre of the sun's disk, the distortion of the lines indicates only vertical motion in the sun's atmosphere ; but, when the spectroscope is directed to the limb of the sun, displacements of the lines indicate horizontal motions in the sun's atmosphere. When a powerful spectroscope is directed to the margin of the sun's disk, so that the slit of the collimator tube shall be perpendicular to the sun's limb, one or more of the dark lines on the disk are seen to be prolonged by a bright line, as shown in Fig. 188. But this prolongation, instead of being straight and narrow, as shown in the figure,

is often widened and distorted in various ways, as shown in Fig. 189. In the left-hand portion of the diagram, the line is deflected towards the red end of the spectrum; this indicates a violent wind on the sun's surface blowing away

Fig. 188.

from us. In the right-hand portion of the diagram, the line is deflected towards the violet end of the spectrum; this indicates a violent wind blowing towards us. In the middle portion of the figure, the line is seen to be bent both ways; this indicates a cyclone, on one side of which the wind would be blowing from us, and on the other side towards us.

The distortions of the solar lines indicate that the wind at the surface of the sun often blows with a velocity of *from one hundred to three hundred miles a second*. The

Fig. 189.

most violent wind known on the earth has a velocity of a hundred miles an hour.

III. THE PHOTOSPHERE AND SUN SPOTS.

THE PHOTOSPHERE.

172. *The Granulation of the Photosphere.* — When the surface of the sun is examined with a good telescope under favorable atmospheric conditions, it is seen to be composed

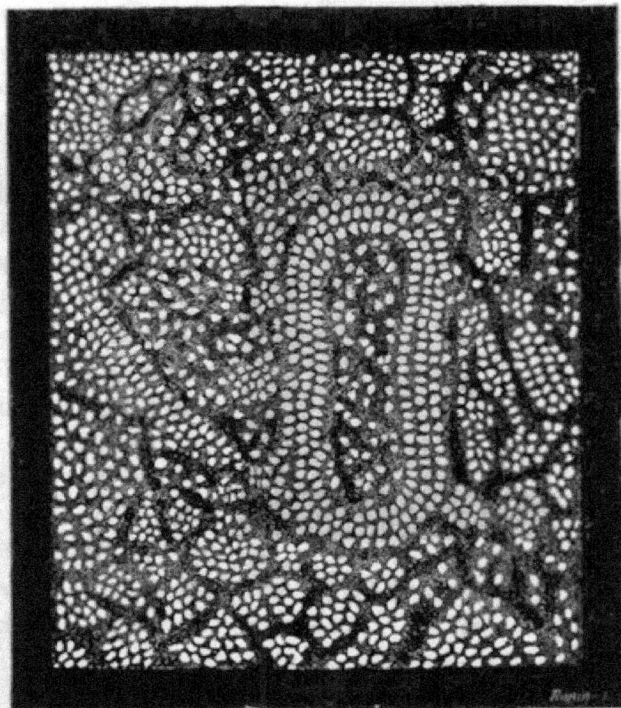

Fig. 190.

of minute grains of intense brilliancy and of irregular form, floating in a darker medium, and arranged in streaks and groups, as shown in Fig. 190. With a rather low power, the general effect of the surface is much like that of rough drawing-paper, or of curdled milk seen from a little distance. With a high power and excellent atmospheric conditions, the *grains* are seen to be irregular, rounded masses, some hundreds of miles in diameter, sprinkled upon a less brilliant background, and appearing somewhat like snow-flakes sparsely scattered over a grayish cloth.   Fig. 191 is a representation of these grains according to Secchi.

With a very powerful telescope and the very best atmos-pheric conditions, the grains themselves are resolved into *granules*, or little luminous dots, not more than a hundred miles or so in diameter, which, by their aggregation, make up the grains, just as they, in their turn, make up the coarser masses of the solar surface.   Professor Langley estimates that these granules constitute about one-fifth of the sun's surface, while they emit at least three-fourths of its light.

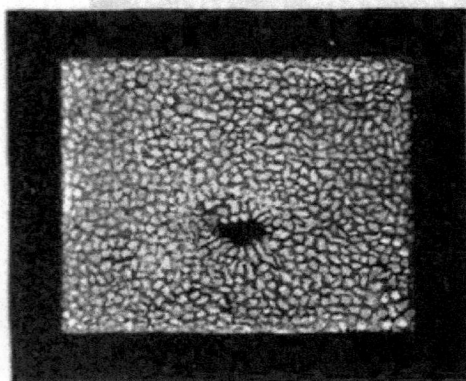

Fig. 191.

173. *Shape of the Grains.* — The grains differ considerably in shape at different times and on differ-ent parts of the sun's surface.   Nasmyth, in 1861, described them as *willow-leaves* in shape, several thousand miles in length, but narrow and with pointed ends.   He figured the surface of the sun as a sort of basket-work formed by the interweaving of such filaments.   To others they have appeared to have the form of *rice-grains*.   On portions of the sun's disk the elemen-tary structure is often composed of long, narrow, blunt-ended filaments, not so much like willow-leaves as like bits of straw lying roughly parallel to each other, — a *thatch-straw* formation, as it has been called.   This is specially common in the immediate neighborhood of the spots.

174. *Nature of the Grains.* — The grains are, undoubt-edly, incandescent *clouds* floating in the sun's atmosphere,

and composed of partially condensed metallic vapors, just as the clouds of our atmosphere are composed of partially condensed aqueous vapor. Rain on the sun is composed of white-hot drops of molten iron and other metals; and these drops are often driven with the wind with a velocity of over a hundred miles a second.

As to the forms of the grains, Professor Young says, " If one were to speculate as to the explanation of the grains and thatch-straws, it might be that the grains are the upper ends of long filaments of luminous cloud, which, over most of the sun's surface, stand approximately vertical, but in the neighborhood of a spot are inclined so as to lie nearly horizontal. This is not certain, though : it may be that the cloud-masses over the more quiet portions of the solar surface are really, as they seem, nearly globular, while near the spots they are drawn out into filamentary forms by atmospheric currents."

175 *Faculæ.* — The *faculæ* are irregular streaks of greater brightness than the general surface, looking much like the flecks of foam on the surface of a stream below a waterfall. They are sometimes from five to twenty thousand miles in length, covering areas immensely larger than a terrestrial continent.

These faculæ are *elevated regions* of the solar surface, ridges and crests of luminous matter, which rise above the general level of the sun's surface, and protrude through the denser portions of the solar atmosphere. When one of these passes over the edge of the sun's disk, it can be seen to project, like a little tooth. Any elevation on the sun to be perceptible at all must measure at least half a second of an arc, or two hundred and twenty-five miles.

The faculæ are most numerous in the neighborhood of the spots, and much more conspicuous near the limb of the sun than near the centre of the disk. Fig. 192 gives the general appearance of the faculæ. and the darkening of the limb of the sun. Near the spots, the faculæ often undergo very rapid change of form, while elsewhere on the disk they change rather slowly, sometimes undergoing little apparent alteration for several days.

176. *Why the Faculæ are most Conspicuous near the Limb of the Sun.* — The reason why the faculæ are most conspicuous near the limb of the sun is this : The luminous surface of the sun is covered with an atmosphere, which, though not very thick compared with the diameter of the sun, is still sufficient to absorb a good deal of light. Light

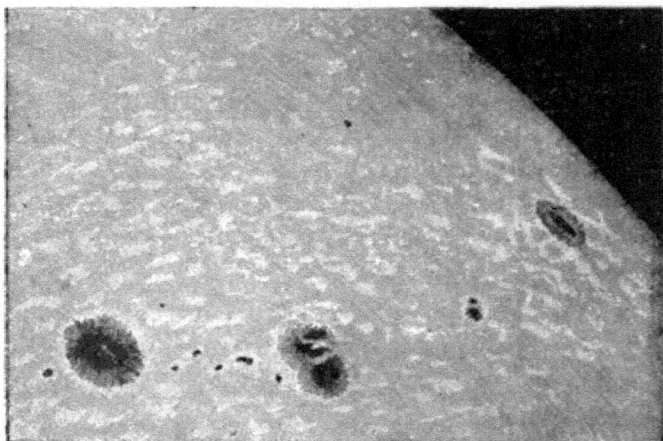

Fig. 192.

coming from the centre of the sun's disk penetrates this atmosphere under the most favorable conditions, and is but slightly reduced in amount. The edges of the disk, on the other hand, are seen through a much greater thickness of atmosphere ; and the light is reduced by absorption some seventy-five per cent. Suppose, now, a facula were sufficiently elevated to penetrate quite through this atmosphere. Its light would be undimmed by absorption on any part of the sun's disk ; but at the centre of the disk it would be seen against a background nearly as bright as itself, while at the margin it would be seen against one only a quarter as bright. It is evident that the light of any facula, owing to the elevation, would be reduced less rapidly as we approach the edge of the disk than that of the general surface of the sun, which lies at a lower level.

SUN-SPOTS.

177. *General Appearance of Sun-Spots.* — The general appearance of a well-formed sun-spot is shown in Fig. 193. The spot consists of a very dark central portion of irregu-

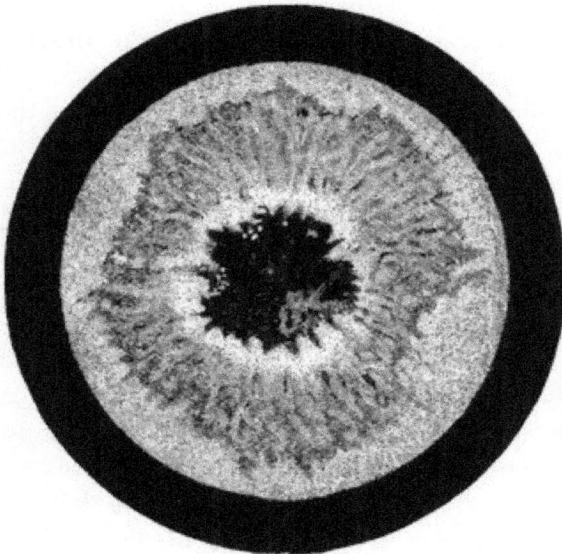

Fig. 193.

lar shape, called the *umbra*, which is surrounded by a less dark fringe, called the *penumbra*. The penumbra is made up, for the most part, of filaments directed radially inward.

There is great variety in the details of form in different sun-spots; but they are generally nearly circular during the middle period of their existence. During the period of their development and of their disappearance they are much more irregular in form.

There is nothing like a gradual shading-off of the penumbra, either towards the umbra on the one side, or towards the photosphere on the other. The penumbra is separated from both the umbra and the photosphere by a sharp line of demarcation. The umbra is much brighter on the inner than on the outer edge, and frequently the photosphere is excessively bright at the margin of the penumbra. The brightness of the inner penumbra seems to be due to the crowding together of the penumbral filaments where they overhang the edge of the umbra.

There is a general antithesis between the irregularities of the outer and inner edges of the penumbra. Where an angle of the penumbral matter crowds in upon the umbra, it is generally matched by a corresponding outward extension into the photosphere, and *vice versa*.

The umbra of the spot is far from being uniformly dark. Many of the penumbral filaments terminate in little detached grains of luminous matter; and there are also fainter veils of a substance less brilliant, but sometimes rose-colored, which seem to float above the umbra. The umbra itself is made up of masses of clouds which are really intensely brilliant, and which appear dark only by contrast with the intenser brightness of the solar surface. Among these clouds are often seen one or more minute circular spots much darker than the rest of the umbra. These darker portions are called *nuclei*. They seem to be the mouths of tubular orifices penetrating to unknown depths. The faint veils mentioned above continually melt away, and are replaced by others in some different position. The bright granules at the tips of the penumbral filaments seem to sink and dissolve, while fresh portions break off to replace them. There is a continual indraught of luminous matter over the whole extent of the penumbra.

At times, though very rarely, patches of intense brightness suddenly break out, remain visible for a few minutes, and move over the spot with velocities as great as a hundred miles *a second.*

The spots change their form and size quite perceptibly from day to day, and sometimes even from hour to hour.

178. *Duration of Sun-Spots.* — The average life of a sun-spot is two or three months : the longest on record is that of a spot observed in 1840 and 1841, which lasted eighteen months. There are cases, however, where the disappearance of a spot is very soon followed by the appearance of another at the same point ; and sometimes this alternate disappearance and re-appearance is several times repeated. While some spots are thus long-lived, others endure only a day or two, and sometimes only a few hours.

179. *Groups of Spots.* — The spots usually appear not singly, but in groups. A large spot is often followed by a train of smaller ones to the east of it, many of which are apt to be irregular in form and very imperfect in structure, sometimes with no umbra at all, often with a penumbra only on one side. In such cases, when any considerable change of form or structure shows itself in the principal spot, it seems to rush westward over the solar surface, leaving its attendants trailing behind. When a large spot divides into two or more, as often happens, the parts usually seem to repel each other, and fly apart with great velocity.

180. *Size of the Spots.* — The spots are sometimes of enormous size. Groups have often been observed covering areas of more than a hundred thousand miles square, and single spots occasionally measure from forty to fifty thousand miles in diameter, the umbra being twenty-five or thirty thousand miles across. A spot, however, measuring thirty thousand miles over all, may be considered a large one. Such a spot can easily be seen without a telescope when the brightness of the sun's surface is reduced by clouds or

ASTRONOMY.

182

nearness to the horizon, or by the use of colored glass.
During the years 1871 and 1872 spots were visible to the
naked eye for a considerable portion of the time. The
largest spot yet recorded was observed in 1858. It had a
breadth of more than a hundred and forty-three thousand
miles, or nearly eighteen times the diameter of the earth,
and covered about a thirty-sixth of the whole surface of
the sun.

Fig. 194 represents a group of sun-spots observed by

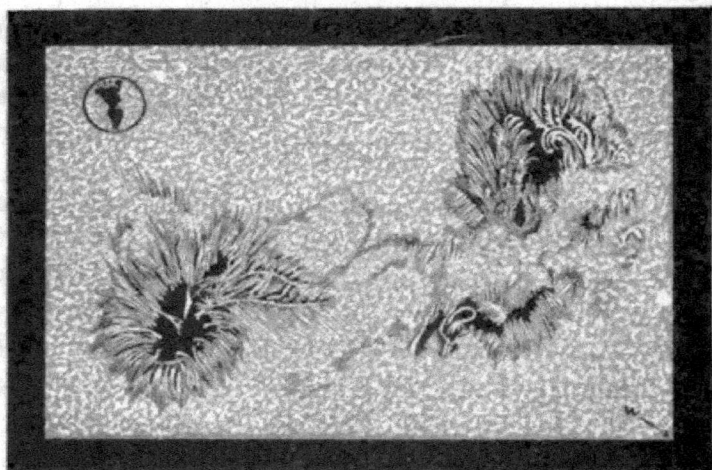

Fig. 194.

Professor Langley, and drawn on the same scale as the small
circle in the upper left-hand corner, which represents the
surface of half of our globe.

181. *The Penumbral Filaments.* — Not unfrequently the
penumbral filaments are curved spirally, indicating a cyclonic
action, as shown in Fig. 195. In such cases the whole spot
usually turns slowly around, sometimes completing an entire
revolution in a few days. More frequently, however, the
spiral motion lasts but a short time ; and occasionally, after
continuing for a while in one direction, the motion is
reversed. Very often in large spots we observe opposite

spiral movements in different portions of the umbra, as
shown in Figs. 196 and 197.

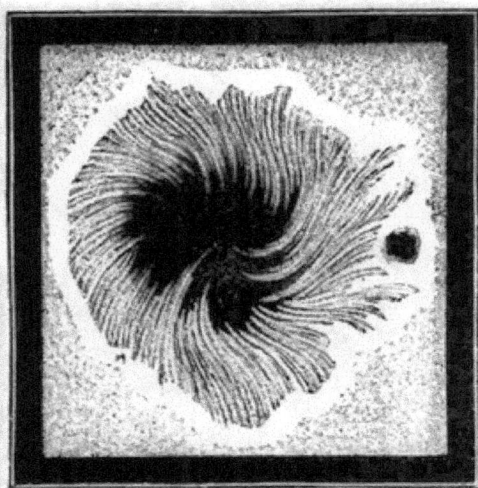

Fig. 195.

Neighboring spots show no tendency to rotate in the

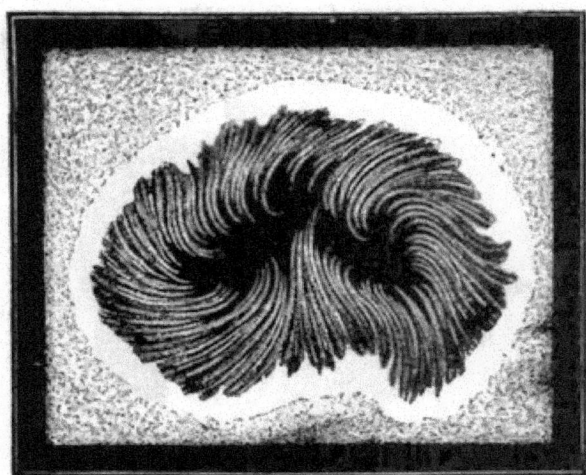

Fig. 196.

same direction. The number of spots in which a decided
cyclonic motion (like that shown in Fig. 198) appears is

comparatively small, not exceeding two or three per cent of the whole.

Fig. 197.

Plate II. represents a typical sun-spot as delineated by

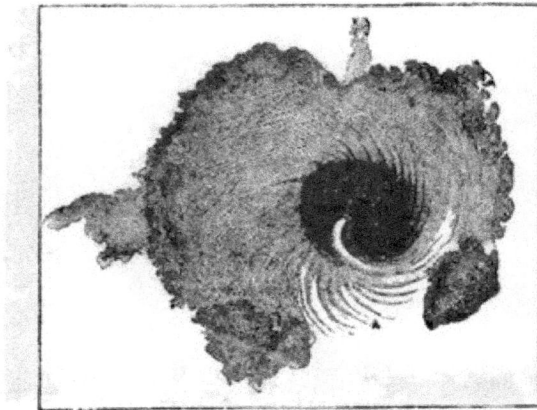

Fig. 198.

Professor Langley. At the left-hand and upper portions of this great spot the filaments present the ordinary appearance,

PLATE II.

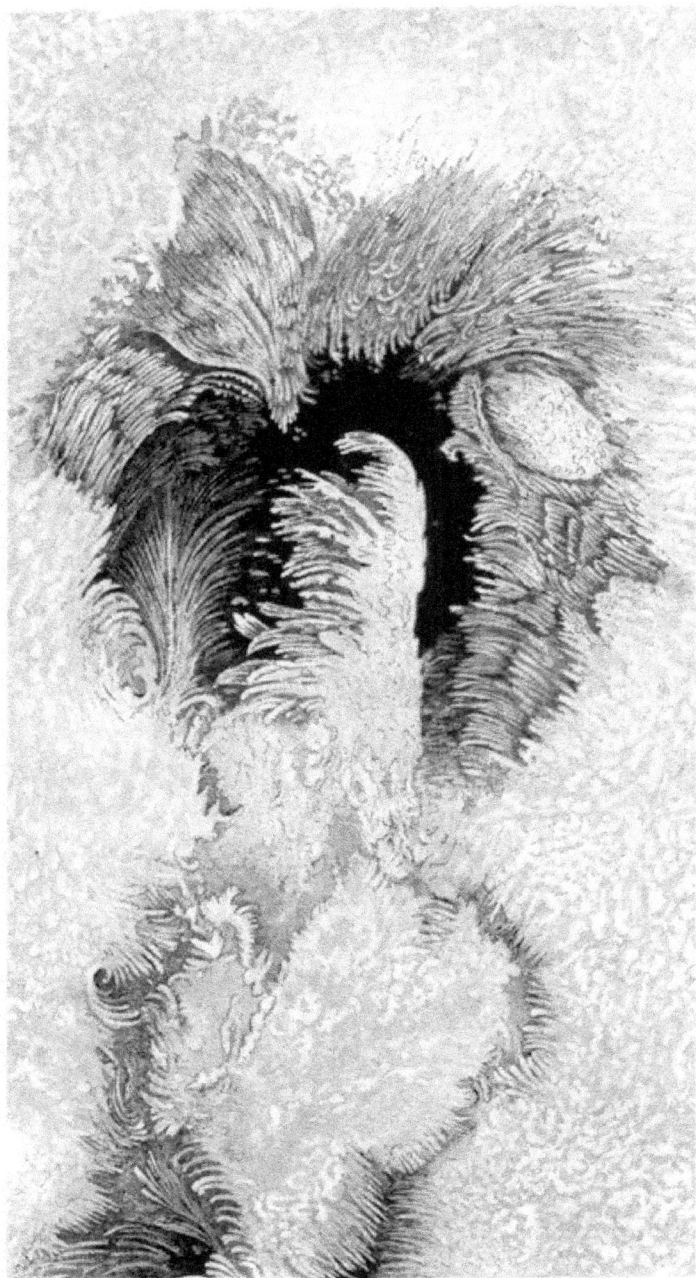

while at the lower edge, and upon the great overhanging branch, they are arranged very differently. The feathery brush below the branch, closely resembling a frost-crystal on a window-pane, is as rare as it is curious, and has not been satisfactorily explained.

182. *Birth and Decay of Sun-Spots.* — The formation of a spot is sometimes gradual, requiring days or even weeks for its full development; and sometimes a single day suffices. Generally, for some time before its appearance, there

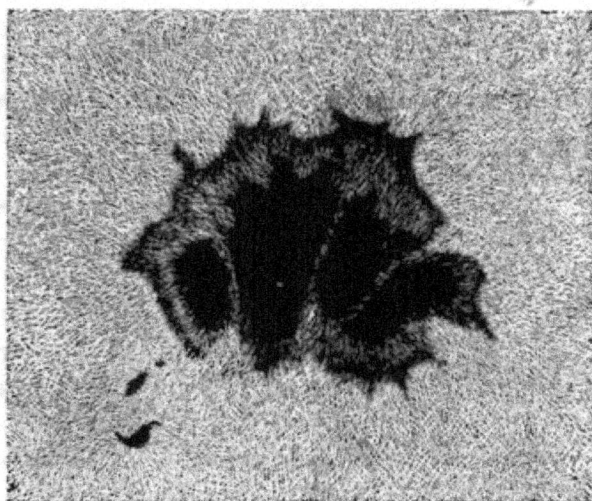

Fig. 199.

is an evident disturbance of the solar surface, indicated especially by the presence of many brilliant faculæ, among which *pores*, or minute black dots, are scattered. These enlarge, and between them appear grayish patches, in which the photospheric structure is unusually evident, as if they were caused by a dark mass lying below a thin veil of luminous filaments. This veil seems to grow gradually thinner, and finally breaks open, giving us at last the complete spot with its penumbra. Some of the pores coalesce with the principal spot, some disappear, and others form the attendant

train before described (179). The spot when once formed
usually assumes a circular form, and remains without striking
change until it disappears. As its end approaches, the
surrounding photosphere seems to crowd in, and overwhelm
the penumbra. Bridges of light (Fig. 199), often much
brighter than the average of the solar surface, push across
the umbra ; the arrangement of the penumbra filaments
becomes confused ; and, as Secchi expresses it, the luminous matter of the photosphere seems to tumble pell-mell
into the chasm, which disappears, and leaves a disturbed
surface marked with faculæ, which, in their turn, gradually
subside.

183. *Motion of Sun-Spots.* — The spots have a regular
motion across the disk of the sun
from east to west, occupying about
twelve days in the transit. A spot
generally appears first on or near
the east limb, and, after twelve or
fourteen days, disappears at the west
limb. At the end of another fourteen days, or more, it re-appears at
the east limb, unless, in the mean

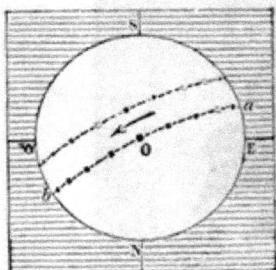

Fig. 200.

time, it has vanished from sight entirely. This motion of
the spots is indicated by the arrow in Fig. 200. The
interval between two successive appearances of the same
spot on the eastern edge of the sun is about twenty-seven
days.

184. *The Rotation of the Sun.* — The spots are evidently
carried around by the rotation of the sun on its axis. It is
evident, from Fig. 201, that the sun will need to make more
than a complete rotation in order to bring a spot again
upon the same part of the disk as seen from the earth.
S represents the sun, and *E* the earth. The arrows indicate
the direction of the sun's rotation. When the earth is at *E*,
a spot at *a* would be seen at the centre of the solar disk.

While the sun is turning on its axis, the earth moves in its orbit from E to E': hence the sun must make a complete rotation, and turn from a to a' in addition, in order to bring the spot again to the centre of the disk. To carry the spot entirely around, and then on to a', requires about twenty-seven days. From this *synodical period* of the spot, as it might be called, it has been calculated that the sun must rotate on its axis in about twenty-five days.

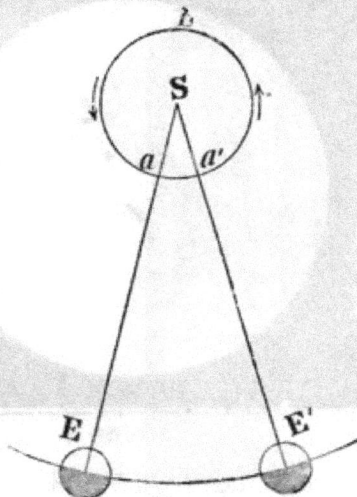

185. *The Inclination of the Sun's Axis.* — The paths described by sun-spots across the solar disk vary with the position of the earth in its orbit, as shown in Fig. 202. We therefore conclude that the sun's axis is not perpendicular to the plane of the earth's orbit. The sun rotates on its axis from west to east, and the axis leans about seven degrees from the perpendicular to the earth's orbit.

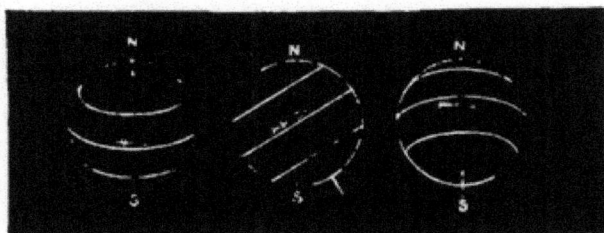

Fig. 201.

Fig. 202.

186. *The Proper Motion of the Spots.* — When the period of the sun's rotation is deduced from the motion of spots in different solar latitudes, there is found to be considerable variation in the results obtained. Thus spots near

188   ASTRONOMY.

the equator indicate that the sun rotates in about twenty-five days; while those in latitude 20° indicate a period about

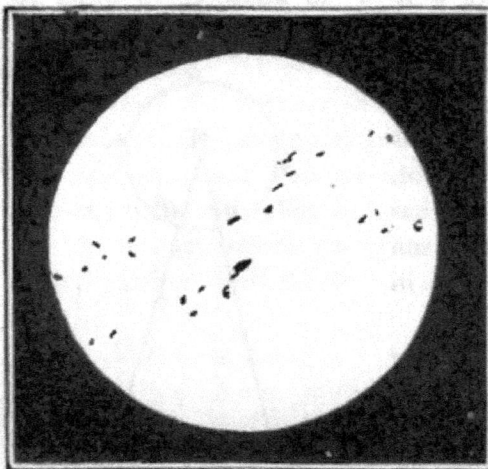

Fig. 203.

eighteen hours. longer; and those in latitude 30° a period of twenty-seven days and a half. Strictly speaking, the sun, as a whole, has no single period of rotation; but different portions of its surface perform their revolutions in different times. The equatorial regions not only move more rapidly in miles per hour than the rest of the solar surface, but they *complete the entire rotation in shorter time.*

There appears to be a peculiar surface-drift in the equatorial regions of the sun, the cause of which is unknown, but which gives the spots a *proper* motion; that is, a motion of their own, independent of the rotation of the sun.

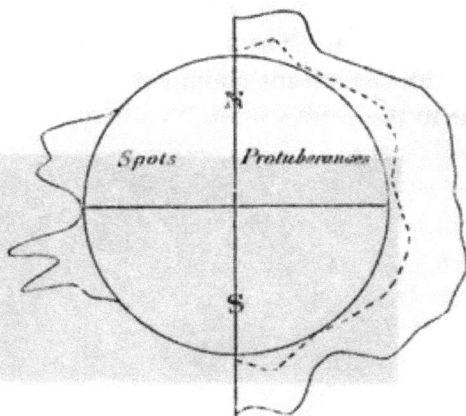

Fig. 204.

187. *Distribution of the Sun-Spots.* — The sun-spots are not distributed uniformly over the sun's surface, but occur mainly in two zones on each side of the equator, and be-

tween the latitudes of 10° and 30°, as shown in Fig. 203. On and near the equator itself they are comparatively rare. There are still fewer beyond 35° of latitude, and only a single spot has ever been recorded more than 45° from the solar equator.

Fig. 204 shows the distribution of the sun-spots observed by Carrington during a period of eight years. The irregular line on the left-hand side of the figure indicates by its height the comparative frequency with which the spots occurred in different latitudes. In Fig. 205 the same thing is indicated by different degrees of darkness in the shading of the belts.

188. *The Periodicity of the Spots.* — Careful observations of the solar spots indicate a period of about eleven years in the spot-producing activity of the sun. During two or three years the spots increase in number and in size ; then they begin to diminish, and reach a minimum five or six years after the maximum. Another period of about six years brings the return of the maximum. The intervals are, however, somewhat irregular.

Fig. 206 gives a graphic representation of the periodicity of the sun-spots. The height of the curve shows the frequency of the sun-spots in the years

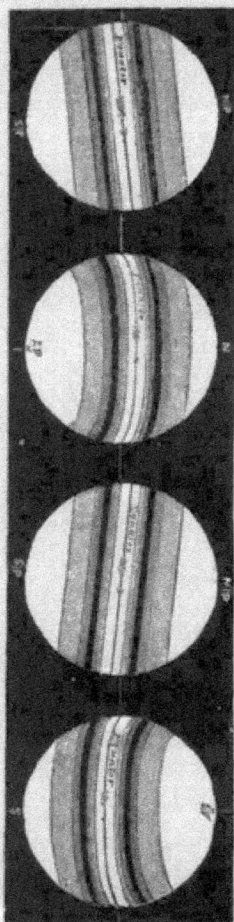

Fig. 205.

given at the bottom of the figure. It appears, from an examination of this sun-spot curve, that the average interval from a minimum to the next following maximum is only about four years and a half, while that from a maxi-

mum to the next following minimum is six years and six-
tenths. The disturbance which produces the sun-spots is
developed suddenly, but dies away
gradually.

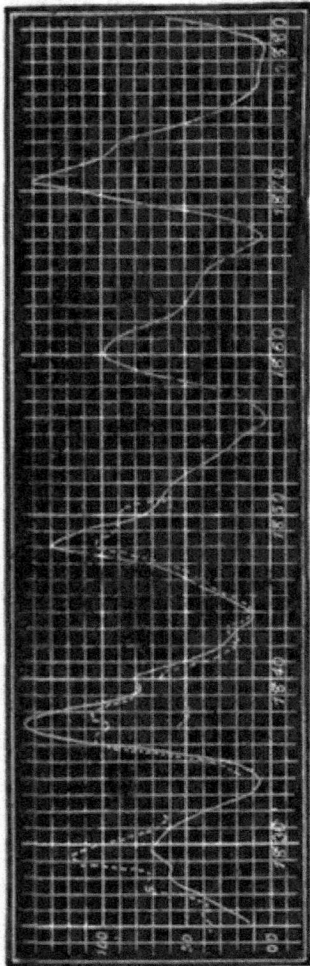

Fig. 206.

189. *Connection between Sun-
Spots and Terrestrial Magnetism.*
— The magnetic needle does not
point steadily in the same direction,
but is subject to various disturbances, some of which are regular,
and others irregular.

(1) One of the most noticeable
of the regular magnetic changes is
the so-called *diurnal oscillation.*
During the early part of the day
the north pole of the needle moves
toward the west in our latitude,
returning to its mean position about
ten P.M., and remaining nearly
stationary during the night. The
extent of this oscillation in the
United States is about fifteen minutes of arc in summer, and not
quite half as much in winter; but
it differs very much in different
localities and at different times, and
the average diurnal oscillation in
any locality increases and decreases
pretty regularly during a period of
about eleven years. The maximum
and minimum of this period of
magnetic disturbance are found to
coincide with the maximum and
minimum of the sun-spot period. This is shown in Fig. 206,
in which the dotted lines indicate the variations in the intensity
of the magnetic disturbance.

(2) Occasionally so-called *magnetic storms* occur, during
which the compass-needle is sometimes violently disturbed,

oscillating five degrees, or even ten degrees, within an hour
or two. These storms are generally accompanied by an aurora,
and an aurora is *always* accompanied by magnetic disturbance.
A careful comparison of aurora observations with those of sun-
spots shows an almost perfect parallelism between the curves
of auroral and sun-spot frequency.

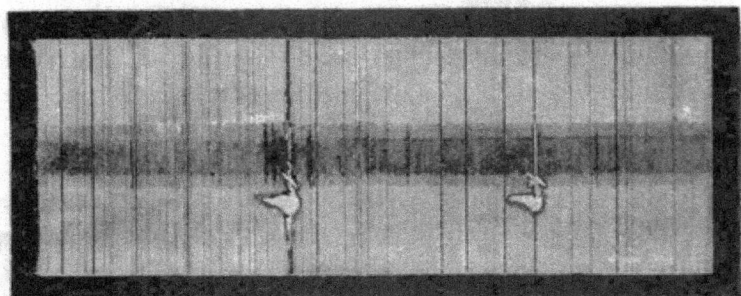

Fig. 207.

(3) A number of observations render it very probable that
every intense disturbance of the solar surface is propagated
to our terrestrial magnetism with the speed of light.

Fig. 207 shows certain of the solar lines as they were
observed by Professor Young on Aug. 3, 1872. The contortions of the *F* line indicated an intense disturbance in the

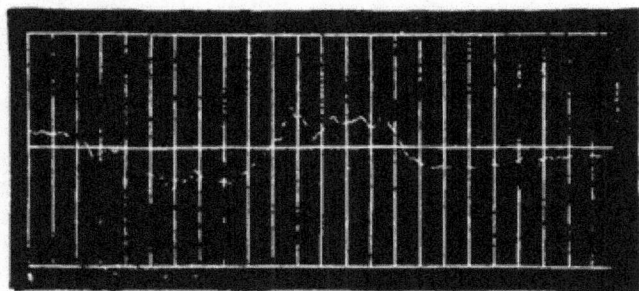

Fig. 208.

atmosphere of the sun. There were three especially notable
paroxysms in this distortion, occurring at a quarter of nine,
half-past ten, and ten minutes of twelve, A.M.

Fig. 208 shows the curve of magnetic disturbance as traced
at Greenwich on the same day. It will be seen from the curve
that it was a day of general magnetic disturbance. At the

times of the three paroxysms, which are given at the bottom
of the figure, it will be observed that there is a peculiar shiver-
ing of the magnetic curve.

190. *The Spots are Depressions in the Photosphere.* —
This fact was first clearly brought out by Dr. Wilson of
Glasgow, in 1769, from observations upon the penumbra of
a spot in November of that year. He found, that when
the spot appeared at the eastern limb, or edge of the sun,
just moving into sight, the penumbra was well marked on
the side of the spot nearest to the edge of the disk ; while
on the other edge of the spot, towards the centre of the
sun, there was no penumbra
visible at all, and the umbra
itself was almost hidden, as if
behind a bank. When the spot
had moved a day's journey
toward the centre of the disk,
the whole of the umbra came
into sight, and the penumbra on
the inner edge of the spot
began to be visible as a narrow
line. After the spot was well
advanced upon the disk, the penumbra was of the same
width all around the spot. When the spot approached the
sun's western limb, the same phenomena were repeated, but
in the inverse order. The penumbra on the *inner* edge of
the spot narrowed much faster than that on the outer, disappeared entirely, and finally seemed to hide from sight
much of the umbra nearly a whole day before the spot
passed from view around the limb. This is precisely what
would occur (as Fig. 209 clearly shows) if the spot were a
saucer-shaped depression in the solar surface, the bottom
of the saucer corresponding to the umbra, and the sloping
sides to the penumbra.

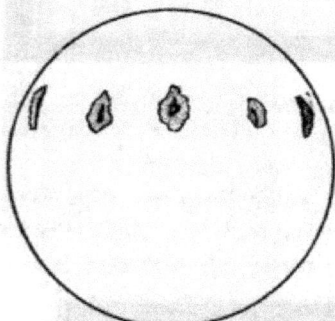

Fig. 209.

191. *Sun-Spot Spectrum.* — When the image of a sun-spot is thrown upon the slit of the spectroscope, the spectrum is seen to be crossed longitudinally by a continuous dark band, showing an increased general absorption in the region of the sun-spot. Many of the spectral lines are greatly thickened, as

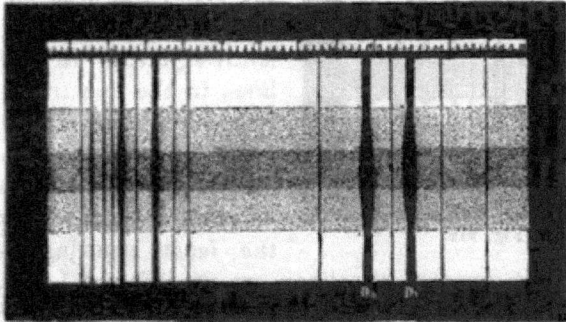

Fig. 210.

shown in Fig. 210. This thickening of the lines shows that the absorption is taking place at a greater depth. New lines and shadings often appear, which indicate, that, in the cooler nucleus of the spot, certain compound vapors exist, which are

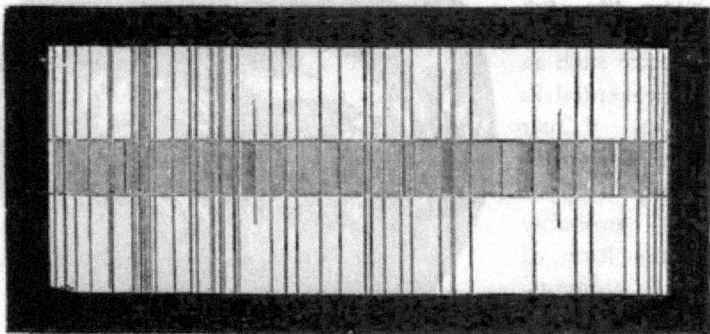

Fig. 211.

dissociated elsewhere on the sun's surface. These lines and shadings are shown in Fig. 211.

It often happens that certain of the spectral lines are reversed in the spectrum of the spot, a thin bright line appearing over the centre of a thick dark one, as shown in Fig. 212. These reversals are due to very bright vapors floating over the spot.

At times, also, the spectrum of a spot indicates violent motion in the overlying gases by distortion and displacement of the lines. This phenomenon occurs oftener at points near

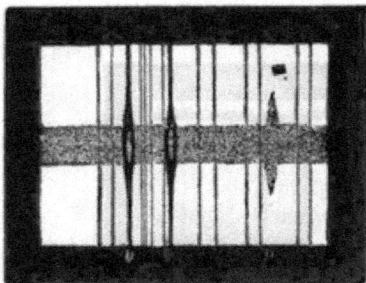

Fig. 212.

the outer edge of the penumbra than over the centre of the spot; but occasionally the whole neighborhood is violently agitated. In such cases, lines in the spectrum side by side are often affected in entirely different ways, one being greatly displaced while its neighbor is not disturbed in the least, showing that the vapors which produce the lines are at different levels in the solar atmosphere, and moving independently of each other.

192. *The Cause and Nature of Sun-Spots.* — According to Professor Young, the arrangement and relations of the photospheric clouds in the neighborhood of a spot are such as are represented in Fig. 213. "Over the sun's surface generally, these clouds probably have the form of vertical columns, as at *a a*. Just outside the spot, the level of the photosphere is

Fig. 213.

the most part, overtopped by eruptions of hydrogen and usually raised into faculæ, as at *b b*. These faculæ are, for metallic vapors, as indicated by the shaded clouds. . . . While the great clouds of hydrogen are found everywhere upon the

sun, these spiky, vivid outbursts of metallic vapors seldom
occur except just in the neighborhood of a spot, and then only
during its season of rapid change. In the penumbra of the
spot the photospheric filaments become more or less nearly
horizontal, as at *pp;* in the umbra at *u* it is quite uncertain
what the true state of affairs may be. We have conjecturally
represented the filaments there as vertical also, but depressed
and carried down by a descending current. Of course, the
cavity is filled by the gases which overlie the photosphere; and
it is easy to see, that, looked at from above, such a cavity
and arrangement of the luminous filaments would present the
appearances actually observed."

Professor Young also suggests that the spots may be depressions in the photosphere caused "by the *diminution of upward
pressure* from below, in consequence of eruptions in the neighborhood; the spots thus being, so to speak, *sinks* in the
photosphere. Undoubtedly the photosphere is not a strictly
continuous shell or crust; but it is *heavy* as compared with the
uncondensed vapors in which it lies, just as a rain-cloud in our
terrestrial atmosphere is heavier than the air; and it is probably continuous enough to have its upper level affected by any
diminution of pressure below. The gaseous mass below the
photosphere supports its weight and the weight of the products
of condensation, which must always be descending in an inconceivable rain and snow of molten and crystallized material.
To all intents and purposes, though nothing but a layer of
clouds, the photosphere thus forms a constricting shell, and
the gases beneath are imprisoned and compressed. Moreover,
at a high temperature the viscosity of gases is vastly increased,
so that quite probably the matter of the solar nucleus resembles pitch or tar in its consistency more than what we usually
think of as a gas. Consequently, any sudden diminution of
pressure would propagate itself slowly from the point where
it occurred. Putting these things together, it would seem, that,
whenever a free outlet is obtained through the photosphere at
any point, thus decreasing the inward pressure, the result would
be the sinking of a portion of the photosphere somewhere in
the immediate neighborhood, to restore the equilibrium; and, if
the eruption were kept up for any length of time, the depres-

sion in the photosphere would continue till the eruption ceased. This depression, filled with the overlying gases, would constitute a spot. Moreover, the line of fracture (if we may call it so) at the edges of the sink would be a region of weakness in the photosphere, so that we should expect a series of eruptions all around the spot. For a time the disturbance, therefore, would grow, and the spot would enlarge and deepen, until, in spite of the viscosity of the internal gases, the equilibrium of pressure was gradually restored beneath. So far as we know the spectroscopic and visual phenomena, none of them contradict this hypothesis. There is nothing in it, however, to account for the distribution of the spots in solar latitudes, nor for their periodicity."

IV. THE CHROMOSPHERE AND PROMINENCES.

193. *The Sun's Outer Atmosphere.* — What we see of the sun under ordinary circumstances is but a fraction of his total bulk. While by far the greater portion of the solar *mass* is included within the photosphere, the larger portion of his *volume* lies without, and constitutes a gaseous envelope whose diameter is at least double, and its bulk therefore sevenfold, that of the central globe.

This outer envelope, though mainly gaseous, is not spherical, but has an exceedingly irregular and variable outline. It seems to be made up, not of regular strata of different density, like our atmosphere, but rather of flames, beams, and streamers, as transient and unstable as those of the aurora borealis. It is divided into two portions by a boundary as definite, though not so regular, as that which separates them both from the photosphere. The outer and far more extensive portion, which in texture and rarity seems to resemble the tails of comets, is known as the *coronal atmosphere*, since to it is chiefly due the *corona*, or glory, which surrounds the darkened sun during an eclipse.

194. *The Chromosphere.* — At the base of the coronal atmosphere, and in contact with the photosphere, is what

resembles a sheet of scarlet fire. It appears as if countless jets of heated gas were issuing through vents over the whole surface, clothing it with flame, which heaves and tosses like the blaze of a conflagration. This is the *chromosphere*, or color-sphere. It owes its vivid redness to the predominance of hydrogen in the flames. The average depth of the chromosphere is not far from ten or twelve seconds, or five thousand or six thousand miles.

195. *The Prominences.* — Here and there masses of this hydrogen, mixed with other substances, rise far above the general level into the coronal regions, where they float like clouds, or are torn to pieces by conflicting currents. These cloud - masses are known as solar *prominences*, or *protuberances*.

196. *Magnitude and Distribution of the Prominences.* — The prominences differ greatly in magnitude. Of the 2,767 observed

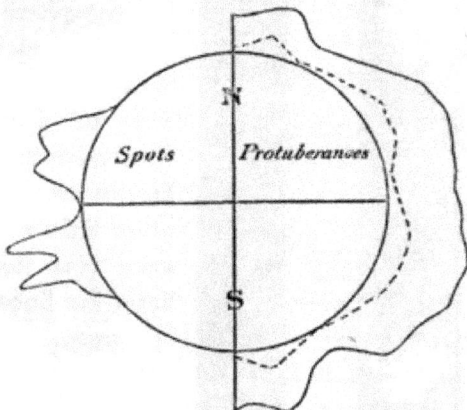

Fig. 214.

by Secchi, 1,964 attained an altitude of eighteen thousand miles; 751, or nearly a fourth of the whole, reached a height of twenty-eight thousand miles; several exceeded eighty-four thousand miles. In rare instances they reach elevations as great as a hundred thousand miles. A few have been seen which exceeded a hundred and fifty thousand miles; and Secchi has recorded one of three hundred thousand miles.

The irregular lines on the right-hand side of Fig. 214 show the proportion of the prominences observed by Secchi, that were seen in different parts of the sun's surface. The outer line shows the distribution of the smaller prominences, and the inner dotted line that of the larger prominences.

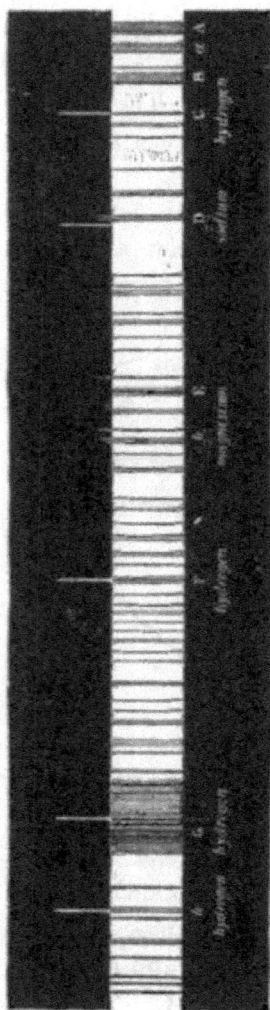

Fig. 215.

By comparing these lines with those on the opposite side of the circle, which show the distribution of the spots, it will be seen, that, while the spots are confined mainly to two belts, the prominences are seen in all latitudes.

197. *The Spectrum of the Chromosphere.* — The spectrum of the chromosphere is comparatively simple. There are eleven lines only which are always present ; and six of these are lines of hydrogen, and the others, with a single exception, are of unknown elements. There are sixteen other lines which make their appearance very frequently. Among these latter are lines of sodium, magnesium, and iron.

Where some special disturbance is going on, the spectrum at the base of the chromosphere is very complicated, consisting of hundreds of bright lines. "The majority of the lines, however, are seen only occasionally, for a few minutes at a time, when the gases and vapors, which generally lie low (mainly in the interstices of the clouds which constitute the photosphere), and below its upper surface, are elevated for the time being by some eruptive action. For the most part, the lines which appear only at such times are simply *reversals* of the more prominent dark lines of the ordinary solar spectrum. But the selection of the lines seems most capricious : one is taken, and another left, though belonging to the same element, of equal intensity, and close beside the first." Some of the main lines of the chromosphere and prominences are shown in Fig. 215.

198. *Method of Studying the Chromosphere and Prominences.* — Until recently, the solar atmosphere could be seen only during a total eclipse of the sun; but now the spectroscope enables us to study the chromosphere and the prominences with nearly the same facility as the spots and faculæ.

The protuberances are ordinarily invisible, for the same reason that the stars cannot be seen in the daytime; they are hidden by the intense light reflected from our own atmosphere. If we could only get rid of this aerial illumination, without at the same time weakening the light of the prominences, the latter would become visible. This the spectroscope enables us to accomplish. Since the air-light is reflected sunshine, it of course presents the same spectrum as sunlight, — a continuous band of color crossed by dark lines. Now, this sort

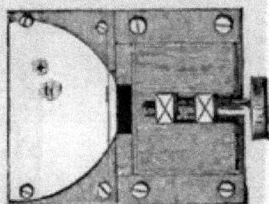

Fig. 216.

of spectrum is weakened by increase of dispersive power (159), because the light is spread out into a longer ribbon, and made to cover a greater area. On the other hand, the spectrum of the prominences, being composed of bright lines, undergoes no such diminution by increased dispersion.

When the spectroscope is used as a means of examining the prominences, the slit is more or less widened. The telescope is directed so that the image of that portion of the solar limb which is to be examined shall be tangent to the opened slit, as in Fig. 216, which represents the slit-plate of the spectroscope of its actual size, with the image of the sun in the proper position for observation.

If, now, a prominence exists at this part of the solar limb, and if the spectroscope itself is so adjusted that the *C* line falls in the centre of the field of view, then one will see something like Fig. 217. "The red portion of the spectrum will

stretch athwart the field of view like a scarlet ribbon with a
darkish band across it; and in that band will appear the prominences, like scarlet clouds, so like our own terrestrial clouds,
indeed, in form and texture, that the resemblance is quite
startling. One might almost think he was looking out through
a partly-opened door upon a sunset sky, except that there is
no variety or contrast of color; all the cloudlets are of the
same pure scarlet hue. Along the edge of the opening is seen
the chromosphere, more brilliant than the clouds which rise
from it or float above it, and, for the most part, made up of
minute tongues and filaments."

199. *Quiescent Prominences.* — The prominences differ
as widely in form
and structure as in
magnitude. The two
principal classes are
the *quiescent, cloud-
formed,* or *hydrogen-
ous,* and the *eruptive,*
or *metallic.*

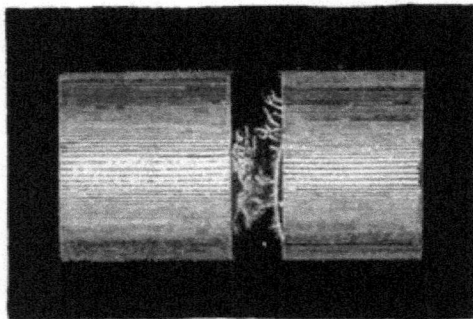

Fig. 217.

The   *quiescent*
prominences resem-
ble almost exactly
our terrestrial clouds, and differ among themselves in the
same manner. They are often of enormous dimensions,
especially in horizontal extent, and are comparatively permanent, often undergoing little change for hours and days.
Near the poles they sometimes remain during a whole solar
revolution of twenty-seven days. Sometimes they appear
to lie upon the limb of the sun, like a bank of clouds in
the terrestrial horizon, probably because they are so far
from the edge that only their upper portions are in sight.
When fully seen, they are usually connected to the chromosphere by slender columns, generally smallest at the base,
and often apparently made up of separate filaments closely

PLATE III.

intertwined, and expanding upward. Sometimes the whole under surface is fringed with pendent filaments. Sometimes they float entirely free from the chromosphere; and in most cases the larger clouds are attended by detached cloudlets. Various forms of quiescent prominences are shown in Plate III. Other forms are given in Figs. 218 and 219.

Their spectrum

Fig. 218.

is usually very simple, consisting of the four lines of hydrogen and the orange D^3: hence the appellation *hydrogenous*. Occasionally the sodium and magnesium lines also appear, even near the tops of the clouds.

200. *Eruptive Prominences.*—The *eruptive* prominences ordinarily consist of brilliant spikes or jets, which

Fig. 219.

change very rapidly in form and brightness. As a rule, their altitude is not more than twenty thousand or thirty thousand

miles ; but occasionally they rise far higher than even the
largest of the quiescent protuberances.   Their spectrum is
very complicated, especially near their base, and often filled
with bright lines.   The most conspicuous lines are those of
sodium, magnesium, barium, iron, and titanium : hence
Secchi calls them *metallic* prominences.

They usually appear in the immediate vicinity of a spot,
never very near the solar poles.   They change with such
rapidity, that the motion can almost be seen with the eye.

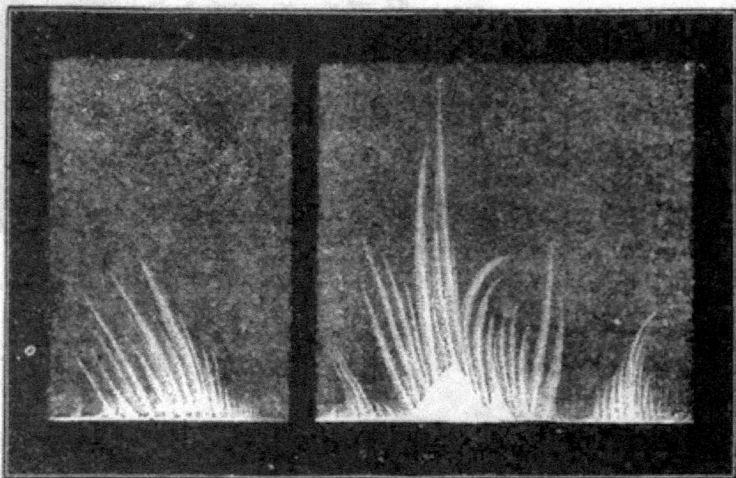

Fig. 220.

Sometimes, in the course of fifteen or twenty minutes, a
mass of these flames, fifty thousand miles high, will undergo
a total transformation ; and in some instances their complete development or disappearance takes no longer time.
Sometimes they consist of pointed rays, diverging in all
directions, as represented in Fig. 220.   "Sometimes they
look like flames, sometimes like sheaves of grain, sometimes like whirling water-spouts capped with a great cloud ;
occasionally they present most exactly the appearance of
jets of liquid fire, rising and falling in graceful parabolas ;
frequently they carry on their edges spirals like the volutes

of an Ionic column; and continually they detach filaments, which rise to a great elevation, gradually expanding and growing fainter as they ascend, until the eye loses
them."

**201. *Change of
Form in Prominences.*
— Fig. 221 represents
a prominence as
seen by Professor
Young, Sept. 7, 1871.
It was an immense
quiescent cloud, a**

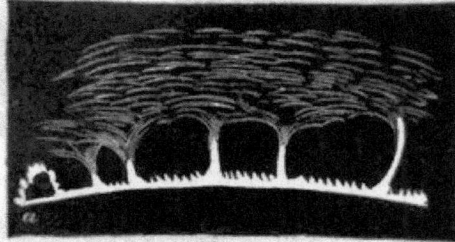

Fig. 221.

hundred thousand miles long and fifty-four thousand miles
high. At *a* there was a brilliant lump, somewhat in the
form of a thunder-head. On returning to the spectroscope less than half an hour
afterwards, he found that the
cloud had been literally blown
into shreds by some inconceivable uprush from beneath.
The prominence then pre-
sented the form shown in
Fig. 222. The *débris* of the
cloud had already attained a
height of a hundred thou-
sand miles. While he was
watching them for the next
ten minutes, they rose, with
a motion almost perceptible
to the eye, till the upper-
most reached an altitude of
two hundred thousand miles. As the filaments rose, they
gradually faded away like a dissolving cloud.

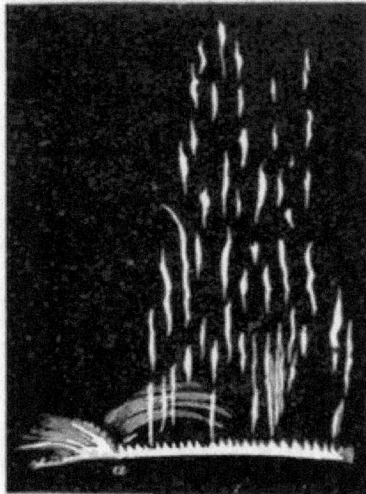

Fig. 222.

Meanwhile the little thunder-head had grown and developed into what appeared to be a mass of rolling and ever-

changing flame.   Figs. 223 and 224 give the appearance

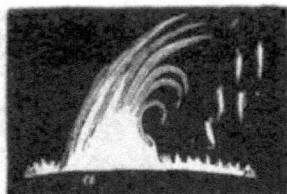

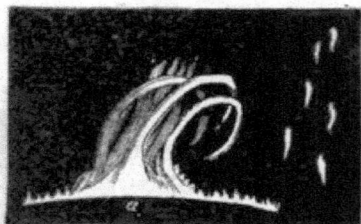

Fig. 223.   Fig. 224.

of this portion of the prominence at intervals of fifteen
minutes.   Other similar eruptions have been observed.

V. THE CORONA.

202. *General Appearance of the Corona.* — At the
time of a total eclipse of the sun, if the sky is clear, the
moon appears as a huge black ball, the illumination at
the edge of the disk being just sufficient to bring out
its rotundity.   " From behind it," to borrow Professor
Young's vivid description, " stream out on all sides radiant
filaments, beams, and sheets of pearly light, which reach
to a distance sometimes of several degrees from the solar
surface, forming an irregular stellate halo, with the black
globe of the moon in its apparent centre.   The portion
nearest the sun is of dazzling brightness, but still less brilliant than the prominences which blaze through it like
carbuncles.   Generally this inner corona has a pretty uniform height, forming a ring three or four minutes of arc
in width, separated by a somewhat definite outline from
the outer corona, which reaches to a much greater distance, and is far more irregular in form.   Usually there are
several *rifts*, as they have been called, like narrow beams of
darkness, extending from the very edge of the sun to the
outer night, and much resembling the cloud-shadows which
radiate from the sun before a thunder-shower ; but the
edges of these rifts are frequently curved, showing them

to be something else than real shadows. Sometimes there are narrow bright streamers, as long as the rifts, or longer. These are often inclined, occasionally are even nearly tangential to the solar surface, and frequently are curved. On the whole, the corona is usually less extensive and brilliant over the solar poles, and there is a recognizable

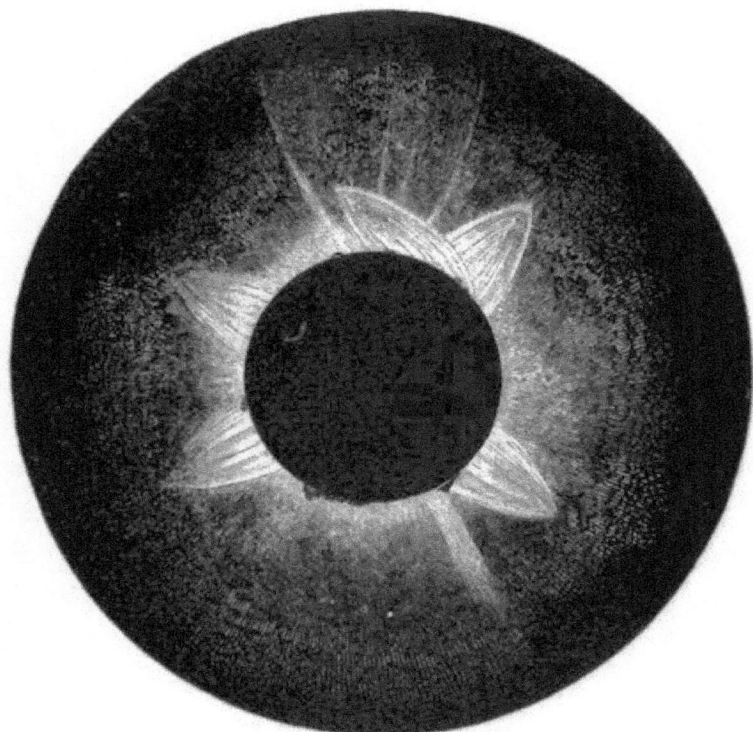

Fig. 225.

tendency to accumulations above the middle latitudes, or spot-zones; so that, speaking roughly, the corona shows a disposition to assume the form of a quadrilateral or four-rayed star, though in almost every individual case this form is greatly modified by abnormal streamers at some point or other."

203. *The Corona as seen at Recent Eclipses.* — The

corona can be seen only at the time of a total eclipse of
the sun, and then for only a few minutes. Its form varies
considerably from one eclipse to another, and apparently
also during the same eclipse. At least, different observers
at different stations depict the same corona under very
different forms. Fig. 225 represents the corona of 1857 as

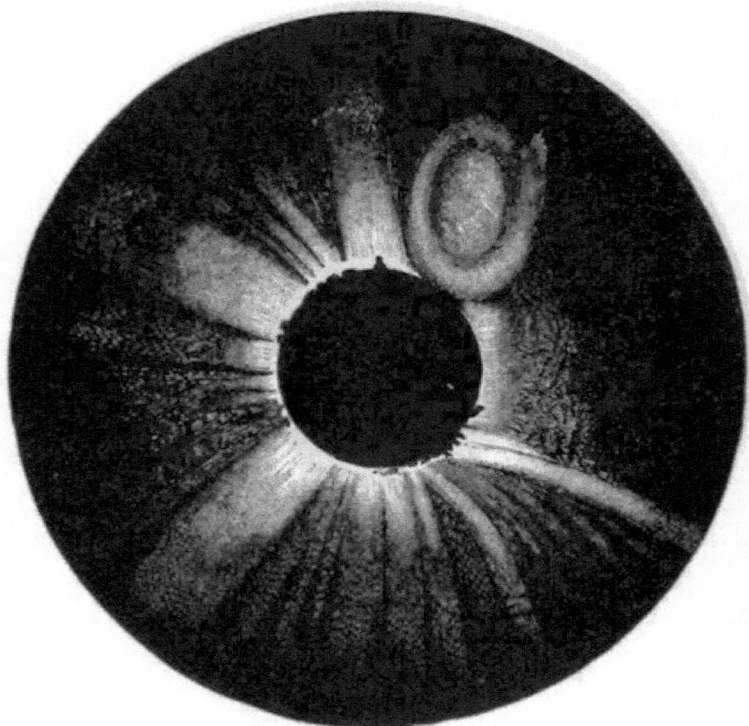

Fig. 226.

observed by Liais. In this view the *petal-like* forms, which
have been noticed in the corona at other times, are especially prominent.

Fig. 226 shows the corona of 1860 as it was observed
by Temple.

Fig. 227 shows the corona of 1867. This is interesting
as being a corona at the time of sun-spot minimum.

Fig. 228 represents the corona of 1868. This is a larger and more irregular corona than usual.

The corona of 1869 is shown in Fig. 229.

Fig. 230 is a view of the corona of 1871 as seen by Capt. Tupman.

Fig. 231 shows the same corona as seen by Fœnander.

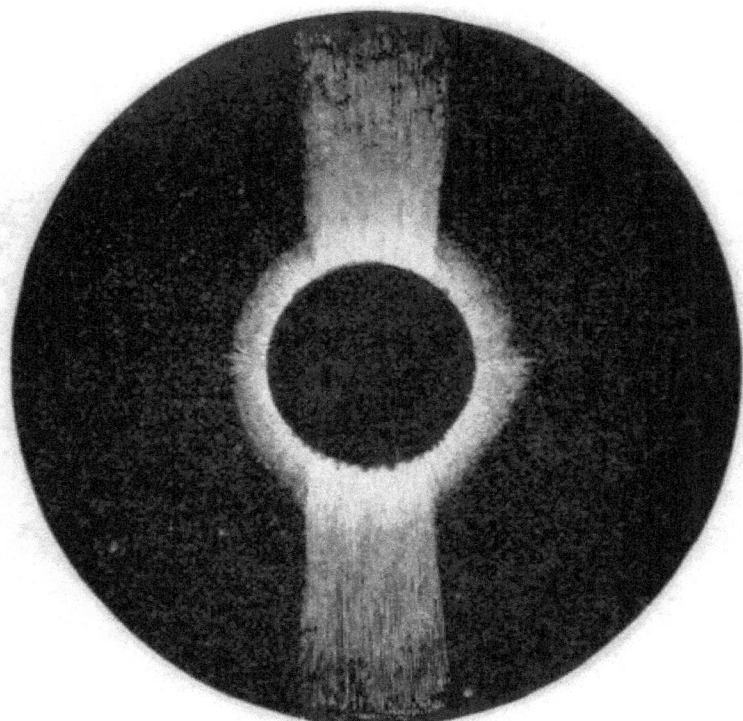

Fig. 227.

Fig. 232 shows the same corona as photographed by Davis.

Fig. 233 shows the corona of 1878 made up from several views as combined by Professor Young.

204. *The Spectrum of the Corona.* — The chief line in the spectrum of the corona is the one usually designated as 1474, and now known as the *coronal* line. It is seen as a dark line

on the disk of the sun; and a spectroscope of great dispersive
power shows this dark line to be closely double, the lower
component being one of the iron lines, and the upper the
coronal line.　This dark line is shown at x, Fig. 234.

Besides this bright line, the hydrogen lines appear faintly
in the spectrum of the corona.　The 1474 line has been

Fig. 228.

sometimes traced with the spectroscope to an elevation of
nearly twenty minutes above the moon's limb, and the hydrogen lines nearly as far; and the lines were just as strong
in the middle of a dark rift as anywhere else.

The substance which produces the 1474 line is unknown
as yet.　It seems to be something with a vapor-density far
below that of hydrogen, which is the lightest substance of
which we have any knowledge.　I can hardly be an "allo-

tropic " form of any terrestrial element, as some scientists have
suggested; for in the most violent disturbances in prominences
and near sun-spots, when the lines of hydrogen, magnesium,
and other metals, are contorted and shattered by the rush of
the contending elements, this line alone remains fine, sharp,
and straight, a little brightened, but not otherwise affected.

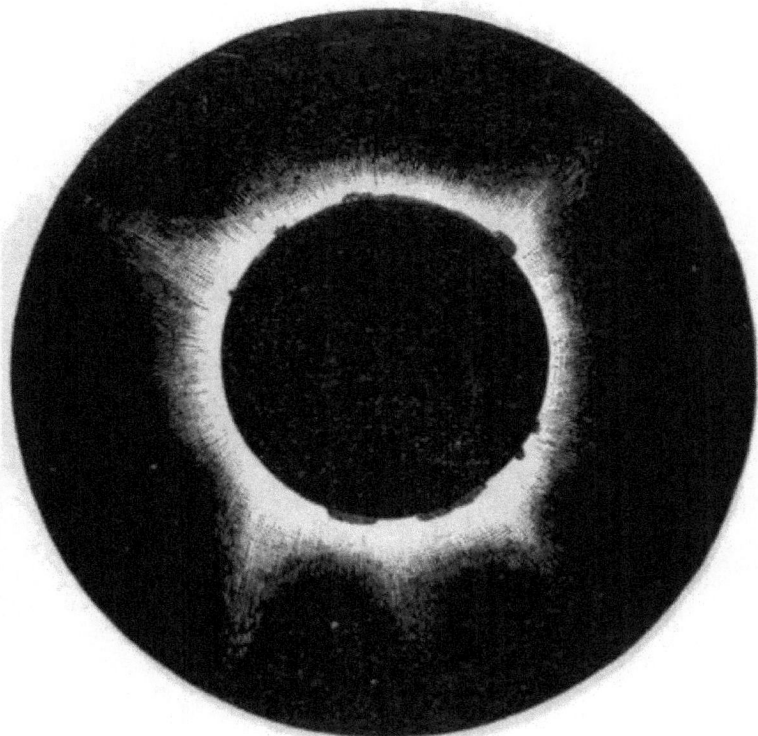

Fig. 229.

For the present it remains, like a few other lines in the spectrum, an unexplained mystery.

Besides bright lines, the corona shows also a faint continuous spectrum, in which have been observed a few of the more
prominent *dark* lines of the solar spectrum.

This shows, that, while the corona may be in the main
composed of glowing gas (as indicated by the bright lines
of its spectrum), it also contains considerable matter in such

a state as to reflect the sunlight, probably in the form of dust
or fog.

V. ECLIPSES.

205. *The Shadows of the Earth and Moon.* — The
shadows cast by the earth and moon are shown in Fig. 235.

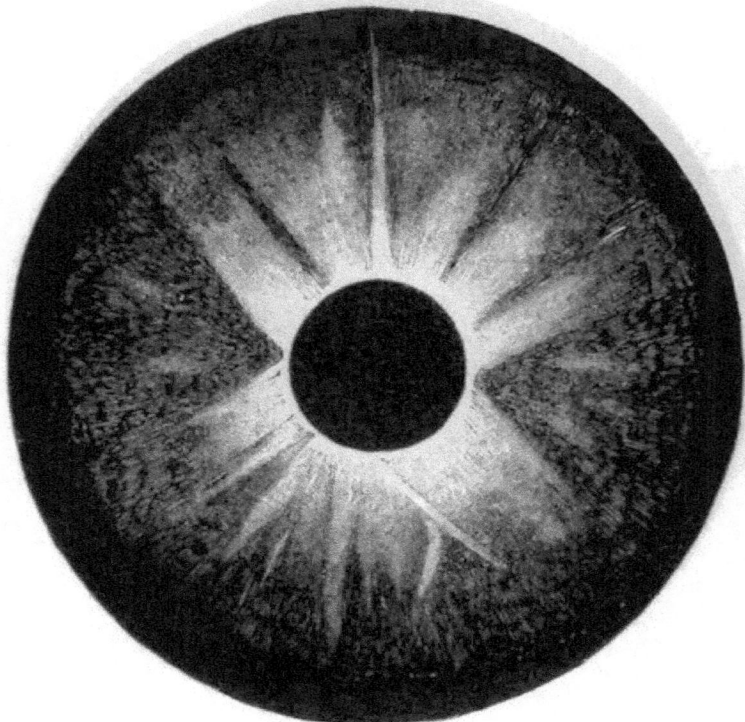

Fig. 230.

Each shadow is seen to be made up of a dark portion
called the *umbra*, and of a lighter portion called the
penumbra. The light of the sun is completely excluded
from the umbra, but only partially from the penumbra.
The umbra is in the form of a cone, with its apex away
from the sun ; though in the case of the earth's shadow
it tapers very slowly. The penumbra surrounds the umbra,

and increases in size as we recede from the sun. The axis
of the earth's shadow lies in the plane of the ecliptic, which
in the figure is the surface of the page. As the moon's
orbit is inclined five degrees to the plane of the ecliptic,
the axis of the moon's shadow will sometimes lie above,

Fig. 231.

and sometimes below, the ecliptic. It will lie on the ecliptic
only when the moon is at one of her nodes.

206. *When there will be an Eclipse of the Moon.* —
The moon is eclipsed *whenever it passes into the umbra
of the earth's shadow.* It will be seen from the figure that
the moon can pass into the shadow of the earth only when
she is in opposition, or *at full.* Owing to the inclination of the moon's orbit to the ecliptic, the moon will pass

either above or below the earth's shadow when she is at full, unless she happens to be near her node at this time : hence there is not an eclipse of the moon every month.

When the moon simply passes into the penumbra of the earth's shadow, the light of the moon is somewhat dimmed,

Fig. 232.

but not sufficiently to attract attention, or to be denominated an eclipse.

207. *The Lunar Ecliptic Limits.* — In Fig. 236 the line AB represents the plane of the ecliptic, and the line CD the moon's orbit. The large black circles on the line AB represent sections of the umbra of the earth's shadow, and the smaller circles on CD represent the moon at full. It will be seen, that, if the moon is full at E, she will just graze the

umbra of the earth's shadow. In this case she will suffer no eclipse. Were the moon full at any point nearer her node, as at *F*, she would pass into the umbra of the earth's shadow, and would be *partially* eclipsed. Were the moon full at *G*, she would pass through the centre of the earth's shadow, and be *totally* eclipsed.

It will be seen from the figure that full moon must occur

Fig. 233.

when the moon is within a certain distance from her node, in order that there may be a lunar eclipse; and this space is called the *lunar ecliptic limits*.

The farther the earth is from the sun, the less rapidly does its shadow taper, and therefore the greater its diameter at the distance of the moon; and, the nearer the moon to the earth, the greater the diameter of the earth's shadow at the distance of the moon. Of course, the greater the diameter of the earth's shadow, the greater the ecliptic limits: hence the lunar ecliptic limits vary somewhat from time to time, according to the distance from the earth to the sun and from the earth to the moon. The limits within which an eclipse is inevitable under all circumstances are called the *minor ecliptic limits;* and those within which an eclipse is possible under some circumstances, the *major ecliptic limits.*

208. *Lunar Eclipses.* — Fig. 237 shows the path of the moon through the earth's shadow in the case of a *partial eclipse.* The magnitude of such an eclipse depends upon the nearness of the moon to her nodes. The magnitude of an eclipse is usually denoted in *digits*, a digit being one-twelfth of the diameter of the moon.

Fig. 238 shows the path of the moon through the earth's shadow in the case of a *total eclipse.* It will be seen from the figure that it is not necessary for the moon to pass through the centre of the earth's shadow in order to have a total eclipse. When the moon passes through the centre of the earth's shadow, the eclipse is both *total* and *central.*

Fig. 234.

At the time of a total eclipse, the moon is not entirely invisible, but shines with a faint copper-colored light. This light is refracted into the shadow by the earth's atmosphere, and its amount varies with the quantity of clouds and vapor in that portion of the atmosphere which the sunlight must graze in order to reach the moon.

The duration of an eclipse varies between very wide limits, being, of course, greatest when the eclipse is central. A total eclipse of the moon may last nearly two hours, or, including the *partial* portions of the eclipse, three or four hours.

Fig. 235.

Every eclipse of the moon, whether total or partial, is

visible at the same time to the whole hemisphere of the
earth which is turned towards the moon; and the eclipse
will have exactly the same magnitude at every point of
observation.

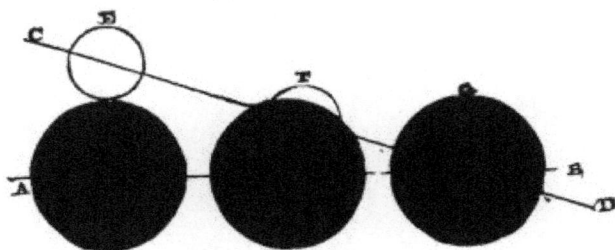

Fig. 236.

209. *When there will be an Eclipse of the Sun.* —
There will be an eclipse of the sun *whenever any portion
of the moon's shadow is thrown on the earth.* It will be
seen from Fig. 235 that this can occur only when the moon

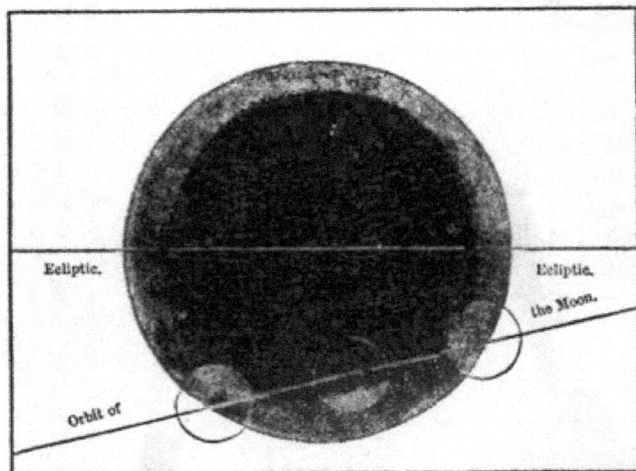

Fig. 237.

is in conjunction, or at *new.* It does not occur every
month, because, owing to the inclination of the moon's orbit
to the ecliptic, the moon's shadow is usually thrown either
above or below the earth at the time of new moon. There

can be an eclipse of the sun only when new moon occurs at or near one of the nodes of her orbit.

210. *Solar Ecliptic Limits.* — The distances from the moon's node within which a new moon would throw some portion of its shadow on the earth so as to produce an eclipse of the sun are called the *solar ecliptic limits.* As in the case of the moon, there are *major* and *minor* ecliptic limits; the former being the limits within which an eclipse of the sun is *possible* under some circumstances, and the latter those under which an eclipse is *inevitable* under all circumstances.

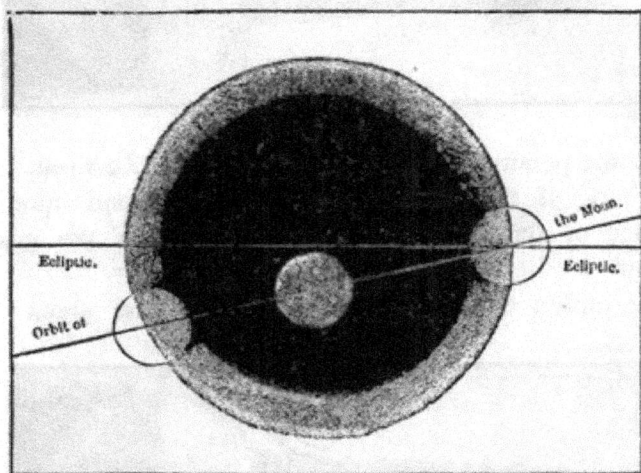

Fig. 238.

The limits within which a solar eclipse may occur are greater than those within which a lunar eclipse may occur. This will be evident from an examination of Fig. 235. Were the moon in that figure just outside of the lines *A B* and *C D*, it will be seen that the penumbra of her shadow would just graze the earth: hence the moon must be somewhere within the space bounded by these lines in order to cause an eclipse of the sun. Now, these lines mark the prolongation to the sun of the cone of the umbra of the earth's shadow: hence, in order to produce an eclipse of the sun, new moon must occur somewhere within this prolongation of the umbra of the earth's shadow. Now, it is evident that the diameter of this cone is greater on the side of the earth toward the sun than on the opposite side: hence the solar ecliptic limits are greater than the lunar ecliptic limits.

211. *Solar Eclipses.* — An observer in the umbra of the moon's shadow would see a *total* eclipse of the sun, while

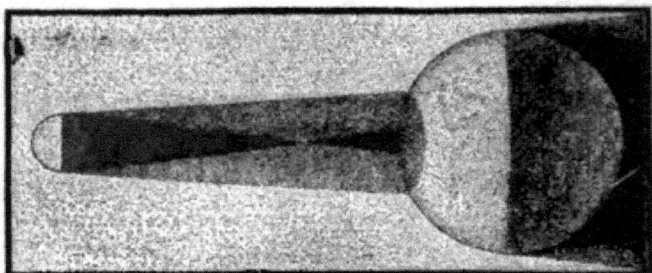

Fig. 239.

one in the penumbra would see only a *partial* eclipse. The magnitude of this partial eclipse would depend upon the distance of the observer from the umbra of the moon's shadow.

The umbra of the moon's shadow is just about long

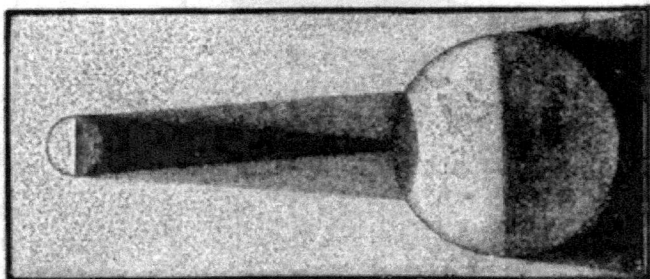

Fig. 240.

enough to reach the earth. Sometimes the point of this shadow falls short of the earth's surface, as shown in Fig. 239, and sometimes it falls upon the earth, as shown in Fig. 240, according to the varying distance of the sun and moon from the earth. The diameter of the umbra at the surface of the earth is seldom more than a hundred miles : hence the belt of a total eclipse is, on the average, not more than a hundred miles wide ; and a total eclipse seldom lasts more than five or six minutes, and sometimes only a few seconds. Owing, however, to the rotation of the earth, the umbra of the moon's shadow may pass over a long reach of the earth's surface. Fig. 241 shows the

Fig. 241.

track of the umbra of the moon's shadow over the earth in the total eclipse of 1860.

Fig. 242 shows the track of the total eclipse of 1871 across India and the adjacent seas.

In a partial eclipse of the sun, more or less of one side of the sun's disk is usually concealed, as shown in Fig. 243. Occasionally, however, the centre of the sun's disk is covered, leaving a bright ring around the margin, as shown in Fig. 244. Such an eclipse is called an *annular* eclipse.

An eclipse can be annular only when the cone of the moon's shadow is too short to reach the earth, and then

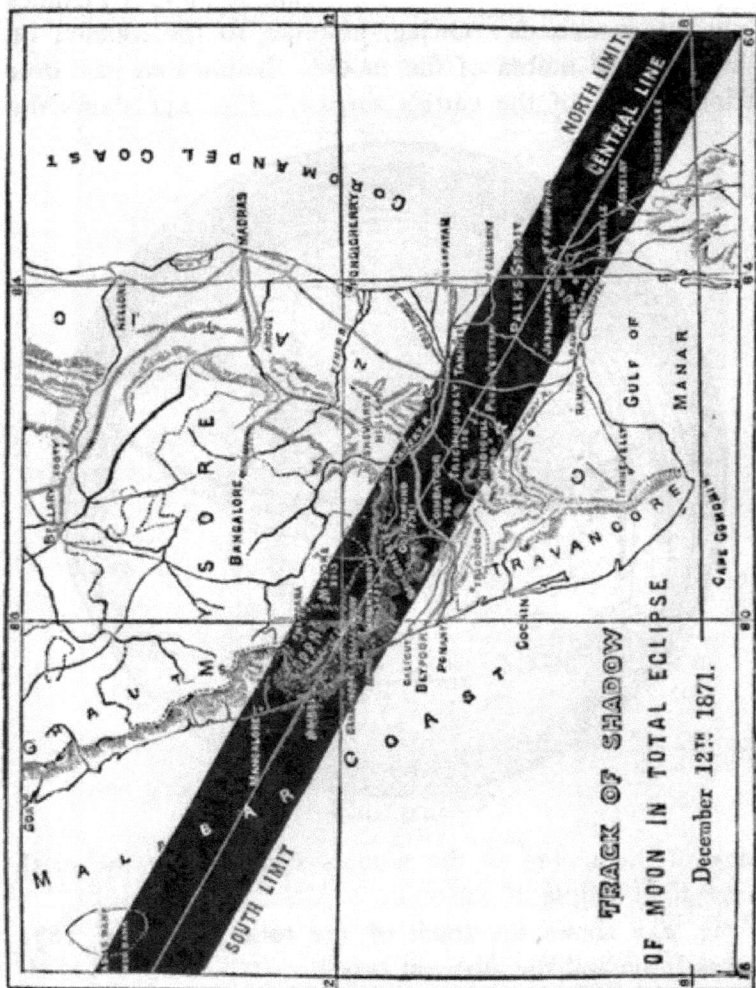

Fig. 242.

only to observers who are in the central portion of the penumbra.

212. *Comparative Frequency of Solar and Lunar Eclipses.* — There are more eclipses of the sun in the year

than of the moon; and yet, at any one place, eclipses of the moon are more frequent than those of the sun.

There are more lunar than solar eclipses, because, as we have seen, the limits within which a solar eclipse may occur are greater than those within which a lunar eclipse may occur. There are more eclipses of the moon visible at any one place than of the sun; because, as we have seen, an eclipse of the

Fig. 243.

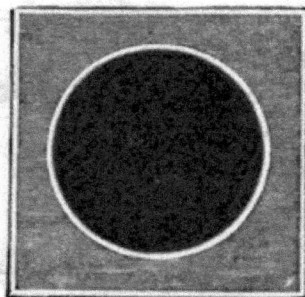

Fig. 244.

moon, whenever it does occur, is visible to a whole hemisphere at a time, while an eclipse of the sun is visible to only a portion of a hemisphere, and a total eclipse to only a very small portion of a hemisphere. A total eclipse of the sun is, therefore, a very rare occurrence at any one place.

The greatest number of eclipses that can occur in a year is seven, and the least number, two. In the former case, five may be of the sun and two of the moon, or four of the sun and three of the moon. In the latter case, both must be of the sun.

VI. THE THREE GROUPS OF PLANETS.

I. GENERAL CHARACTERISTICS OF THE GROUPS.

213. *The Inner Group.* — The *inner group* of planets is composed of *Mercury*, *Venus*, the *Earth*, and *Mars*; that is, of all the planets which lie between the asteroids

and the sun. The planets of this group are comparatively small and dense. So far as known, they rotate on their axes in about twenty-four hours, and they are either entirely without moons, or are attended by comparatively few.

The comparative sizes and eccentricities of the orbits of

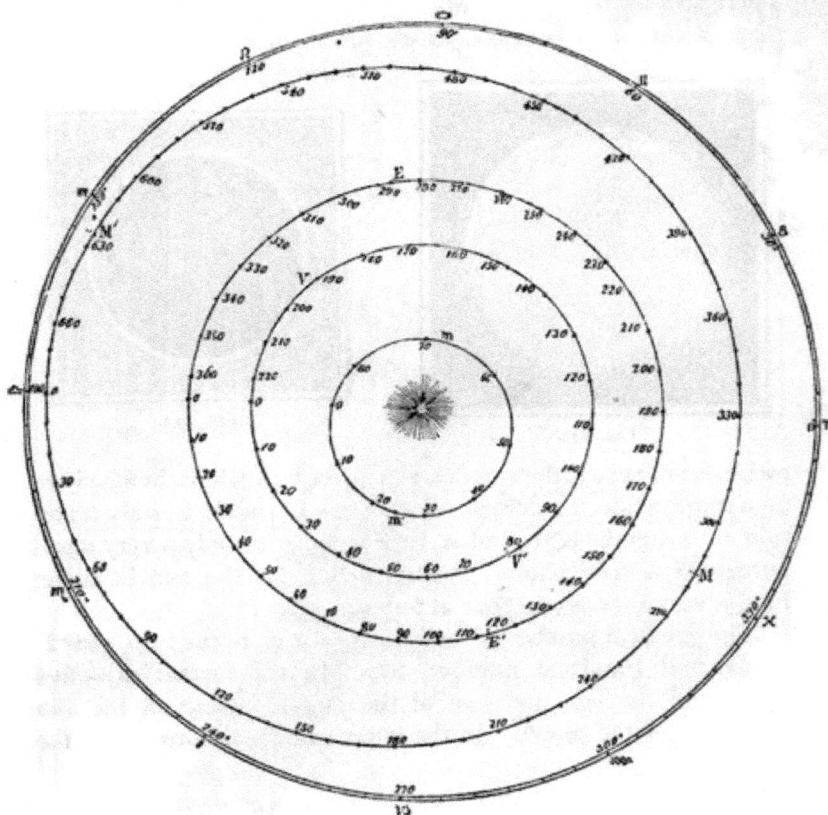

Fig. 245.

this group are shown in Fig. 245. The dots round the orbits show the position of the planets at intervals of ten days.

214. *The Outer Group.* — The *outer group* of planets is composed of *Jupiter, Saturn, Uranus,* and *Neptune*. These planets are all very large and of slight density. So far as known, they rotate on their axes in about ten hours,

and are accompanied with complicated systems of moons.
Fig. 246, which represents the comparative sizes of the
planets, shows at a glance the immense difference between
those of the inner and outer group. Fig. 247 shows the
comparative sizes and eccentricities of the orbits of the
outer planets. The dots round the orbits show the position
of the planets at intervals
of a thousand days.

215. *The Asteroids.* —
Between the inner and
outer groups of planets
there is a great number
of very small planets
known as the *minor plan-
ets*, or *asteroids*. Over
two hundred planets be-
longing to this group
have already been dis-
covered. Their orbits are
shown by the dotted lines
in Fig. 247. The sizes
of the four largest of
these planets, compared
with the earth, are shown
in Fig. 248.
The asteroids of this

Fig. 246.

group are distinguished from the other planets, not only by
their small size, but by the great eccentricities and inclina-
tions of their orbits. If we except Mercury, none of the
larger planets has an eccentricity amounting to one-tenth
the diameter of its orbit (43), nor is any orbit inclined more
than two or three degrees to the ecliptic ; but the inclina-
tions of many of the minor planets exceed ten degrees, and
the eccentricities frequently amount to an eighth of the
orbital diameter. The orbit of Pallas is inclined thirty-four

degrees to the ecliptic, while there are some planets of
this group whose orbits nearly coincide with the plane of
the ecliptic.

Fig. 249 shows one of the most and one of the least

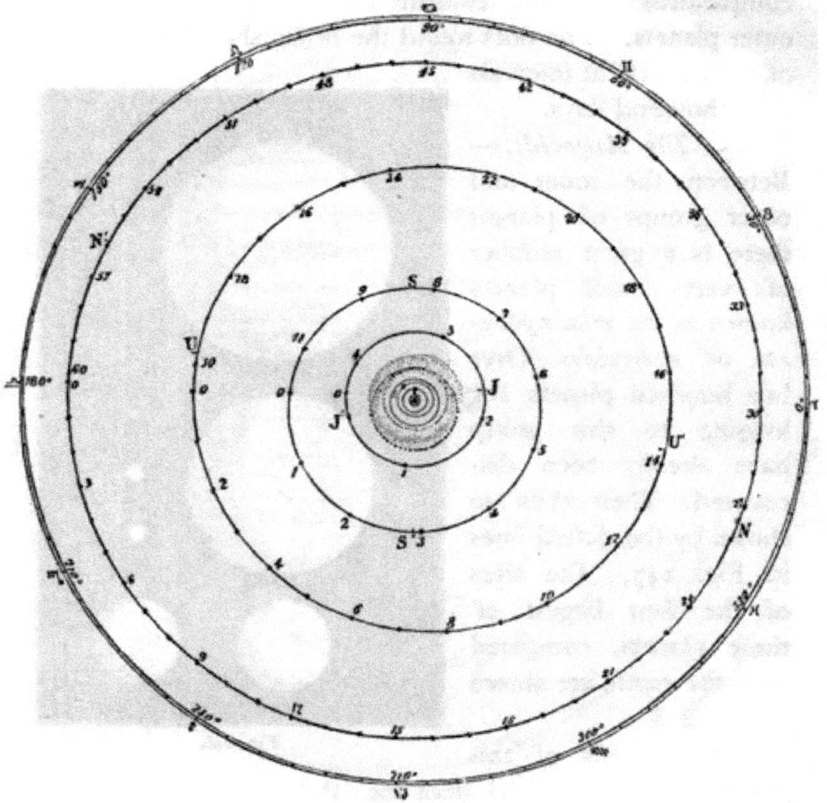

Fig. 247.

eccentric of the orbits of this group as compared with that
of the earth.

The intricate complexity of the orbits of the asteroids is
shown in Fig. 250.

II. THE INNER GROUP OF PLANETS.

MERCURY.

216. *The Orbit of Mercury.* — The orbit of Mercury is more eccentric than that of any of the larger planets, and it has also a greater inclination to the eclip- tic. Its eccentricity (43) is a little over a fifth, and its inclination to the ecliptic somewhat over seven degrees. The mean distance of Mer- cury from the sun is

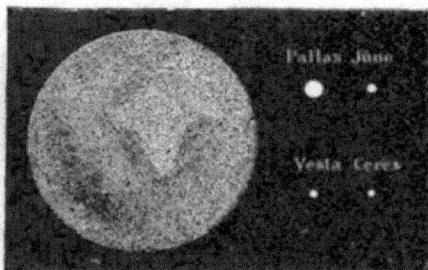

Fig. 248.

about thirty-five million miles ; but, owing to the great eccentricity of its orbit, its distance from the sun varies from about forty- three million miles at aphelion to about twenty-eight million at perihe- lion.

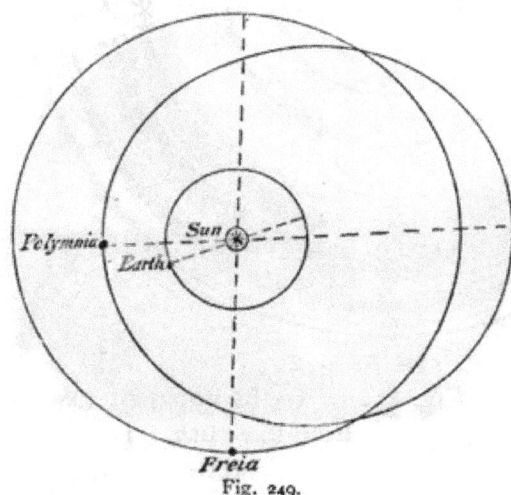

Fig. 249.

217. *Distance of Mercury from the Earth.* — It is evi- dent, from Fig. 251, that an infe- rior planet, like Mercury, is the whole diameter of its orbit nearer the earth at inferior conjunction than at superior conjunction : hence Mercury's distance from the earth varies considerably. Owing to the great eccentricity of its orbit, its distance from the earth at inferior conjunction also varies considerably. Mercury is nearest to the earth when its inferior conjunction occurs at its own aphelion and at the earth's perihelion.

218. *Apparent Size of Mercury.* — Since Mercury's distance from the earth is variable, the apparent size of the

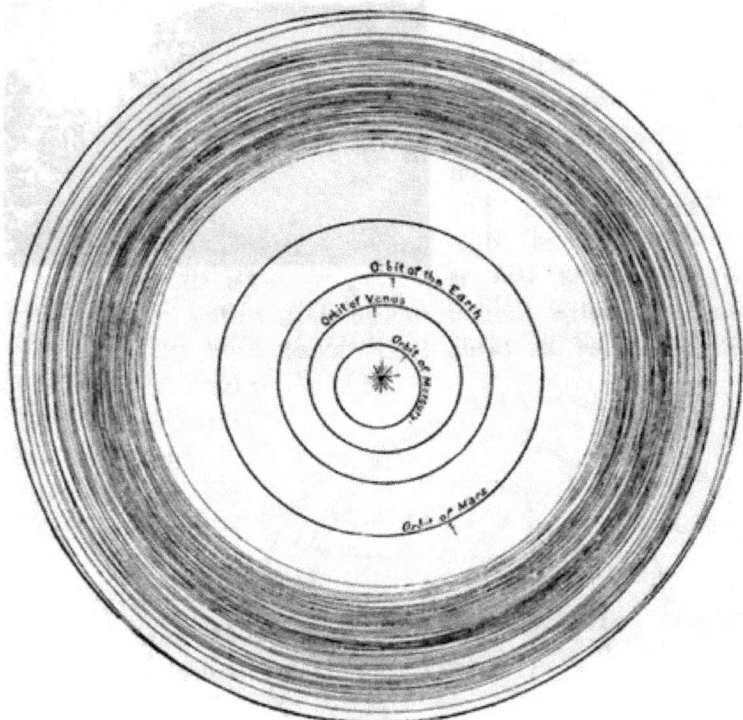

Fig. 250.

planet is also variable. Fig. 252 shows its apparent size at its extreme and mean distances from the earth. Its apparent diameter varies from five seconds to twelve seconds.

219. *Volume and Density of Mercury.* — The real diameter of Mercury is about three thousand miles. Its size, compared with that of the earth, is shown in Fig. 253. The earth is about sixteen times as large as Mer-

cury; but Mercury is about one-fifth more dense than the earth.

220. Greatest Elongation of Mercury. — Mercury, being an *inferior* planet (or one within the orbit of the earth), appears to oscillate to and fro across the sun. Its greatest apparent distance from the sun, or its *greatest elongation*, varies considerably. The farther Mercury is from the sun, and the nearer the earth is to Mercury, the greater is its angular distance from the sun at the time of its

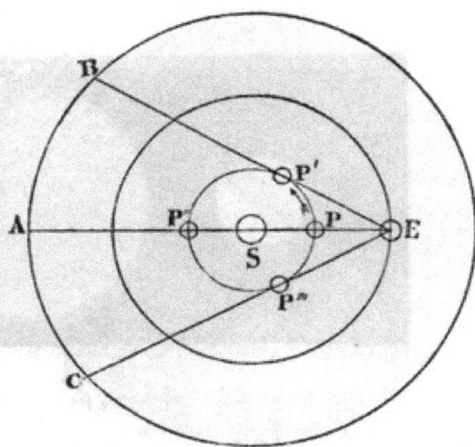

Fig. 251.

greatest elongation. Under the most favorable circumstances, the greatest elongation amounts to about twenty-eight degrees, and under the least favorable to only sixteen or seventeen degrees.

221. Sidereal and Synodical Periods of Mercury. — Mercury accomplishes a complete revolution around the sun in about eighty-eight days; but it takes it a hundred and sixteen days to pass from its greatest elongation east to the same elongation again. The orbital motion of this planet is at the rate of nearly thirty miles a second.

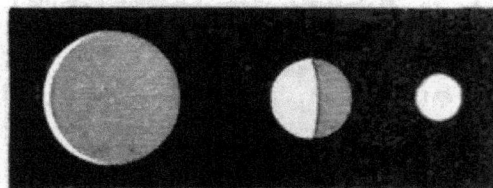

Fig. 252.

In Fig. 251, P''' represents elongation east of the sun, and P' elongation west. It will be seen that it is much farther from P' around to P''' than from P''' on to P'. Mercury is only about forty-eight days in passing from greatest elongation east to greatest elongation west, while it is about sixty-eight days in passing back again.

222. *Visibility of Mercury.* — Mercury is too close to

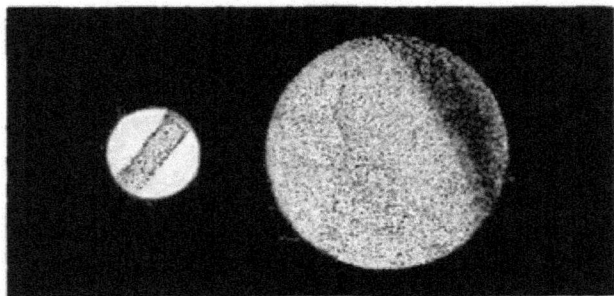

Fig. 253.

the sun for favorable observation. It is never seen long after sunset, or long before sunrise, and never far from the horizon. When visible at all, it must be sought for low down in the west shortly after sunset, or low in the east shortly before sunrise, according as the planet is at its east or west elongation. It is often visible to the naked eye in our latitude; but the illumination of the twilight sky, and the excess of vapor in our atmosphere near the horizon, combine to make the telescopic study of the planet difficult and unsatisfactory.

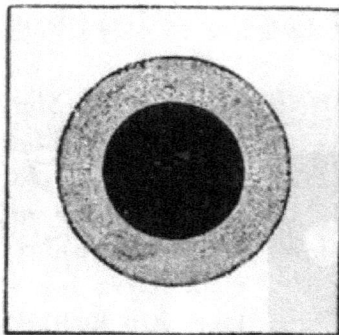

Fig. 254.

223. *The Atmosphere and Surface of Mercury.* — Mercury seems to be surrounded by a dense atmosphere. One proof of the existence of such an atmosphere is furnished at the time of the planet's *transit* across the disk of the sun, which occasionally happens. The planet is then seen

surrounded by a border, as shown in Fig. 254. A bright spot has also been observed on the dark disk of the planet during a transit, as shown in Fig. 255. The border around the planet seems to be due to the action of the planet's atmosphere; but it is difficult to account for the bright spot.

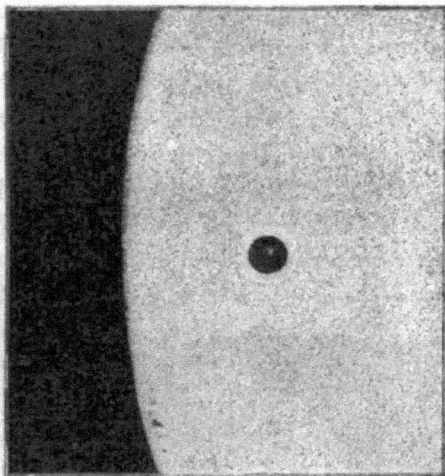

Fig. 255.

Schröter, a celebrated German astronomer, at about the beginning of the present century, thought that he detected spots and shadings on the disk of the planet, which indicated both the presence of an atmosphere and of elevations. The shading along the terminator, which seemed to indicate the presence of a twilight, and therefore of an atmosphere, are shown in Fig. 256. It also shows the blunted

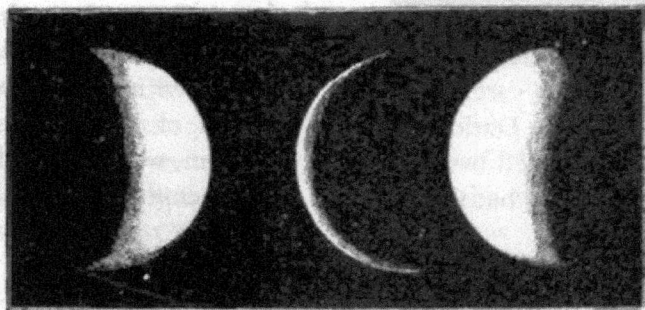

Fig. 256.

aspect of one of the cusps, which Schröter noticed at times, and which he attributed to the shadow of a mountain, estimated to be ten or twelve miles high. Fig. 257 shows

this mountain near the upper cusp, as Schröter believed he
saw it in the year 1800. By watching certain marks upon
the disk of Mercury, Schröter came to the conclusion that
the planet rotates on its axis in about twenty-four hours.
Modern observers, with more powerful telescopes, have
failed to verify Schröter's observations as to the indications
of an atmosphere and of elevations. Nothing is known
with certainty about the rotation of the planet.

The border around Mercury, and the bright spot on its
disk at the time of the transit of the planet across the sun,
have been seen since Schröter's time, and the existence of
these phenomena is now well established; but astronomers
are far from being agreed as to
their cause.

224. *Intra-Mercurial Planets.*
—It has for some time been
thought probable that there is a
group of small planets between
Mercury and the sun; and at various times the discovery of such
bodies has been announced. In
1859 a French observer believed
that he had detected an intra-

Fig. 257.

Mercurial planet, to which the name of *Vulcan* was given,
and for which careful search has since been made, but without success. During the total eclipse of 1878 Professor
Watson observed two objects near the sun, which he thought
to be planets; but this is still matter of controversy.

VENUS.

225. *The Orbit of Venus.*—The orbit of Venus has
but slight eccentricity, differing less from a circle than that
of any other large planet. It is inclined to the ecliptic somewhat more than three degrees. The mean distance of the
planet from the sun is about sixty-seven million miles.

226. *Distance of Venus from the Earth.* — The distance of Venus from the earth varies within much wider limits than that of Mercury. When Venus is at inferior conjunction, her distance from the earth is ninety-two million miles *minus* sixty-seven million miles, or twenty-five million miles; and when at superior conjunction it is ninety-two million miles *plus* sixty-seven million miles, or a hundred and fifty-nine million miles. Venus is considerably more than *six times* as far off at superior conjunction as at inferior conjunction.

227. *Apparent Size of Venus.* — Owing to the great

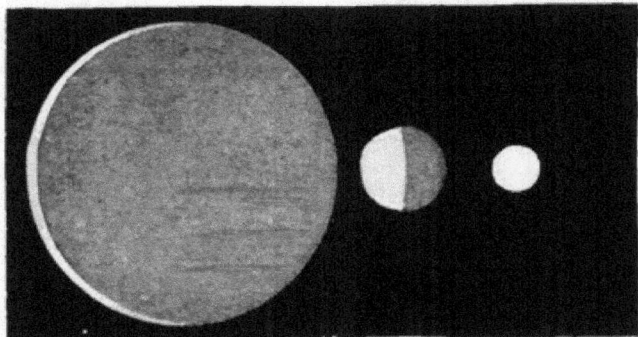

Fig. 258.

variation in the distance of Venus from the earth, her apparent diameter varies from about ten seconds to about sixty-six seconds. Fig. 258 shows the apparent size of Venus at her extreme and mean distances from the earth.

228. *Volume and Density of Venus.* — The real size of Venus is about the same as that of the earth, her diameter being only about three hundred miles less. The comparative sizes of the two planets are shown in Fig. 259. The density of Venus is a little less than that of the earth.

229. *The Greatest Elongation of Venus.* — Venus, like Mercury, appears to oscillate to and fro across the sun. The angular value of the greatest elongation of Venus varies but slightly, its greatest value being about forty-seven degrees.

230. *Sidereal and Synodical Periods of Venus.* — The *sidereal* period of Venus, or that of a complete revolution around the sun, is about two hundred and twenty-five days ; her orbital motion being at the rate of nearly twenty-two miles a second. Her *synodical* period, or the time it takes her to pass around from her greatest eastern elongation to the same elongation again, is about five hundred and eighty-four days, or eighteen months. Venus is a hundred and forty-six days, or nearly five months, in passing from her greatest elongation east through inferior conjunction to her greatest elongation west.

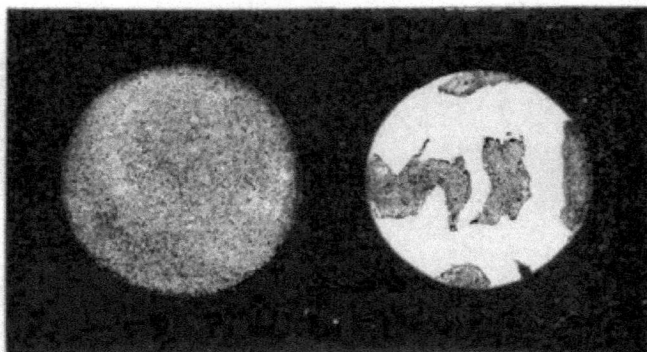

Fig. 259.

231. *Venus as a Morning and an Evening Star.* — For a period of about nine months, while Venus is passing from superior conjunction to her greatest eastern elongation, she will be east of the sun, and will therefore set after the sun. During this period she is the *evening star*, the *Hesperus* of the ancients. While passing from inferior conjunction to superior conjunction, Venus is west of the sun, and therefore rises before the sun. During this period of nine months she is the *morning star*, the *Phosphorus*, or *Lucifer*, of the ancients.

232. *Brilliancy of Venus.* — Next to the sun and moon, Venus is at times the most brilliant object in the heavens, being bright enough to be seen in daylight, and to cast

a distinct shadow at night. Her brightness, however, varies considerably, owing to her phases and to her varying distance from the earth. She does not appear brightest when at full, for she is then farthest from the earth, at superior conjunction; nor does she appear brightest when nearest the earth, at inferior conjunction, for her phase is then a thin crescent (see Fig. 258). She is most conspicuous while passing from her greatest eastern elongation to her greatest western elongation. After she has passed her eastern elongation, she becomes brighter and brighter till she is within about forty degrees of the sun. Her phase at this point in her orbit is shown in Fig. 260. Her brilliancy then begins to wane, until she comes too near the sun to be visible. When she re-appears on the west of the sun, she again becomes more brilliant; and her brilliancy increases till she is about forty degrees from the sun, when she is again at her brightest. Venus passes

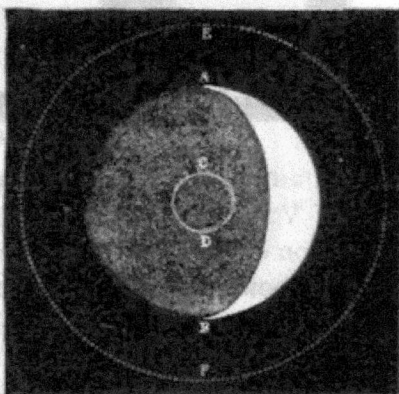

Fig. 260.

from her greatest brilliancy as an evening star to her greatest brilliancy as a morning star in about seventy-three days. She has the same phase, and is at the same distance from the earth, in both cases of maximum brilliancy. Of course, the brilliancy of Venus when at the maximum varies somewhat from time to time, owing to the eccentricities of the orbits of the earth and of Venus, which cause her distance from the earth, at her phase of greatest brilliancy, to vary. She is most brilliant when the phase of her greatest brilliancy occurs when she is at her aphelion and the earth at its perihelion.

233. *The Atmosphere and Surface of Venus.* — Schröter believed that he saw shadings and markings on Venus similar to those on Mercury, indicating the presence of an atmosphere and of elevations on the surface of the planet. Fig. 261 represents the surface of Venus as it appeared

Fig. 261.

to this astronomer. By watching certain markings on the disk of Venus, Schröter came to the conclusion that Venus rotates on her axis in about twenty-four hours.

It is now generally conceded that Venus has a dense atmosphere ; but Schröter's observations of the spots on her disk have not been verified by modern astronomers, and we really know nothing certainly of her rotation.

Fig. 262.

234. *Transits of Venus.* — When Venus happens to be near one of the nodes of her orbit when she is in inferior conjunction, she makes a transit across the sun's disk. These transits occur in pairs, separated by an interval of over a hundred years. The two transits of each pair are separated by an interval of eight years, the dates of the most recent being 1874 and 1882. Venus, like Mercury, appears surrounded with a border on passing across the sun's disk, as shown in Fig. 262.

MARS.

235. *The Orbit of Mars.* — The orbit of Mars is more eccentric than that of any of the larger planets, except Mercury; its eccentricity being about one-eleventh. The inclination of the orbit to the ecliptic is somewhat under two degrees. The mean distance of Mars from the sun is about a hundred and forty million miles; but, owing to the eccentricity of his orbit, the distance varies from a hundred and fifty-three million miles to a hundred and twenty-seven million miles.

236. *Distance of Mars from the Earth.* — It will be seen, from Fig. 263, that a *superior* planet (or one outside the orbit of the earth), like Mars, is nearer the earth, by the whole diameter of the earth's orbit, when in opposition than

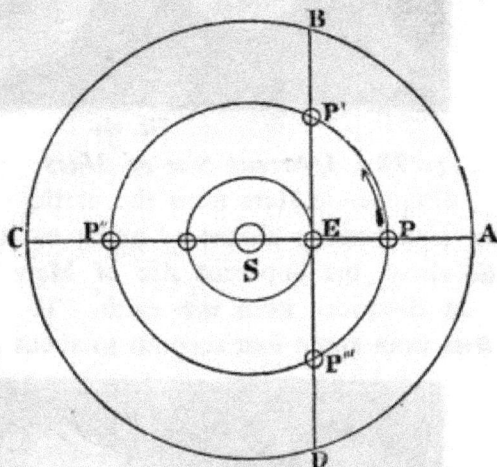

Fig. 263.

when in conjunction. The mean distance of Mars from the earth, at the time of opposition, is a hundred and forty million miles *minus* ninety-two million miles, or forty-eight million miles. Owing to the eccentricity of the orbit of the earth and of Mars, the distance of this planet when in opposition varies considerably. When the earth is in aphelion, and Mars in perihelion, at the time of opposition, the distance of the planet from the earth is only about thirty-three million miles. On the other hand, when the earth is in perihelion, and Mars in aphelion, at the time of opposition, the distance of the planet is over sixty-two million miles.

The mean distance of Mars from the earth when in conjunction is a hundred and forty million miles *plus* ninety-two million miles, or two hundred and thirty-two million miles. It will therefore be seen that Mars is nearly five times as far off at conjunction as at opposition.

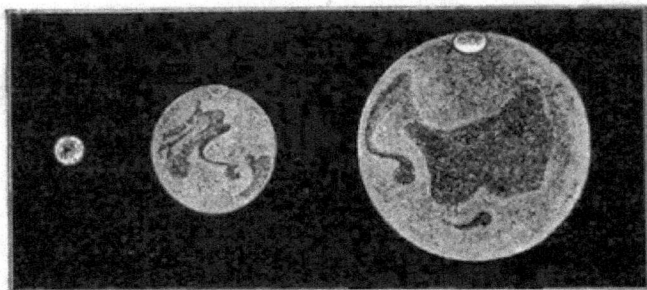

Fig. 264.

237. *The Apparent Size of Mars.* — Owing to the varying distance of Mars from the earth, the apparent size of the planet varies almost as much as that of Venus. Fig. 264 shows the apparent size of Mars at its extreme and mean distances from the earth. The apparent diameter varies from about four seconds to about thirty seconds.

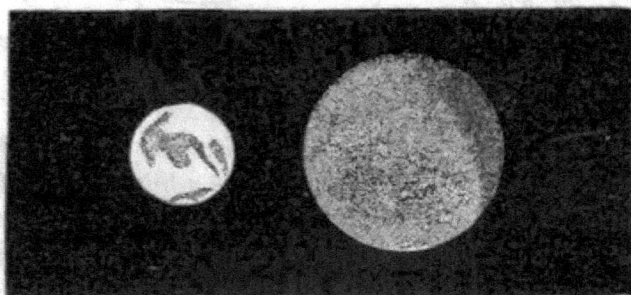

Fig. 265.

238. *The Volume and Density of Mars.* — Among the larger planets Mars is next in size to Mercury. Its real diameter is somewhat more than four thousand miles, and its bulk is about one-seventh of that of the earth. Its size, compared with that of the earth, is shown in Fig. 265.

PLATE IV.

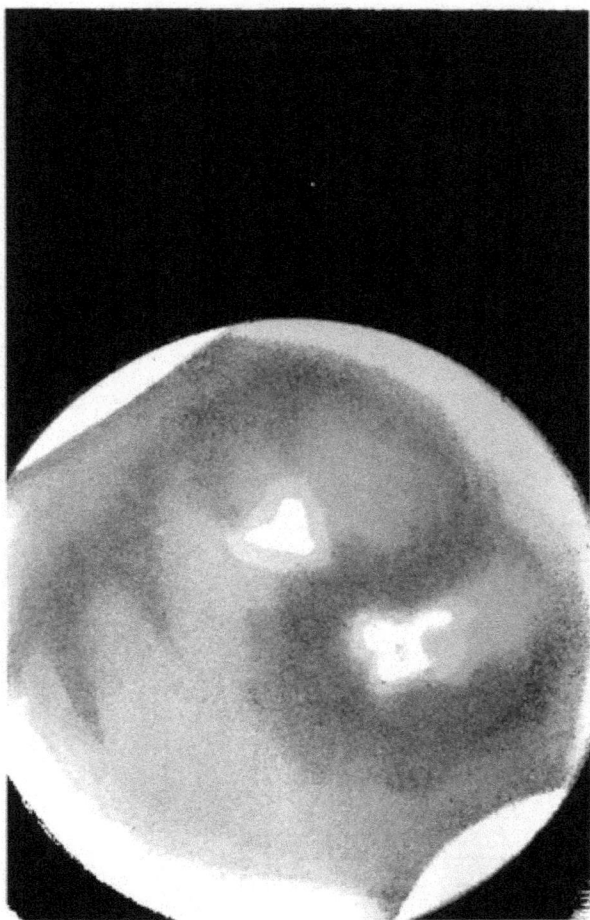

The density of Mars is only about three-fourths of that of the earth.

239. *Sidereal and Synodical Periods of Mars.* — The *sidereal* period of Mars, or the time in which he makes a complete revolution around the sun, is about six hundred and eighty-seven days, or nearly twenty-three months; but he is about seven hundred and eighty days in passing from opposition to opposition again, or in performing a *synodical* revolution. Mars moves in his orbit at the rate of about fifteen miles a second.

240. *Brilliancy of Mars.* — When near his opposition, Mars is easily recognized with the naked eye by his fiery-red light. He is much more brilliant at some oppositions than at others, for reasons already explained (236), but always shines brighter than an ordinary star of the first magnitude.

241. *Telescopic Appearance of Mars.* — When viewed with a good telescope (see Plate IV.), Mars is seen to be covered with dusky, dull-red patches, which are supposed to be continents, like those of our own globe. Other portions, of a greenish hue, are believed to be tracts of water. The ruddy color, which overpowers the green, and makes the whole planet seem red to the naked eye, was believed by Sir J. Herschel to be due to an ochrey tinge in the general soil, like that of the red sandstone districts on the earth. In a telescope, Mars appears less red, and the higher the power the less the intensity of the color. The disk, when well seen, is mapped out in a way which gives at once the impression of land and water. The bright part is red inclining to orange, sometimes dotted with brown and greenish points. The darker spaces, which vary greatly in depth of tone, are of a dull gray-green, having the aspect of a fluid which absorbs the solar rays. The proportion of land to water on the earth appears to be reversed on Mars. On the earth every continent is an island; on Mars all seas are lakes. Long, narrow straits are more common than on the

earth ; and wide expanses of water, like our Atlantic Ocean,
are rare.   (See Fig. 266.)

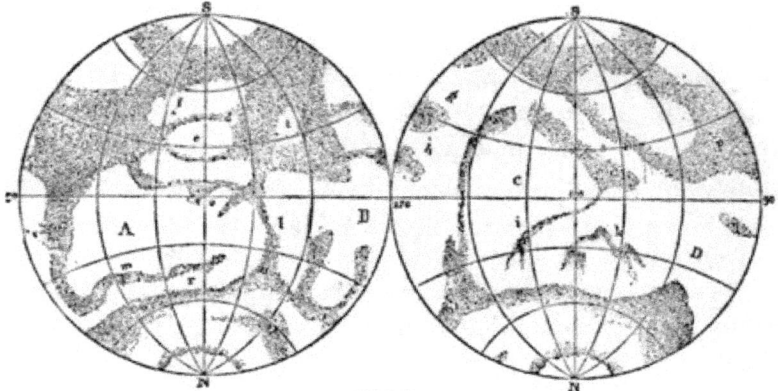

Fig. 266.

Fig. 267 represents a chart of the surface of Mars, which

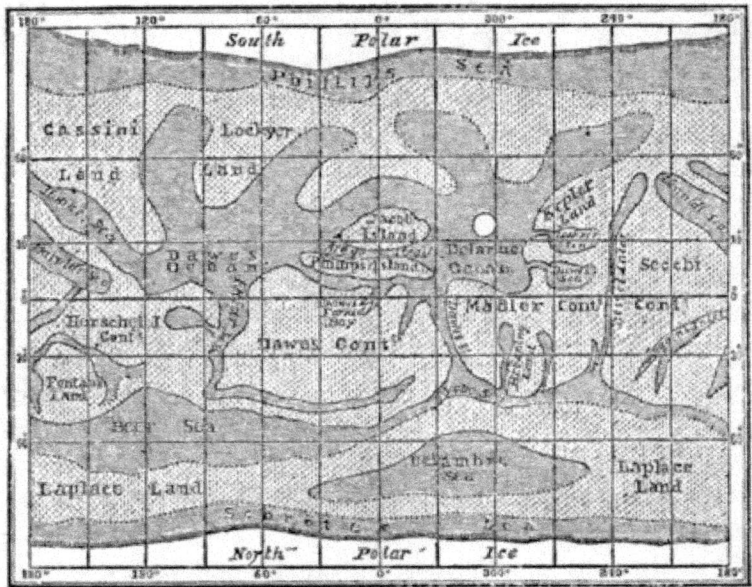

Fig. 267.

has been constructed from careful telescopic observation.
The outlines, as seen in the telescope, are, however, much

less distinct than they are represented here; and it is by no means certain that the light and dark portions are bodies of land and water.

In the vicinity of the poles brilliant white spots may be noticed, which are considered by many astronomers to be masses of snow. This conjecture is favored by the fact that they appear to diminish under the sun's influence at the beginning of the Martial summer, and to increase again on the approach of winter.

242. *Rotation of Mars.*— On watching Mars with a telescope, the spots on the disk are found to move (as shown in Fig. 268) in a manner which indicates that the

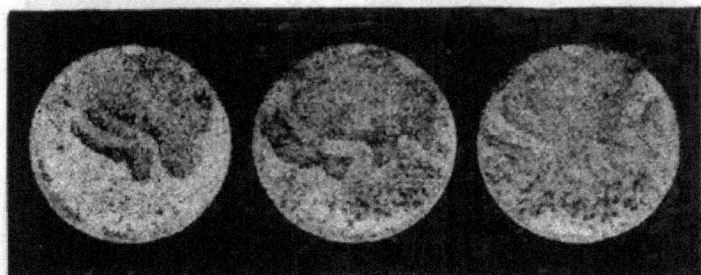

Fig. 268.

planet rotates in about twenty-four hours on an axis inclined about twenty-eight degrees from a perpendicular to the plane of its orbit. The inclination of the axis is shown in Fig. 269. It is evident from the figure that the variation in the length of day and night, and the change of seasons, are about the same on Mars as on the earth. The changes will, of course, be somewhat greater, and the seasons will be about twice as long.

243. *The Satellites of Mars.*— In 1877 Professor Hall of the Washington Observatory discovered that Mars is accompanied by two small moons, whose orbits are shown in Fig. 270. The inner satellite has been named *Phobos*, and the outer one *Deimos*. It is estimated that the diameter of the outer moon is from five to ten miles, and that of the inner one from ten to forty miles.

Phobos is remarkable for its nearness to the planet and the rapidity of its revolution, which is performed in seven hours thirty-eight minutes. Its distance from the centre of

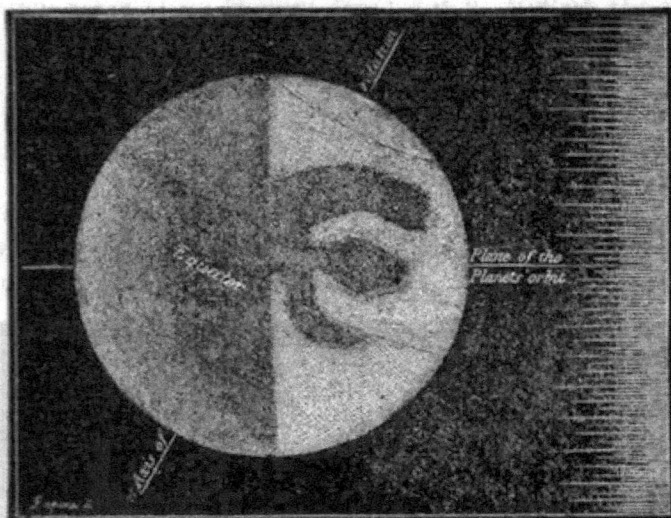

Fig. 269.

the planet is about six thousand miles, and from the surface less than four thousand. Astronomers on Mars, with telescopes and eyes like ours, could readily find out whether

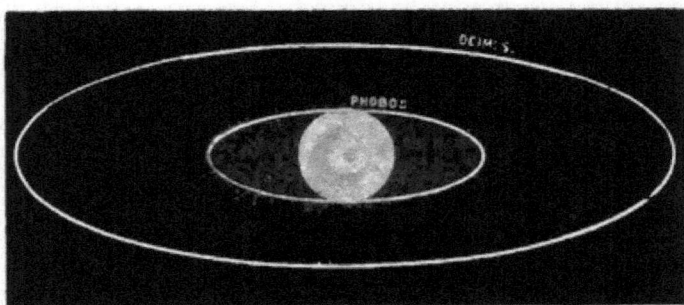

Fig. 270.

this satellite is inhabited, the distance being less than one-sixtieth of that of our moon.

It will be seen that Phobos makes about three revolutions

to one rotation of the planet. It will, of course, rise in the west; though the sun, the stars, and the other satellite rise in the east. Deimos makes a complete revolution in about thirty hours.

III. THE ASTEROIDS.

244. *Bode's Law of Planetary Distances.* — There is a very remarkable law connecting the distances of the planets from the sun, which is generally known by the name of *Bode's Law.* Attention was drawn to it in 1778 by the astronomer Bode, but he was not really its author.

To express this law we write the following series of numbers : —

$$0, \ 3, \ 6, \ 12, \ 24, \ 48, \ 96 ;$$

each number, with the exception of the first, being double the one which precedes it. If we add 4 to each of these numbers, the series becomes —

$$4, \ 7, \ 10, \ 16, \ 28, \ 52, \ 100 ;$$

which series was known to Kepler. These numbers, with the exception of 28, are sensibly proportional to the distances of the principal planets from the sun, the actual distances being as follows : —

Mercury.	Venus.	Earth.	Mars.		Jupiter.	Saturn.
3·9	7·2	10	15·2		52·9	95·4

245. *The First Discovery of the Asteroids.* — The great gap between Mars and Jupiter led astronomers, from the time of Kepler, to suspect the existence of an unknown planet in this region ; but no such planet was discovered till the beginning of the present century. *Ceres* was discovered Jan. 1, 1801, *Pallas* in 1802, *Juno* in 1804, and *Vesta* in 1807. Then followed a long interval of thirty-eight years before *Astræa*, the fifth of these minor planets, was discovered in 1845.

246. *Olbers's Hypothesis.* — After the discovery of Pallas,

Olbers suggested his celebrated hypothesis, that the two bodies might be fragments of a single planet which had been shattered by some explosion. If such were the case, the orbits of all the fragments would at first intersect each other at the point where the explosion occurred. He therefore thought it likely that other fragments would be found, especially if a search were kept up near the intersection of the orbits of Ceres and Pallas.

Professor Newcomb makes the following observations concerning this hypothesis : —

" The question whether these bodies could ever have formed a single one has now become one of cosmogony rather than of astronomy. If a planet were shattered, the orbit of each fragment would at first pass through the point at which the explosion occurred, however widely they might be separated through the rest of their course; but, owing to the secular changes produced by the attractions of the other planets, this coincidence would not continue. The orbits would slowly move away, and after the lapse of a few thousand years no trace of a common intersection would be seen. It is therefore curious that Olbers and his contemporaries should have expected to find such a region of intersection, as it implied that the explosion had occurred within a few thousand years. The fact that the required conditions were not fulfilled was no argument against the hypothesis, because the explosion might have occurred millions of years ago ; and in the mean time the perihelion and node of each orbit would have made many entire revolutions, so that the orbits would have been completely mixed up. . . . A different explanation of the group is given by the nebular hypothesis; so that Olbers's hypothesis is no longer considered by astronomers."

247. *Later Discoveries of Asteroids.* — Since 1845 over two hundred asteroids have been discovered. All these are so small, that it requires a very good telescope to see them ; and even in very powerful telescopes they appear as mere points of light, which can be distinguished from the stars only by their motions.

To facilitate the discovery of these bodies, very accurate maps have been constructed, including all the stars down to the thirteenth magnitude in the neighborhood of the ecliptic. A reduced copy of one of these maps is shown in Fig. 271.

Furnished with a map of this kind, and with a telescope powerful enough to show all the stars marked on it, the

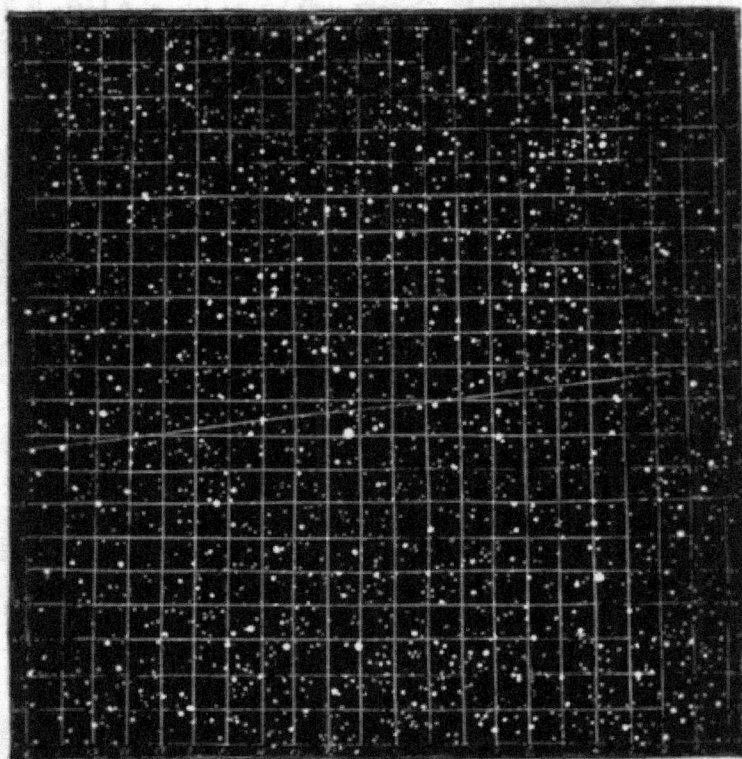

Fig. 271.

observer who is searching for these small planets will place in the field of view of his telescope six spider-lines at right angles to each other, and at equal distances apart, in such a manner that several small squares will be formed, embracing just as much of the heavens as do those shown in the map. He will then direct his telescope to the region of the sky he wishes to examine, represented by the map, so as to be able to compare successively each square with the corre-

sponding portion of the sky. Fig. 272 shows at the right
hand the squares in the telescopic field of view, and at the
left hand the corresponding squares of the map.

He can then assure himself if the numbers and positions of
the stars mapped, and of the stars observed, are identical. If
he observes in the field of view a luminous point which is not
marked in the map, it is evident that either the new body is a
star of variable brightness which was not visible at the time

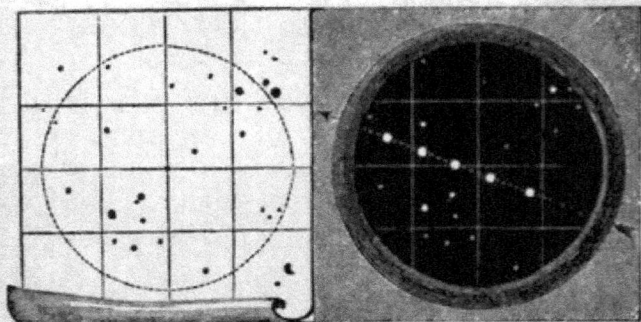

Fig. 272.

the map was made, or it is a planet, or perhaps a comet. If
the new body remains fixed at the same point, it is the former;
but, if it changes its position with regard to the neighboring
stars, it is the latter. The motion is generally so sensible, that
in the course of one evening the change of position may be
detected; and it can soon be determined, by the direction and
rate of the motion, whether the body is a planet or a comet.

IV. OUTER GROUP OF PLANETS.

JUPITER.

248. *Orbit of Jupiter.* — The orbit of Jupiter is inclined
only a little over one degree to the ecliptic ; and its eccentricity is only about half of that of Mars, being less than
one-twentieth. The mean distance of Jupiter from the sun
is about four hundred and eighty million miles ; but, owing
to the eccentricity of his orbit, his actual distance from the
sun ranges from four hundred and fifty-seven to five hundred and three million miles.

249. *Distance of Jupiter from the Earth.* — When Jupiter is in opposition, his mean distance from the earth is four hundred and eighty million miles *minus* ninety-two million miles, or three hundred and eighty-eight million miles, and, when he is in conjunction, four hundred and eighty million miles *plus* ninety-two million miles, or five hundred and seventy-two million miles. It will be seen that he is less than twice as far off in conjunction as in opposition, and that the ratio of his greatest to his least distance is very much less than in the case of Venus and Mars. This is owing to his very much greater distance from the sun. Owing to the eccentricities of the orbits of the

Fig. 273.

earth and of Jupiter, the greatest and least distances of Jupiter from the earth vary somewhat from year to year.

250. *The Brightness and Apparent Size of Jupiter.* — The apparent diameter of Jupiter varies from about fifty seconds to about thirty seconds. His apparent size at his extreme and mean distances from the earth is shown in Fig. 273.

Jupiter shines with a brilliant white light, which exceeds that of every other planet except Venus. The planet is, of course, brightest when near opposition.

251. *The Volume and Density of Jupiter.* — Jupiter is the "giant planet" of our system, his mass largely exceeding that of all the other planets combined. His mean

diameter is about eighty-five thousand miles; but the equatorial exceeds the polar diameter by five thousand miles.
In volume he exceeds our earth about thirteen hundred
times, but in mass only about two hundred and thirteen
times. His specific gravity is, therefore, far less than that
of the earth, and even less than that of water. The comparative size of Jupiter and the earth is shown in Fig. 274.

252. *The Sidereal and Synodical Periods of Jupiter.* —
It takes Jupiter nearly twelve years to make a *sidereal* revo-

Fig. 274.

lution, or a complete revolution around the sun, his orbital
motion being at the rate of about eight miles a second.
His *synodical* period, or the time of his passage from opposition to opposition again, is three hundred and ninety-eight
days.

253. *The Telescopic Aspect of Jupiter.* — There are no
really permanent markings on the disk of Jupiter; but his
surface presents a very diversified appearance. The earlier
telescopic observers descried dark belts across it, one north
of the equator, and the other south of it. With the increase of telescopic power, it was seen that these bands

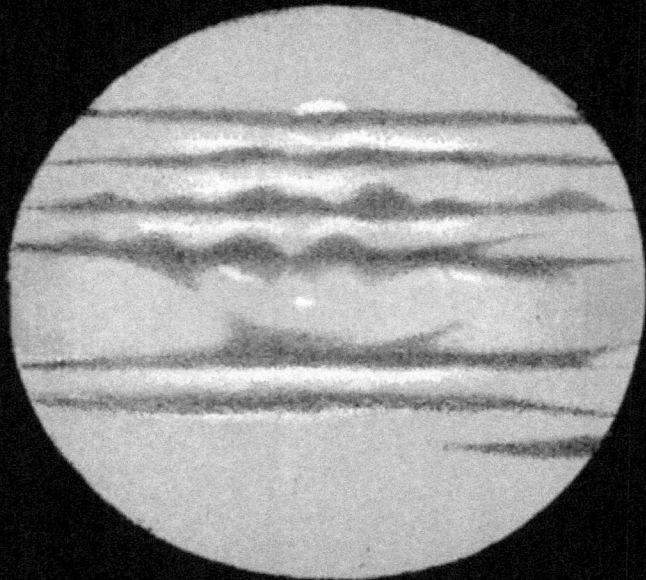

were of a more complex structure than had been supposed, and consisted of stratified, cloud-like appearances, varying greatly in form and number. These change so rapidly, that the face of the planet rarely presents the same appearance on two successive nights. They are most strongly marked at some distance on each side of the planet's equator, and thus appear as two belts under a low magnifying power.

Both the outlines of the belts, and the color of portions of the planet, are subject to considerable changes. The equatorial regions, and the spaces between the belts generally, are often of a rosy tinge. This color is sometimes strongly marked, while at other times hardly a trace of it can be seen. A general telescopic view of Jupiter is given in Plate V.

254. *The Physical Constitution of Jupiter.* — From the changeability of the belts, and of nearly all the visible features of Jupiter, it is clear that what we see on that planet is not the solid nucleus, but cloud-like formations, which cover the entire surface to a great depth. The planet appears to be covered with a deep and dense atmosphere, filled with thick masses of clouds and vapor. Until recently this cloud-laden atmosphere was supposed to be somewhat like that of our globe ; but at present the physical constitution of Jupiter is believed to resemble that of the sun rather than that of the earth. Like the sun, he is brighter in the centre than near the edges, as is shown in the transits of the satellites over his disk. When the satellite first enters on the disk, it commonly seems like a bright spot on a dark background ; but, as it approaches the centre, it appears like a dark spot on the bright surface of the planet. The centre is probably two or three times brighter than the edges. This may be, as in the case of the sun, because the light near the edge passes through a greater depth of atmosphere, and is diminished by absorption.

It has also been suspected that Jupiter shines partly by

his own light, and not wholly by reflected sunlight. The planet cannot, however, emit any great amount of light; for, if it did, the satellites would shine by this light when they are in the shadow of the planet, whereas they totally disappear. It is possible that the brighter portions of the surface are from time to time slightly self-luminous.

Again : the interior of Jupiter seems to be the seat of an activity so enormous that it can be ascribed only to intense

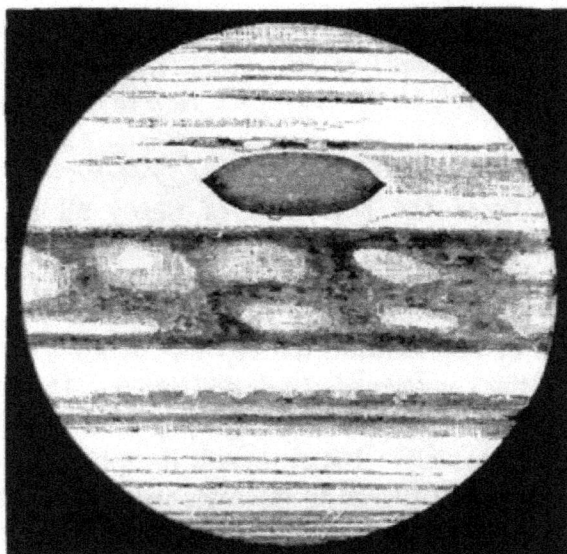

Fig. 275.

heat. Rapid movements are always occurring on his surface, often changing its aspect in a few hours. It is therefore probable that Jupiter is not yet covered by a solid crust, and that the fiery interior, whether liquid or gaseous, is surrounded by the dense vapors which cease to be luminous on rising into the higher and cooler regions of the atmosphere. Figs. 275 and 276 show the disk of Jupiter as it appeared in December, 1881.

255. *Rotation of Jupiter.* — Spots are sometimes visible

which are much more permanent than the ordinary markings on the belts. The most remarkable of these is "the

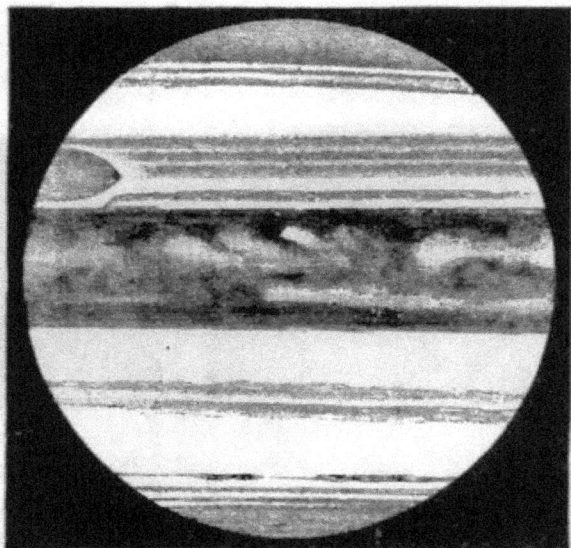

Fig. 276.

great red spot," which was first observed in July, 1878,
and is still to be seen in February, 1882. It is shown
just above the centre of the disk in Fig. 275. By watch-

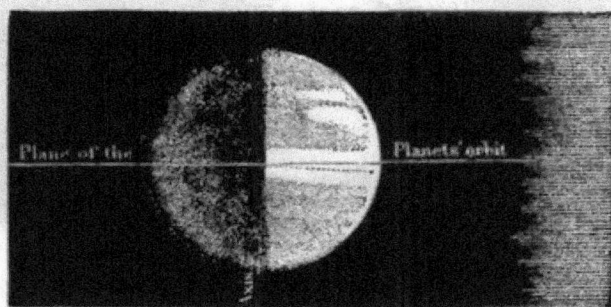

Fig. 277.

ing these spots from day to day, the time of Jupiter's axial
rotation has been found to be about nine hours and fifty
minutes.

The axis of Jupiter deviates but slightly from a perpendicular to the plane of its orbit, as is shown in Fig. 277.

THE SATELLITES OF JUPITER.

256. *Jupiter's Four Moons.*— Jupiter is accompanied

Fig. 278.

by four moons, as shown in Fig. 278. The diameters of
these moons range from about twenty-two hundred to thirty-
seven hundred miles. The second from the planet is the
smallest, and the third the largest. The smallest is about
the size of our moon ; the largest considerably exceeds

Fig. 279.

Mercury, and almost rivals Mars, in bulk. The sizes of
these moons, compared with those of the earth and its
moon, are shown in Fig. 279.

The names of these satellites, in the order of their distance from the planet, are *Io, Europa, Ganymede,* and *Cal-*

listo. Their times of revolution range from about a day and three-fourths up to about sixteen days and a half. Their orbits are shown in Fig. 280.

257. *The Variability of Jupiter's Satellites.* — Remarkable variations in the light of these moons have led to the supposition that violent changes are taking place on their surfaces. It was formerly believed, that, like our moon,

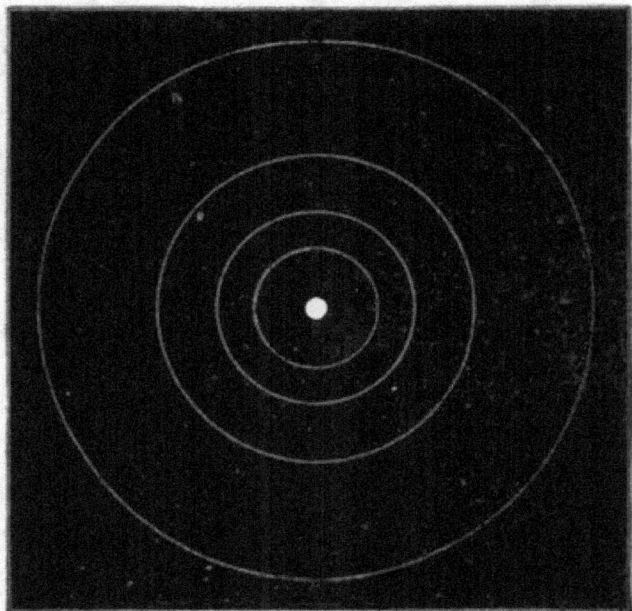

Fig. 280.

they always present the same face to the planet, and that the changes in their brilliancy are due to differences in the luminosity of parts of their surface which are successively turned towards us during a revolution ; but careful measurements of their light show that this hypothesis does not account for the changes, which are sometimes very sudden. The satellites are too distant for examination of their surfaces with the telescope : hence it is impossible to give any certain explanation of these phenomena.

258. *Eclipses of Jupiter's Satellites.* — Jupiter, like the earth, casts a shadow away from the sun, as shown in

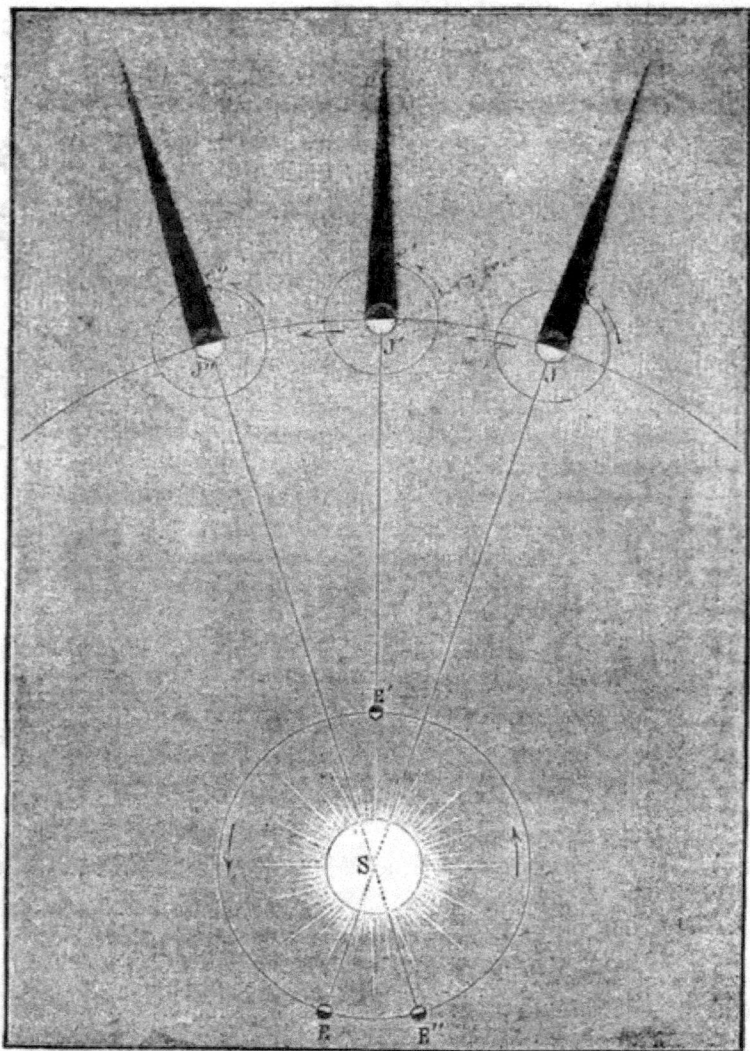

Fig. 281.

Fig. 281 ; and, whenever one of his moons passes into this shadow, it becomes eclipsed. On the other hand, whenever one of the moons throws its shadow on Jupiter, the sun is eclipsed to that part of the planet which lies within the shadow.

To the inhabitants of Jupiter (if there are any, and if

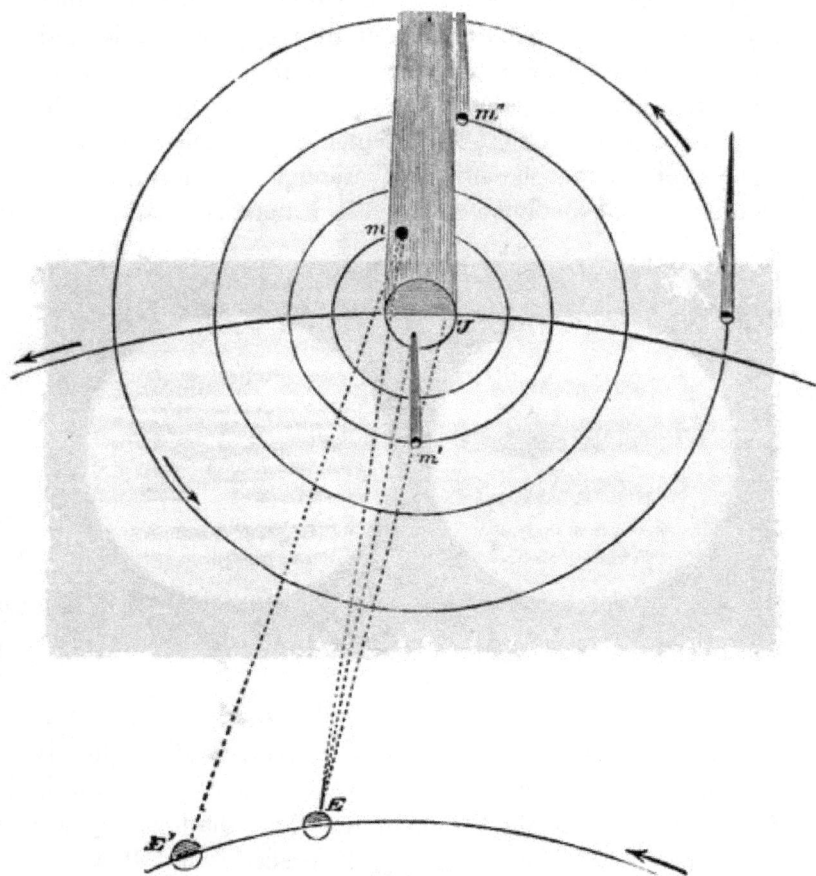

Fig. 282.

they can see through the clouds) these eclipses must be very familiar affairs ; for in consequence of the small incli- nations of the orbits of the satellites to the planet's equator, and the small inclination of the latter to the plane of Jupiter's orbit, all the satellites, except the most distant one, are eclipsed in every revolution. A spectator on Jupiter might therefore witness during the planetary year forty-five hundred eclipses of the moons, and about the same number of the sun.

259. *Transits of Jupiter's Satellites.* — Whenever one of Jupiter's moons passes in front of the planet, it is said to make a *transit* across his disk. When a moon is making a transit, it presents its bright hemisphere towards the earth, as will be seen from Fig. 282 : hence it is usually seen as a bright spot on the planet's disk; though sometimes, on the brighter central portions of the disk, it appears dark.

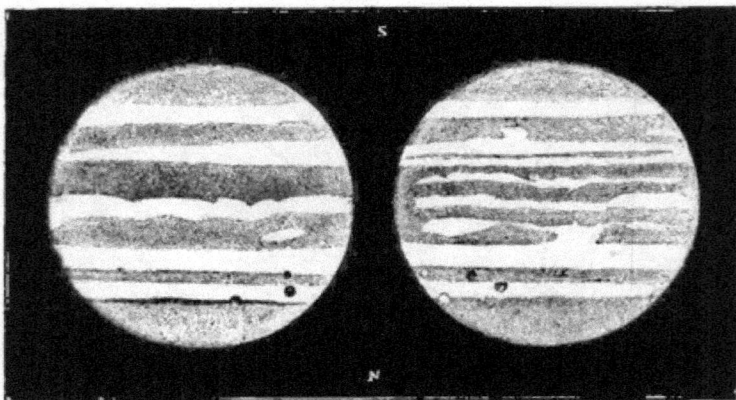

Fig. 283.

It will be seen from Fig. 282 that the shadow of a moon does not fall upon the part of the planet's disk that is covered by the moon : hence we may observe the transit of both the moon and its shadow. The shadow appears as a small black spot, which will precede or follow the moon according to the position of the earth in its orbit. Fig. 283 shows two moons of Jupiter in transit.

260. *Occultations of Jupiter's Satellites.* — The eclipse of a moon of Jupiter must be carefully distinguished from the *occultation* of a moon by the planet. In the case of an eclipse, the moon ceases to be visible, because the mass

of Jupiter is interposed between the sun and the moon,
which ceases to be luminous, because the sun's light is cut
off; but, in the case of an occultation, the moon gets into
such a position that the body of Jupiter is interposed between it and the earth, thus rendering the moon invisible
to us. The third satellite, m'' (Fig. 282), is invisible from
the earth E, having become *occulted* when it passed behind
the planet's disk; but
it will not be *eclipsed*
until it passes into the
shadow of Jupiter.

261. *Jupiter without
Satellites.*—It occasion-
ally happens that every
one of Jupiter's satel-
lites will disappear at
the same time, either
by being eclipsed or
occulted, or by being in
transit. In this event,
Jupiter will appear with-
out satellites. This oc-
curred on the 21st of
August, 1867. The po-

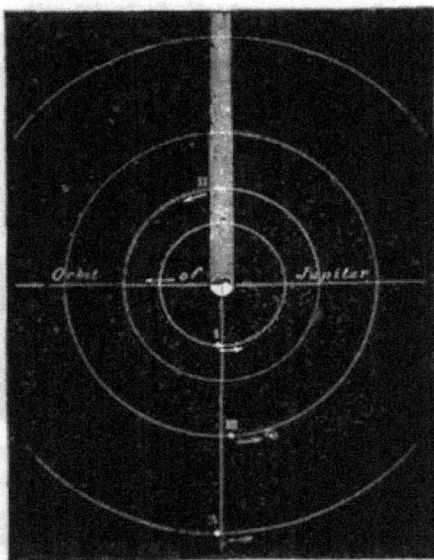

Fig. 284.

sition of Jupiter's satellites at this time is shown in
Fig. 284.

SATURN.

THE PLANET AND HIS MOONS.

262. *The Orbit of Saturn.*—The orbit of Saturn is
rather more eccentric than that of Jupiter, its eccentricity
being somewhat more than one-twentieth. Its inclination
to the ecliptic is about two degrees and a half. The mean
distance of Saturn from the sun is about eight hundred and
eighty million miles. It is about a hundred million miles
nearer the sun at perihelion than at aphelion.

263. *Distance of Saturn from the Earth.* — The mean distance of Saturn from the earth at opposition is eight hundred and eighty million miles *minus* ninety-two million miles, or seven hundred and eighty-eight million ; and at conjunction, eight hundred and eighty million miles *plus* ninety-two million, or nine hundred and seventy-two million. Owing to the eccentricity of the orbit of Saturn, his distance from the earth at opposition and at conjunction varies by about a hundred million miles at different times ; but he is so immensely far away, that this is only a small fraction of his mean distance.

264. *Apparent Size and Brightness of Saturn.* — The apparent diameter of Saturn varies from about twenty seconds to about fourteen seconds. His apparent size at his

Fig. 285.

extreme and mean distances from the earth is shown in Fig. 285.

The planet generally shines with the brilliancy of a moderate first-magnitude star, and with a dingy, reddish light, as if seen through a smoky atmosphere.

265. *Volume and Density of Saturn.* — The real diameter of Saturn is about seventy thousand miles, and its volume over seven hundred times that of the earth. The comparative size of the earth and Saturn is shown in Fig. 286. This planet is a little more than half as dense as Jupiter.

266. *The Sidereal and Synodical Periods of Saturn.* — Saturn makes a complete revolution round the sun in a period of about twenty-nine years and a half, moving in his orbit at the rate of about six miles a second. The

planet passes from opposition to opposition again in a period of three hundred and seventy-eight days, or thirteen days over a year.

267. *Physical Constitution of Saturn.* — The physical constitution of Saturn seems to resemble that of Jupiter; but, being twice as far away, the planet cannot be so well studied. The farther an object is from the sun, the less it is illuminated; and, the farther it is from the earth, the

Fig. 286.

smaller it appears: hence there is a double difficulty in examining the more distant planets. Under favorable circumstances, the surface of Saturn is seen to be diversified with very faint markings; and, with high telescopic powers, two or more very faint streaks, or belts, may be discerned parallel to its equator. These belts, like those of Jupiter, change their aspect from time to time; but they are so faint that the changes cannot be easily followed. It is only on rare occasions that the time of rotation can be determined from a study of the markings.

268. *Rotation of Saturn.* — On the evening of Dec. 7, 1876, Professor Hall, who had been observing the satellites of Saturn with the great Washington telescope (18), saw a brilliant white spot near the equator of the planet. It seemed as if an immense eruption of incandescent matter had suddenly burst up from the interior. The spot gradually spread itself out into a long light streak, of which the brightest point was near the western end. It remained visible until January, when it became faint and ill-defined, and the planet was lost in the rays of the sun.

Fig. 287.

From all the observations on this spot, Professor Hall found the period of Saturn to be ten hours fourteen minutes, reckoning by the brightest part of the streak. Had the middle of the streak been taken, the time would have been less, because the bright matter seemed to be carried along in the direction of the planet's rotation. If this motion was due to a wind, the velocity of the current must have been between fifty and a hundred miles an hour. The axis of Saturn is inclined twenty-seven degrees from the perpendicular to its orbit.

269. *The Satellites of Saturn.* — Saturn is accompanied by eight moons. Seven of these are shown in Fig. 287. The names of these satellites, in the order of their distances from the planet, are given in the accompanying table : —

Number.	NAME.	Distance from Planet in Miles.	Sidereal Period.		Discoverer.	Date of Discovery.
			d. h. m.	d.		
1	Mimas . .	120,800	0 22 37	0.94	Herschel . .	Sept. 17, 1789.
2	Enceladus .	155,000	1 8 53	1.37	Herschel . .	Aug. 28, 1789.
3	Tethys . .	191,900	1 21 18	1.88	Cassini . .	March, 1684.
4	Dione . . .	245,800	2 17 41	2.73	Cassini . .	March, 1684.
5	Rhea . . .	343,400	4 12 25	4.51	Cassini . .	Dec. 23, 1672.
6	Titan . . .	796,100	15 22 41	15.94	Huyghens .	March 25, 1655.
7	Hyperion .	963,300	21 7 7	21.29	Bond . . .	Sept. 16, 1848.
8	Japetus . .	2,313,800	79 7 53	79.33	Cassini . .	October, 1671.

The apparent brightness or visibility of these satellites follows the order of their discovery. The smallest telescope will show Titan, and one of very moderate size will show Japetus in the western part of its orbit. An instrument of four or five inches aperture will show Rhea, and perhaps Tethys and Dione; while seven or eight inches are required for Enceladus, even at its greatest elongation from the planet.

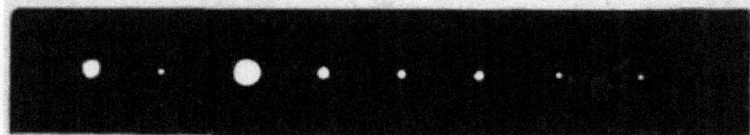

Fig. 288.

Mimas can rarely be seen except at its greatest elongation, and then only with an aperture of twelve inches or more. Hyperion can be detected only with the most powerful telescopes, on account of its faintness and the difficulty of distinguishing it from minute stars.

Japetus, the outermost satellite, is remarkable for the fact, that while, in one part of its orbit, it is the brightest of the satellites except Titan, in the opposite part it is almost as

ASTRONOMY.

faint as Hyperion, and can be seen only in large telescopes. When west of the planet, it is bright; when east of it, faint. This peculiarity has been accounted for by supposing that the satellite, like our moon, always presents the same face to the planet, and that one side of it is white and the other intensely black; but it is doubtful whether any known substance is so black as one side of the satellite must be to account for such extraordinary changes of brilliancy.

Titan, the largest of these satellites, is about the size of the largest satellite of Jupiter. The relative sizes of

Fig. 290.

the satellites are shown in Fig. 288, and their orbits in Fig. 289.

Fig. 290 shows the transit of one of the satellites, and of its shadow, across the disk of the planet.

THE RINGS OF SATURN.

270. *General Appearance of the Rings.* — Saturn is surrounded by a thin flat ring lying in the plane of its equator. This ring is probably less than a hundred miles thick. The part of it nearest Saturn reflects little sunlight to us; so that it has a dusky appearance, and is not easily seen, although it is not quite so dark as the sky seen between it and the planet. The outer edge of this dusky portion of the ring is at a distance from Saturn of between two and three times the earth's diameter. Outside of this dusky part of

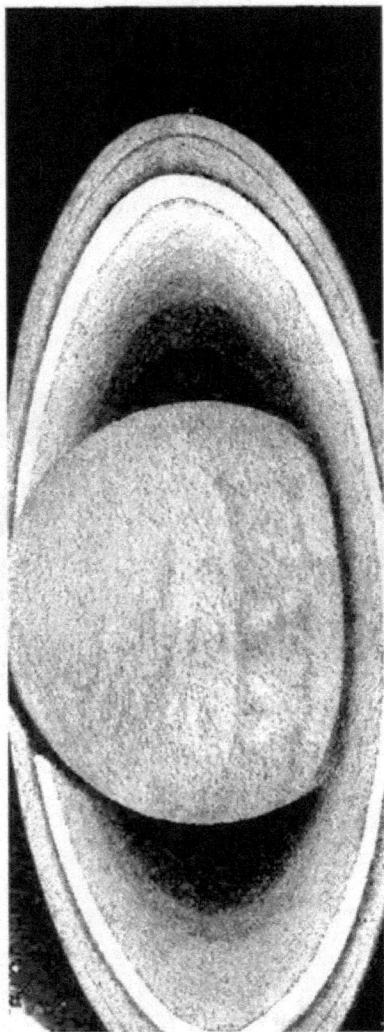

the ring is a much brighter portion, and outside of this another, which is somewhat fainter, but still so much brighter than the dusky part as to be easily seen. The width of the brighter parts of the ring is over three times the earth's diameter. To distinguish the parts, the outer one is called ring *A*, the middle one ring *B*, and the dusky one ring *C*. Between *A* and *B* is an apparently open space, nearly two thousand miles wide, which looks like a black line on the ring. Other divisions in the ring have been noticed at times; but this is the only one always seen with good telescopes at times when either side of the ring is in view from the earth. The general telescopic appearance of the ring is shown in Fig. 291.

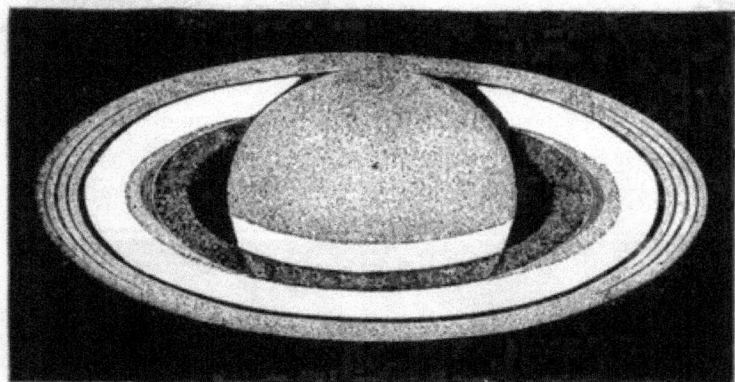

Fig. 292.

Fig. 292 shows the divisions of the rings as they were seen by Bond.

271. *Phases of Saturn's Ring.* — The ring is inclined to the plane of the planet's orbit by an angle of twenty-seven degrees. The general aspect from the earth is nearly the same as from the sun. As the planet revolves around the sun, the axis and plane of the ring keep the same direction in space, just as the axis of the earth and the plane of the equator do.

When the planet is in one part of its orbit, we see the

upper or northern side of the ring at an inclination of twenty-seven degrees, the greatest angle at which the ring can ever be seen. This phase of the ring is shown in Fig. 293.

Fig. 293.

When the planet has moved through a quarter of a revolution, the edge of the ring is turned towards the sun and the earth; and, owing to its extreme thinness, it is visible only in the most powerful telescopes as a fine line

Fig. 294.

of light, stretching out on each side of the planet. This phase of the ring is shown in Fig. 294.

All the satellites, except Japetus, revolve very nearly in the plane of the ring: consequently, when the edge of the ring is turned towards the earth, the satellites seem to swing from one side of the planet to the other in a straight line, running along the thin edge of the ring like beads on a string. This phase affords the best opportunity of seeing

Fig. 295.

the inner satellites, Mimas and Enceladus, which at other times are obscured by the brilliancy of the ring.

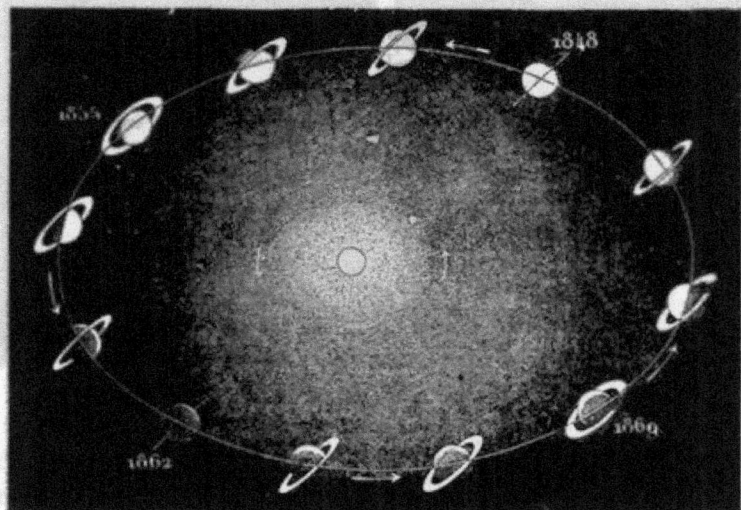

Fig. 296.

Fig. 295 shows a phase of the ring intermediate between the last two.

When the planet has moved ninety degrees farther, we

again see the ring at an angle of twenty-seven degrees; but
now it is the lower or southern side which is visible. When
it has moved ninety degrees farther, the edge of the ring
is again turned towards the earth and sun.

The successive phases of Saturn's ring during a complete
revolution are shown in Fig. 296.

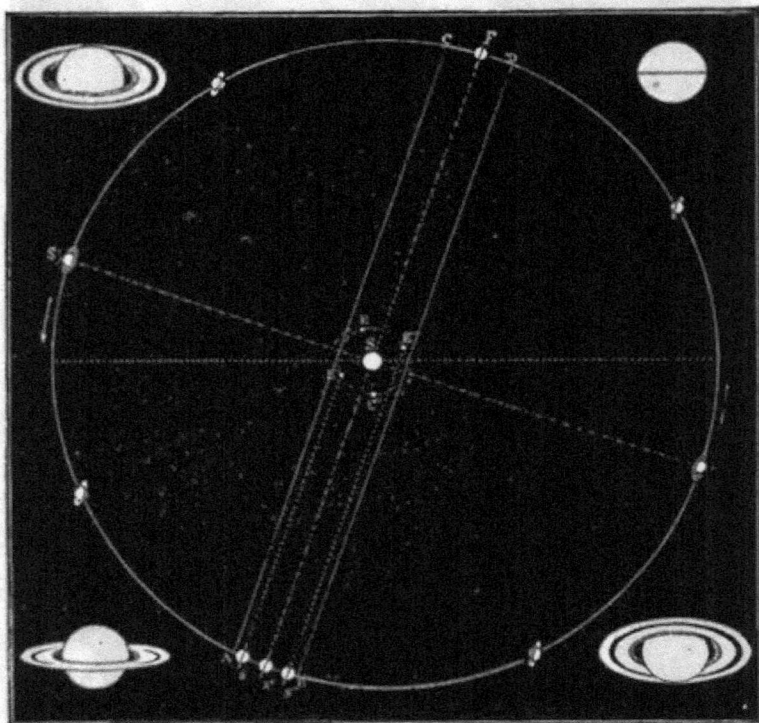

Fig. 297.

It will be seen that there are two opposite points of
Saturn's orbit in which the rings are turned edgewise to
us, and two points half-way between the former in which
the ring is seen at its maximum inclination of about twenty-
seven degrees. Since the planet performs a revolution in
twenty-nine years and a half, these phases occur at average
intervals of about seven years and four months.

272. *Disappearance of Saturn's Ring.* — It will be seen from Fig. 297 that the plane of the ring may not be turned towards the sun and the earth at exactly the same time, and also that the earth may sometimes come on one side of the plane of the ring while the sun is shining on the other. In the figure, E, E', E''. and E''' is the orbit of the earth. When Saturn is at S', or opposite, at F, the plane of the ring will pass through the sun, and then only the edge of the ring will be illumined. Were Saturn at S, and the earth at E', the plane of the ring would pass through the earth. This would also be the case were the earth at E''', and Saturn at S''.

Fig. 298.

Were Saturn at S or at S'', and the earth farther to the left or to the right, the sun would be shining on one side of the ring while we should be looking on the other. In all these cases the ring will disappear entirely in a telescope of ordinary power. With very powerful telescopes the ring will appear, in the first two cases, as a thin line of light (Fig. 298). It will be seen that all these cases of disappearance must take place when Saturn is in the parts of his orbit intercepted between the parallel lines $A C$ and $B D$. These lines are tangent to the earth's orbit, which they enclose, and are parallel to the plane of Saturn's ring. As Saturn passes away from these two lines on either side, the rings appear more and more open. When the dark side of the ring is in view, it appears as a

black line crossing the planet; and on such occasions the sunlight reflected from the outer and inner edges of the rings *A*
and *B* enables us to see traces of the ring on each side of
Saturn, at least in places where two such reflections come
nearly together. Fig. 299 illustrates this reflection from the
edges at the divisions of the rings.

273. *Changes in Saturn's Ring.* — The question whether
changes are going on in the rings of Saturn is still unsettled.
Some observers have believed that they saw additional divisions in the rings from time to time; but these may have been
errors of vision, due partly to the shading which is known to
exist on portions of the ring.

Fig. 299.

Professor Newcomb says, "As seen with the great Washington equatorial in the autumn of 1874, there was no great or
sudden contrast between the inner or dark edge of the bright
ring and the outer edge of the dusky ring. There was some
suspicion that the one shaded into the other by insensible
gradations. No one could for a moment suppose, as some
observers have, that there was a separation between these two
rings. All these considerations give rise to the question
whether the dusky ring may not be growing at the expense
of the inner bright ring."

Struve, in 1851, advanced the startling theory that the inner
edge of the ring was gradually approaching the planet, the

whole ring spreading inwards, and making the central opening
smaller. The theory was based upon the descriptions and
drawings of the rings by the astronomers of the seventeenth
century, especially Huyghens, and the measures made by later
astronomers up to 1851. This supposed change in the dimen-
sion of the ring is shown in Fig. 300.

274. *Constitution of Saturn's Ring.*—The theory now generally held by astronomers is, that the ring is composed of a
cloud of satellites too small to be separately seen in the telescope, and too close together to admit of visible intervals
between them. The ring looks solid, because its parts are
too small and too numerous to be seen singly. They are like
the minute drops of water that make up clouds and fogs,
which to our eyes seem like solid masses. In the dusky ring
the particles may be so scattered that we can see through

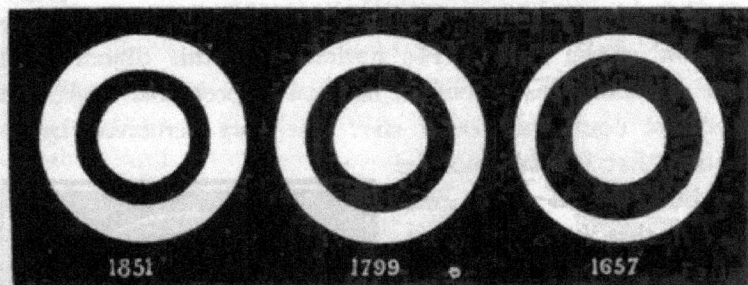

Fig. 300.

the cloud, the duskiness being due to the blending of light and
darkness. Some believe, however, that the duskiness is caused
by the darker color of the particles rather than by their being
farther apart.

URANUS.

275. *Orbit and Dimensions of Uranus.*—Uranus, the
smallest of the outer group of planets, has a diameter of
nearly thirty-two thousand miles. It is a little less dense
than Jupiter, and its mean distance from the sun is about
seventeen hundred and seventy millions of miles. Its orbit
has about the same eccentricity as that of Jupiter, and is
inclined less than a degree to the ecliptic. Uranus makes

a revolution around the sun in eighty-four years, moving at
the rate of a little over four miles a second.   It is visible
to the naked eye as a star of the sixth magnitude.

As seen in a large telescope, the planet has a decidedly
sea-green color ; but no markings have with certainty been
detected on its disk, so that
nothing is really known with
regard to its rotation.   Fig.
301 shows the comparative
size of Uranus and the
earth.

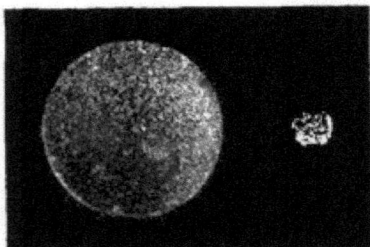

276. *Discovery of Uranus.*
— This planet was discovered

Fig. 301.

by Sir William Herschel in March, 1781.   He was engaged
at the time in examining the small stars of the constellation
Gemini, or the Twins.   He noticed that this object which
had attracted his attention had an appreciable disk, and
therefore could not be a star.   He also perceived by its
motion that it could not be
a nebula ; he therefore concluded that it was a comet,
and announced his discovery
as such.   On attempting to
compute its orbit, it was
soon found that its motions
could be accounted for only
on the supposition that it
was moving in a circular
orbit at about twice the distance of Saturn from the
sun.   It was therefore recognized as a new planet, whose
discovery nearly doubled the dimensions of the solar system
as it was then known.

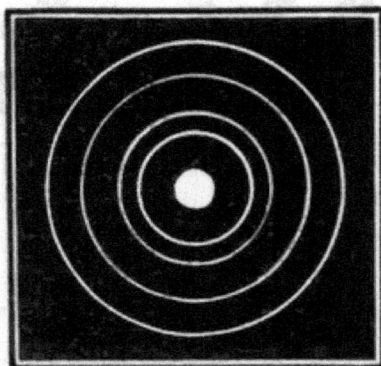

Fig. 302.

277. *The Name of the Planet.* — Herschel, out of compli
ment to his patron, George III., proposed to call the new

planet *Georgium Sidus* (the Georgian Star); but this name found little favor. The name of *Herschel* was proposed, and continued in use in England for a time, but did not meet with general approval. Various other names were suggested, and finally that of *Uranus* was adopted.

278. *The Satellites of Uranus.* — Uranus is accompanied by four satellites, whose orbits are shown in Fig. 302. These satellites are remarkable for the great inclination of their orbits to the plane of the planet's orbit, amounting to about eighty degrees, and for their *retrograde* motion ; that is, they move *from east to west*, instead of from west to east, as in the case of all the planets and of all the satellites previously discovered.

NEPTUNE.

279. *Orbit and Dimensions of Neptune.* — So far as known, Neptune is the most remote member of the solar system, its mean distance from the sun being twenty-seven hundred and seventy-five million miles. This distance is considerably less than twice that of Uranus. Neptune revolves around the sun in a period of a little less than a hundred and sixty-five years. Its orbit has but slight eccentricity, and is inclined less than two degrees to the ecliptic. This planet is considerably larger than Uranus, its diameter being nearly thirty-five thousand miles. It is somewhat less dense than Uranus. Neptune is invisible to the naked eye, and no telescope has revealed any markings on its disk : hence nothing is certainly known as to its rotation. Fig. 303 shows the comparative size of Neptune and the earth.

280. *The Discovery of Neptune.* — The discovery of Neptune was made in 1846, and is justly regarded as one of the grandest triumphs of astronomy.

Soon after Uranus was discovered, certain irregularities in its motion were observed, which could not be explained. It is well known that the planets are all the while disturbing each other's motions, so that none of them describe perfect ellipses. These mutual disturbances are called *perturbations*. In the case of Uranus it was found, that, after making due allowance for the action of all the known planets, there were still certain perturbations in its course which had not been accounted for. This led astronomers to the suspicion that these might be caused by an unknown planet. Leverrier in France, and Adams in England, independently of each other, set themselves the difficult problem of computing the position and magnitude of a planet which would produce these perturbations. Both, by a most laborious computation, showed that the perturbations were such as would be produced by a planet revolving about the sun at about twice the distance of Uranus, and having a mass somewhat greater than that of this planet; and both pointed out the same part of the heavens as that in which the planet ought to be found at that time. Almost immediately after they had announced the conclusion to which they had arrived, the planet was found with the telescope. The astronomer who was searching for the planet at the suggestion of Leverrier was the first to recognize it: hence Leverrier has obtained the chief credit of the discovery.

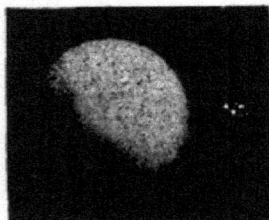

Fig. 303.

The observed planet is proved to be nearer than the one predicted by Leverrier and Adams, and therefore of smaller magnitude.

281. *The Observed Planet not the Predicted One.*— Professor Peirce always maintained that the planet found by observation was not the one whose existence had been predicted by Leverrier and Adams, though its action would completely explain all the irregularities in the motion of Uranus. His last

statement on this point is as follows : " My position is, that there were *two possible planets*, either of which might have

caused the observed irregular motions of Uranus. Each planet excluded the other; so that, if one was, the other was not. They coincided in direction from the earth at certain epochs, once in six hundred and fifty years. It was at one of these epochs that the prediction was made, and at no other time for six centuries could the prediction of the one planet have revealed the

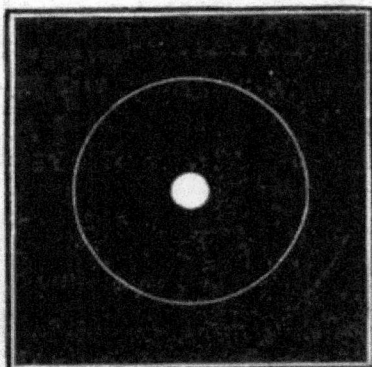

Fig. 304.

other. The observed planet was not the predicted one."

282. *Bode's Law Disproved.* — The following table gives the distances of the planets according to Bode's law, their actual distances, and the error of the law in each case : —

PLANET.	Numbers of Bode.	Actual Distances.	Errors.
Mercury	0 + 4 = 4	3.9	0.1
Venus	3 + 4 = 7	7.2	0.2
Earth	6 + 4 = 10	10.0	0.0
Mars.	12 + 4 = 16	15.2	0.8
Minor planets . .	24 + 4 = 28	20 to 35	
Jupiter	48 + 4 = 52	52.0	0.0
Saturn	96 + 4 = 100	95.4	4.6
Uranus	192 + 4 = 196	191.9	4.1
Neptune	384 + 4 = 388	300 6	87.4

It will be seen, that, before the discovery of Neptune, the agreement was so close as to indicate that this was an actual law of the distances ; but the discovery of this planet completely disproved its existence.

283. *The Satellite of Neptune.* — Neptune is accompanied by at least one moon, whose orbit is shown in Fig. 304. The orbit of this satellite is inclined about thirty degrees to the plane of the ecliptic, and the motion of the satellite is retrograde, or from east to west.

VII.   COMETS AND METEORS.

I.   COMETS.

GENERAL PHENOMENA OF COMETS.

284. *General Appearance of a Bright Comet.* — Comets bright enough to be seen with the naked eye are composed of three parts, which run into each other by insensible gradations. These are the *nucleus*, the *coma*, and the *tail*.

The *nucleus* is the bright centre of the comet, and appears to the eye as a star or planet.

The *coma* is a nebulous mass surrounding the nucleus on all sides. Close to the nucleus it is almost as bright as the nucleus itself; but it gradually

Fig. 305.

shades off in every direction. The nucleus and coma combined appear like a star shining through a small patch of fog; and these two together form what is called the *head* of the comet.

The *tail* is a continuation of the coma, and consists of a

stream of milky light, growing wider and fainter as it recedes from the head, till the eye is unable to trace it.

The general appearance of one of the smaller of the brilliant comets is shown in Fig. 305.

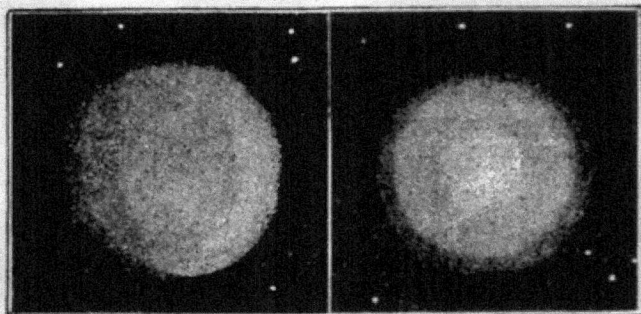

Fig. 306.

285. *General Appearance of a Telescopic Comet.* — The great majority of comets are too faint to be visible with the naked eye, and are called *telescopic* comets. In these comets there seems to be a development of coma at the expense of nucleus and tail. In some cases the telescope fails to reveal any nucleus at all in one of these comets; at other times the nucleus is so faint and ill-defined as to be barely distinguishable. Fig. 306 shows a telescopic comet without any nucleus at all, and

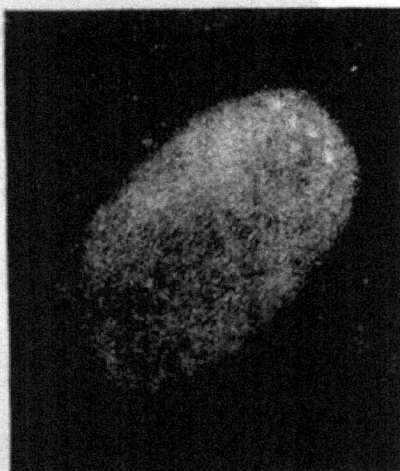

Fig. 307.

another with a slight condensation at the centre. In these comets it is generally impossible to distinguish the coma from the tail, the latter being either entirely invisible, as in

Fig. 306, or else only an elongation of the coma, as shown

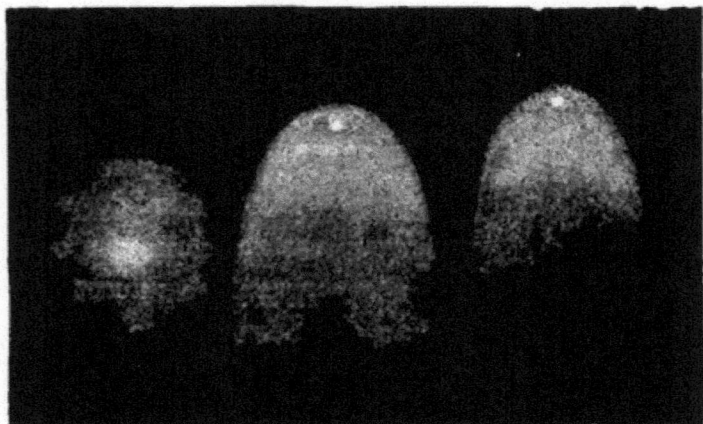

Fig. 308.

in Fig. 307. Many comets appear simply as patches of

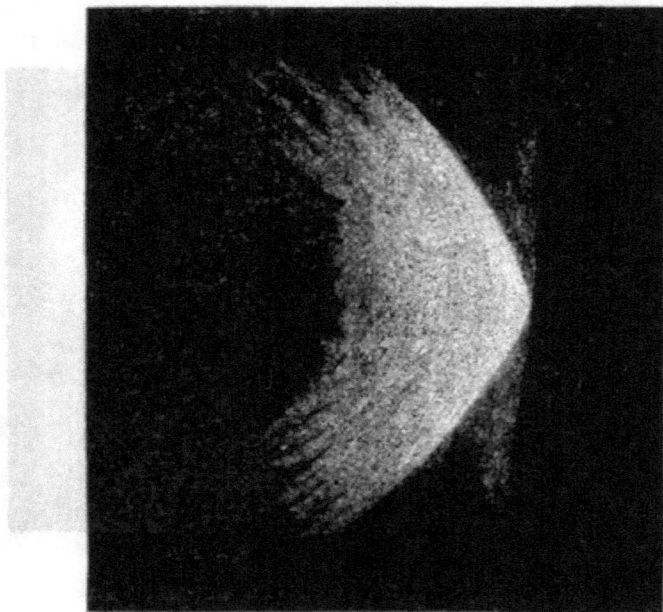

Fig. 309.

foggy light of more or less irregular form.

286. *The Development of Telescopic Comets on their Approach to the Sun.* — As a rule, all comets look nearly alike when they first come within the reach of the telescope. They appear at first as little foggy patches, without any tail, and often without any visible nucleus. As they approach the sun their peculiarities are rapidly developed. Fig. 308 shows such a comet as first seen, and the gradual development of its nucleus, head, and tail, as it approaches the sun.

If the comet is only a small one, the tail developed

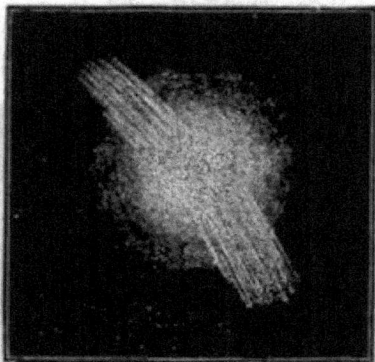

Fig. 310.

is small; but these small appendages have a great variety of form in different comets. Fig. 309 shows the singular form into which *Encke's* comet was developed in 1871.

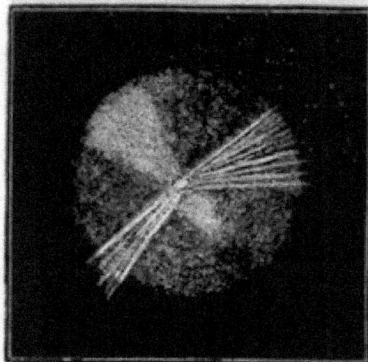

Fig. 311.

Figs. 310 and 311 show other peculiar developments of telescopic comets.

287. *Development of Brilliant Comets on their Approach to the Sun.* — Brilliant comets, as well as telescopic comets, appear nearly alike when they come into the view of the telescope; and it is only on their approach to the sun that their distinctive features are developed. Not only do these comets, when they first come into view, resemble each other, but they also bear a close resemblance to telescopic comets.

As the comet approaches the sun, bright vaporous jets,
two or three in number, are emitted from the nucleus on
the side of the sun and in the direction of the sun.   These
jets, though directed towards the sun, are soon more or less
carried backward, as if repelled by the sun.   Fig. 312
shows a succession of views of these jets as they were
developed in the case of *Halley's* comet in 1835.

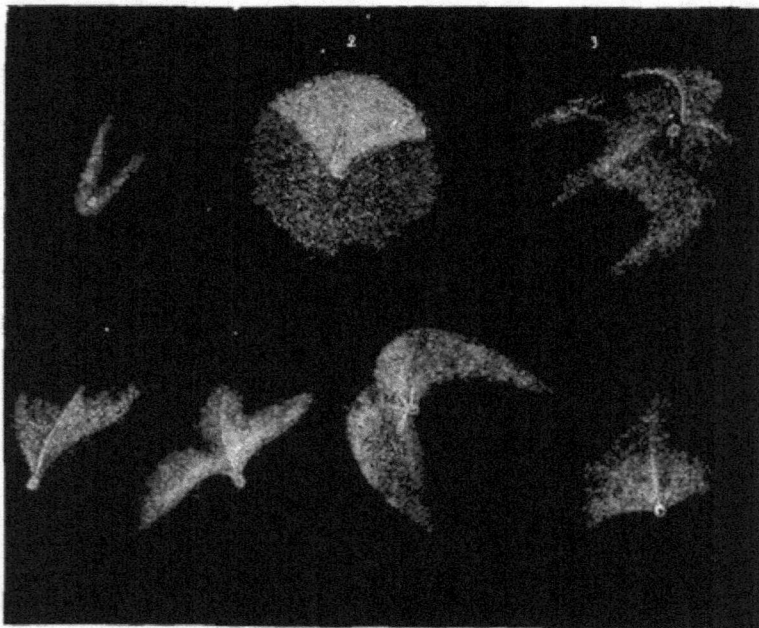

Fig. 312.

The jets in this case seemed to have an oscillatory motion.
At 1 and 2 they seemed to be attracted towards the sun,
and in 3 to be repelled by him.   In 4 and 5 they seemed
to be again attracted, and in 6 to be repelled, but in a
reverse direction to that in 3.   In 7 they appeared to be
again attracted.   Bessel likened this oscillation of the jets
to the vibration of a magnetic needle when presented to
the pole of a magnet.

In the case of larger comets these luminous jets are surrounded by one or more envelops, which are thrown off in succession as the comet approaches the sun. The formation of these envelops was a conspicuous feature of *Donati's* comet of 1858. A rough view of the jets and the surrounding envelops is given in Fig. 313. Fig. 314 gives a view of the envelops without the jets.

288. *The Tails of Comets.* — The *tails* of brilliant comets are rapidly formed as the comet approaches the sun, their increase in length often being at the rate of several million miles a day. These appendages seem to be formed entirely out of the matter which is emitted from the nucleus in the luminous jets which are at first directed towards the sun. The tails of comets are, however, always directed away from the sun, as shown in Fig. 315.

It will be seen that the comet, as it approaches the sun, travels head foremost; but as it leaves the sun it goes tail foremost.

Fig. 313.

The apparent length of the tail of a comet depends partly upon its real length, partly upon the distance of the comet, and partly upon the direction of the axis of the tail with reference to the line of vision. The longer the tail, the nearer the comet; and the more nearly at right angles to the line of vision is the axis of the tail, the greater is the apparent length of the tail. In the majority of cases the tails of comets measure only a few degrees; but, in the case of many comets recorded in history, the tail has extended half way across the heavens.

The tail of a comet, when seen at all, is usually several million miles in length; and in some instances the tail is long enough to reach across the orbit of the earth, or twice as far as from the earth to the sun.

The tails of comets are apparently hollow, and are sometimes a million of miles in diameter. So great, however, is the tenuity of the matter in them, that the faintest stars

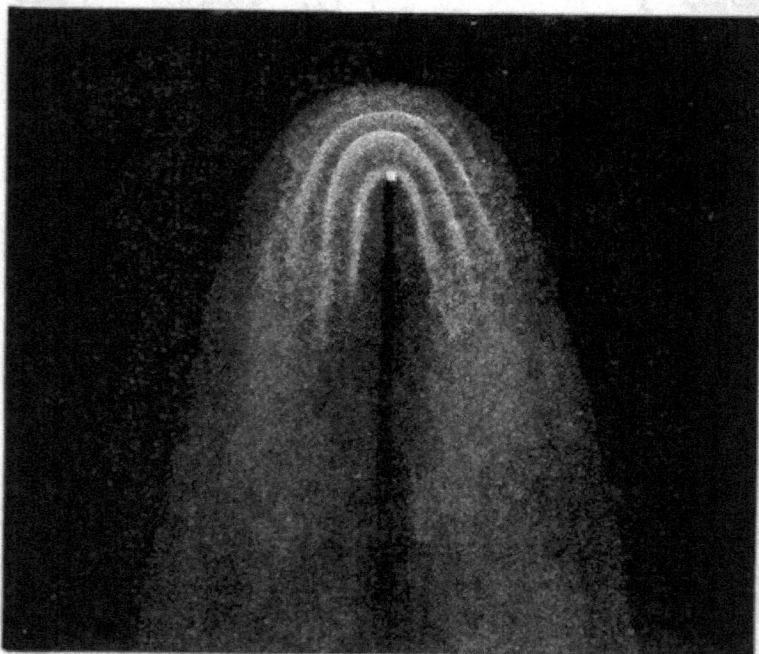

Fig. 314.

are seen through it without any apparent obscuration. See Fig. 316, which is a view of the great comet of 1264.

The tails of comets are sometimes straight, as in Fig. 316, but usually more or less curved, as in Fig. 317, which is a view of *Donati's* comet as it appeared at one time. The tail of a comet is occasionally divided into a number of streamers, as in Figs. 318 and 319. Fig. 318 is a view of the great comet of 1744, and Fig. 319 of the great comet of 1861. No. 1, in Fig. 320, is a view of the comet of 1577; No. 2, of the comet of 1680; and No. 3, of the comet of 1769.

Fig. 321 shows some of the forms which the imagination of a superstitious age saw depicted in comets, when these heavenly visitants were thought to be the forerunners of wars, pestilence, famine, and other dire calamities.

289. *Visibility of Comets.* — Even the brightest comets are visible only a short time near their perihelion passage. When near the sun, they sometimes become very brilliant, and on rare occasions have been visible even at mid-day. It is seldom that a comet can be seen, even with a powerful telescope, during its perihelion passage, unless its perihelion is either inside of the earth's orbit, or but little outside of it.

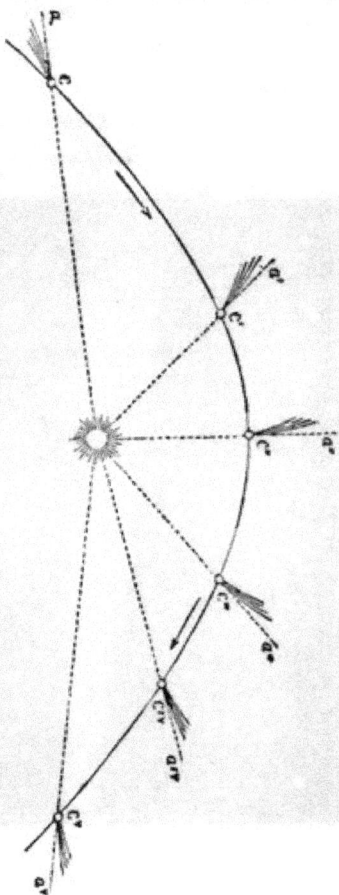

Fig. 315.

MOTION AND ORIGIN OF COMETS.

290. *Recognition of a Telescopic Comet.* — It is impossible to distinguish telescopic comets by their appearance from another class of heavenly bodies known as *nebulæ*. Such comets can be recognized only by their motion.

Thus, in Fig. 322, the upper and lower bodies look exactly alike ; but the upper one is found to remain stationary, while the lower one moves across the field of view. The upper one is thus shown to be a nebula, and the lower one a comet.

291. *Orbits of Comets.* — All comets are found to move in *very eccentric ellipses,* in *parabolas,* or in *hyperbolas.*

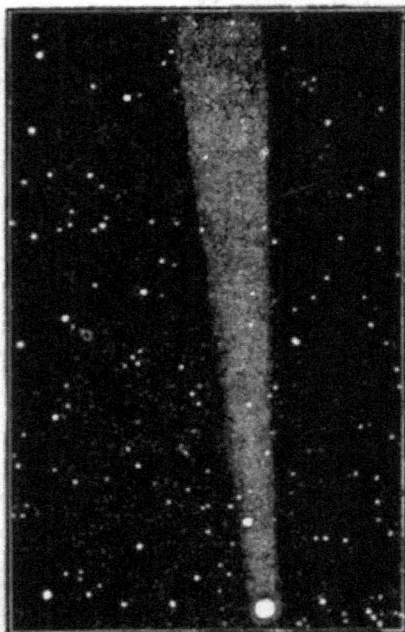

Fig. 316.

Since an ellipse is a *closed* curve (48), all comets that move in ellipses, no matter how eccentric, are permanent members of the solar system, and will return to the sun at intervals of greater or less length, according to the size of the ellipses and the rate of the comet's motion.

Parabolas and hyperbolas being *open* curves (48), comets that move in either of these orbits are only temporary members of our solar system. After passing the sun, they move off into space, never to return, unless deflected hither by the action of some heavenly body which they pass in their journey.

Since a comet is visible only while it is near the sun, it is impossible to tell, by the form of the portion of the orbit which it describes during the period of its visibility, whether it is a part of a very elongated ellipse, a parabola, or a hyperbola. Thus in Fig. 323 are shown two orbits, one of which is a very elongated ellipse, and the other a parabola. The

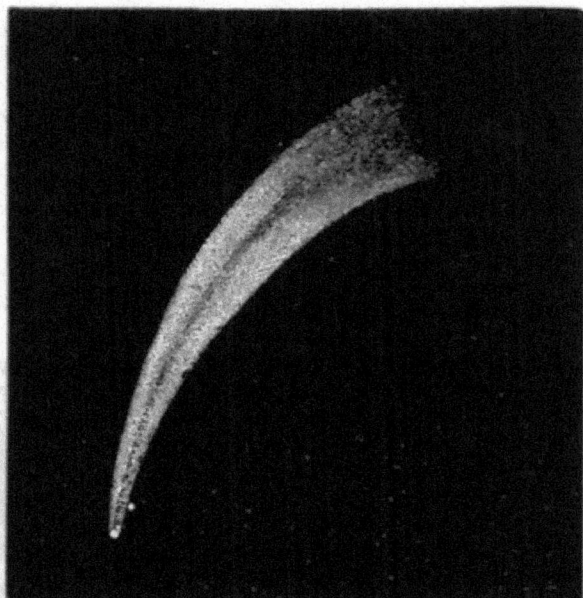

Fig. 317.

part *ab*, in each case, is the portion of the orbit described by the comet during its visibility. While describing the dotted

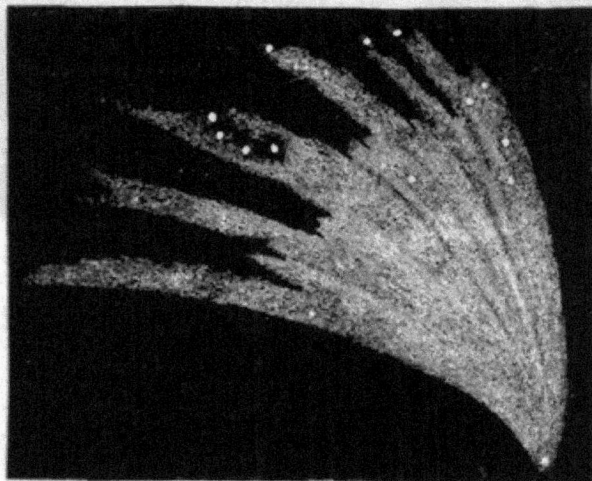

Fig. 318.

portions of the orbit, the comet is invisible. Now it is impossible to distinguish the form of the visible portion in the two orbits. The same would be true were one of the orbits a hyperbola.

Whether a comet will describe an ellipse, a parabola, or a hyperbola, can be determined only by its *velocity*, taken in connection with its *distance from the sun*. Were a comet ninety-two and a half million miles from the sun, moving away from the sun at the rate of twenty-six miles a second, it would have just the velocity necessary to describe a *parabola*. Were it moving with a greater velocity, it would necessarily describe

Fig. 319.

a *hyperbola*, and, with a less velocity, an *ellipse*. So, at any distance from the sun, there is a certain velocity which would cause a comet to describe a parabola; while a greater velocity would cause it to describe a hyperbola, and a less velocity to describe an ellipse. If the comet is moving in an ellipse, the less its velocity, the less the eccentricity of its orbit: hence, in order to determine the form of the orbit of any comet, it is only necessary to ascertain its distance from the sun, and its velocity at any given time.

Fig. 320.

Comets move in every direction in their orbits, and these orbits have every conceivable inclination to the ecliptic.

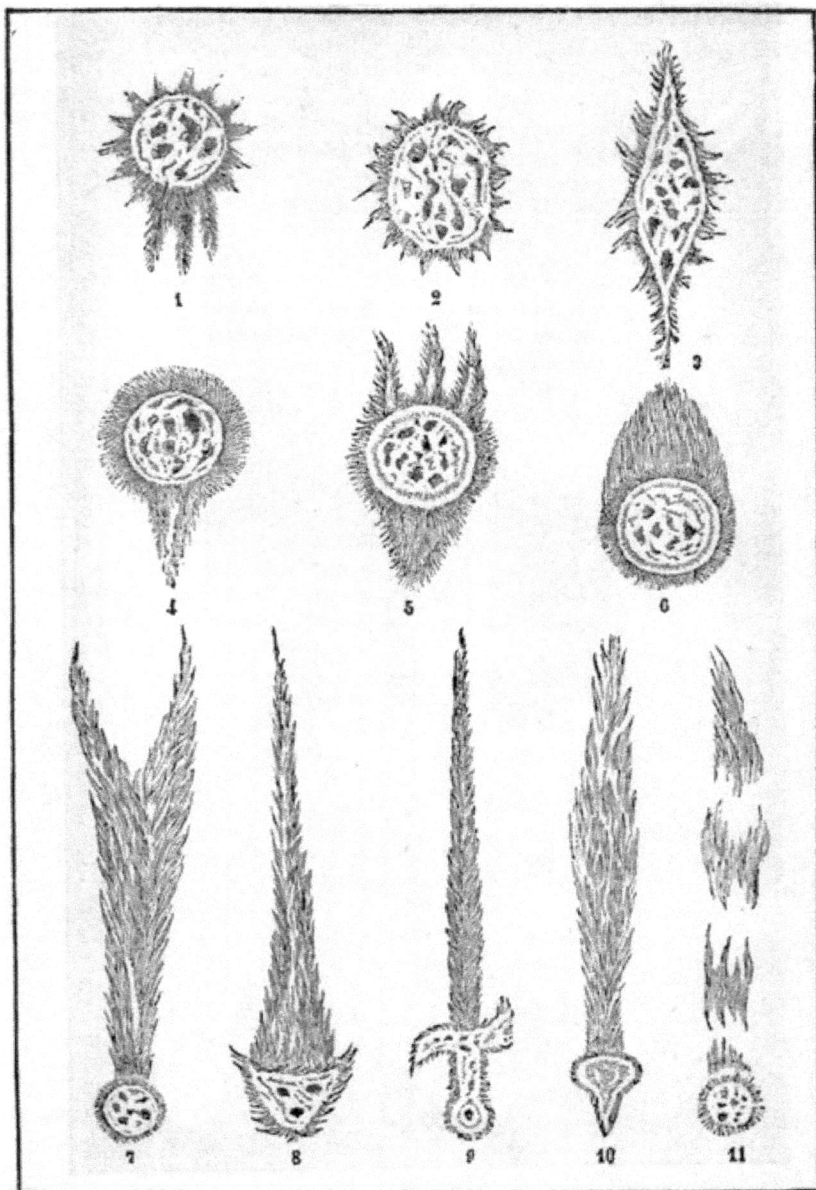

Fig. 321.

292. *Periodic Comets.* — There are quite a number of

comets which are known to be *periodic*, returning to the
sun at regular intervals in elliptic orbits. Some of these
have been observed at sev-
eral returns, so that their
period has been determined
with great certainty. In the
case of others the perio-
dicity is inferred from the
fact that the velocity fell
so far short of the parabolic
limit that the comet must
move in an ellipse. The
number of known periodic
comets is increasing every

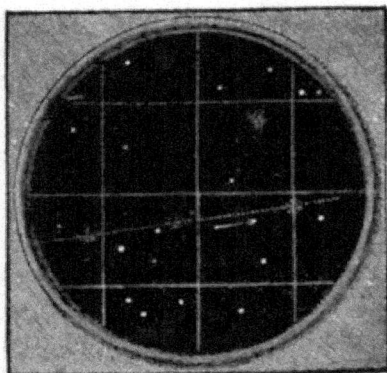

Fig. 322.

year, three having been added to the list in 1881.

The velocity of most comets is so near the parabolic limit
that it is not possible to decide, from observations, whether it
falls short of it, or exceeds it. In the case of a few comets
the observations indi-
cate a minute excess of
velocity: but this cannot
be confidently asserted.
It is not, therefore, abso-
lutely certain that any
known comet revolves
in a hyperbolic orbit;
and thus it is possible
that all comets belong
to our system, and will
ultimately return to it.
It is, however, certain,
that, in the majority of
cases, the return will be
delayed for many cen-

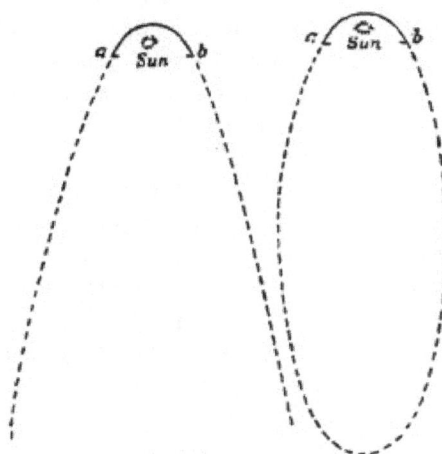

Fig. 323.

turies, and perhaps for many thousand years.

293. *Origin of Comets.* — It is now generally believed that
the original home of the comets is in the stellar spaces outside

of our solar system, and that they are drawn towards the sun, one by one, in the long lapse of ages. Were the sun unaccompanied by planets, or were the planets immovable, a comet thus drawn in would whirl around the sun in a parabolic orbit, and leave it again never to return, unless its path were again deflected by its approach to some star. But, when a comet is moving in a parabola, the slightest *retardation* would change its orbit to an ellipse, and the slightest *acceleration* into a hyperbola. Owing to the motion of the several planets in their orbits, the velocity of a comet would be changed on passing each of them. Whether its velocity would be accelerated or retarded, would depend upon the way in which it passed. Were the comet accelerated by the action of the planets, on its passage through our system, more than it was retarded by them, it would leave the system with a more than parabolic orbit, and would therefore move in a hyperbola. Were it, on the contrary, retarded more than accelerated by the action of the planets, its velocity would be reduced, so that the comet would move in a more or less elongated ellipse, and thus become a permanent member of the solar system.

In the majority of cases the retardation would be so slight that it could not be detected by the most delicate observation, and the comet would return to the sun only after the expiration of tens or hundreds of thousands of years; but, were the comet to pass very near one of the larger planets, the retardation might be sufficient to cause the comet to revolve in an elliptical orbit of quite a short period. The orbit of a comet thus captured by a planet would have its aphelion point near the orbit of the planet which captured it. Now, it happens that each of the larger planets has a family of comets whose aphelia are about its own distance from the sun. It is therefore probable that these comets have been captured by the action of these planets. As might be expected from the gigantic size of Jupiter, the Jovian family of comets is the largest. The orbits of several of the comets of this group are shown in Fig. 324.

294. *Number of Comets.* — The number of comets recorded as visible to the naked eye since the birth of Christ

is about five hundred, while about two hundred telescopic comets have been observed since the invention of the telescope. The total number of comets observed since the Christian era is therefore about seven hundred. It is certain, however, that only an insignificant fraction of all existing comets have ever been observed. Since they can be

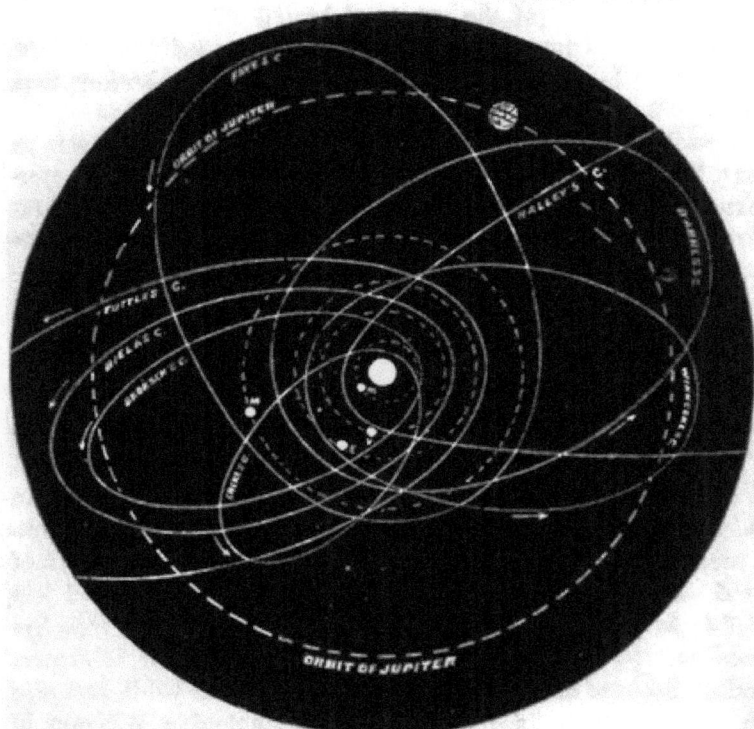

Fig. 324.

seen only when near their perihelion, and since it is probable that the period of most of those which have been observed is reckoned by thousands of years (if, indeed, they ever return at all), our observations must be continued for many thousand years before we have seen all which come within range of our telescopes. Besides, as already stated (289), a comet can seldom be seen unless its perihelion is either

inside the orbit of the earth, or but little outside of it; and
it is probable that the perihelia of the great majority of
comets are beyond this limit of visibility.

REMARKABLE COMETS.

295. *The Comet of 1680.* — The great comet of 1680, shown
in Fig. 320, is one of the most celebrated on record. It was
by his study of its motions that Newton proved the orbit of
a comet to be one of the conic sections, and therefore that
these bodies move under the influence of gravity. This comet
descended almost in a direct line to the sun, passing nearer to
that luminary than any comet before known. Newton estimated, that, at its perihelion point, it was exposed to a temperature two thousand times that of red-hot iron. During its
perihelion passage it was exceedingly brilliant. Halley suspected that this comet had a period of five hundred and
seventy-five years, and that its first recorded appearance was
in 43 B.C., its third in 1106, and its fourth in 1680. If this is
its real period, it will return in 2255. The comet of 43 B.C.
made its appearance just after the assassination of Julius
Cæsar. The Romans called it the *Julian Star*, and regarded
it as a celestial chariot sent to convey the soul of Cæsar to the
skies. It was seen two or three hours before sunset, and continued visible for eight successive days. The great comet of
1106 was described as an object of terrific splendor, and was
visible in close proximity to the sun. The comet of 1680 has
become celebrated, not only on account of its great brilliance,
and on account of Newton's investigation of its orbit, but also
on account of the speculation of the theologian Whiston in
regard to it. He accepted five hundred and seventy-five years
as its period, and calculated that one of its earlier apparitions
must have occurred at the date of the flood, which he supposed
to have been caused by its near approach to the earth; and he
imagined that the earth is doomed to be destroyed by fire on
some future encounter with this comet.

296. *The Comet of 1811.* — The great comet of 1811, a view
of which is given in Fig. 325, is, perhaps, the most remarkable
comet on record. It was visible for nearly seventeen months,

and was very brilliant, although at its perihelion passage it was over a hundred million miles from the sun. Its tail was a hundred and twenty million miles in length, and several million miles through. It has been calculated that its aphelion point is about two hundred times as far from the sun as its perihelion point, or some seven times the distance of Neptune from the sun. Its period is estimated at about three thousand years. It was an object of superstitious terror, especially in the East. The Russians regarded it as presaging Napoleon's great and fatal war with Russia.

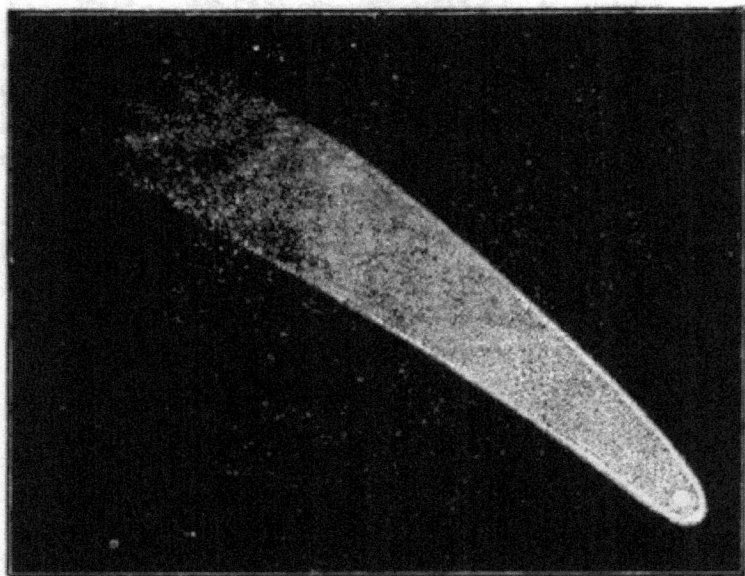

Fig. 325.

297. *Halley's Comet.* — Halley's comet has become one of the most celebrated of modern times. It is the first comet whose return was both predicted and observed. It made its appearance in 1682. Halley computed its orbit, and compared it with those of previous comets, whose orbits he also computed from recorded observations. He found that it coincided so exactly with that of the comet observed by Kepler in 1607, that there could be no doubt of the identity of the two orbits. So close were they together, that, were they both drawn in the

heavens, the naked eye would almost see them joined into one line. There could therefore be no doubt that the comet of 1682 was the same that had appeared in 1607. and that it moved in an elliptic orbit, with a period of about seventy-five years.

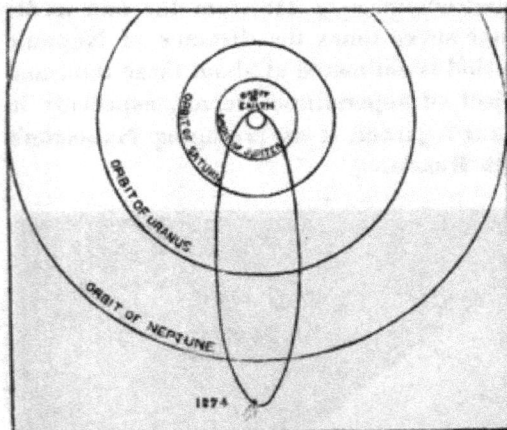

Fig. 326.

He found that this comet had previously appeared in 1531 and in 1456; and he predicted that it would return about 1758. Its actual return was retarded somewhat by the action of the planets on it in its passage through the solar system. It, however, appeared again in 1759, and a third time in 1835. Its next appearance will be about 1911. The orbit of this comet is shown in Fig. 326. Fig. 327 shows the comet as it appeared to the naked eye, and

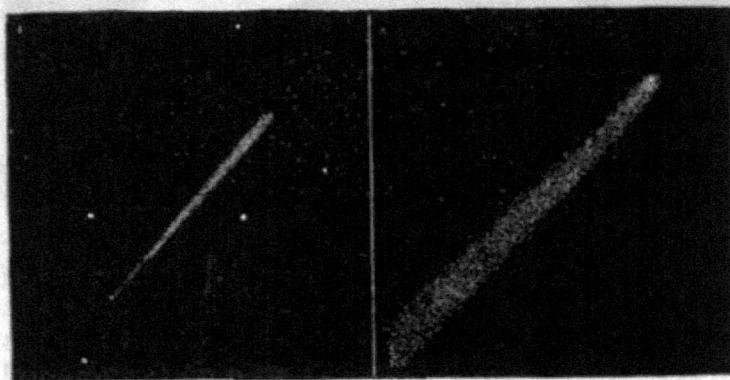

Fig. 327.

in a telescope of moderate power, in 1835. This comet appears to be growing less brilliant. In 1456 it appeared as a comet of great splendor; and coming as it did in a very superstitious age, soon after the fall of Constantinople. and during the threatened invasion of Europe by the Turks, it caused great alarm. Fig. 328 shows the changes undergone by the nucleus of this comet during its perihelion passage in 1835.

298. *Encke's Comet.* — This telescopic comet, two views of which are given in Figs. 329 and 330, appeared in 1818. Encke computed its orbit, and found it to lie wholly within the orbit of Jupiter (Fig. 324), and the period to be about three years and a third. By comparing the intervals between the succes-

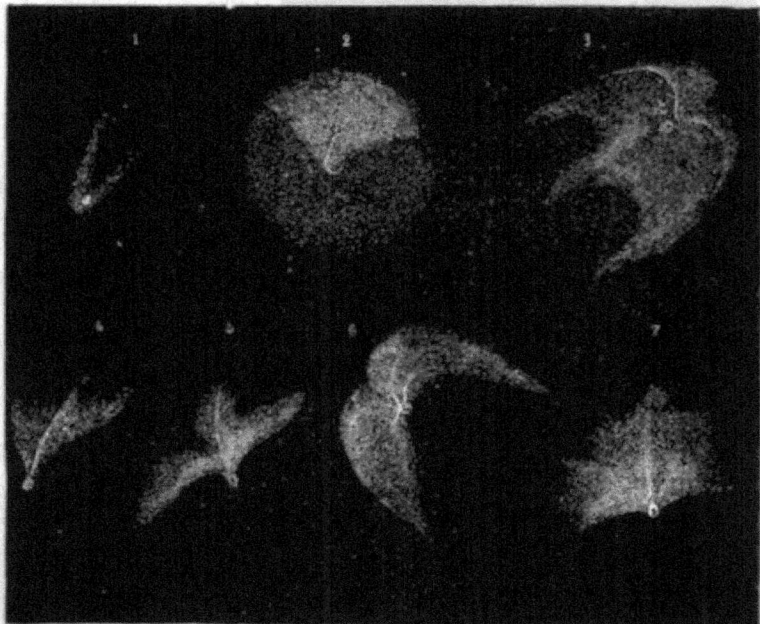

Fig. 328.

sive returns of this comet, it has been ascertained that its orbit is continually growing smaller and smaller. To account for the retardation of this comet, Olbers announced his cele-
'brated hypothesis, that the celestial spaces are filled with a subtile *resisting medium*. This hypothesis was adopted by Encke, and has been accepted by certain other astronomers; but it has by no means gained universal assent.

299. *Biela's Comet.* — This comet appeared in 1826, and was found to have a period of about six years and two thirds. On its return in 1845, it met with a singular, and as yet unex-

plained, accident, which has rendered the otherwise rather insignificant comet famous. In November and December of that year it was observed as usual, without any thing remarka-

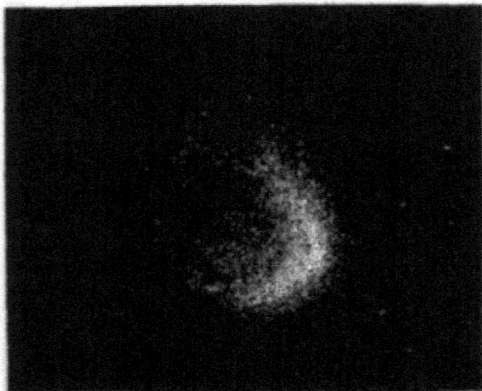

Fig. 329.

ble about it; but, in January of the following year, it was found to have been divided into two distinct parts, so as to appear as two comets instead of one. The two parts were at first of very unequal brightness; but, during the following month, the smaller of the two increased in brilliancy until it equalled its companion; it then grew fainter till it entirely disappeared, a month before its companion. The two parts were about two hundred thousand miles apart.

Fig. 331 shows these two parts as they appeared on the 19th of February, and Fig. 332 as they appeared on the 21st of February. On its return in 1852, the comets were found still to be double; but the two components were now about a million and a half miles apart. They are shown in Fig. 333 as they appeared at

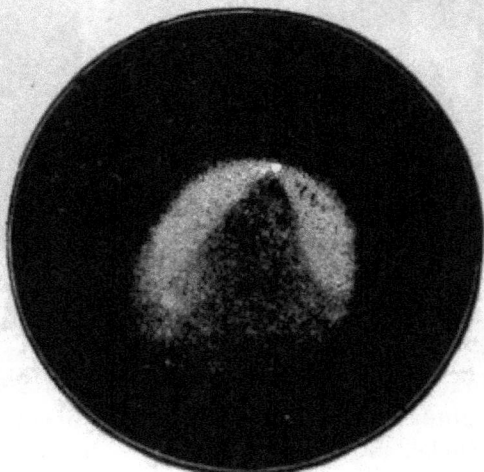

Fig. 330.

this time. Sometimes one of the parts appeared the brighter, and sometimes the other; so that it was impossible to decide which was really the principal comet. The two portions passed out of view in September, and have not been seen since; although in 1872 the position of the comet would have been especially favorable for observation. The comet appears to have become completely broken up.

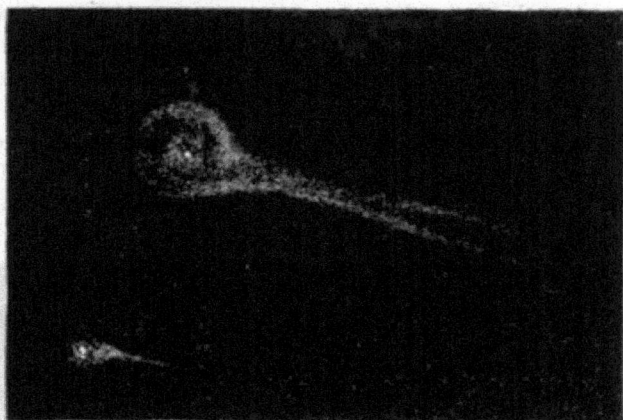

Fig. 331.

300. *The Comet of 1843.* — The great comet of 1843, a view of which is given in Fig. 334, was favorably situated for observation only in southern latitudes. It was exceedingly brilliant,

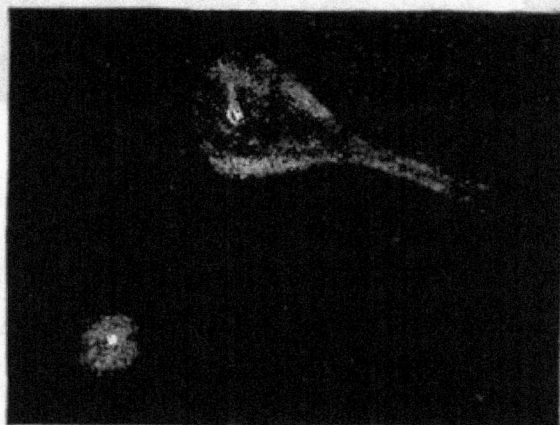

Fig. 332.

and was easily seen in full daylight, in close proximity to the sun. The apparent length of its tail was sixty-five degrees, and its real length a hundred and fifty million miles, or nearly

twice the distance from the earth to the sun.   This comet is
especially remarkable on account of its near approach to the
sun.   At the time of its perihelion passage the distance of
the comet from the photosphere of the sun was less than
one-fourteenth of the diameter of the sun.   This distance was
only one-half that of the comet of 1680 when at its perihelion.
When at perihelion, this comet was plunging through the sun's
outer atmosphere at the rate of one million, two hundred and
eighty thousand miles an hour.   It passed half way round the
sun in the space of *two hours*, and its tail was whirled round
through a hundred and eighty degrees in that brief time.   As

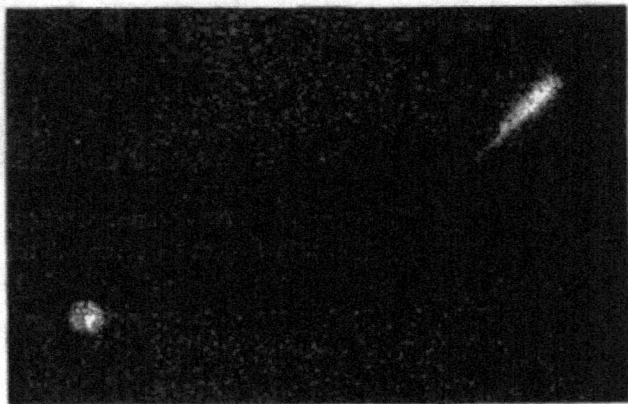

Fig. 333.

the tail extended almost double the earth's distance from the
sun, the end of the tail must have traversed in two hours a
space nearly equal to the circumference of the earth's orbit, —
a distance which the earth, moving at the rate of about twenty
miles a second, is *a whole year* in passing.   It is almost impossible to suppose that the matter forming this tail remained the
same throughout this tremendous sweep.

301. *Donati's Comet.* — The great comet of 1858, known as
Donati's comet, was one of the most magnificent of modern
times.   When at its brightest it was only about fifty million
miles from the earth.   Its tail was then more than fifty million miles long.   Had the comet at this time been directly
between the earth and sun, the earth must have passed through

its tail; but this did not occur. The orbit of this comet was found to be decidedly elliptic, with a period of about two thou· sand years. This comet is especially celebrated on account of the careful telescopic observations of its nucleus and coma at the time of its perihelion passage. Attention has already been called (287) to the changes it underwent at that time. Its tail was curved, and of a curious feather-like form, as shown in Fig. 335. At times it developed lateral streamers, as shown in Fig. 336. Fig. 337 shows the head of the comet as it was seen by Bond of the Harvard Observatory, whose delineations of this comet have been justly celebrated.

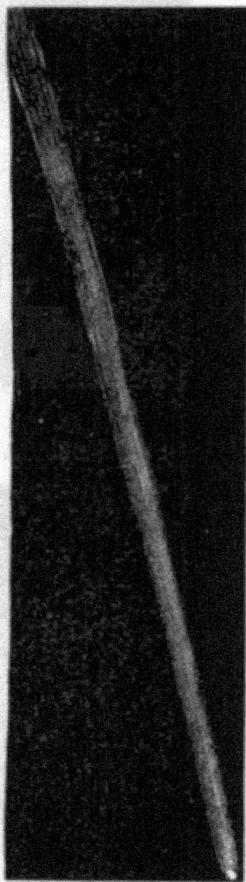

Fig. 334.

302. *The Comet of 1861.* — The great comet of 1861 is remarkable for its great brilliancy, for its peculiar fan-shaped tail. and for the probable passage of the earth through its tail. Sir John Herschel declared that it far exceeded in brilliancy any comet he had ever seen, not excepting those of 1811 and 1858. Secchi found its tail to be a hundred and eighteen degrees in length. the largest but one on record. Fig. 338 shows this comet as it appeared at one time. Fig. 339 shows the position of the earth at *E*. in the tail of this comet, on the 30th of June, 1861. Fig. 340 shows the probable passage of the earth through the tail of the comet on that date. As the tail of a comet doubtless consists of something much less dense than our atmosphere, it is not surprising that no noticeable effect was produced upon us by the encounter, if it occurred.

303. *Coggia's Comet.* — This comet, which appeared in 1874, looked very large, because it came very near the earth. It was

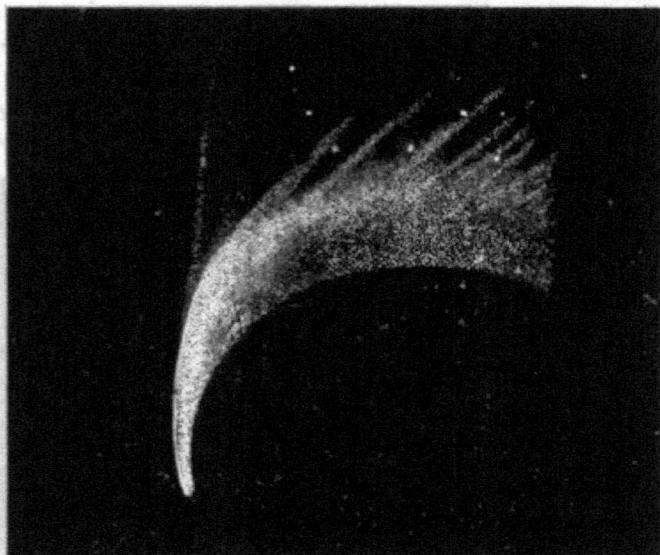

Fig. 335.

not at all brilliant. Its nucleus was carefully studied, and was

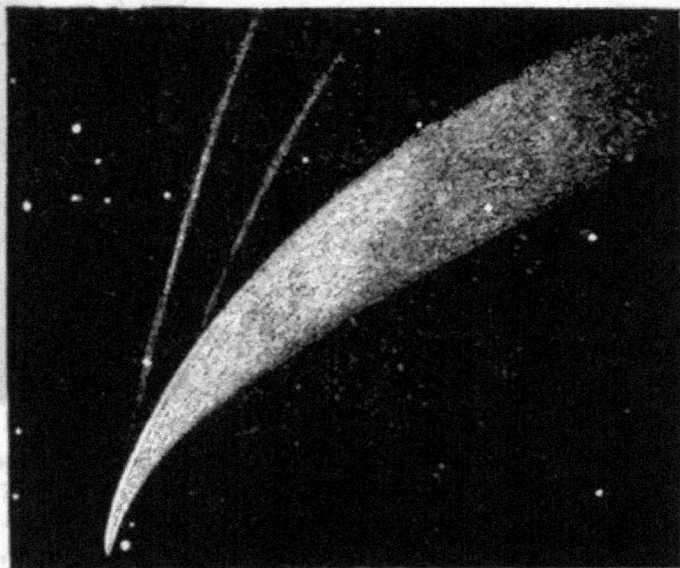

Fig. 336.

found to develop a series of envelops similar to those of
Donati's comet. Figs. 341 and 342 are two views of the head

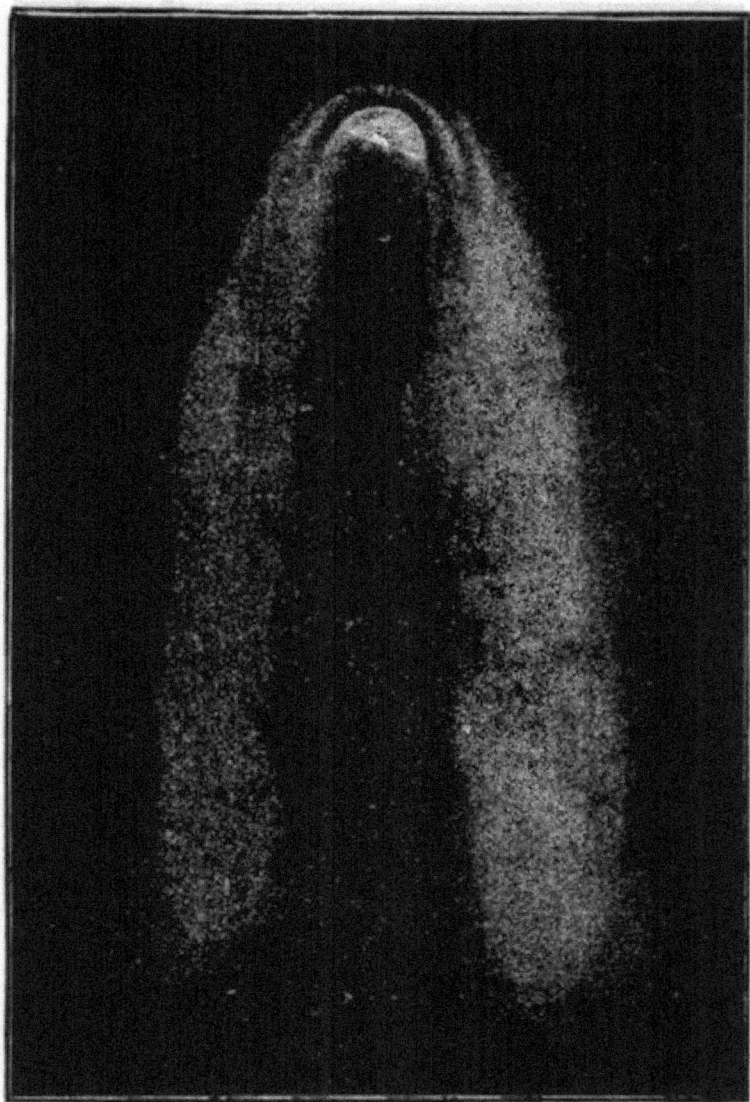

Fig. 337.

of this comet. Fig. 343 shows the system of envelops that
were developed during its perihelion passage.

304. *The Comet of June, 1881.* — This comet, though far from being one of the largest of modern times, was still very

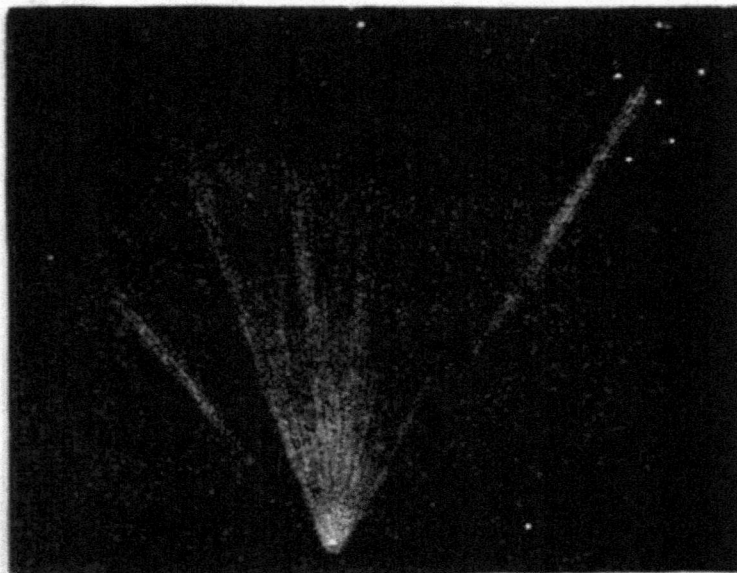

Fig. 338.

brilliant. It will ever be memorable as the first brilliant comet which has admitted of careful examination with the spectroscope.

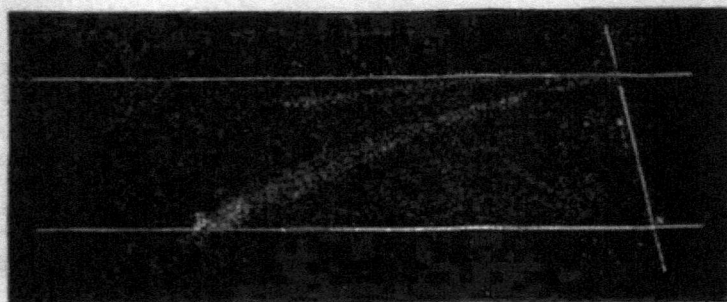

Fig. 339.

CONNECTION BETWEEN METEORS AND COMETS.

305. *Shooting-Stars.* — On watching the heavens any clear night, we frequently see an appearance as of a star

shooting rapidly through a short space in the sky, and then suddenly disappearing. Three or four such *shooting-stars* may, on the average, be observed in the course of an hour. They are usually seen only a second or two ; but they sometimes move slowly, and are visible much longer. These stars begin to be visible at an average height of about seventy-five miles, and they disappear at an average height of about fifty miles. They are occasionally seen as high as a hundred and fifty miles, and continue to be visible till within thirty miles of the earth. Their visible paths

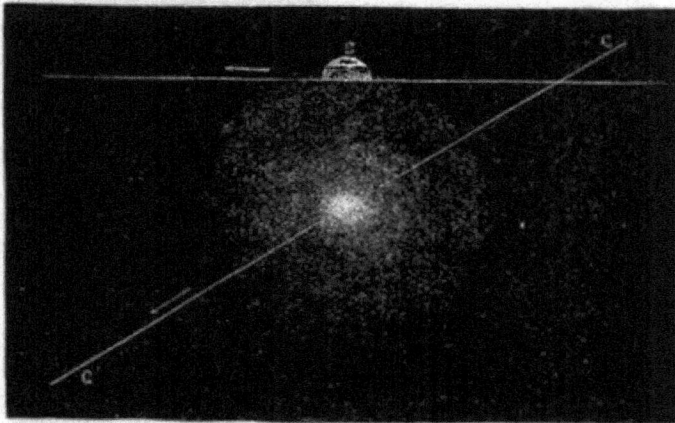

Fig. 340.

vary from ten to a hundred miles in length, though they are occasionally two hundred or three hundred miles long. Their average velocity, relatively to the earth's surface, varies from ten to forty-five miles a second.

The average number of shooting-stars visible to the naked eye at any one place is estimated at about *a thousand an hour;* and the average number large enough to be visible to the naked eye, that traverse the atmosphere daily, is estimated at *over eight millions.* The number of telescopic shooting-stars would of course be much greater.

Occasionally, shooting-stars leave behind them a trail of

light which lasts for several seconds. These trails are sometimes straight, as shown in Fig. 344, and sometimes curved,
as in Figs. 345 and 346. They often disappear like trails
of smoke, as shown in Fig. 347.

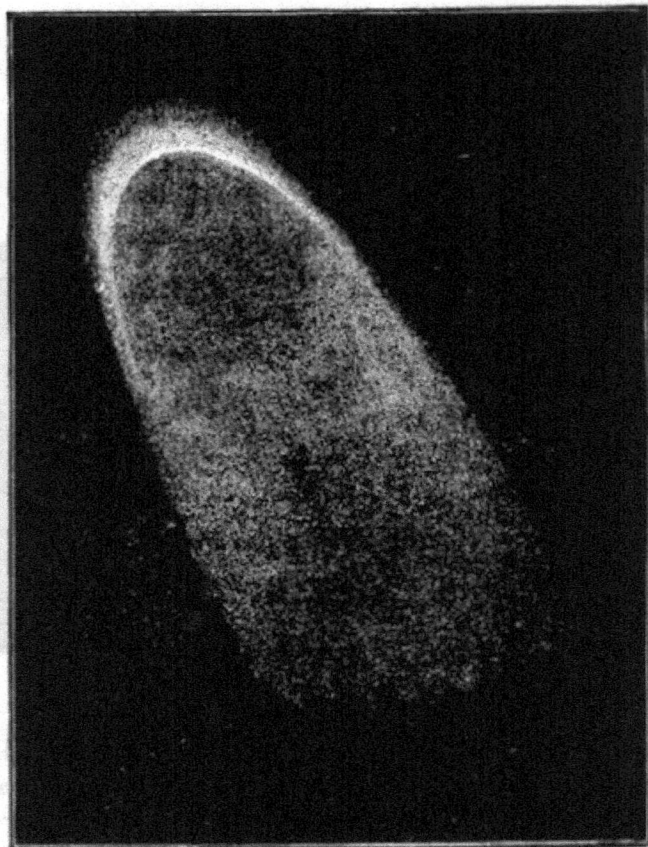

Fig. 341.

Shooting-stars are seen to move in all directions through
the heavens. Their apparent paths are, however, generally
inclined downward, though sometimes upward; and after
midnight they come in the greatest numbers from that
quarter of the heavens toward which the earth is moving
in its journey around the sun.

306. *Meteors.* — Occasionally these bodies are brilliant enough to illuminate the whole heavens. They are then called *meteors*, although this term is equally applicable

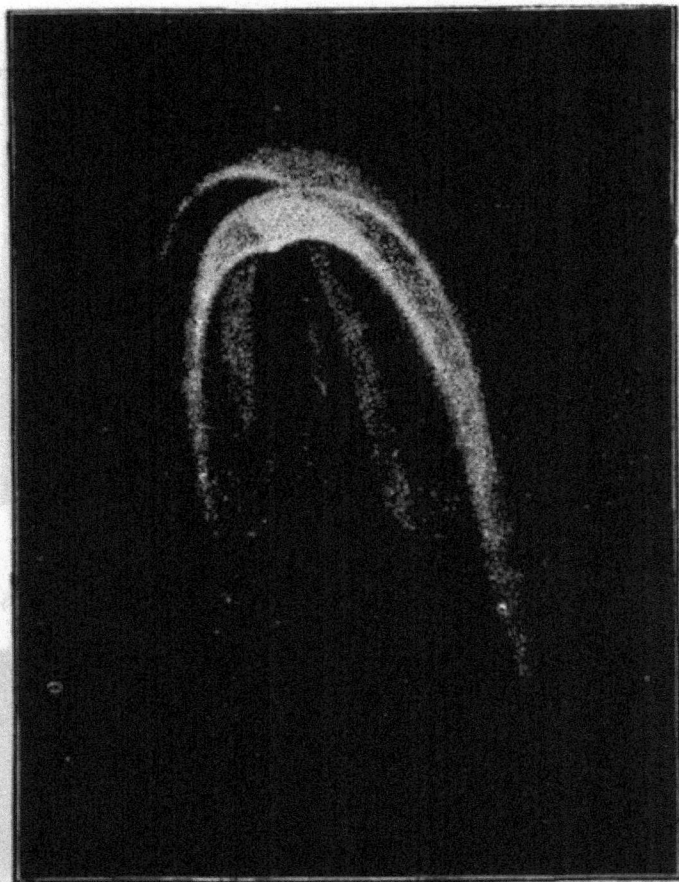

Fig. 342.

to ordinary shooting-stars. Such a meteor is shown in Fig. 348.

Sometimes these brilliant meteors are seen to explode, as shown in Fig. 349; and the explosion is accompanied with a loud detonation, like the discharge of cannon.

Ordinary shooting-stars are not accompanied by any

audible sound, though they are sometimes seen to break in pieces. Meteors which explode with an audible sound are called *detonating meteors*.

Fig. 343.

307. *Aerolites.* — There is no certain evidence that any deposit from ordinary shooting-stars ever reaches the sur-

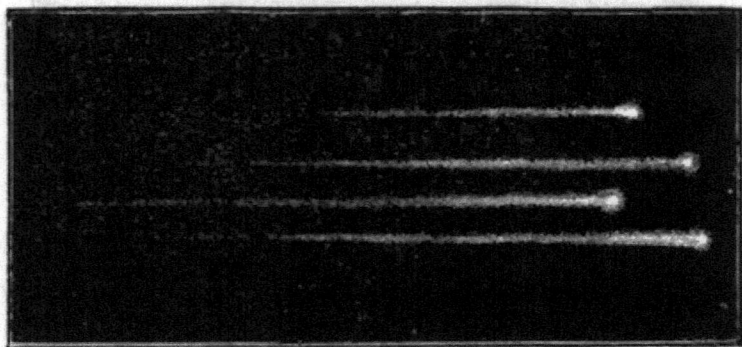

Fig. 344.

face of the earth; though a peculiar dust has been found in certain localities, which has been supposed to be of meteoric origin, and which has been called *meteoric dust*.

But solid bodies occasionally descend to the earth from beyond our atmosphere. These generally penetrate a foot or more into the earth, and, if picked up soon after their fall, are found to be warm, and sometimes even hot. These

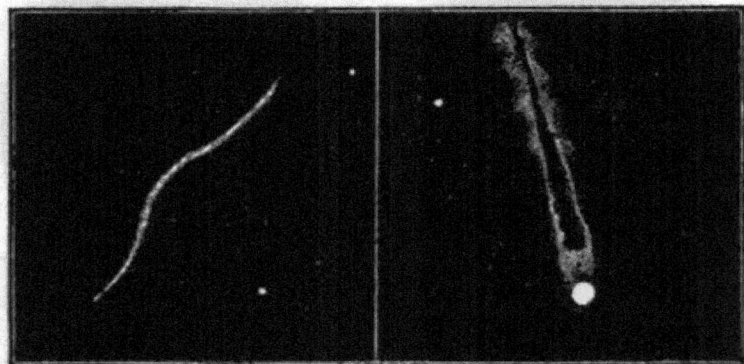

Fig. 345.

bodies are called *aerolites*. When they have a stony appearance, and contain but little iron, they are called *meteoric stones;* when they have a metallic appearance, and are composed largely of iron, they are called *meteoric iron.*

There are eighteen well-authenticated cases in which aerolites have fallen in the United States during the last sixty

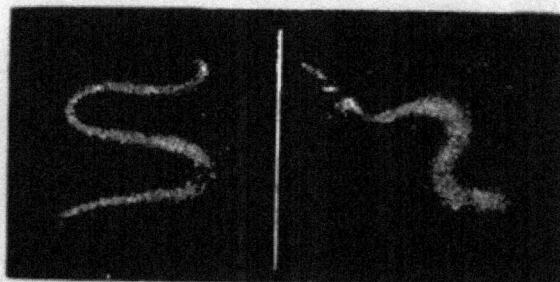

Fig. 346.

years, and their aggregate weight is twelve hundred and fifty pounds. The entire number of known aerolites the date of whose fall is well determined is two hundred and sixty-one. There are also on record seventy-four cases of which the date

is more or less uncertain.   There have also been found eighty-
six masses, which, from their peculiar composition, are believed
to be aerolites, though their fall was not seen.   The weight

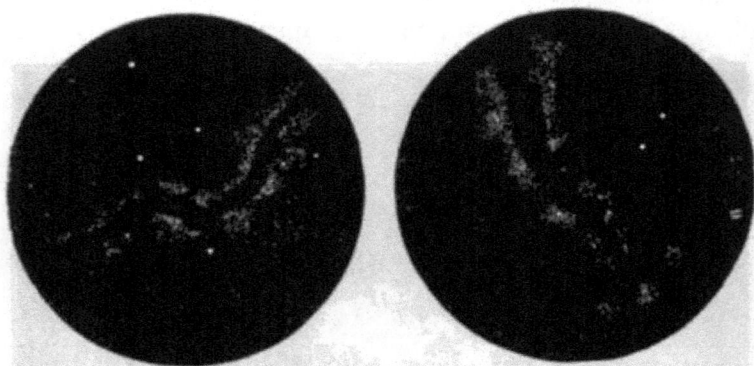

Fig. 347.

of these masses varies from a few pounds to several tons.
The entire number of aerolites of which we have any knowledge is therefore about four hundred and twenty.

Fig. 348.

Aerolites are composed of the same elementary substances
as occur in terrestrial minerals, not a single new element
having been found in their analysis.   Of the sixty or more

elements now recognized by chemists, about twenty have been found in aerolites.

While aerolites contain no new elements, their appearance is quite peculiar; and the compounds found in them are so

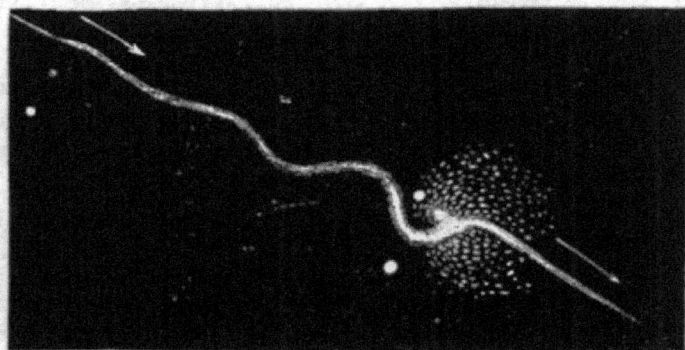

Fig. 349.

peculiar as to enable us by chemical analysis to distinguish an aerolite from any terrestrial substance.

Iron ores are very abundant in nature, but iron in the metallic state is exceedingly rare. Now, aerolites invariably contain metallic iron, sometimes from ninety to ninety-six per cent. This iron is malleable, and may be readily worked into

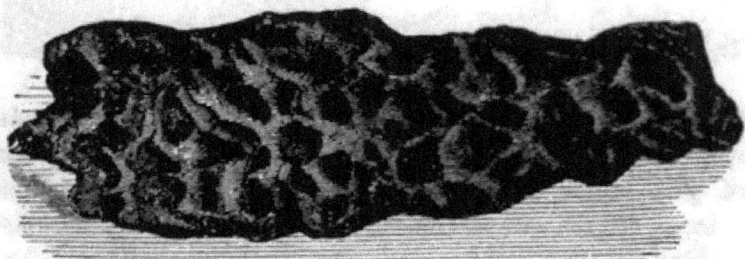

Fig. 350.

cutting instruments. It always contains eight or ten per cent of nickel, together with small quantities of cobalt, copper, tin, and chromium. This composition *has never been found in any terrestrial mineral.* Aerolites also contain, usually in small amount, a compound of iron, nickel, and phosphorus, which has never been found elsewhere.

Meteorites often present the appearance of having been fused on the surface to a slight depth, and meteoric iron is found to have a peculiar crystalline structure. The external appearance of a piece of meteoric iron found near Lockport, N.Y., is shown in Fig. 350. Fig. 351 shows the peculiar internal structure of meteoric iron.

308. *Meteoroids.* — Astronomers now universally hold that shooting-stars, meteors, and aerolites are all minute bodies, revolving, like the comets, about the sun. They

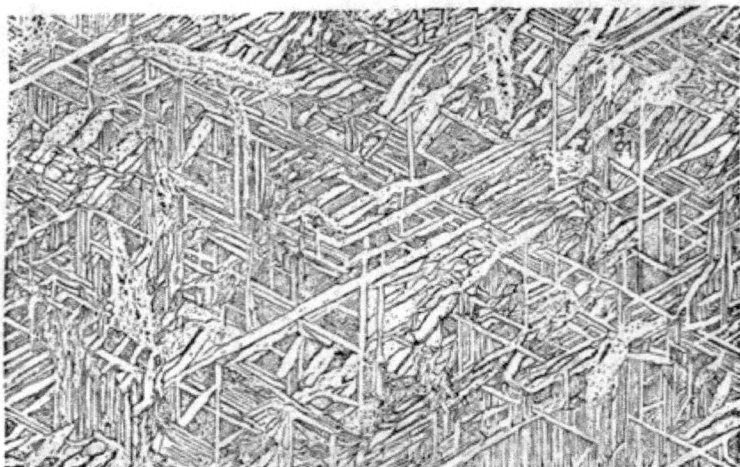

Fig. 351.

are moving in every possible direction through the celestial spaces. They may not average more than one in a million of cubic miles, and yet their total number exceeds all calculation. Of the nature of the minuter bodies of this class nothing is certainly known. The earth is continually encountering them in its journey around the sun. They are burned by passing through the upper regions of our atmosphere, and the shooting-star is simply the light of that burning. These bodies, which are invisible till they plunge into the earth's atmosphere, are called *meteoroids.*

309. *Origin of the Light of Meteors.* — When one of

these meteoroids enters our atmosphere, the resistance of
the air arrests its motion to some extent, and so converts
a portion of its energy of motion into that of heat. The
heat thus developed is sufficient to raise the meteoroid and
the air around it to incandescence, and in most cases
either to cause the meteoroid to burn up, or to dissipate it
as vapor. The luminous vapor thus formed constitutes the
luminous train which occasionally accompanies a meteor,
and often disappears as a puff of smoke. When a meteoroid is large enough and refractory enough to resist the
heat to which it is exposed, its motion is sufficiently arrested,
on entering the lower layers of our atmosphere, to cause
it to fall to the earth. We then have an *aerolite*. A
brilliant meteor differs from a shooting-star simply in magnitude.

310. *The Intensity of the Heat to which a Meteoroid is
Exposed.* — It has been ascertained by experiment that a body
moving through the atmosphere at the rate of a hundred and
twenty-five feet a second raises the temperature of the air
immediately in front of it one degree, and that the temperature
increases as the square of the velocity of the moving body;
that is to say, that, with a velocity of two hundred and fifty
feet, the temperature in front of the body would be raised
four degrees; with a velocity of five hundred feet, sixteen
degrees; and so on. To find, therefore, the temperature to
which a meteoroid would be exposed in passing through our
atmosphere, we have merely to divide its velocity in feet per
second by a hundred and twenty-five, and square the quotient.
With a velocity of forty-four miles a second in our atmosphere,
a meteoroid would therefore be exposed to a temperature of
between three and four million degrees. The air acts upon
the body as if it were raised to this intense heat. At such a
temperature small masses of the most refractory or incom-
bustible substances known to us would flash into vapor with
the evolution of intense light and heat.

If one of these meteoric bodies is large enough to pass

through the atmosphere and reach the earth, without being volatilized by the heat, we have an aerolite. As it is only a few seconds in making the passage, the heat has not time to penetrate far into its interior, but is expended in melting and vaporizing the outer portions. The resistance of the denser strata of the atmosphere to the motion of the aerolite sometimes becomes so enormous that the body is suddenly rent to pieces with a loud detonation. It seems like an explosion produced by some disruptive action within the mass; but there can be little doubt that it is due to the velocity — perhaps ten, twenty, or thirty miles a second — with which the body strikes the air.

If, on the other hand, the meteoroid is so small as to be burned up or volatilized in the upper regions of the atmosphere, we have a common shooting-star, or a meteor of greater or less brilliancy.

311. *Meteoric Showers.* — On ordinary nights only four or five shooting-stars are seen in an hour, and these move in every direction. Their orbits lie in all possible positions, and are seemingly scattered at random. Such meteors are called *sporadic* meteors. On occasional nights, shooting-stars are more numerous, and all move in a common direction. Such a display is called a *meteoric shower.* These showers differ greatly in brilliancy; but during any one shower the meteors all appear to radiate from some one point in the heavens. If we mark on a celestial globe the apparent paths of the meteors which fall during a shower, or if we trace them back on the celestial sphere, we shall find that they all meet in the same point, as shown in Fig. 352. This point is called the *radiant point.* It always appears in the same position, wherever the observer is situated, and does not partake of the diurnal motion of the earth. As the stars move towards the west, the radiant point moves with them. The point in question is purely an effect of perspective, being the "vanishing point" of the parallel lines in which the meteors are actually moving.

These lines are seen, not in their real direction in space, but as projected on the celestial sphere. If we look upwards, and watch snow falling through a calm atmosphere, the flakes which fall directly towards us do not seem to move at all, while the surrounding flakes seem to diverge from them on all sides. So, in a meteoric shower, a meteor coming directly towards the observer does not seem

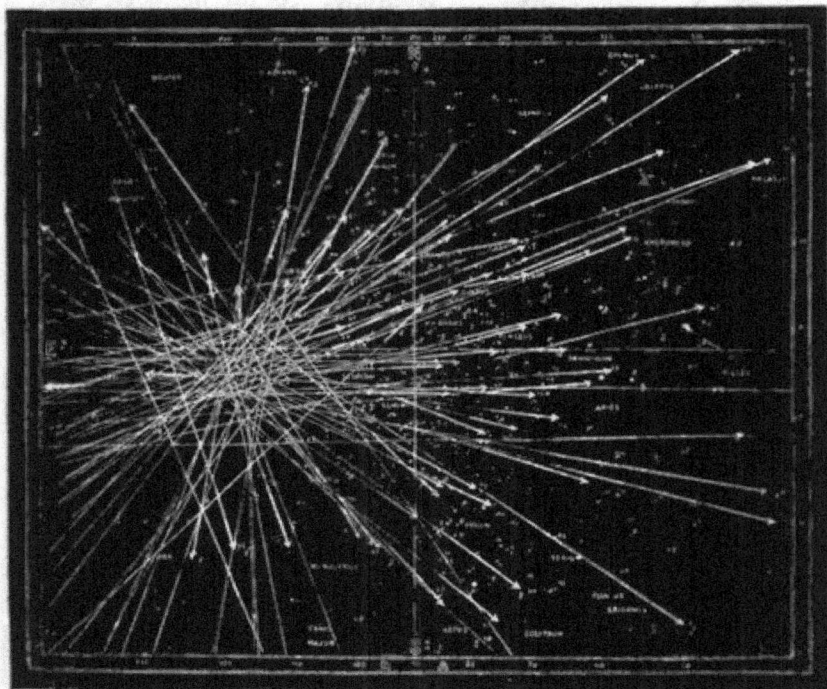

Fig. 352.

to move at all, and marks the point from which all the others seem to radiate.

312. *The August Meteors.* — A meteoric shower of no great brilliancy occurs annually about the 10th of August. The radiant point of this shower is in the constellation *Perseus*, and hence these meteors are often called the *Perseids*. The orbit of these meteoroids has been pretty accurately determined, and is shown in Fig. 353.

It will be seen that the perihelion point of this orbit is at about the distance of the earth from the sun ; so that the earth encounters the meteors once a year, and this takes place in the month of August. The orbit is a very eccentric ellipse, reaching far beyond Neptune. As the meteoric display is about equally brilliant every year, it seems probable that the meteoroids form a stream quite uniformly distributed throughout the whole orbit. It probably takes one of the meteoroids about a hundred and twenty-four years to pass around this orbit.

313. *The November Meteors.* —A somewhat brilliant meteoric shower also occurs annually, about the 13th of November. The radiant point of these meteors is in the constellation *Leo*, and hence they are often called the *Leonids*. Their orbit has been determined with great accuracy, and is shown in Fig. 354. While the November meteors are not usually very numerous or bright, a remarkably brilliant display of them has been seen once in about thirty-three or thirty-four years : hence we infer, that, while there are some meteoroids scattered throughout the whole extent of the orbit, the great majority are massed in

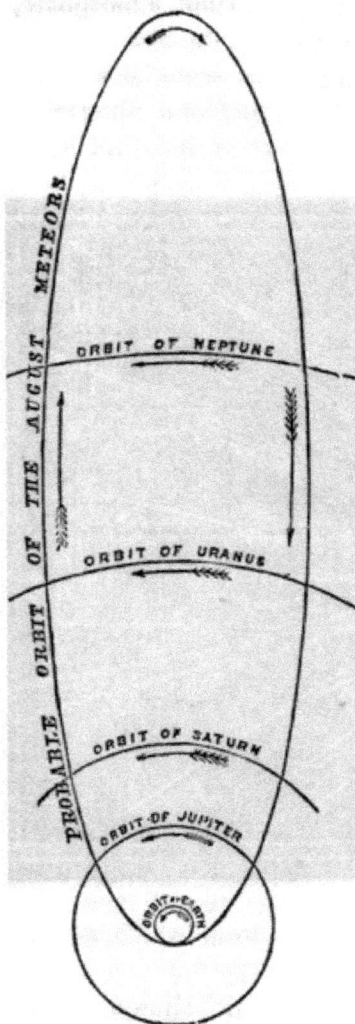

Fig. 353.

a group which traverses the orbit in a little over thirty-three years. A conjectural form of this condensed group is shown in Fig. 355. The group is so large that it takes it two or three years to pass the perihelion point : hence there may be a brilliant meteoric display two or three years in succession.

The last brilliant display of these meteors was in the years 1866 and 1867. The display was visible in this country only a short time before sunrise, and therefore did not attract general attention. The display of 1833 was remarkably brilliant in this country, and caused great consternation among the ignorant and superstitious.

314. *Connection between Meteors and Comets.* — It has been found that a comet which appeared in 1866, and which is designated as 1866, I., has exactly the same orbit and period as the No-

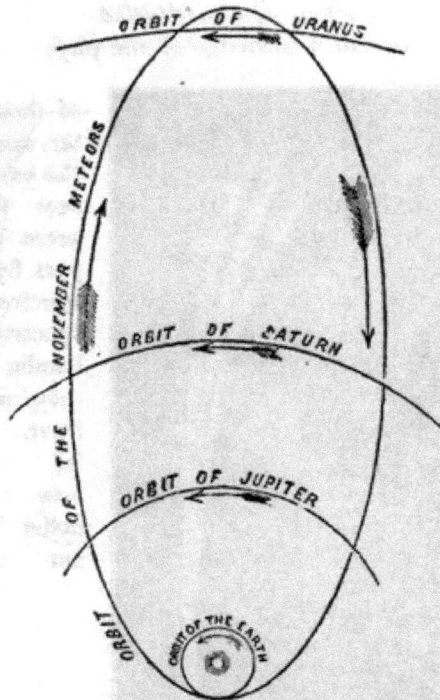

Fig. 354.

vember meteors, and that another comet. known as the 1862, III., has the same orbit as the August meteors. It has also been ascertained that a third comet, 1861, I., has the same orbit as a stream of meteors which the earth encounters in April. Furthermore, it was found, in 1872, that there was a small stream of meteors following in the train of the lost comet of Biela. These various orbits of comets and meteoric streams are shown in Fig. 356. The coincidence of the orbits of comets and of meteoric streams indicates that these two classes of bodies are very closely related. They undoubtedly have a common origin. The fact that there is a stream of meteors in the train of Biela's comet has led to the supposition that comets may become gradually disintegrated into meteoroids.

PHYSICAL AND CHEMICAL CONSTITUTION OF COMETS.

315. *Physical Constitution of Telescopic Comets.* — We have no certain knowledge of the physical constitution of telescopic comets. They are usually tens of thousands of miles in diameter, and yet of such tenuity that the smallest stars can readily be seen through them. It would seem that they must shine in part by reflected light; yet the spectroscope shows that their spectrum is composed of bright bands, which would indicate that they are composed, in part at least, of incandescent gases. It is, however, difficult to conceive how these gases become sufficiently heated to be luminous; and at the same time such gases would reflect no sunlight.

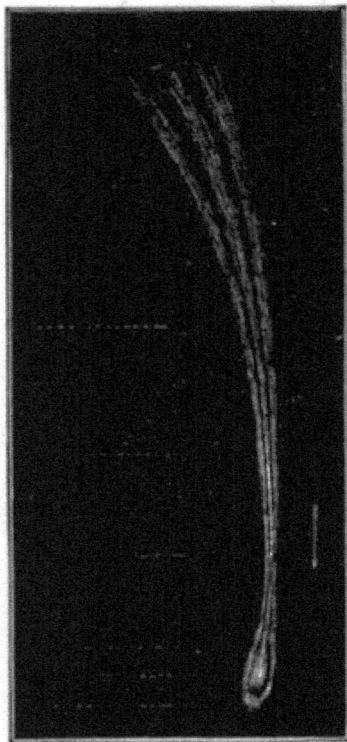

It seems probable that these comets are really made up of a combination of small, solid particles in the form of minute meteoroids, and of gases which are, perhaps, rendered luminous by electric discharges of slight intensity.

Fig. 355.

316. *Physical Constitution of Large Comets.* — In the case of large comets the nucleus is either a dense mass of solid matter several hundred miles in diameter, or a dense group of meteoroids. Professor Peirce estimated that the density

of the nucleus is at least equal to that of iron. As such a comet approaches the sun, the nucleus is, to a slight extent, vaporized, and out of this vapor is formed the coma and the tail.

That some evaporating process is going on from the nucleus of the comet is proved by the movements of the tail. It is evident that the tail cannot be an appendage carried along with the comet, as it seems to be. It is impossible that there should be any cohesion in matter of such tenuity that the smallest stars could be seen through a million of miles of it, and which is, moreover, continually changing its form. Then,

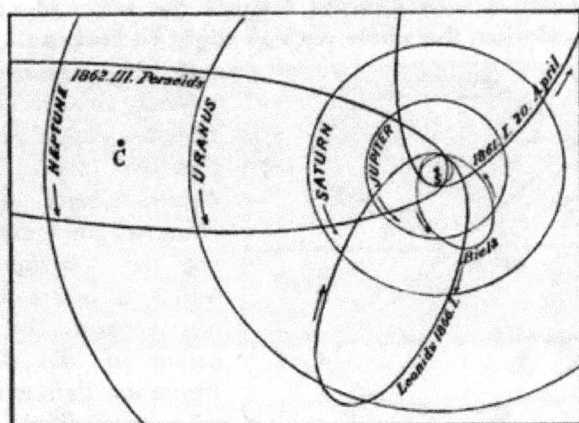

Fig. 356.

again, as a comet is passing its perihelion, the tail appears to be whirled from one side of the sun to another with a rapidity which would tear it to pieces if the movement were real. The tail seems to be, not something attached to the comet, and carried along with it, but a stream of vapor issuing from it, like smoke from a chimney. The matter of which it is composed is continually streaming outwards, and continually being replaced by fresh vapor from the nucleus.

The vapor, as it emanates from the nucleus, is repelled by the sun with a force often two or three times as great as the ordinary solar attraction. The most probable explanation of this phenomenon is, that it is a case of electrical repulsion, the sun and the particles of the cometary mist being similarly

electrified. With reference to this electrical theory of the
formation of comets' tails, Professor Peirce makes the following observation: "In its approach to the sun, the surface of
the nucleus is rapidly heated: it is melted and vaporized, and
subjected to frequent explosions. The vapor rises in its atmosphere with a well-defined upper surface, which is known to
observers as an *envelop*. . . . The electrification of the cometary mist is analogous to that of our own thunder-clouds. Any
portion of the coma which has received the opposite kind of
electricity to the sun and to the repelled tail will be attracted.
This gives a simple explanation of the negative tails which have
been sometimes seen directed towards the sun. In cases of
violent explosion, the whole nucleus might be broken to pieces,
and the coma dashed
around so as to give
varieties of tail, and even
multiple tails. There
seems, indeed, to be no
observed phenomenon of
the tail or the coma
which is not consistent
with a reasonable modifi-
cation of the theory."
Professor Peirce regard-
ed comets simply as the
largest of the meteoroids.

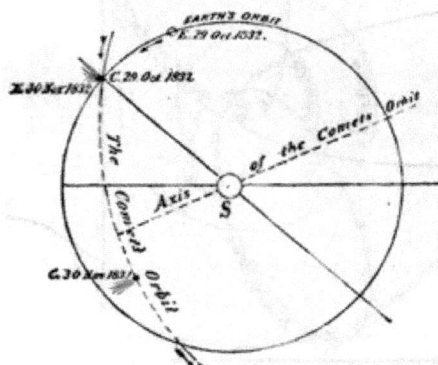

Fig. 357

They appear to shine partly by reflected sunlight, and partly
by their own proper light, which seems to be that of vapor
rendered luminous by an electric discharge of slight intensity.

317. *Collision of a Comet and the Earth.* — It sometimes
happens that the orbit of a comet intersects that of the earth,
as is shown in Fig. 357, which shows a portion of the orbit
of Biela's comet, with the positions of the comet and of the
earth in 1832. Of course, were a comet and the earth both to
reach the intersection of their orbits at the same time, a collision of the two bodies would be inevitable. With reference
to the probable effect of such a collision, Professor Newcomb
remarks, —

"The question is frequently asked, What would be the

effect if a comet should strike the earth? This would depend upon what sort of a comet it was, and what part of the comet came in contact with our planet. The latter might pass through the tail of the largest comet without the slightest effect being produced; the tail being so thin and airy that a million miles thickness of it looks only like gauze in the sunlight. It is not at all unlikely that such a thing may have happened without ever being noticed. A passage through a telescopic comet would be accompanied by a brilliant meteoric shower, probably a far more brilliant one than has ever been recorded. No more serious danger would be encountered than that arising from a possible fall of meteorites; but a collision between the nucleus of a large comet and the earth might be a serious

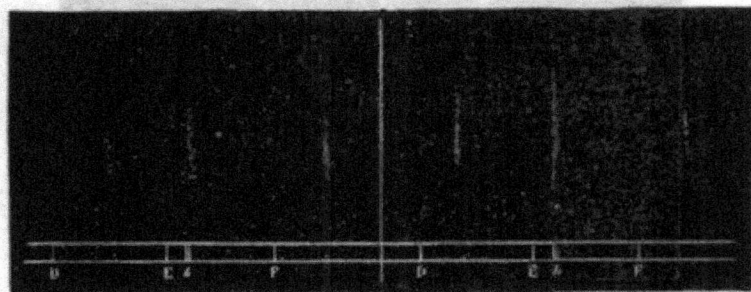

Fig. 358.

matter. If, as Professor Peirce supposes, the nucleus is a solid body of metallic density, many miles in diameter, the effect where the comet struck would be terrific beyond conception. At the first contact in the upper regions of the atmosphere, the whole heavens would be illuminated with a resplendence beyond that of a thousand suns, the sky radiating a light which would blind every eye that beheld it, and a heat which would melt the hardest rocks. A few seconds of this, while the huge body was passing through the atmosphere, and the collision at the earth's surface would in an instant reduce every thing there existing to fiery vapor, and bury it miles deep in the solid earth. Happily, the chances of such a calamity are so minute that they need not cause the slightest uneasiness. There is hardly a possible form of death which is not a thousand times more probable than this. So small is the earth in

comparison with the celestial spaces, that if one should shut
his eyes, and fire a gun at random in the air, the chance of
bringing down a bird would be better than that of a comet of
any kind striking the earth."

318. *The Chemical Constitution of Comets.* — Fig. 358 shows
the bands of the spectrum of a telescopic comet of 1873, as
seen by two different observers. Fig. 359 shows the spectrum
of the coma and tail of the comet of 1874; and the spectrum
of the bright comet of 1881 showed the same three bands for

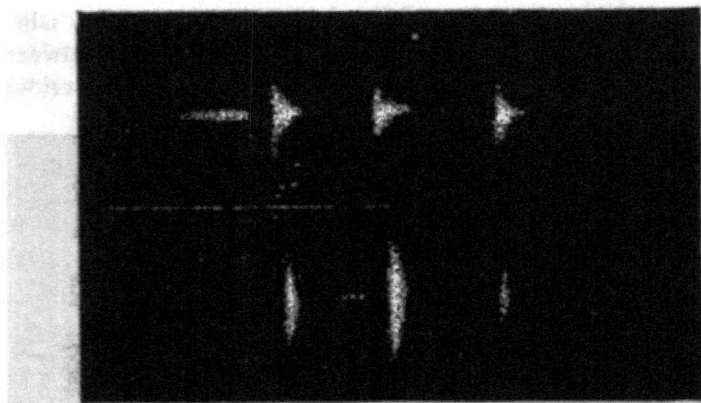

Fig. 359.

the coma and tail. Now, these three bands are those of certain hydrocarbon vapors: hence it would seem that the coma
and tails of comets are composed chiefly of such vapors (315).

II. THE ZODIACAL LIGHT.

319. *The General Appearance of the Zodiacal Light.* —
The phenomenon known as the *zodiacal light* consists of a
very faint luminosity, which may be seen rising from the
western horizon after twilight on any clear winter or spring
evening, also from the eastern horizon just before daybreak
in the summer or autumn. It extends out on each side
of the sun, and lies nearly in the plane of the ecliptic. It
grows fainter the farther it is from the sun, and can generally be traced to about ninety degrees from that luminary,

Fig. 360.

when it gradually fades away. In a very clear, tropical atmosphere, it has been traced all the way across the heavens from east to west, thus forming a complete ring. The general appearance of this column of light, as seen in the morning, in the latitude of Europe, is shown in Fig. 360.

Taking all these appearances together, they indicate that it is due to a lens-shaped appendage surrounding the sun, and extending a little beyond the earth's orbit. It lies nearly in the plane of the ecliptic ; but its exact position is not easily determined.   Fig. 361 shows the general form and position of this solar appendage, as seen in the west.

Fig. 361.

320. *The Visibility of the Zodiacal Light.* — The reason why the zodiacal light is more favorably seen in the evening during the winter and spring than in the summer and fall is evident from Fig. 362, which shows the position of the ecliptic and the zodiacal light with reference to the western horizon at the time of sunset in March and in September. It will be seen that in September the axis of the light forms a small angle with the horizon, so that the phenomenon is visible only a short time after sunset and low down where it is difficult to distinguish it from the glimmer of the twilight : while in March, its axis being nearly perpendicular to the horizon, the light may be observed for some hours after sunset

and well up in the sky. Fig. 363 gives the position of the ecliptic and of the zodiacal light with reference to the eastern horizon at the time of sunrise, and shows why the zodiacal light is seen to better advantage in the morning during the summer and fall than during the winter and spring. It will be observed that here the angle made by the axis of the light with the horizon is small in March, while it is large in September; the conditions represented in the preceding figure being thus reversed.

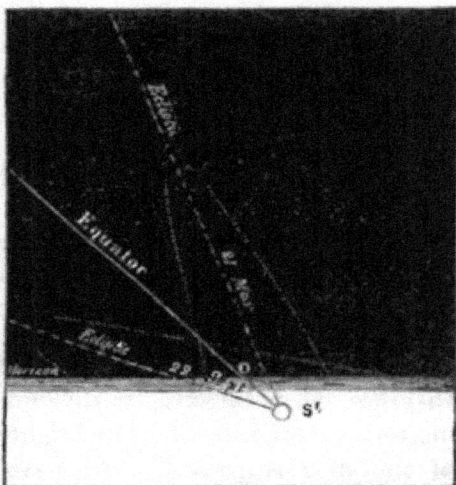

Fig. 362.

321. Nature of the Zodiacal Light. — Various attempts have been made to explain the phenomena of the zodiacal light; but the most probable theory is, that it is due to an immense number of meteors which are revolving around the sun, and which lie mostly within the earth's orbit. Each of these meteors reflects a sensible portion of sunlight, but is far too small to be separately visible. All of these meteors together would, by their combined reflection, produce a kind of pale, diffused light.

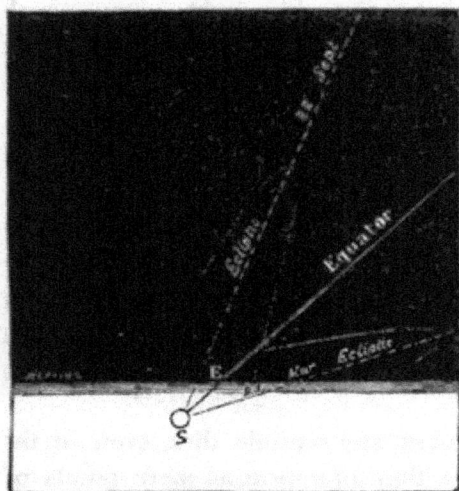

Fig. 363.

III.

THE STELLAR UNIVERSE.

I. GENERAL ASPECT OF THE HEAVENS.

322. *The Magnitude of the Stars.* — The stars that are visible to the naked eye are divided into six classes, according to their brightness. The brightest stars are called stars of the *first magnitude;* the next brightest, those of the *second magnitude;* and so on to the *sixth magnitude.* The last magnitude includes the faintest stars that are visible to the naked eye on the most favorable night. Stars which are fainter than those of the sixth magnitude can be seen only with the telescope, and are called *telescopic stars.* Telescopic stars are also divided into magnitudes; the division extending to the *sixteenth* magnitude, or the faintest stars that can be seen with the most powerful telescopes.

The classification of stars according to magnitudes has reference only to their brightness, and not at all to their actual size. A sixth magnitude star may actually be larger than a first magnitude star; its want of brilliancy being due to its greater distance, or to its inferior luminosity, or to both of these causes.

None of the stars present any sensible disk, even in the most powerful telescope : they all appear as mere points of light. The larger the telescope, the greater is its power of revealing faint stars; not because it makes these stars appear larger, but because of its greater light-gathering power. This power increases with the size of the object-glass of the telescope, which plays the part of a gigantic pupil of the eye.

The classification of the stars into magnitudes is not made in accordance with any very accurate estimate of their brightness. The stars which are classed together in the same magnitude are far from being equally bright.

The stars of each lower magnitude are about two-fifths as bright as those of the magnitude above. The ratio of diminution is about a third from the higher magnitude down to the fifth. Were the ratio two-fifths exact, it would take about

2½ stars of the 2d magnitude to make one of the 1st.
6 stars of the 3d magnitude to make one of the 1st.
16 stars of the 4th magnitude to make one of the 1st.
40 stars of the 5th magnitude to make one of the 1st.
100 stars of the 6th magnitude to make one of the 1st.
10,000 stars of the 11th magnitude to make one of the 1st.
1,000,000 stars of the 16th magnitude to make one of the 1st.

323. *The Number of the Stars.* — The total number of stars in the celestial sphere visible to the average naked eye is estimated, in round numbers, at five thousand; but the number varies much with the perfection and the training of the eye and with the atmospheric conditions. For every star visible to the naked eye, there are thousands too minute to be seen without telescopic aid. Fig. 364 shows a portion of the constellation of the Twins as seen with the naked eye; and Fig. 365 shows the same region as seen in a powerful telescope.

Fig. 364.

Struve has estimated that the total number of stars visible with Herschel's twenty-foot telescope was about twenty million. The number that can be seen with the great telescopes of modern times has not been carefully estimated, but is probably somewhere between thirty million and fifty million.

The number of stars between the north pole and the circle thirty-five degrees south of the equator is about as follows: —

Of the 1st magnitude about . . . . . 14 stars.
Of the 2d magnitude about . . . . . 48 stars.
Of the 3d magnitude about . . . . . 152 stars.
Of the 4th magnitude about . . . . . 313 stars.
Of the 5th magnitude about . . . . . 854 stars.
Of the 6th magnitude about . . . . . 2010 stars.

Total visible to naked eye . . . . . 3391 stars.

Fig. 365.

The number of stars of the several magnitudes is approximately in inverse proportion to that of their brightness, the ratio being a little greater in the higher magnitudes, and probably a little less in the lower ones.

324. *The Division of the Stars into Constellations.*—
A glance at the heavens is sufficient to show that the stars
are not distributed uniformly over the sky. The larger ones
especially are collected into more or less irregular groups.
The larger groups are called *constellations.* At a very early
period a mythological figure was allotted to each constellation ; and these figures were drawn in such a way as to
include the principal stars of each constellation. The
heavens thus became covered, as it were, with immense
hieroglyphics.

There is no historic record of the time when these figures
were formed, or of the principle in accordance with which they
were constructed. It is probable that the imagination of the
earlier peoples may, in many instances, have discovered some
fanciful resemblance in the configuration of the stars to the
forms depicted. The names are still retained, although the
figures no longer serve any astronomical purpose. The constellation Hercules, for instance, no longer represents the figure
of a man among the stars, but a certain portion of the heavens
within which the ancients placed that figure. In star-maps
intended for school and popular use it is still customary to
give these figures; but they are not generally found on maps
designed for astronomers.

325. *The Naming of the Stars.*—The brighter stars have
all proper names, as *Sirius, Procyon, Arcturus, Capella,
Aldebaran*, etc. This method of designating the stars was
adopted by the Arabs. Most of these names have dropped
entirely out of astronomical use, though many are popularly
retained. The brighter stars are now generally designated
by the letters of the Greek alphabet. — *alpha, beta, gamma*,
etc., — to which is appended the genitive of the name of
the constellation, the first letter of the alphabet being used
for the brightest star, the second for the next brightest, and
so on. Thus *Aldebaran* would be designated as *Alpha
Tauri*. In speaking of the stars of any one constellation,

we simply designate them by the letters of the Greek alphabet, without the addition of the name of the constellation, which answers to a person's surname, while the Greek letter answers to his Christian name. The names of the seven stars of the "Dipper" are given in Fig. 366. When the letters of the Greek alphabet are exhausted, those of the Roman alphabet are employed. The fainter stars in a constellation are usually designated by some system of numbers.

326. *The Milky-Way, or Galaxy.* — The Milky-Way is

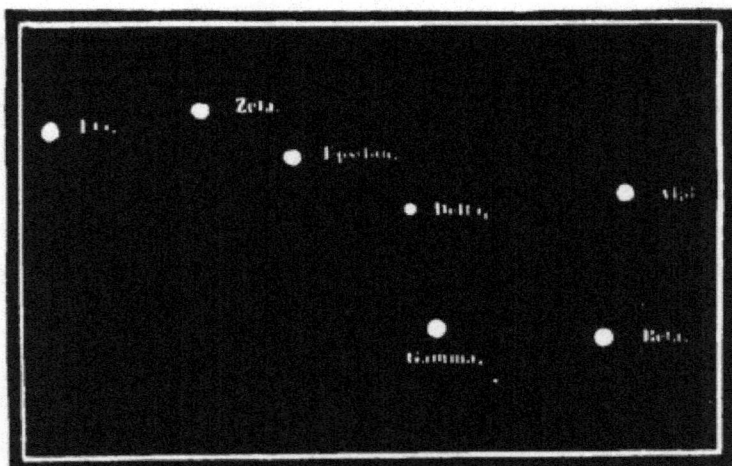

Fig. 366.

a faint luminous band, of irregular outline, which surrounds the heavens with a great circle, as shown in Fig. 367. Through a considerable portion of its course it is divided into two branches, and there are various vacant spaces at different points in this band; but at only one point in the southern hemisphere is it entirely interrupted.

The telescope shows that the Galaxy arises from the light of countless stars too minute to be separately visible with the naked eye. The telescopic stars, instead of being uniformly distributed over the celestial sphere, are mostly

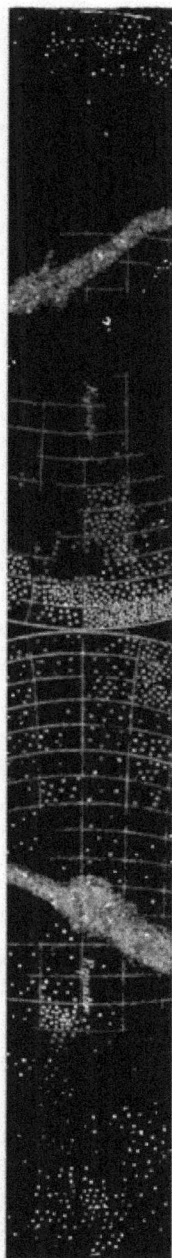

Fig. 367.

condensed in the region of the Galaxy. They are fewest in the regions most distant from this belt, and become thicker as we approach it. The greater the telescopic power, the more marked is the condensation. With the naked eye the condensation is hardly noticeable ; but with the aid of a very small telescope, we see a decided thickening of the stars in and near the Galaxy, while the most powerful telescopes show that a large majority of the stars lie actually in the Galaxy. If all the stars visible with a twelve-inch telescope were blotted out, we should find that the greater part of those remaining were in the Galaxy.

The increase in the number of the stars of all magnitudes as we approach the plane of the Milky-Way is shown in Fig. 368. The curve acb shows by its height the distribution of the stars above the ninth magnitude, and the curve ACB those of all magnitudes.

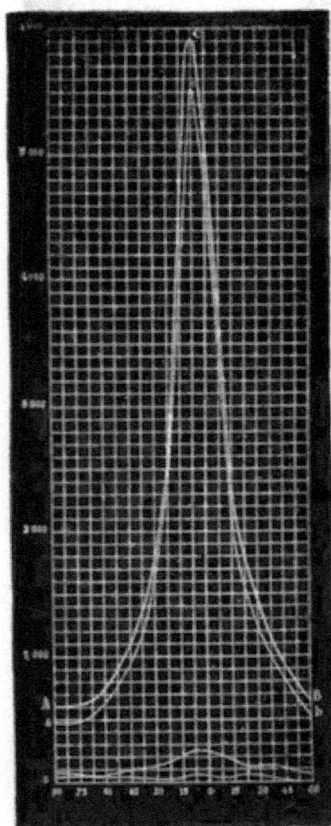

Fig. 368.

327. *Star-Clusters.* — Besides this gradual and regular condensation towards the Galaxy, occasional aggregations of stars into *clusters* may be seen. Some of these are visible to the naked eye, sometimes as separate stars, like the "Seven Stars," or Pleiades, but more commonly as patches of diffused light, the stars being too small to be seen separately. The number visible in powerful telescopes is, however, much

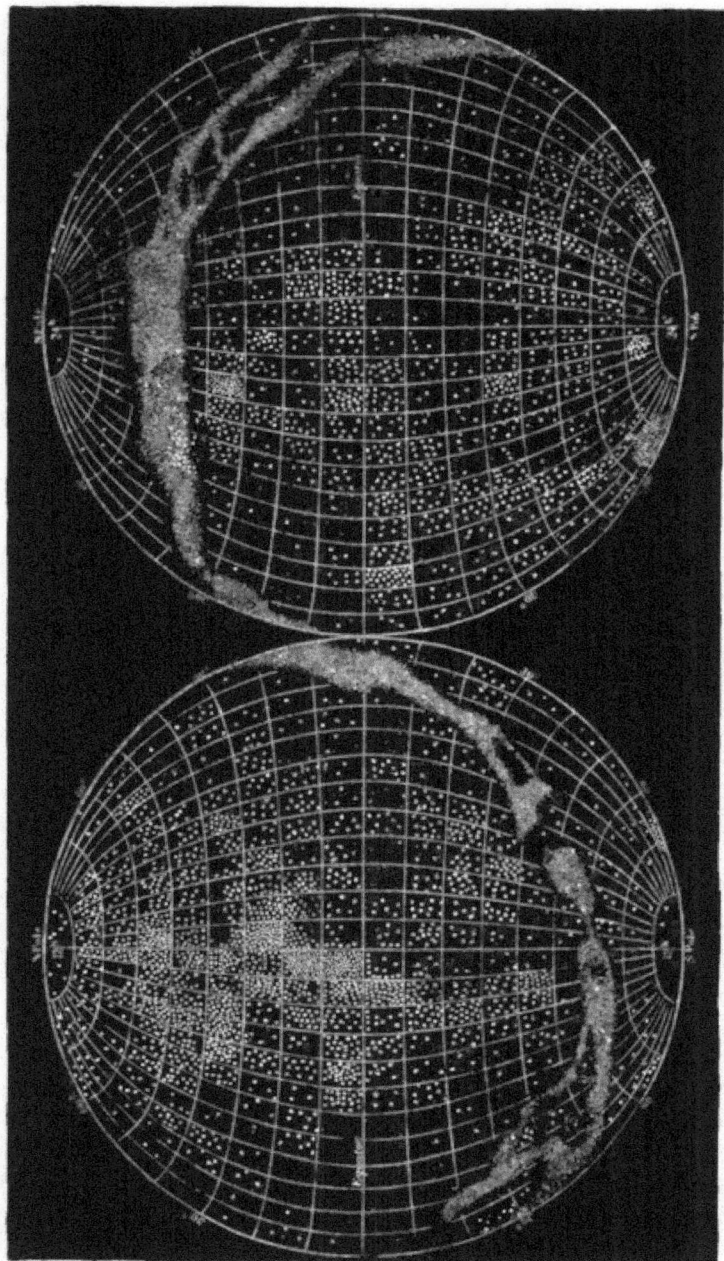

Fig. 369.

greater. Sometimes hundreds or even thousands of stars are visible in the field of view at once, and sometimes the number is so great that they cannot be counted.

328. *Nebulæ.* — Another class of objects which are found in the celestial spaces are irregular masses of soft, cloudy light, known as *nebulæ*. Many objects which look like nebulæ in small telescopes are shown by more powerful instruments to be really star-clusters. But many of these objects are not composed of stars at all, being immense masses of gaseous matter.

The general distribution of nebulæ is the reverse of that of the stars. Nebulæ are thickest where stars are thinnest. While stars are most numerous in the region of the Milky-Way, nebulæ are most abundant about the poles of the Milky-Way. This condensation of nebulæ about the poles of the Milky-Way is shown in Figs. 367 and 369, in which the points represent, not stars, but nebulæ.

II. THE STARS.

THE CONSTELLATIONS.

329. *The Great Bear.* — The Great Bear, or *Ursa Major*, is one of the circumpolar constellations (4), and contains one of the most familiar *asterisms*, or groups of stars, in our sky; namely, the *Great Dipper*, or *Charles's Wain*. The positions and names of the seven prominent stars in it are shown in Fig. 370. The two stars Alpha and Beta are called the *Pointers*. This asterism is sometimes called the *Butcher's Cleaver*. The whole constellation is shown in Fig. 371. A rather faint star marks the nose of the bear, and three equidistant pairs of faint stars mark his feet.

330. *The Little Bear, Draco, and Cassiopeia.* — These are all circumpolar constellations. The most important star of the Little Bear, or *Ursa Minor*, is *Polaris*, or the *Pole Star*. This star may be found by drawing a line from Beta to Alpha of the Dipper, and prolonging it as shown in Fig. 372. This explains why these stars are called the *Pointers*. The Pole Star, with

the six other chief stars of the Little Bear, form an asterism

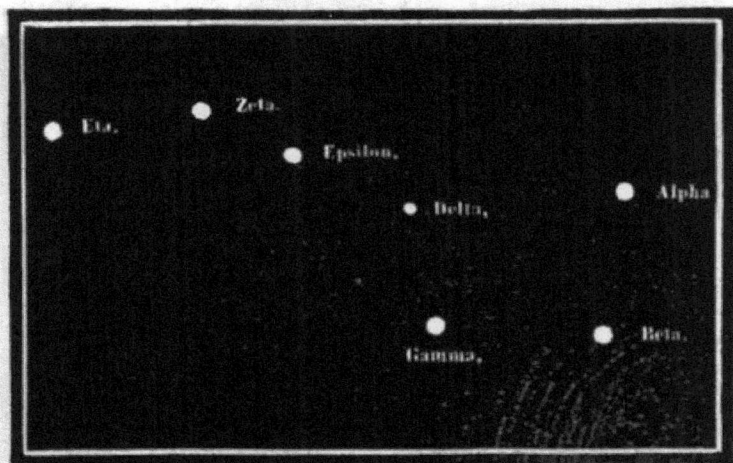

Fig. 370.

called the *Little Dipper*. These six stars are joined with
Polaris by a dotted line in Fig. 372.

Fig. 371.

The stars in a serpentine line between the two Dippers are
the chief stars of *Draco*, or the *Dragon;* the trapezium mark-

ing its head.   Fig. 373 shows the constellations of
and Draco as usually figured.

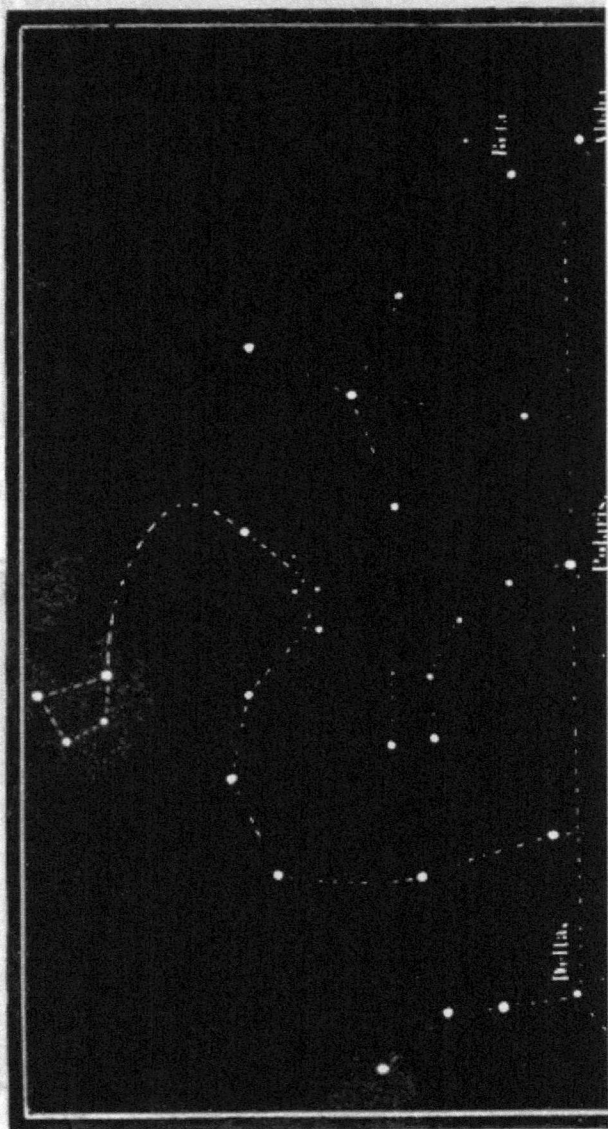

Fig. 372.

To find *Cassiopeia*, draw a line from Delta of th

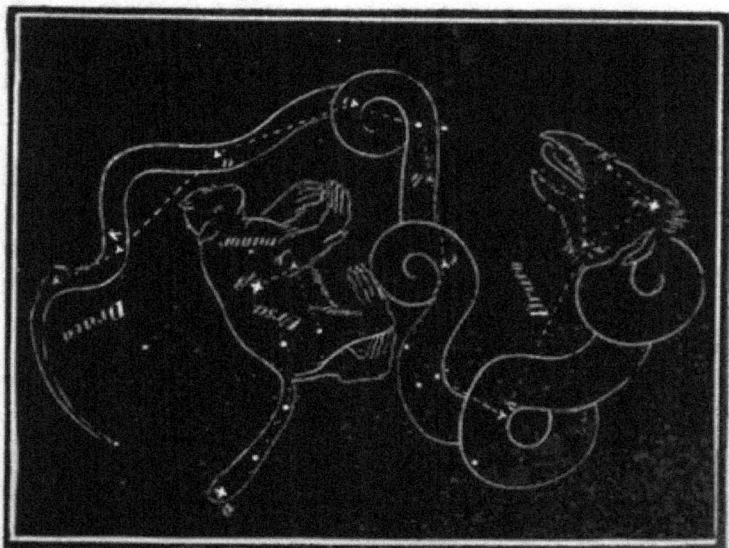

Fig. 373.

Polaris, and prolong it about an equal distance beyond, as

Fig. 374.

shown in Fig. 372. This line will pass near Alpha of Cassiopeia. The five principal stars of this constellation form an irregular *W*, opening towards the pole. Between Cassiopeia and Draco are five rather faint stars, which form an irregular *K*. These are the principal stars of the constellation *Cepheus*. These two constellations are shown in Fig. 374.

331. *The Lion, Berenice's Hair, and the Hunting-Dogs.* — A line drawn from Alpha to Beta of the Dipper, and prolonged as shown in Fig. 375, will pass between the two stars *Denebola* and *Regulus* of *Leo*, or the *Lion*. Regulus forms a *sickle* with

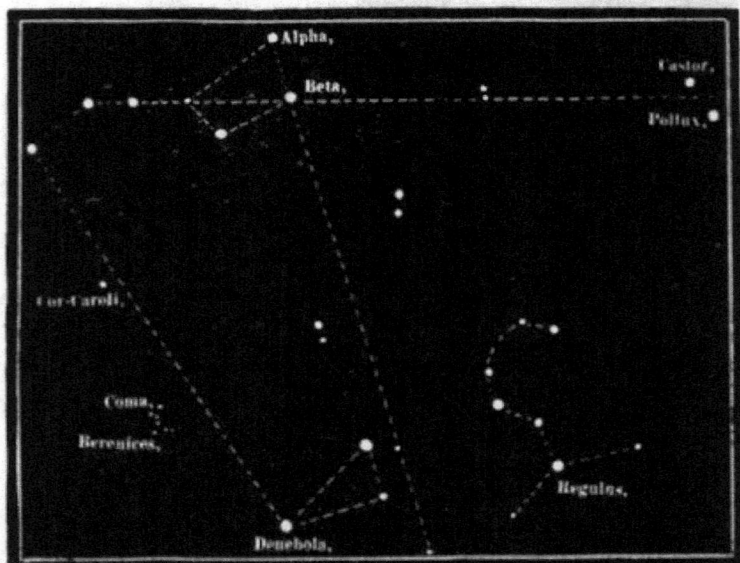

Fig. 375.

several other faint stars, and marks the heart of the lion. Denebola is at the apex of a right-angled triangle, which it forms with two other stars, and marks the end of the lion's tail. This constellation is visible in the evening from February to July, and is figured in Fig. 376.

In a straight line between Denebola and Eta, at the end of the Great Bear's tail, are, at about equal distances, the two small constellations of *Coma Berenices*, or *Berenice's Hair*, and *Canes Venatici*, or the *Hunting-Dogs*. These are shown in Fig. 377. The dogs are represented as pursuing the bear, urged on by the huntsman *Boötes*.

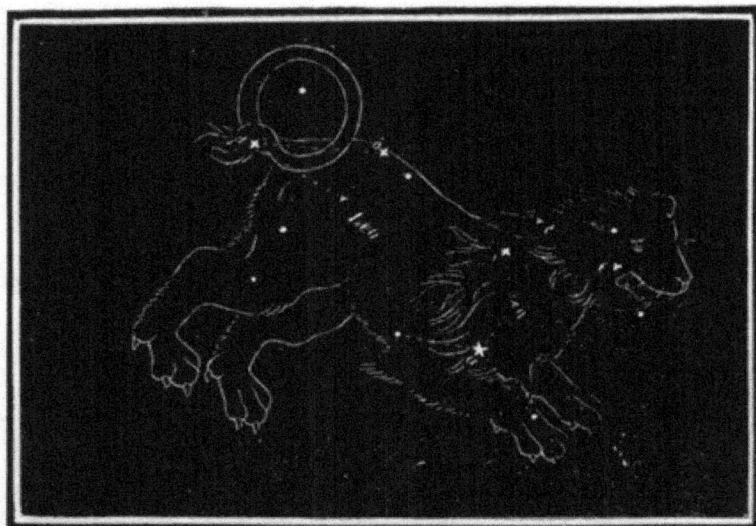

Fig. 376.

332. *Boötes, Hercules, and the Northern Crown. — Arc*

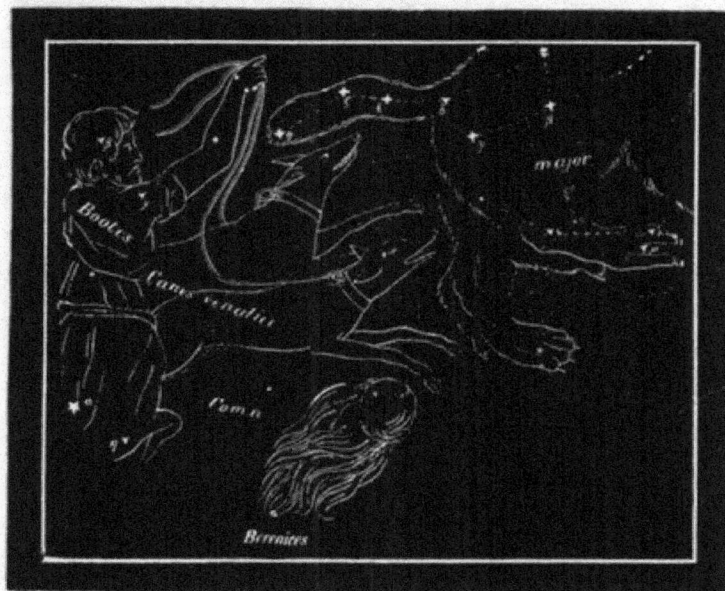

Fig. 377.

turus, the principal star of *Boötes*, may be found by drawing

a line from Zeta to Eta of the Dipper, and then prolonging
it with a slight bend, as shown in Fig. 378. Arcturus and
Polaris form a large isosceles triangle with a first-magnitude
star called *Vega*. This triangle encloses at one corner the
principal stars of Boötes, and the head of the Dragon near
the opposite side. The side running from Arcturus to Vega
passes through *Corona Borealis*, or the *Northern Crown*, and

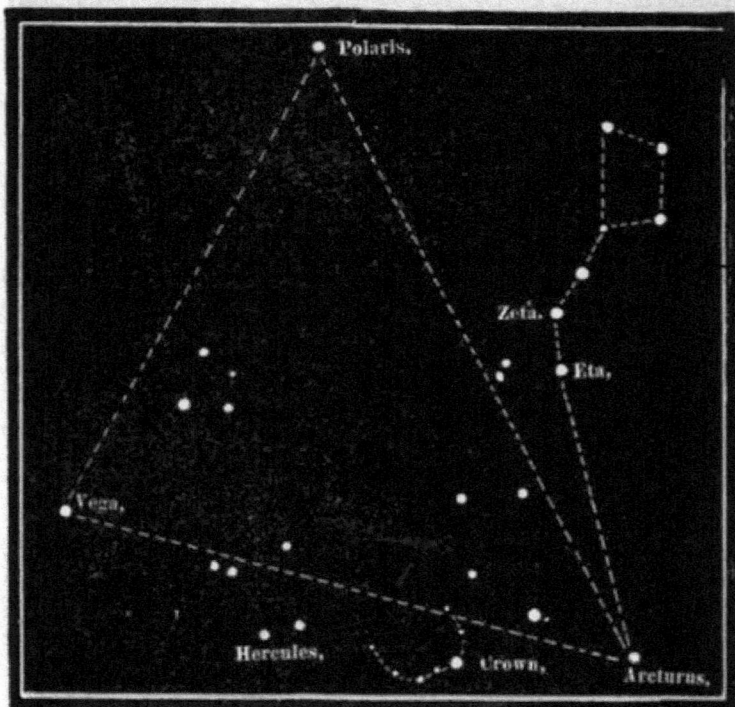

Fig. 378.

the body of *Hercules*, which is marked by a quadrilateral of
four stars.

Boötes, who is often represented as a husbandman, *Corona
Borealis*, and *Hercules*, are delineated in Fig. 379. These
constellations are visible in the evening from May to September.

333. *The Lyre, the Swan, the Eagle, and the Dolphin.* —
Altair, the principal star of *Aquila*, or the *Eagle*, lies on the
opposite side of the Milky-Way from Vega. Altair is a first-

magnitude star, and has a faint star on each side of it, as

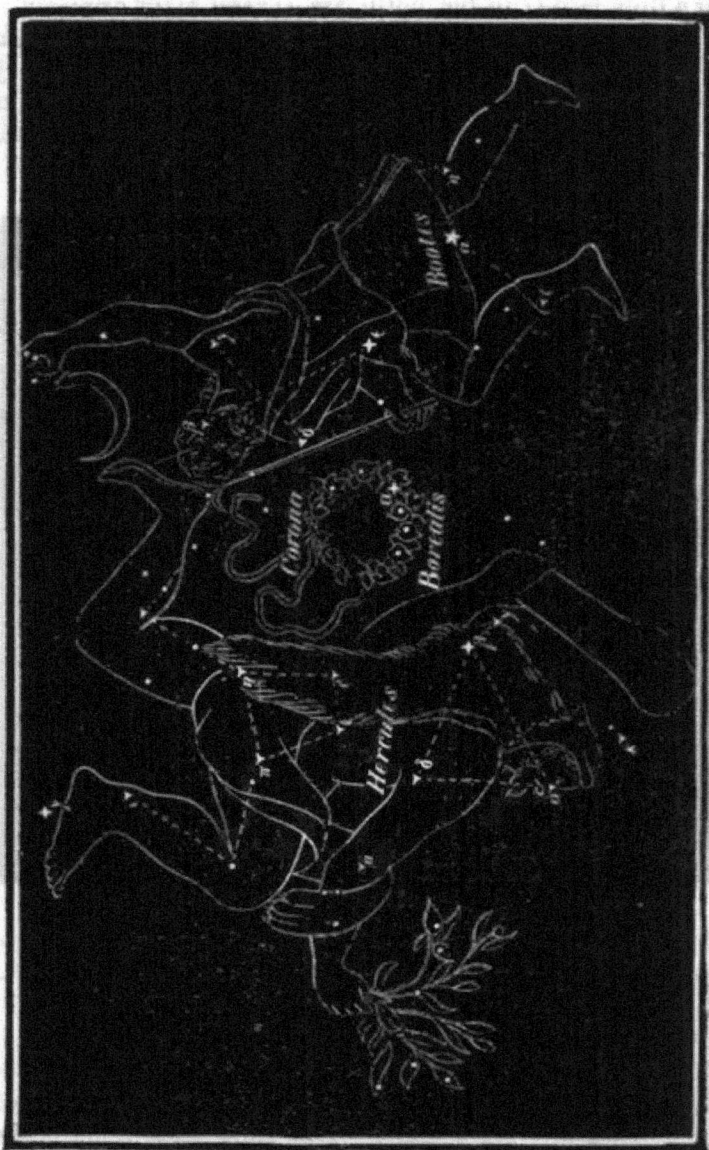

Fig. 379.

shown in Fig. 380. Vega, also of the first magnitude, is the principal star of *Lyra*, or the *Lyre*. Between these two stars, and a little farther to the north, are several stars arranged in the form of an immense cross. The bright star at the head of this cross is called *Deneb*. The cross lies in the Milky-Way, and contains the chief stars of the constellation *Cygnus*, or the *Swan*. A little to the north of Altair are four stars in the form of a diamond. This asterism is popularly known as *Job's*

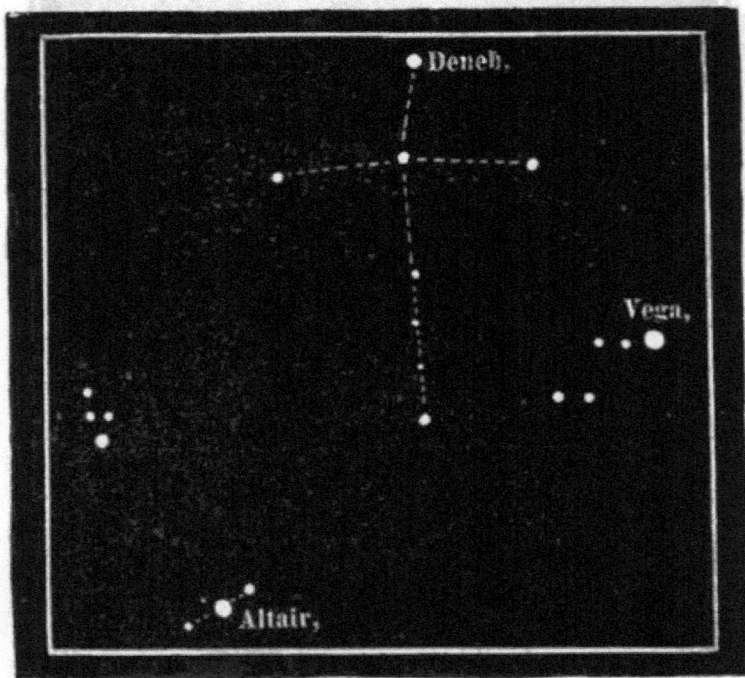

Fig. 380.

Coffin. These four stars are the chief stars of *Delphinus*, or the *Dolphin*. These four constellations are shown together in Fig. 381. The *Swan* is visible from June to December, in the evening.

334. *Virgo.* — A line drawn from Alpha to Gamma of the Dipper, and prolonged with a slight bend at Gamma, will reach to a first-magnitude star called *Spica* (Fig. 382). This is the chief star of the constellation *Virgo*, or the *Virgin*, and forms a large isosceles triangle with *Arcturus* and *Denebola*.

Virgo is represented in Fig. 383. To the right of this con-

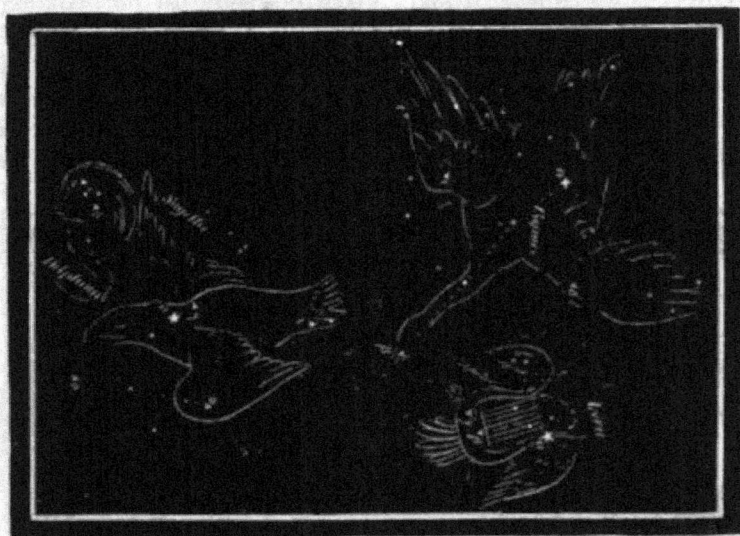

Fig. 381.

stellation, as shown in the figure, there are four stars which

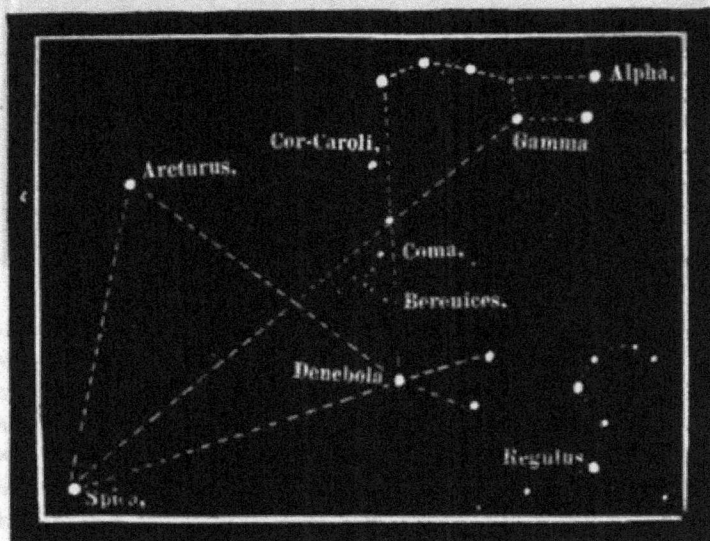

Fig. 382.

form a trapezium, and mark the constellation *Corvus*, or the

Crow. This bird is represented as standing on the body of *Hydra*, or the *Water-Snake*. *Virgo* is visible in the evening, from April to August.

335. *The Twins.* — A line drawn from Delta to Beta of the Dipper, and prolonged as shown in Fig. 384, passes between two bright stars called *Castor* and *Pollux*. The latter of these is usually reckoned as a first-magnitude star. These are the

Fig. 383.

principal stars of the constellation *Gemini*, or the *Twins*, which is shown in Fig. 385. The constellation *Canis Minor*, or the *Little Dog*, is shown in the lower part of the figure. There are two conspicuous stars in this constellation, the brightest of which is of the first magnitude, and called *Procyon*.

The region to which we have now been brought is the richest of the northern sky, containing no less than seven first-magnitude stars. These are *Sirius, Procyon, Pollux, Capella, Aldebaran, Betelgeuse,* and *Rigel.* They are shown in Fig. 386.

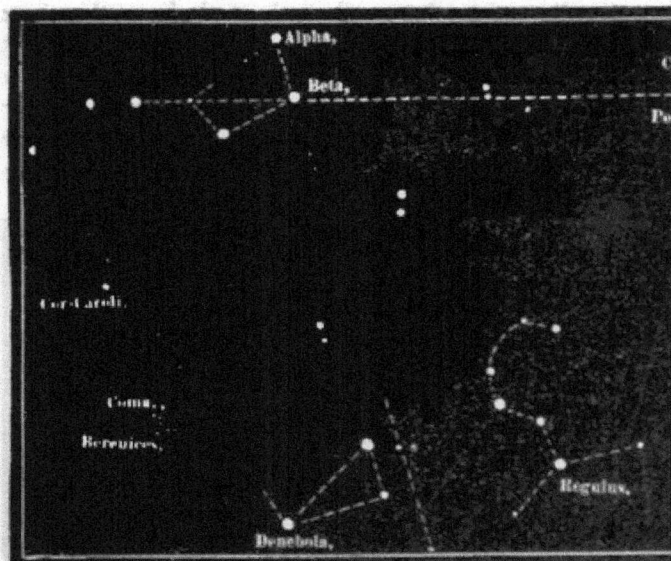

Fig. 384.

Betelgeuse and *Rigel* are in the constellation *Orion*,

about equally distant to the north and south from the three
stars forming the *belt* of Orion. Betelgeuse is a red star.
Sirius is the brightest star in the heavens, and belongs to the
constellation *Canis Major*, or the *Great Dog.* It lies to the
east of the belt of Orion. *Aldebaran* lies at about the same
distance to the west of the belt. It is a red star, and belongs

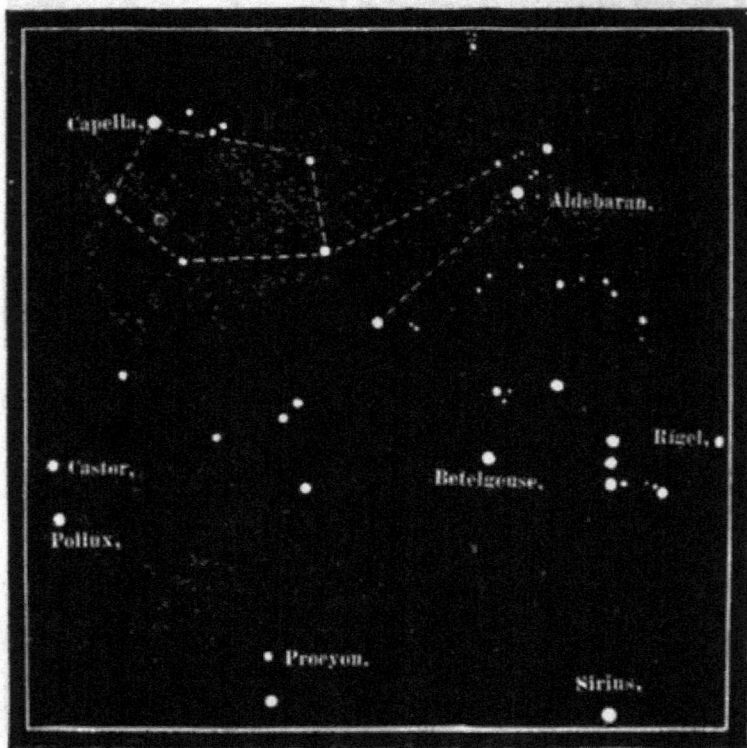

Fig. 386.

to the constellation *Taurus,* or the *Bull. Capella* is in the
constellation *Auriga*, or the *Wagoner.* These stars are visible
in the evening, from about December to April.

336. *Orion and his Dogs, and Taurus.* — *Orion* and his
Dogs are shown in Fig. 387, and *Orion* and *Taurus* in Fig. 388.
Aldebaran marks one of the eyes of the bull, and is often called
the *Bull's Eye.* The irregular *V* in the face of the bull is
called the *Hyades,* and the cluster on the shoulder the *Pleiades.*

337. *The Wagoner.* — The constellation *Auriga*, or the *Wagoner* (sometimes called the *Charioteer*), is shown in Fig. 389. *Capella* marks the *Goat*, which he is represented as carrying on his back, and the little right-angled triangle of stars near it the *Kids.* The five chief stars of this constellation form a large, irregular pentagon. Gamma of *Auriga* is

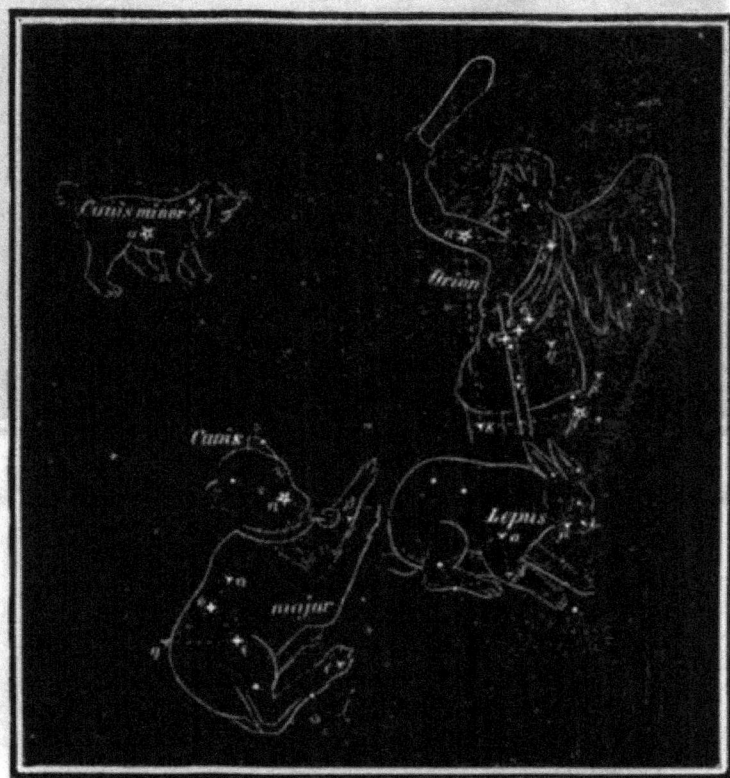

Fig. 387.

also Beta of *Taurus*, and marks one of the horns of the *Bull*.

338. *Pegasus, Andromeda, and Perseus.* — A line drawn from Polaris near to Beta of *Cassiopeia* will lead to a bright second-magnitude star at one corner of a large square (Fig. 390). Alpha belongs both to the *Square of Pegasus* and to *Andromeda*. Beta and Gamma, which are connected with Alpha in the figure by a dotted line, also belong to Andromeda. *Algol,*

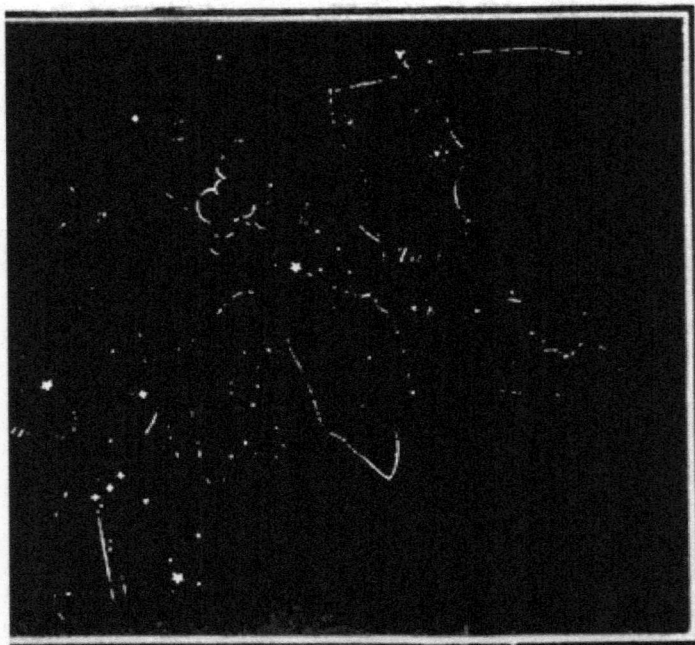

Fig. 388.

forms, with the last-named stars and with the *Square of*

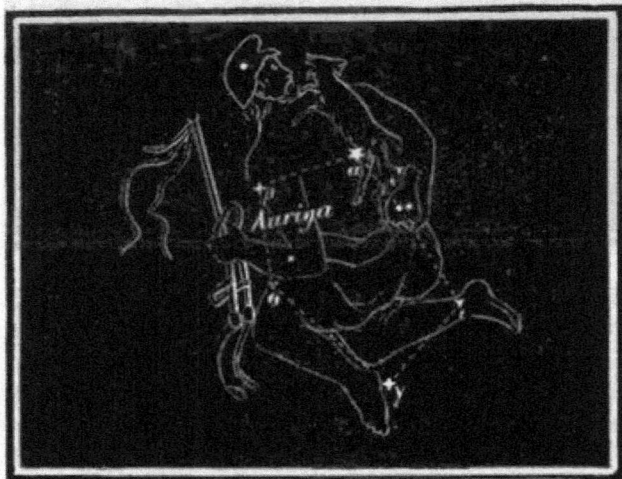

Fig. 389.

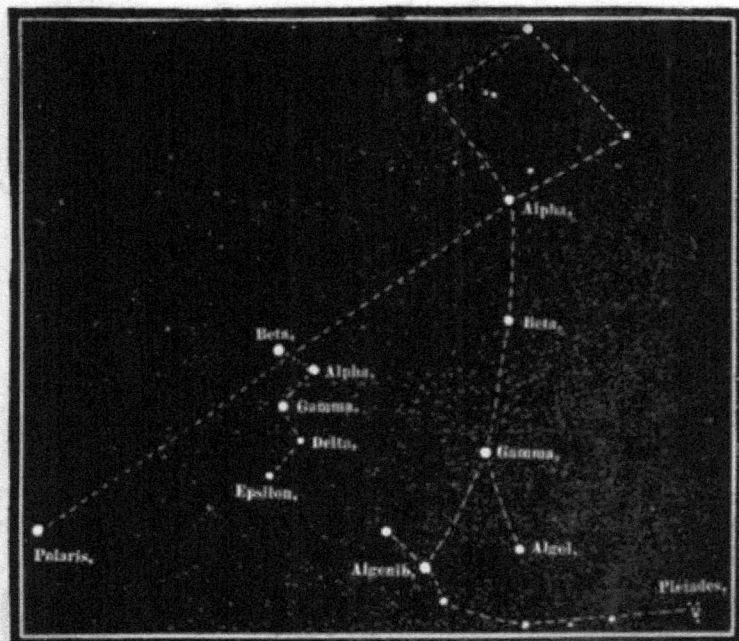

Fig. 390.

Pegasus, an asterism similar in configuration to the *Great*

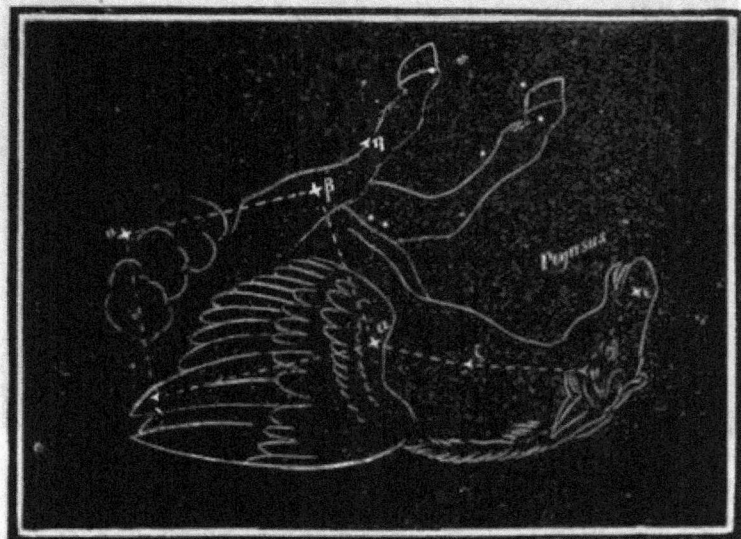

Fig. 391.

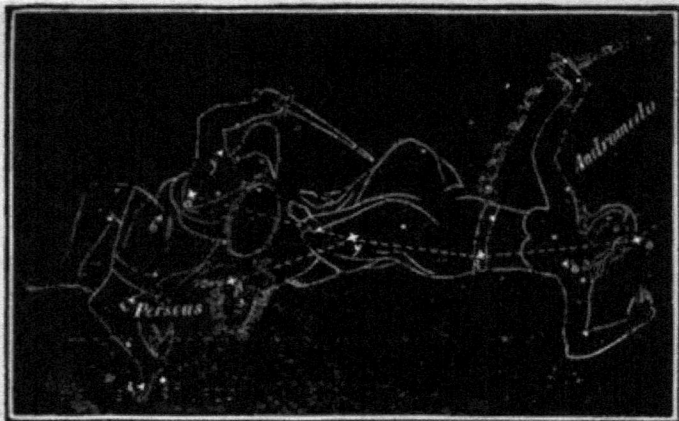

Fig. 390.

Dipper, belongs to *Perseus*. *Algenib*, which is reached by
bending the line at Gamma in the opposite direction, is the
principal star of *Perseus*.

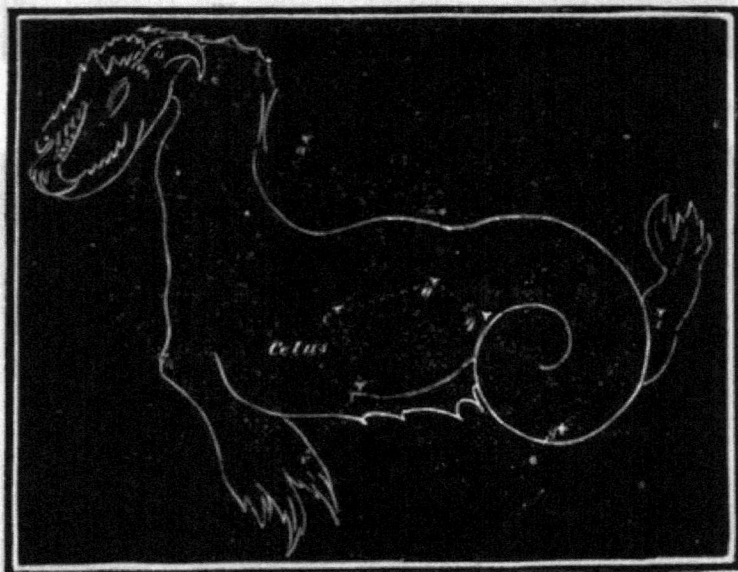

Fig. 393.

Pegasus is shown in Fig. 391, and *Andromeda* in Fig. 392.
Cetus, the *Whale*, or the *Sea Monster*, shown in Fig. 393,
belongs to the same mythological group of constellations.

339. *Scorpio*, *Sagittarius*, *and Ophiuchus*. — During the summer months a brilliant constellation is visible, called *Scorpio*, or the *Scorpion*. The configuration of the chief stars of this constellation is shown in Fig. 394. They bear some resemblance to a boy's kite. The brightest star is of the first magnitude, and called *Antares* (from *anti*, instead of, and *Ares*, the Greek name of Mars), because it rivals Mars in redness. The stars in the tail of the Scorpion are visible in our latitude only under very favorable circumstances. This constellation

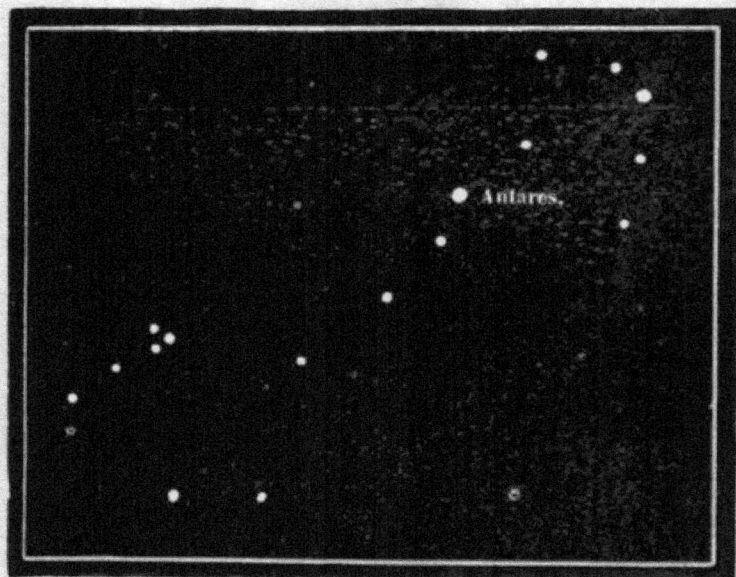

Fig. 394.

is shown in Fig. 395, together with *Sagittarius* and *Ophiuchus*. *Sagittarius*, or the *Archer*, is to the east of *Scorpio*. It contains no bright stars, but is easily recognized from the fact that five of its principal stars form the outline of an inverted dipper, which, from the fact of its being partly in the Milky-Way, is often called the *Milk Dipper*.

Ophiuchus, or the *Serpent-Bearer*, is a large constellation, filling all the space between the head of *Hercules* and *Scorpio*. It is difficult to trace, since it contains no very brilliant stars. This constellation and *Libra*, or the *Balances*, which is

Fig. 395.

the zodiacal constellation to the west of Scorpio, are shown
in Fig. 396.

Fig. 396.

340. *Capricornus, Aquarius, and the Southern Fish.*—The

Fig. 397.

two zodiacal constellations to the east of Sagittarius are *Capri-*

cornus and *Aquarius*. *Capricornus* contains three pairs of small stars, which mark the head, the tail, and the knees of the animal.

Aquarius is marked by no conspicuous stars. An irregular line of minute stars marks the course of the stream of water which flows from the Water-Bearer's Urn into the mouth of the *Southern Fish*. This mouth is marked by the first-magnitude star *Fomalhaut*. These constellations are shown in Fig. 397.

341. *Pisces and Aries.* — The remaining zodiacal constellations are *Pisces*, or the *Fishes*, *Aries*, or the *Ram* (Fig. 398), and *Cancer*, or the *Crab*.

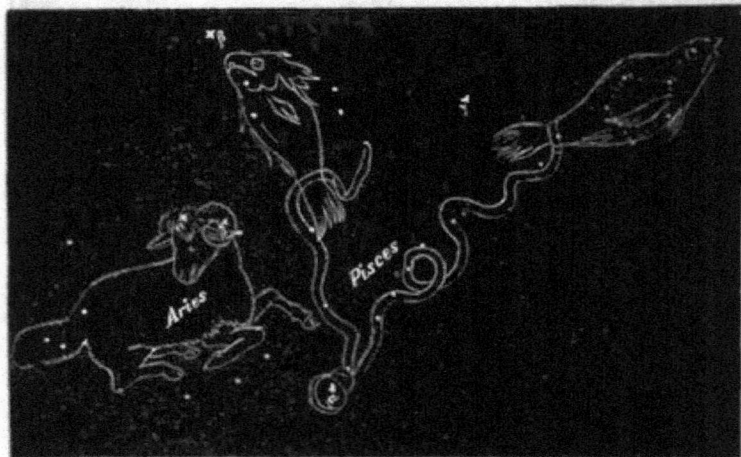

Fig. 398.

The *Fishes* lie under *Pegasus* and *Andromeda*, but contain no bright stars. *Aries* (between *Pisces* and *Taurus*) is marked by a pair of stars on the head, — one of the second, and one of the third magnitude. *Cancer* (between *Leo* and *Gemini*) has no bright stars, but contains a remarkable cluster of small stars called *Præsepe*, or the *Beehive*.

CLUSTERS.

342. *The Hyades.* — The *Hyades* are a very open cluster in the face of *Taurus* (334). The three brightest stars of this cluster form a letter *V*, the point of the *V* being on the nose, and the open ends at the eyes. This cluster is shown in Fig.

399. The name, according to the most probable etymology, means *rainy;* and they are said to have been so called because their rising was associated with wet weather. They were usually considered the daughters of Atlas, and sisters of the Pleiades, though sometimes referred to as the nurses of Bacchus.

343. *The Pleiades.* — The *Pleiades* constitute a celebrated

Fig. 399.

group of stars, or a miniature constellation, on the shoulder of *Taurus*. Hesiod mentions them as "the seven virgins of Atlas born," and Milton calls them "the seven Atlantic sisters." They are referred to in the Book of Job. The Spaniards term them "the little nanny-goats;" and they are sometimes called "the hen and chickens."

Usually only six stars in this cluster can be seen with the naked eye, and this fact has given rise to the legend of the

Fig. 400.

"lost Pleiad." On a clear, moonless night, however, a good

eye can discern seven or eight stars, and some observers have distinguished as many as eleven. Fig. 400 shows the *Pleiades*

Fig. 401.

as they appear to the naked eye under the most favorable circumstances. Fig. 401 shows this cluster as it appears in a powerful telescope. With such an instrument more than five hundred stars are visible.

344. *Cluster in the Sword-handle of Perseus.* — This is a somewhat dense double cluster. It is visible to the naked eye, appearing as a hazy star. A line drawn from *Algenib*, or *Alpha* of *Perseus* (338), to *Delta* of *Cassiopeia* (330), will pass through this cluster at about two-thirds the distance from the former. This double cluster is one of the most brilliant objects in the heavens, with a telescope of moderate power.

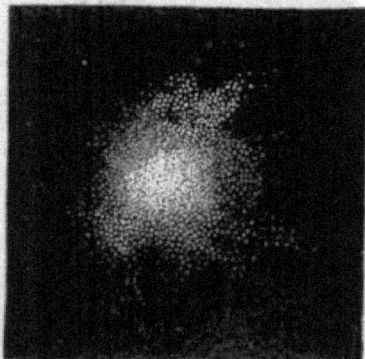
Fig. 402.

345. *Cluster of Hercules.* — The celebrated globular cluster of *Hercules* can be seen only with a telescope of considerable power, and to resolve it into

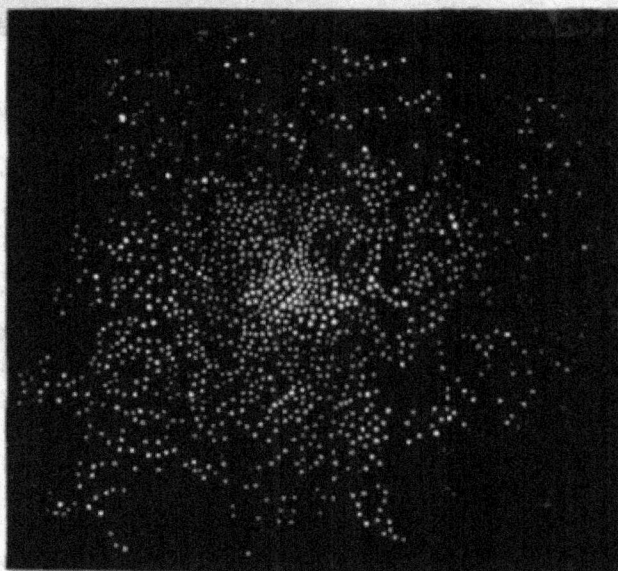
Fig. 403.

distinct stars (as shown in Fig. 402) requires an instrument of the very highest class.

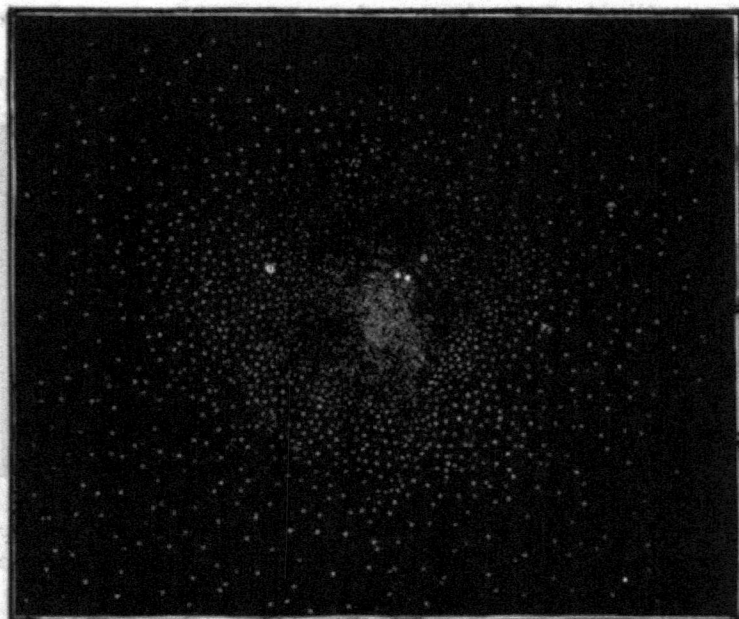

Fig. 404.

346. *Other Clusters.* — Fig. 403 shows a magnificent globular cluster in the constellation *Aquarius.* Herschel describes it as appearing like a heap of sand, being composed of thousands of stars of the fifteenth magnitude.

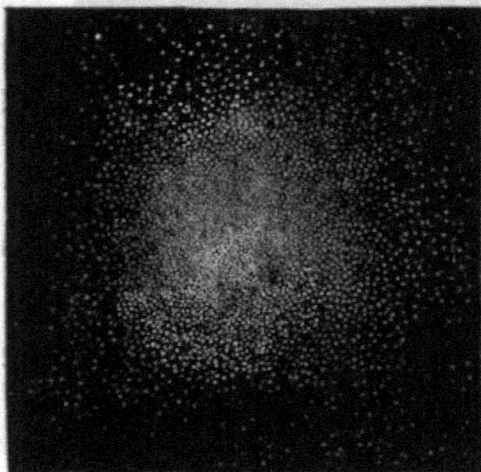

Fig. 405.

Fig. 404 shows a cluster in the constellation *Toucan,* which Sir John Herschel describes as a most glorious globular cluster, the stars of the fourteenth magnitude being immensely numerous. There is a marked condensation of light at the centre.

Fig. 405 shows a cluster in the *Centaur*, which, according to the same astronomer, is beyond comparison the richest and largest object of the kind in the heavens, the stars in it being literally innumerable. Fig. 406 shows a cluster in *Scorpio*, remarkable for the peculiar arrangement of its component stars.

Star clusters are especially abundant in the region of the Milky-Way, the law of their distribution being the reverse of that of the nebulæ.

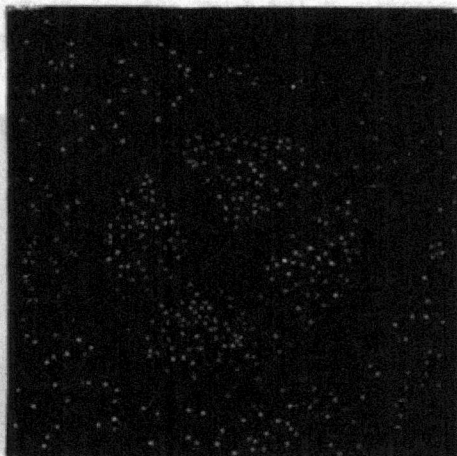

Fig. 406.

DOUBLE AND MULTIPLE STARS.

347. *Double Stars*. — The telescope shows that many stars which appear single to the naked eye are really *double*, or composed of a pair of stars lying side by side. There are several pairs of stars in the heavens which lie so near

Fig. 407.

Fig. 408.

together that they almost seem to touch when seen with the naked eye.

Pairs of stars are not considered double unless the components are so near together that they both appear in the

field of view when examined with a telescope. In the
majority of the pairs classed as double stars the distance
between the components ranges from half a second to
fifteen seconds.

Epsilon Lyræ is a good
example of a pair of
stars that can barely be
separated with a good
eye. Figs. 407 and 408
show this pair as it ap-
pears in telescopes mag-
nifying respectively four
and fifteen times; and
Fig. 409 shows it as seen
in a more powerful tele-
scope, in which each of

Fig. 409.

the two components of the pair is seen to be a truly double
star.

348. *Multiple Stars.* — When a star is resolved into
more than two components by a telescope, it is called a
multiple star. Fig. 410 shows a *triple* star in *Pegasus.*

Fig. 410.

Fig. 411.

Fig. 411 shows a quadruple star in *Taurus.* Fig. 412
shows a *sextuple* star, and Fig. 413 a *septuple* star. Fig.
414 shows the celebrated septuple star in *Orion*, called
Theta Orionis, or the *trapezium* of Orion.

349. *Optically Double and Multiple Stars.* — Two or more stars which are really very distant from each other, and which have no physical connection whatever, may appear to be near together, because they happen to lie in the same direction, one behind the other. Such accidental combinations are called *optically* double or multiple stars.

Fig. 412. Fig. 413.

350. *Physically Double and Multiple Stars.* — In the majority of cases the components of double and multiple stars are in reality comparatively near together, and are bound together by gravity into a physical system. Such combinations are called *physically* double and multiple stars. The components of these systems all revolve around their common centre of gravity. In many instances their orbits and periods of revolution have been ascertained by observation and

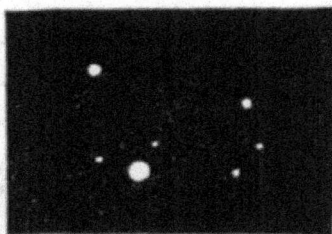

Fig. 414.

calculation. Fig. 415 shows the orbit of one of the components of a double star in the constellation *Hercules*.

351. *Colors of Double and Multiple Stars.* — The components of double and multiple stars are often highly colored, and frequently the components of the same system are of different colors. Sometimes one star of a binary system is *white*, and the other *red;* and sometimes a *white*

star is combined with a *blue* one.   Other colors found in combination in these systems are *red* and *blue, orange* and *green, blue* and *green, yellow* and *blue, yellow* and *red*, etc.

If these double and multiple stars are accompanied by

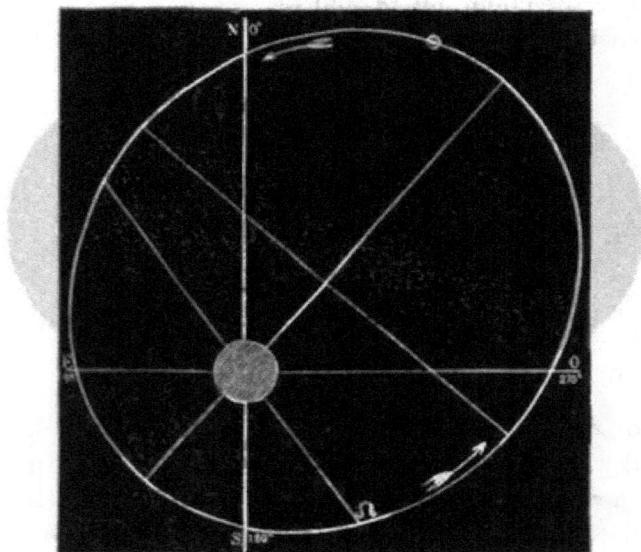

Fig. 415.

planets, these planets will sometimes have two or more suns in the sky at once.   On alternate days they may have suns of different colors, and perhaps on the same day two suns of different colors.   The effect of these changing colored lights on the landscape must be very remarkable.

NEW AND VARIABLE STARS.

352. *Variable Stars.* — There are many stars which undergo changes of brilliancy, sometimes slight, but occasionally very marked.   These changes are in some cases apparently irregular, and in others *periodic*.   All such stars are said to be *variable*, though the term is applied especially to those stars whose variability is *periodic*.

353. *Algol.* — *Algol*, a star of *Perseus*, whose position is shown in Fig. 416, is a remarkable variable star of a short period. Usually it shines as a faint second-magnitude star; but at intervals of a little less than three days it fades to the fourth magnitude for a few hours, and then regains its former brightness. These changes were first noticed some two centuries ago, but it was not till 1782 that they were accurately observed. The period is now known to be two days, twenty hours, forty-nine minutes. It takes about four hours and a half to fade away, and four hours more to recover its brilliancy. Near the beginning and end of the variations, the change is very slow, so that there are not more than five or six hours during which an ordinary observer would see that the star was less bright than usual.

This variation of light was at first explained by supposing that a large dark planet was revolving round Algol, and passed over its face at every revolution, thus cutting off a portion of its light; but there are small irregularities in the variation, which this theory does not account for.

Fig. 416.

354. *Mira.*—Another remarkable variable star is *Omicron Ceti*, or *Mira* (that is, the *wonderful* star). It is generally invisible to the naked eye; but at intervals of about eleven months it shines forth as a star of the second or third magnitude. It is about forty days from the time it becomes visible until it attains its greatest brightness, and is then about two months in fading to invisibility; so that its increase of brilliancy is more rapid than its waning. Its period is quite irregular, ranging from ten to twelve months; so that the times of its appearance cannot be predicted

with certainty. Its maximum brightness is also variable,
being sometimes of the second magnitude, and at others
only of the third or fourth.

355. *Eta Argus.* — Perhaps the most extraordinary variable star in the heavens is *Eta Argus,* in the constellation
Argo, or the *Ship,* in the southern hemisphere (Fig. 417).
The first careful observations of its variability were made
by Sir John Herschel while at the Cape of Good Hope.
He says, "It was on the 16th of December, 1837, that,
resuming the photometrical comparisons, my astonishment
was excited by the appearance of a new candidate for dis-
tinction among the very brightest stars of the first magni-

Fig. 417.

tude in a part of the heavens
where, being perfectly familiar
with it, I was certain that no
such brilliant object had before
been seen. After a momentary
hesitation, the natural consequence of a phenomenon so
utterly unexpected, and refer-
ring to a map for its configuration with other conspicuous
stars in the neighborhood, I

became satisfied of its identity with my old acquaintance,
Eta Argus. Its light was, however, nearly tripled. While
yet low, it equalled Rigel, and, when it attained some
altitude, was decidedly greater." It continued to increase
until Jan. 2, 1838, then faded a little till April following,
though it was still as bright as Aldebaran. In 1842 and
1843 it blazed up brighter than ever, and in March of the
latter year was second only to *Sirius.* During the twenty-
five years following it slowly but steadily diminished. In
1867 it was barely visible to the naked eye; and the next
year it vanished entirely from the unassisted view, and has
not yet begun to recover its brightness. The curve in

Fig. 418 shows the change in brightness of this remarkable star. The numbers at the bottom show the years of the century, and those at the side the brightness of the star.

356. *New Stars.* — In several cases stars have suddenly appeared, and even become very brilliant; then, after a longer or shorter time, they have faded away and disappeared. Such stars are called *new* or *temporary* stars. For a time it was supposed that such stars were actually new. They are now, however, classified by astronomers among the variable stars, their changes being of a very irregular and fitful character. There is scarcely a doubt that they were all in the heavens as very small stars before

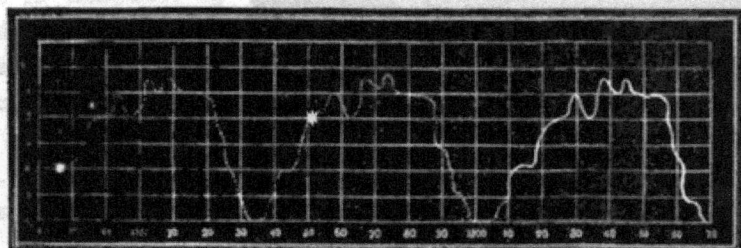

Fig. 418.

they blazed forth in so extraordinary a manner, and that they are in the same places still. There is a wide difference between these irregular variations, or the breaking-forth of light on a single occasion in the course of centuries, and the regular and periodic changes in the case of a star like *Algol;* but a long series of careful observation has resulted in the discovery of stars of nearly every degree of irregularity between these two extremes. Some of them change gradually from one magnitude to another, in the course of years, without seeming to follow any law whatever; while in others some slight tendency to regularity can be traced. *Eta Argus* may be regarded as a connecting link between new and variable stars.

357. *Tycho Brahe's Star.* — An apparently new star

suddenly appeared in *Cassiopeia* in 1572. It was first seen by Tycho Brahe, and is therefore associated with his name. Its position in the constellation is shown in Fig. 419. It was first seen on Nov. 11, when it had already attained the first magnitude. It became rapidly brighter, soon rivalling Venus in splendor, so that good eyes could discern it in full daylight. In December it began to wane, and gradually faded until the following May, when it disappeared entirely.

A star showed itself in the same part of the heavens in 945 and in 1264. If these were three appearances of the same star, it must be reckoned as a periodic star with a period of a little more than three hundred years.

Fig. 419.

358. *Kepler's Star.* — In 1604 a new star was seen in the constellation *Ophiuchus.* It was first noticed in October of that year, when it was of the first magnitude. In the following winter it began to fade, but remained visible during the whole year 1605. Early in 1606 it disappeared entirely. A very full history of this star was written by Kepler.

One of the most remarkable things about this star was its brilliant scintillation. According to Kepler, it displayed all the colors of the rainbow, or of a diamond cut with multiple facets, and exposed to the rays of the sun. It is thought that this star also appeared in 393. 798, and 1203; if so, it is a variable star with a period of a little over four hundred years.

359. *New Star of 1866.* — The most striking case of this kind in recent times was in May, 1866, when a star of the second magnitude suddenly appeared in *Corona Borealis*. On the 11th and 12th of that month it was observed independently by at least five observers in Europe and America. The fact that none of these new stars were noticed until they had nearly or quite attained their greatest brilliancy renders it probable that they all blazed up very suddenly.

360. *Cause of the Variability of Stars.* — The changes in the brightness of variable and temporary stars are probably due to operations similar to those which produce the spots and prominences in our sun. We have seen (188) that the frequency of solar spots shows a period of eleven years, during one portion of which there are few or no spots to be seen, while during another portion they are numerous. If an observer so far away as to see our sun like a star could from time to time measure its light exactly, he would find it to be a variable star with a period of eleven years, the light being least when we see most spots, and greatest when few are visible. The variation would be slight, but it would nevertheless exist. Now, · we have reason to believe that the physical constitution of the sun and the stars is of the same general nature. It is therefore probable, that, if we could get a nearer view of the stars, we should see spots on their disks as we do on the sun. It is also likely that the varying physical constitution of the stars might give rise to great differences in the number and size of the spots; so that the light of some of these suns might vary to a far greater degree than that of our own sun does. If the variations had a regular period, as in the case of our sun, the appearances to a distant observer would be precisely what we see in the case of a periodic variable star.

The spectrum of the new star of 1866 was found to be a continuous one. crossed by bright lines, which were apparently due to glowing hydrogen. The continuous spectrum was also crossed by dark lines, indicating that the light had passed through an atmosphere of comparatively cool gas. Mr. Huggins

infers from this that there was a sudden and extraordinary out-
burst of hydrogen gas from the star, which by its own light,
as well as by heating up the whole surface of the star, caused
the extraordinary increase of brilliancy. Now, the spectroscope shows that the red flames of the solar chromosphere
(197) are largely composed of hydrogen; and it is not unlikely
that the blazing-forth of this star arose from an action similar
to that which produces these flames, only on an immensely
larger scale.

DISTANCE OF THE STARS.

361. *Parallax of the Stars.* — Such is the distance of
the stars, that only in a comparatively few instances has any
displacement of these bodies been detected when viewed
from opposite parts of the earth's orbit, that is, from points
a hundred and eighty-five million miles apart; and in no
case can this displacement be detected except by the most
careful and delicate measurement. Half of the above displacement, or the displacement of the star as seen from
the earth instead of the sun, is called the *parallax* of the
star. In no case has a parallax of one second as yet been
detected.

362. *The Distance of the Stars.* — The distance of a star
whose parallax is one second would be 206,265 times the
distance of the earth from the sun, or about nineteen million
million miles. It is quite certain that no star is nearer than
this to the earth. Light has a velocity which would carry
it seven times and a half around the earth in a second; but
it would take it more than three years to reach us from
that distance. Were all the stars blotted out of existence
to-night, it would be at least three years before we should
miss a single one.

Alpha Centauri, the brightest star in the constellation
of the *Centaur*, is, so far as we know, the nearest of the
fixed stars. It is estimated that it would take its light about
three years and a half to reach us. It has also been esti-

mated that it would take light over sixteen years to reach us from *Sirius*, about eighteen years to reach us from *Vega*, about twenty-five years from *Arcturus*, and over forty years from the *Pole-Star*. In many instances it is believed that it would take the light of stars hundreds of years to make the journey to our earth, and in some instances even thousands of years.

PROPER MOTION OF THE STARS.

363. *Why the Stars appear Fixed.* — The stars seem to retain their relative positions in the heavens from year to

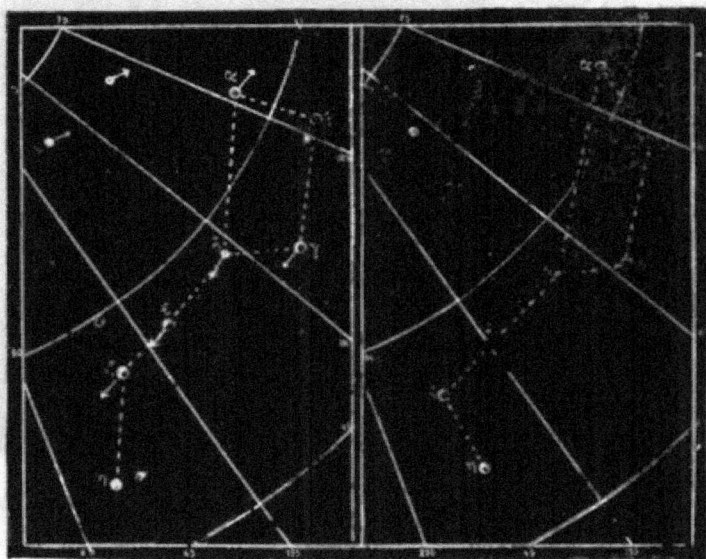

Fig. 420.

year, and from age to age; and hence they have come universally to be denominated as *fixed*. It is, however, now well known that the stars, instead of being really stationary, are moving at the rate of many miles a second; but their distance is so enormous, that, in the majority of cases, it would be thousands of years before this rate of motion would produce a sufficient displacement to be noticeable to the unaided eye.

364. *Secular Displacement of the Stars.* — Though the proper motion of the stars is apparently slight, it will, in the course of many ages, produce a marked change in the configuration of the stars. Thus, in Fig. 420, the left-hand portion shows the present configuration of the stars of the Great Dipper. The small arrows attached to the stars show the direction and comparative magnitudes of their motion. The right-hand portion of the figure shows these

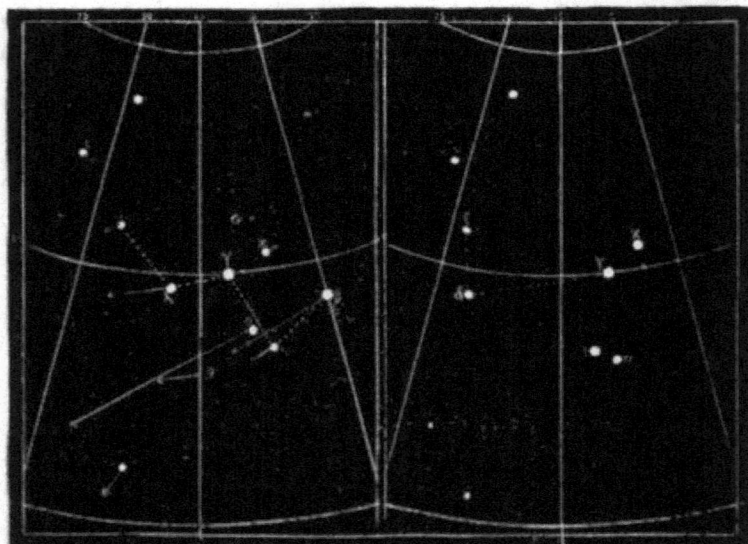

Fig. 421.

stars as they will appear thirty-six thousand years from the present time.

Fig. 421 shows in a similar way the present configuration and proper motion of the stars of *Cassiopeia*, and also these stars as they will appear thirty-six thousand years hence.

Fig. 422 shows the same for the constellation *Orion*.

365. *The Secular Motion of the Sun.* — The stars in all parts of the heavens are found to move in all directions and with all sorts of velocities. When, however, the motions

of the stars are averaged, there is found to be an apparent proper motion common to all the stars. The stars in the

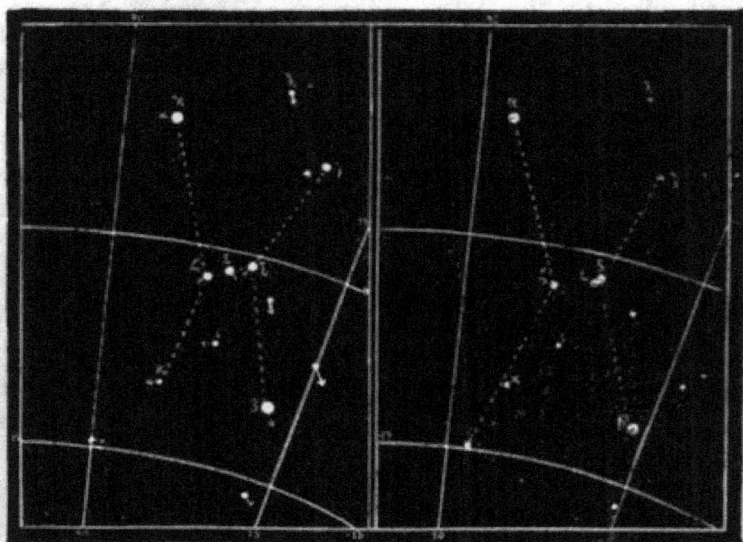

Fig. 422.

neighborhood of *Hercules* appear to be approaching us, and those in the opposite part of the heavens appear to be receding from us. In other words, all the stars appear to be moving away from Hercules, and towards the opposite part of the heavens.

Fig. 423.

This apparent motion common to all the stars is held by astronomers to be due to the real motion of the sun through space. The point in the heavens towards which our sun is moving at the present time is indicated by the small circle in the constellation Hercules in Fig. 423. As the sun moves, he carries the earth and all the planets along with him. Fig. 424 shows the direction of the sun's motion

Fig. 424.

with reference to the ecliptic and to the axis of the earth. Fig. 425 shows the earth's path in space; and Fig. 426 shows the paths of the earth, the moon, Mercury, Venus, and Mars in space.

Whether the sun is actually moving in a straight line, or around some distant centre, it is impossible to determine at the present time. It is estimated that the sun is moving along his path at the rate of about a hundred and fifty million miles a year. This is about five-sixths of the diameter of the earth's orbit.

366. *Star - Drift.* — In several instances, groups of stars have a common proper motion entirely different from that of the stars around and among them. Such groups probably form connected systems, in the motion of

Fig. 425.

which all the stars are carried along together without any great change in their relative positions. The most remarkable case of this kind occurs in the constellation *Taurus.* A large majority of the brighter stars in the region between *Aldebaran* and the *Pleiades* have a common proper motion of about ten seconds per century towards the east. Proctor has shown that five out of the seven stars which form the Great Dipper have a common proper

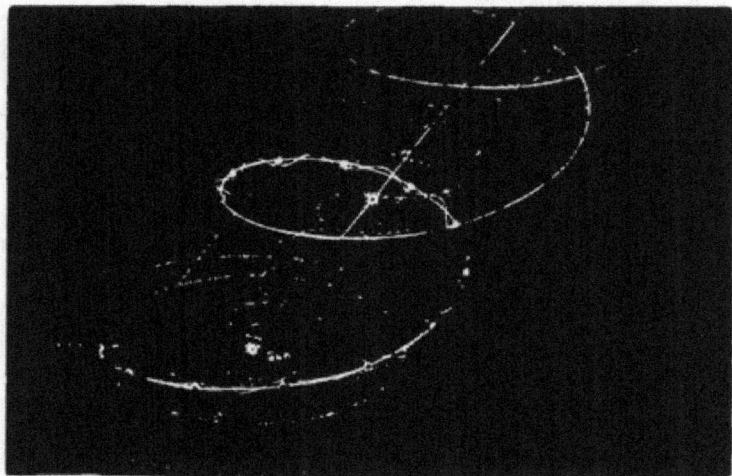

Fig. 426.

motion, as shown in Fig. 427 (see also Fig. 420). He proposes for this phenomenon the name of *Star-Drift*.

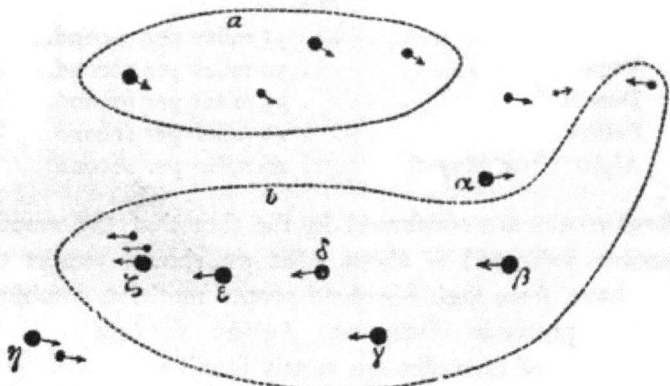

Fig. 427.

367. *Motion of Stars along the Line of Sight.* — A motion of a star in the direction of the line of sight would produce no displacement of the star that could be detected with the

telescope; but it would cause a change in the brightness of
the star, which would become gradually fainter if moving from
us, and brighter if approaching us. Motion along the line
of sight has, however, been detected by the use of the telespectroscope (152), owing to the fact that it causes a displacement of the spectral lines. As has already been explained
(169), a displacement of a spectral line towards the red end
of the spectrum indicates a motion away from us, and a displacement towards the violet end, a motion towards us.

By means of these displacements of the spectral lines,
Huggins has detected motion in the case of a large number
of stars, and calculated its rate : —

STARS RECEDING FROM US.

Sirius . . . . 20 miles per second.
Betelgeuse . . . . . . 22 miles per second.
Rigel . . . . 15 miles per second.
Castor . . . . 25 miles per second.
Regulus . . . . 15 miles per second.

STARS APPROACHING US.

Arcturus . . . . . . 55 miles per second.
Vega . . . . 50 miles per second.
Deneb . . . . 39 miles per second.
Pollux . . . . 49 miles per second.
Alpha Ursæ Majoris . . . 46 miles per second.

These results are confirmed by the fact that the amount
of motion indicated is about what we should expect the
stars to have, from their observed proper motions, combined .
with their probable distances. Again : the stars in the
neighborhood of Hercules are mostly found to be approaching the earth, and those which lie in the opposite direction
to be receding from it ; which is exactly the effect which
would result from the sun's motion through space. The
five stars in the Dipper, which have a common proper

ASTRONOMY. 371

motion, are also found to have a common motion in the
line of sight. But the displacement of the spectral lines
is so slight, and its measurement so difficult, that the velocities in the above table are to be accepted as only an
approximation to the true values.

CHEMICAL AND PHYSICAL CONSTITUTION OF THE STARS.

368. *The Constitution of the Stars Similar to that of
the Sun.* — The stellar spectra bear a general resemblance
to that of the sun, with characteristic differences. These
spectra all show Fraunhofer's lines, which indicate that
their luminous surfaces are surrounded by atmospheres containing absorbent vapors, as in the case of the sun. The
positions of these lines indicate that the stellar atmospheres
contain elements which are also found in the sun's, and
on the earth.

369. *Four Types of Stellar Spectra.* — The spectra of
the stars have been carefully observed by Secchi and Huggins. They have found that stellar spectra may be reduced
to four types, which are shown in Fig. 428. In the spectrum of *Sirius*, a representative of *Type I.*, very few lines
are represented ; but the lines are very thick.

Next we have the solar spectrum, which is a representative of *Type II.*, one in which more lines are represented. In *Type III.* fluted spaces begin to appear,
and in *Type IV.*, which is that of the red stars, nothing
but fluted spaces is visible , and this spectrum shows that
something is at work in the atmosphere of those red
stars different from what there is in the simpler atmosphere
of *Type I.*

Lockyer holds that these differences of spectra are due
simply to differences of temperature. According to him,
the red stars, which give the fluted spectra, are of the
lowest temperature ; and the temperature of the stars of

the different types gradually rises till we reach the first
type, in which the temperature is so high that the dis-

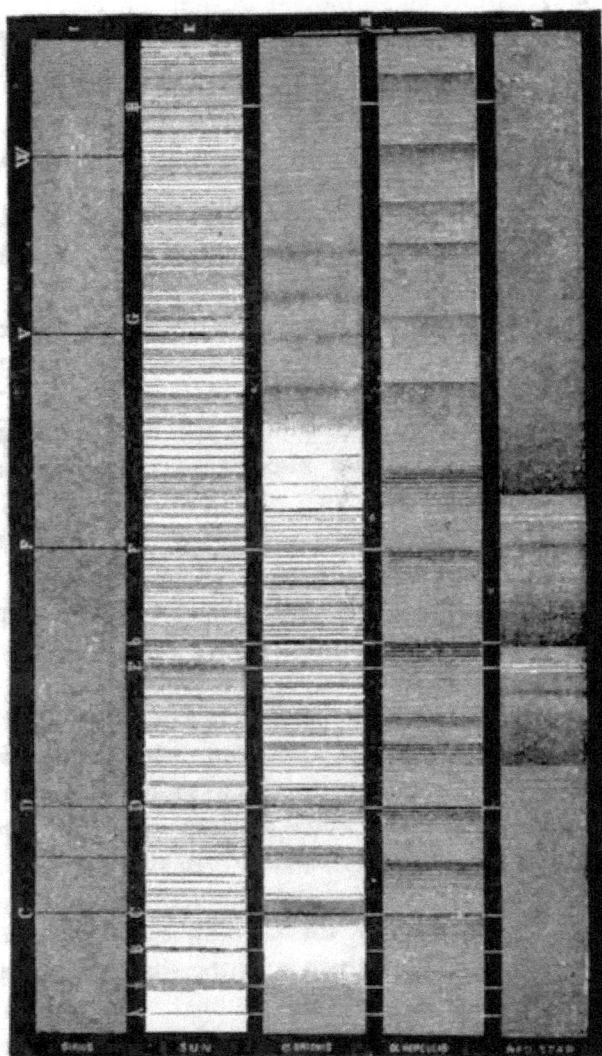

Fig. 428.

sociation (161) of the elements is nearly if not quite
complete.

III. NEBULÆ.

CLASSIFICATION OF NEBULÆ.

370. *Planetary Nebulæ.* — Many nebulæ (328) present a well-defined circular disk, like that of a planet, and are therefore called *planetary* nebulæ. Specimens of planetary nebulæ are shown in Fig. 429.

371. *Circular and Elliptical Nebulæ.* — While many nebulæ are circular in form, others are elliptical. The former are called *circular* nebulæ, and the latter *elliptical* nebulæ. Elliptical nebulæ have been discovered of every degree of eccentricity. Examples of various circular and elliptical nebulæ are given in Fig. 430.

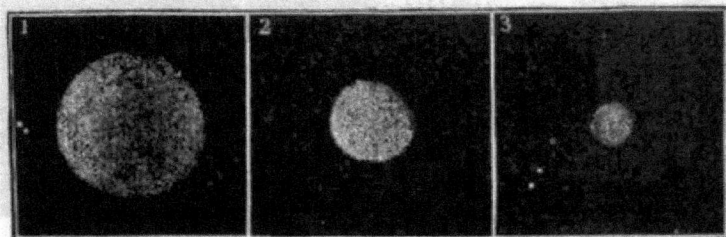

Fig. 429.

372. *Annular Nebulæ.* — Occasionally ring-shaped nebulæ have been observed, sometimes with, and sometimes without, nebulous matter within the ring. They are called *annular* nebulæ. They are both circular and elliptical in form. Several specimens of this class of nebulæ are given in Fig. 431.

373. *Nebulous Stars.* — Sometimes one or more minute stars are enveloped in a nebulous haze, and are hence called *nebulous stars.* Several of these nebulæ are shown in Fig. 432.

374. *Spiral Nebulæ.* — Very many nebulæ disclose a more or less spiral structure, and are known as *spiral* nebulæ. They are illustrated in Fig. 433. There are, how-

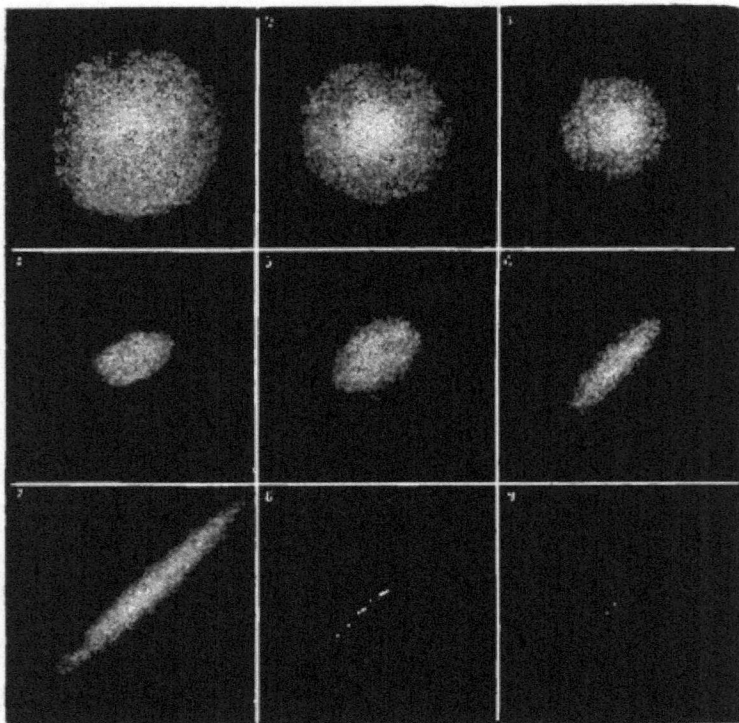

Fig. 430.

ever, a great variety of spiral forms. We shall have occasion to speak of these nebulæ again (381–383).

375. *Double and Multiple Nebulæ.* — Many *double* and

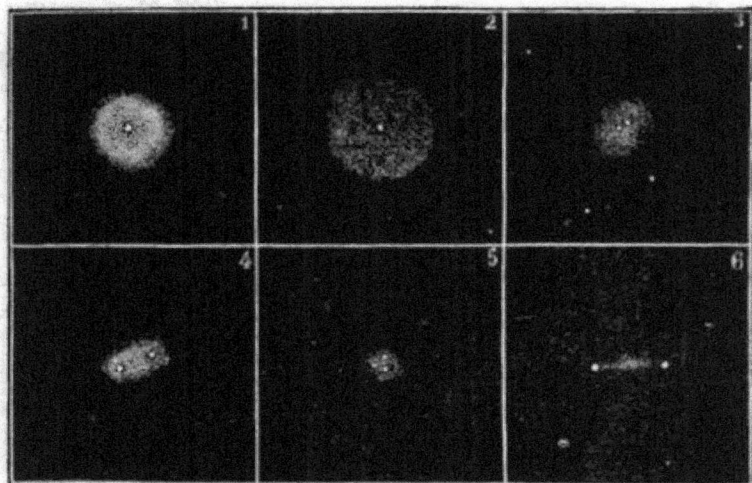

Fig. 432.

multiple nebulæ have been observed, some of which are
represented in Fig. 434.

Fig. 435 shows what appears to be a double annular
nebula. Fig. 436 gives two views of a double nebula.

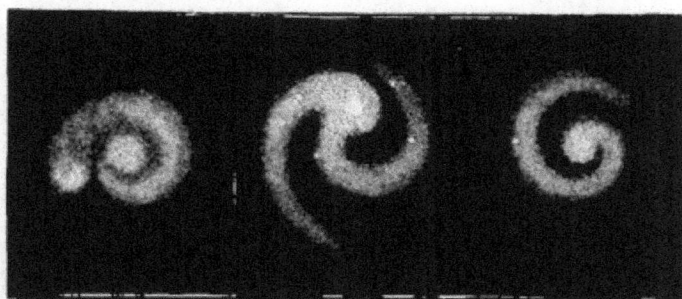

Fig. 433.

The change of position in the components of this double
nebula indicates a motion of revolution similar to that of
the components of double stars.

IRREGULAR NEBULÆ.

376. *Irregular Forms.* — Besides the more or less regular forms of nebulæ which have been classified as indicated

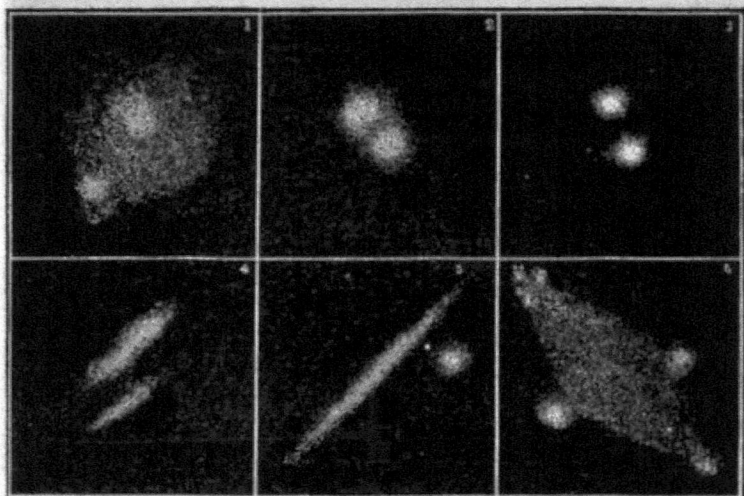

Fig. 434.

above, there are many of very irregular shapes, and some of these are the most remarkable nebulæ in the heavens. Fig. 437 shows a curiously shaped nebula, seen by Sir John Herschel in the southern heavens; and Fig. 438, one in *Taurus*, known as the *Crab* nebula.

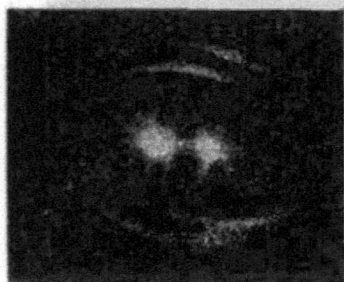

Fig. 435.

377. *The Great Nebula of Andromeda.* — This is one of the few nebulæ that are visible to the naked eye. We see at a glance that it is not a star, but a mass of diffused light. Indeed, it has sometimes been very naturally mistaken for a comet. It was first described by Marius in 1614, who compared its light to

that of a candle shining through horn. This gives a very good idea of the impression it produces, which is that of a translucent object illuminated by a brilliant light behind it. With a small telescope it is easy to imagine it to be a solid like horn; but with a large one the effect is more like fog or mist with a bright body in its midst. Unlike most of the nebulæ, its spectrum is a continuous one, similar

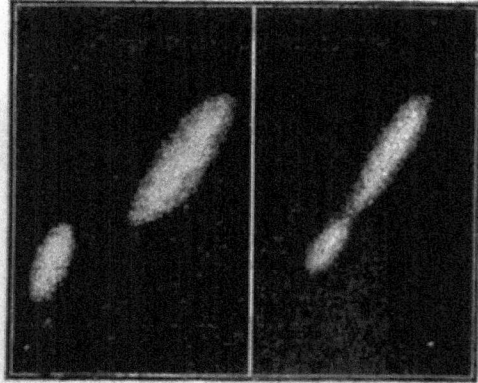

Fig. 436.

to that from a heated solid, indicating that the light emanates, not from a glowing gas, but from matter in the solid or liquid state. This would suggest that it is really

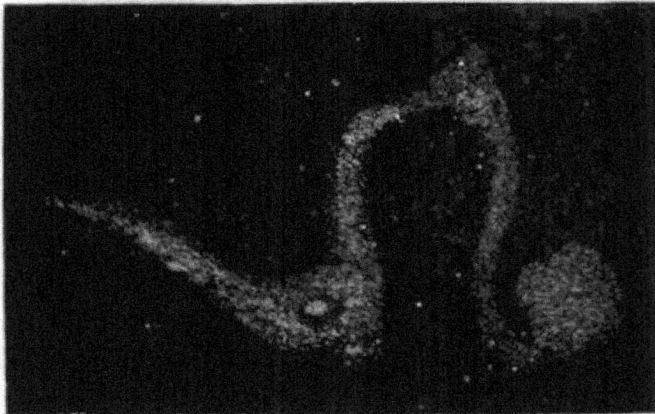

Fig. 437.

an immense star-cluster, so distant that the highest telescopic power cannot resolve it; yet in the largest telescopes it looks less resolvable, and more like a gas, than in those of moderate size. If it is really a gas, and if the spectrum is continuous throughout the whole extent of the nebula, either it must shine by reflected light, or the gas must be subjected to a great pressure almost to its outer limit, which is hardly possible. If the light is reflected, we cannot determine whether it comes from a single

Fig. 438.

bright star, or a number of small ones scattered through the nebula.

With a small telescope this nebula appears elliptical, as in Fig. 439. Fig. 440 shows it as it appeared to Bond, in the Cambridge refractor.

378. *The Great Nebula of Orion.* — The nebula which, above all others, has occupied the attention of astrono-

ASTRONOMY.

ASTRONOMY.

mers, and excited the wonder of observers, is the *great nebula of Orion*, which surrounds the middle star of the three which form the sword of Orion. A good eye will perceive that this star, instead of looking like a bright point, has a hazy appearance, due to the surrounding nebula. This object was first described by Huyghens in 1659, as follows : —

"There is one phenomenon among the fixed stars worthy of mention, which, so far as I know, has hitherto been

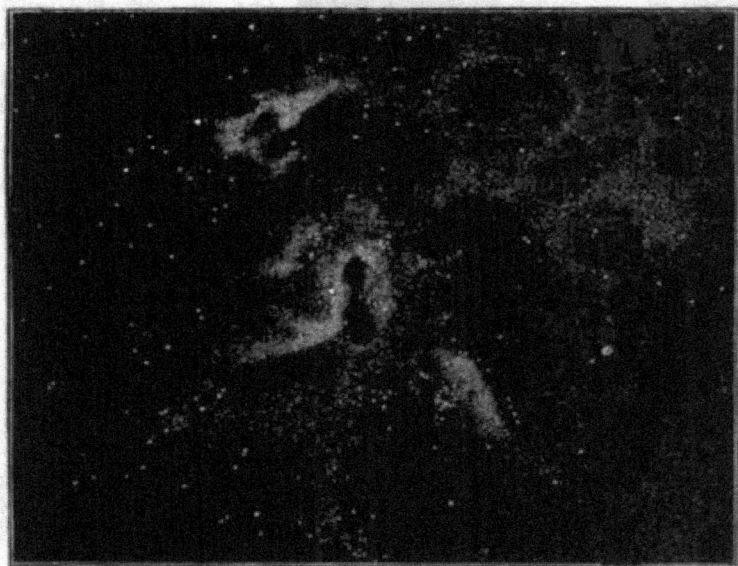

Fig. 442.

noticed by no one, and indeed cannot be well observed except with large telescopes. In the sword of Orion are three stars quite close together. In 1656, as I chanced to be viewing the middle one of these with the telescope, instead of a single star, twelve showed themselves (a not uncommon circumstance). Three of these almost touched each other, and with four others shone through a nebula, so that the space around them seemed far brighter than the rest of the heavens, which was entirely clear, and appeared quite black; the effect being that of an opening in the sky, through which a brighter region was visible."

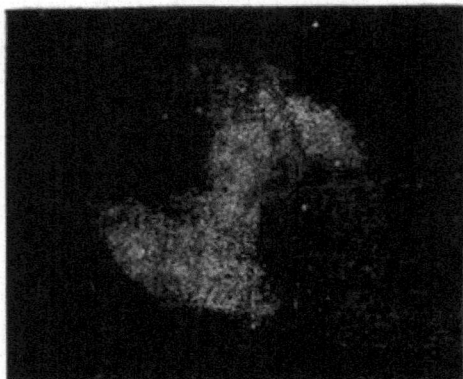

Fig. 443.

The representation of this nebula in Fig. 441 is from a drawing made by Bond. In brilliancy and variety of detail it exceeds any other nebula visible in the northern hemisphere. In its centre are four stars, easily distinguished by a small telescope with a magnifying power of forty or fifty, together with two

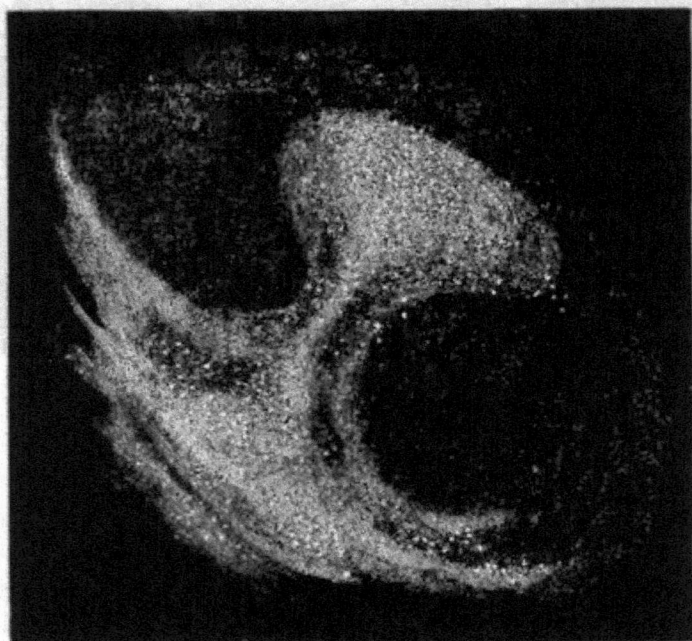

Fig. 444.

smaller ones, requiring a nine-inch telescope to be well seen. Besides these, the whole nebula is dotted with stars.

In the winter of 1864–65 the spectrum of this nebula was examined independently by Secchi and Huggins, who found that it consisted of three bright lines, and hence concluded that the nebula was composed, not of stars, but of glowing gas. The position of one of the lines was near that of a line of nitrogen, while another seemed to coincide with a hydrogen line. This would suggest that the nebula is a mixture of hydrogen and nitrogen gas; but of this we cannot be certain.

379. *The Nebula in Argus.* — There is a nebula (Fig. 442) surrounding the variable star *Eta Argus* (355), which is remarkable as exhibiting variations of brightness and of outline.

In many other nebulæ, changes have been suspected; but the indistinctness of outline which characterizes most of these ob-

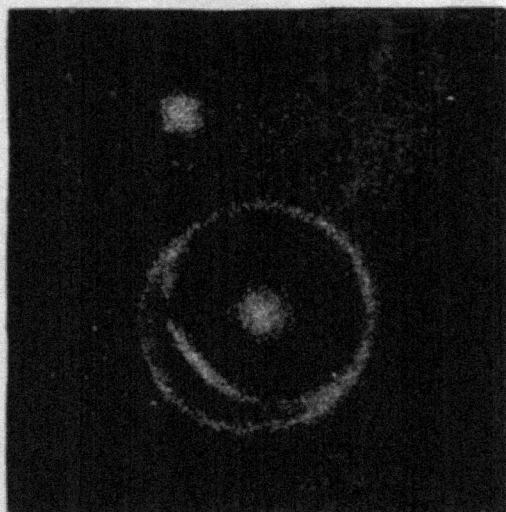

Fig. 445.

jects, and the very different aspect they present in telescopes of different powers, render it difficult to prove a change beyond a doubt.

380. *The Dumb-Bell Nebula.* — This nebula was named from its peculiar shape. It is a good illustration of the change in the appearance of a nebula when viewed with different magnifying powers. Fig. 443 shows it as it appeared in Herschel's telescope, and Fig. 444 as it appears in the great Parsonstown reflector (20).

SPIRAL NEBULÆ.

381. *The Spiral Nebula in Canes Venatici.* — The great spiral nebula in the constellation *Canes Venatici*, or the

Fig. 446.

Hunting-Dogs, is one of the most remarkable of its class. Fig. 445 shows this nebula as it appeared in Herschel's telescope, and Fig. 446 shows it as it appears in the Parsonstown reflector.

382. *Condensation of Nebulæ.* — The appearance of the

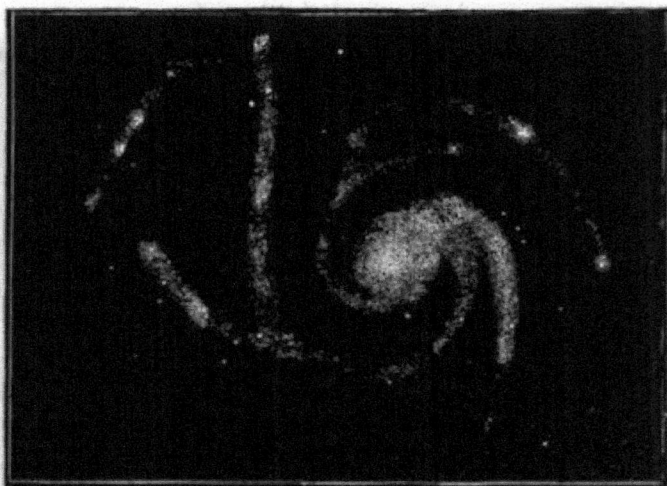

Fig. 447.

nebula just mentioned suggests a body rotating on its axis, and undergoing condensation at the same time.

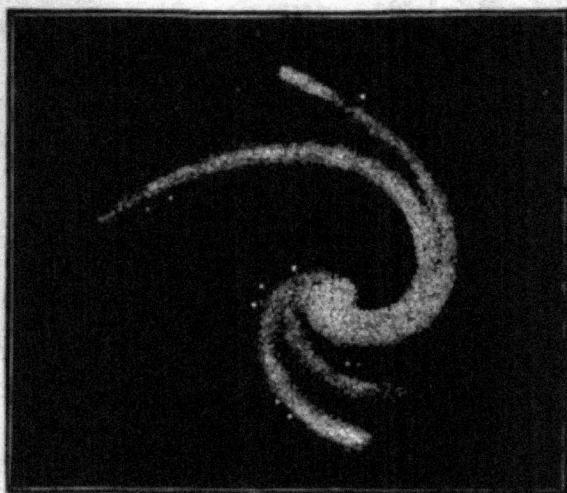

Fig. 448.

It is now a generally received theory that nebulæ are the material out of which stars are formed. According to this

theory, tne stars originally existed as nebulæ, and all nebulæ
will ultimately become condensed into stars.

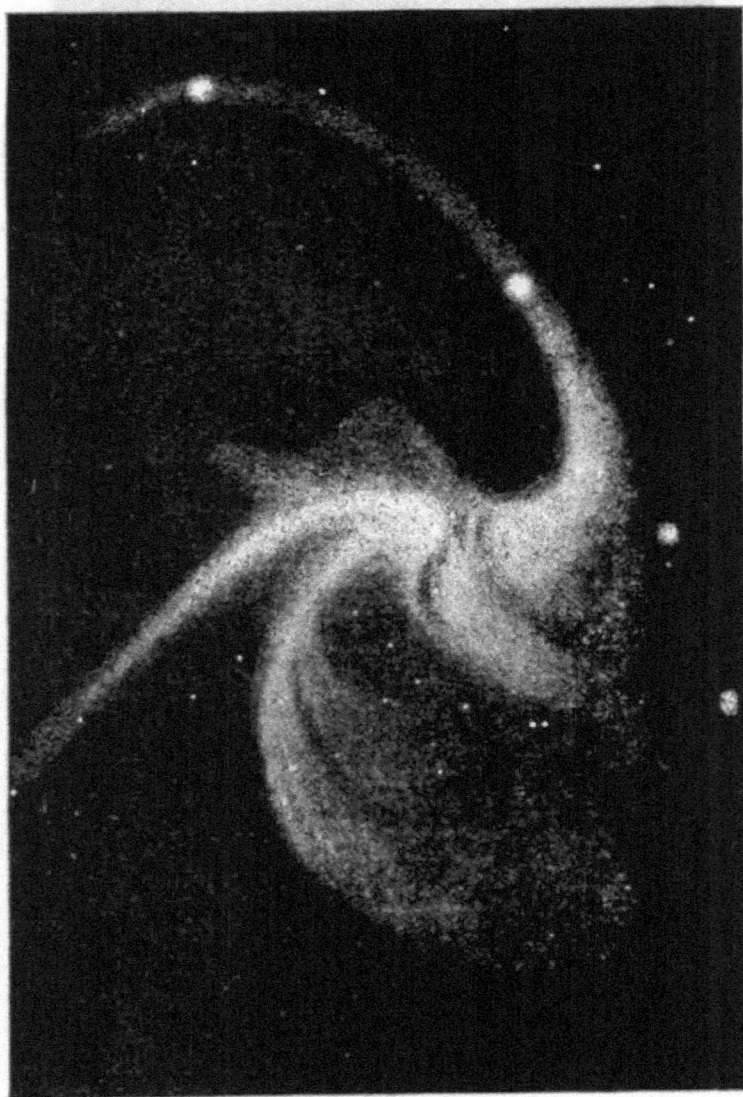

Fig. 449.

383. *Other Spiral Nebulæ.* — Fig. 447 represents a spiral

nebula of the *Great Bear.* This nebula seems to have several centres of condensation. Fig. 448 is a view of a spiral

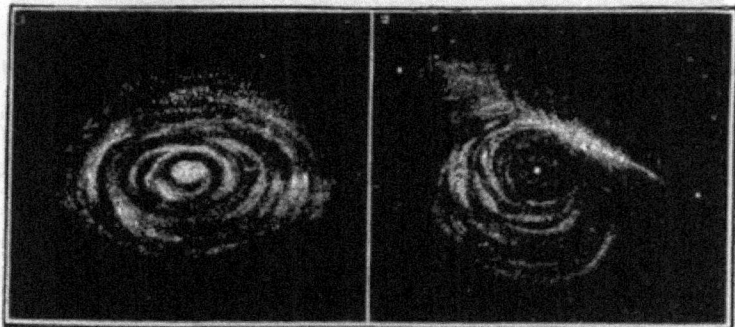

Fig. 450.

nebula in *Cepheus,* and Fig. 449 of a singular spiral nebula in the *Triangle.* This also appears to have several points

Fig. 451.

of condensation. Figs. 450 and 451 represent oval and elliptical nebulæ having a spiral structure.

Fig. 452.

THE MAGELLANIC CLOUDS.

384. *Situation and General Appearance of the Magellanic Clouds.* — The *Magellanic clouds* are two nebulous-looking bodies near the southern pole of the heavens, as shown in the right-hand portion of Fig. 452. In the appearance and brightness of their light they resemble portions of the Milky-Way.

The larger of these clouds is called the *Nubecula Major.* It is visible to the naked eye in strong moonlight, and covers a space about two

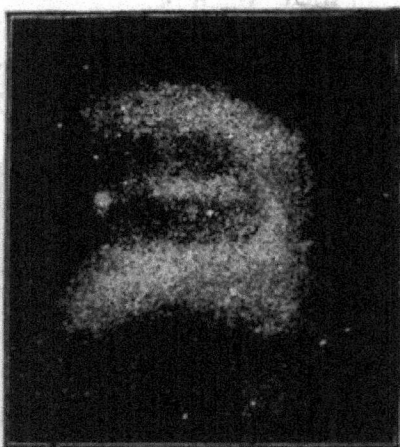

Fig. 453.

hundred times the surface of the moon. It is shown in Fig. 453. The smaller cloud is called the *Nubecula Minor.* It has only about a fourth the extent of the larger cloud, and is considerably less brilliant. It is visible to the naked eye, but it disappears in full moonlight. This cloud is shown in Fig. 454. The region around this cloud is singularly bare of stars; but the magnificent cluster of

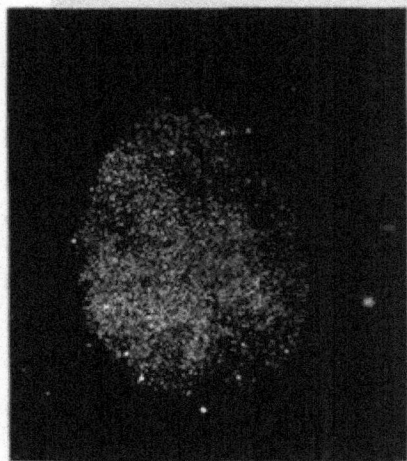

Fig. 454.

Toucan, already described (346), is near, and is shown a little to the right of the cloud in the figure.

385. *Structure of the Nubecula.* — Fig. 455 shows the structure of these clouds as revealed by a powerful tele-scope. The general ground of both consists of large tracts and patches of nebulosity in every stage of resolution, — from that which is irresolvable with eighteen inches of reflecting aperture, up to perfectly separated stars, like the Milky-Way and clustering groups. There are also nebulæ in abundance, both regular and irregular, globular clusters

Fig. 455.

in every state of condensation, and objects of a nebulous character quite peculiar, and unlike any thing in other regions of the heavens. In the area occupied by the *nubecula major* two hundred and seventy-eight nebulæ and clusters have been enumerated, besides fifty or sixty outliers, which ought certainly to be reckoned as its appendages, being about six and a half per square degree; which very far exceeds the average of any other part of the nebulous heavens. In the *nubecula minor* the concentration of such objects is less, though still very striking. The nebuculæ, then, combine, each within its own area, characters which in the rest of the heavens are no less strikingly separated; namely, those of the galactic and the nebular system. Globular clusters (except in one region of small extent) and nebulæ of regular elliptic forms are comparatively rare in the Milky-Way, and are found congregated in the greatest abundance in a part of the heavens the most remote possible from that circle; whereas in the nubeculæ they are indiscriminately mixed with the general starry ground, and with irregular though small nebulæ.

THE NEBULAR HYPOTHESIS.

386. *The Basis of the Nebular Hypothesis.* — We have seen that the planets all revolve around the sun from west to east in nearly the same plane, and that the sun rotates on his axis from west to east. The planets, so far as known, rotate on their axes from west to east; and all the moons, except those of Uranus and Neptune, revolve around their planets from west to east. These common features in the motion of the sun, moons, and planets, point to the conclusion that they are of a common origin.

387. *Kant's Hypothesis.* — Kant, the celebrated German philosopher, seems to have the best right to be regarded as the founder of the modern nebular hypothesis. His reasoning has been concisely stated thus: "Examining the solar system, we find two remarkable features presented to our consideration. One is, that six planets and nine satellites [the entire number then known] move around the sun in circles, not only in the same direction in which the sun himself revolves on his axis, but very nearly in the same plane. This common feature of the motion of so many bodies could not by any reasonable possibility have been a result of chance: we are therefore forced to believe that it must be the result of some common cause originally acting on all the planets.

"On the other hand, when we consider the spaces in which the planets move, we find them entirely void, or as good as void; for, if there is any matter in them, it is so rare as to be without effect on the planetary motions. There is, therefore, no material connection now existing between the planets through which they might have been forced to take up a common direction of motion. How, then, are we to reconcile this common motion with the absence of all material connection? The most natural way is to suppose that there was once some such connection, which brought about the uniformity of motion which we observe; that the materials of which the planets are formed once filled the whole space between them. There was no formation in this chaos, the formation of separate bodies by the mutual gravitation of parts of the mass being a later occurrence. But, naturally, some parts of the mass would be more dense than others, and would thus gather around them the rare matter which filled the intervening spaces. The larger collections thus formed would draw the smaller ones into them, and this process would continue until a few round bodies had taken the place of the original chaotic mass."

Kant, however, failed to account satisfactorily for the motion of the sun and planets. According to his system, all the bodies formed out of the original nebulous mass should have been drawn to a common centre so as to form one sun, instead of a system of revolving bodies like the solar system.

388. *Herschel's Hypothesis.* — The idea of the gradual transmutation of nebulæ into stars seems to have been suggested to Herschel, not by the study of the solar system, but by that of the nebulæ themselves. Many of these bodies he believed to be immense masses of phosphorescent vapor: and he conceived that these must be gradually condensing, each around its own centre, or around the parts where it is most dense, until it should become a star, or a cluster of stars. On classifying the nebulæ, it seemed to him that he could see this process going on before his eyes. There were the large, faint, diffused nebulæ, in which the condensation had hardly begun; the smaller but brighter ones, which had become so far condensed that the central parts would soon begin to form into stars; yet others, in which stars had actually begun to form; and, finally, star-clusters in which the condensation was complete. The spectroscopic revelations of the gaseous nature of

the true nebulæ tend to confirm the theory of Herschel, that these masses will all, at some time, condense into stars.

389. *Laplace's Hypothesis.* — Laplace was led to the nebular hypothesis by considering the remarkable uniformity in the direction of the rotation of the planets. Believing that this could not have been the result of chance, he sought to investigate its cause. This, he thought, could be nothing else than the atmosphere of the sun, which once extended so far out as to fill all the space now occupied by the planets. He begins with the sun, surrounded by this immense fiery atmosphere. Since the sum total of rotary motion now seen in the planetary system must have been there from the beginning, he conceives the immense vaporous mass forming the sun and his atmosphere to have had a slow rotation on its axis. As the intensely hot mass gradually cooled, it would contract towards the centre. As it contracted, its velocity of rotation would, by the laws of mechanics, constantly increase; so that a time would arrive, when, at the outer boundary of the mass, the centrifugal force due to the rotation would counterbalance the attractive force of the central mass. Then those outer portions would be left behind as a revolving ring, while the next inner portions would continue to contract until the centrifugal and attractive forces were again balanced, when a second ring would be left behind; and so on. Thus, instead of a continuous atmosphere, the sun would be surrounded by a series of concentric revolving rings of vapor. As these rings cooled, their denser materials would condense first; and thus the ring would be composed of a mixed mass, partly solid and partly vaporous, the quantity of solid matter constantly increasing, and that of vapor diminishing. If the ring were perfectly uniform, this condensation would take place equally all around it, and the ring would thus be broken up into a group of small planets, like the asteroids. But if, as would more likely be the case, some portions of the ring were much denser than others, the denser portions would gradually attract the rarer portions, until, instead of a ring, there would be a single mass composed of a nearly solid centre, surrounded by an immense atmosphere of fiery vapor. This condensation of the ring of vapor around a single point would not change the amount of rotary motion that had existed

in the ring. The planet with its atmosphere would therefore be in rotation; and would be, on a smaller scale, like the
original solar mass surrounded by its atmosphere. In the
same way that the latter formed itself first into rings, which
afterwards condensed into planets, so the planetary atmospheres, if sufficiently extensive, would form themselves into
rings, which would condense into satellites. In the case of
Saturn, however, one of the rings was so uniform throughout,
that there was no denser portion to attract the rest around it:
and thus the ring of Saturn retained its annular form.

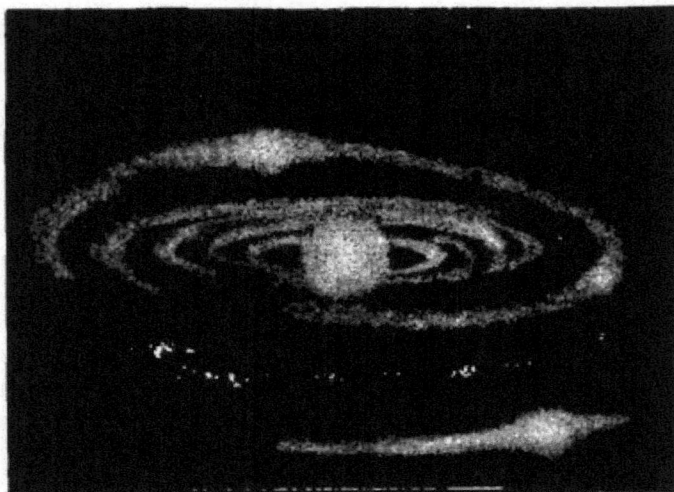

Fig. 456.

Such is the celebrated nebular hypothesis of Laplace. It
starts, not with a purely nebulous mass, but with the sun, surrounded by an immense atmosphere, out of which the planets
were formed by gradual condensation. Fig. 456 represents
the condensing mass according to this theory.

390. *The Modern Nebular Hypothesis.* — According to the
nebular hypothesis as held at the present time, the sun, planets, and meteoroids originated from a purely nebulous mass.
This nebula first condensed into a nebulous star, the star being
the sun, and its surrounding nebulosity being the fiery atmosphere of Laplace. The original nebula must have been put
into rotation at the beginning. As it contracted and became

condensed through the loss of heat by radiation into space, and under the combined attraction of gravity, cohesion, and affinity, its speed of rotation increased; and the nebulous envelop became, by the centrifugal force, flattened into a thin disk, which finally broke up into rings, out of which were formed the planets and their moons. According to Laplace, the rings which were condensed into the planets were thrown off in succession from the equatorial region of the condensing nebula; and so the outer planets would be the older. According to the more modern idea, the nebulous mass was first flattened into a disk, and subsequently broken up into rings, in such a way that there would be no marked difference in the ages of the planets. The sun represents the central portion of the original nebula, and the comets and meteoroids its outlying portion. At the sun the condensation is still going on, and the meteoroids appear to be still gradually drawn in to the sun and planets.

The whole store of energy with which the original solar nebula was endowed existed in it in the potential form. By the condensation and contraction this energy was gradually transformed into the kinetic energy of molar motion and of heat; and the heat became gradually dissipated by radiation into space. This transformation of potential energy into heat is still going on at the sun, the centre of the condensing mass, by the condensation of the sun itself, and by the impact of meteors as they fall into it.

It has been calculated, that, by the shrinking of the sun to the density of the earth, the transformation of potential energy into heat would generate enough heat to maintain the sun's supply, at the present rate of dissipation, for seventeen million years. A shrinkage of the sun which would generate all the heat he has poured into space since the invention of the telescope could not be detected by the most powerful instruments yet constructed.

The least velocity with which a meteoroid could strike the sun would be two hundred and eighty miles a second; and it is easy to calculate how much heat would be generated by the collision. It has been shown, that, were enough meteoroids to fall into the sun to develop its heat, they would not increase his mass appreciably during a period of two thousand years.

The sun's heat is undoubtedly developed by contraction and the fall of meteoroids; that is to say, by the transformation of the potential energy of the original nebula into heat.

It must be borne in mind that the nebular hypothesis is simply a supposition as to the way in which the present solar system may have been developed from a nebula endowed with a motion of rotation and with certain tendencies to condensation. Of course nothing could have been developed out of the nebula, the germs of which had not been originally implanted in it by the Creator.

IV. THE STRUCTURE OF THE STELLAR UNIVERSE.

391. *Sir William Herschel's View.* — Sir William Herschel assumed that the stars are distributed with tolerable uniformity throughout the space occupied by our stellar system. He

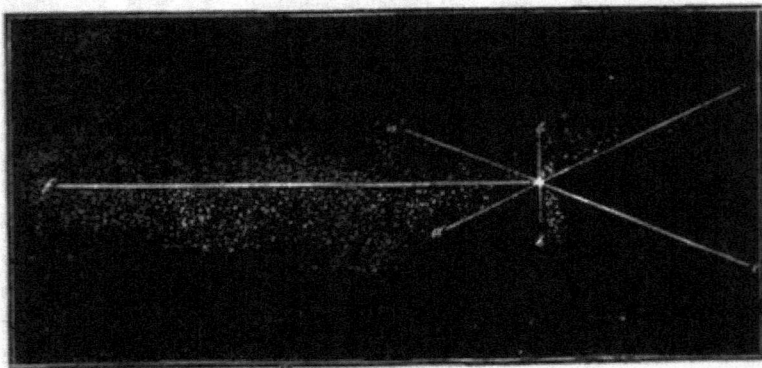

Fig. 457.

accounted for the increase in the number of stars in the field of view as he approached the plane of the Milky-Way, not by the supposition that the stars are really closer together in and about this plane, but by the supposition that our stellar system is in the form of a flat disk cloven at one side, and with our sun near its centre. A section of this disk is shown in Fig. 457.

An observer near *S*, with his telescope pointed in the direction of *Sb*, would see comparatively few stars within the field of view, because looking through a comparatively thin stratum of stars. With his telescope pointed in the direction *Sa*, he would see many more stars within his field of view, even though the stars were really no nearer together, because he would be looking through a thicker stratum of stars. As he directed his telescope more and more nearly in the direction *Sf*, he would be looking through a thicker and thicker stratum of stars, and hence he would see a greater and greater number of them in the field of view, though they were everywhere in the disk distributed at uniform distances. He assumed, also, that the stars are all tolerably

uniform in size, and that certain stars appear smaller than others, only because they are farther off. He supposed the faint stars of the Milky-Way to be merely the most distant stars of the stellar disk; that they are really as large as the other stars, but appear small owing to their great distance. The disk was assumed to be cloven on

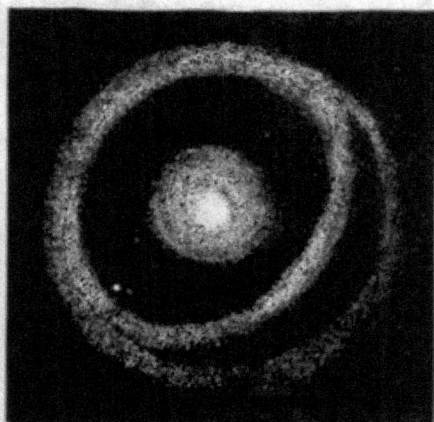

Fig. 458.

one side, to account for the division of the Milky-Way through nearly half of its course. This theory of the structure of the stellar universe is often referred to as the *cloven disk* theory.

392. *The Cloven Ring Theory.* — According to Mädler, the stars of the Milky-Way are entirely separated from the other stars of our system, belonging to an outlying ring, or system of rings. To account for the division of the Milky-Way, the ring is supposed to be cloven on one side: hence this theory is often referred to as the *cloven ring* theory. According to this hypothesis, the stellar system viewed from without would present an appearance somewhat like that in Fig. 458. The outlying ring cloven on one side would represent the stars

of the Milky-Way; and the luminous mass at the centre, the
remaining stars of the system.

393. *Proctor's View.*— According to Proctor, the Milky-
Way is composed of an irregular spiral stream of minute stars
lying in and among the larger stars of our system, as represented in Fig. 459. The spiral stream is shown in the inner

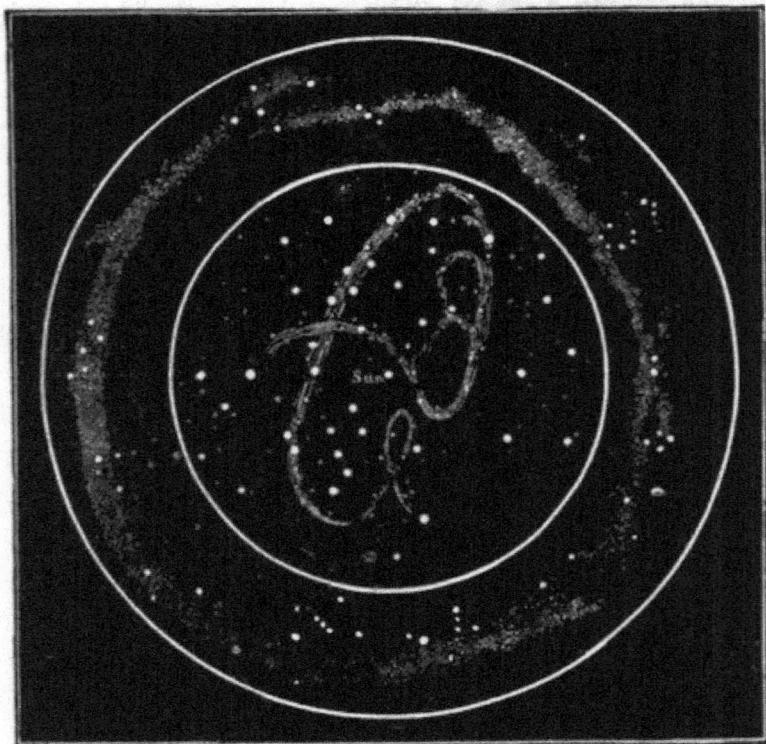

Fig. 459.

circle as it really exists among the stars, and in the outer
circle as it is seen projected upon the sky. According to this
view, the stars of the Milky-Way appear faint, not because
they are distant, but because they are really small.

394. *Newcomb's View.*— According to Newcomb, the stars
of our system are all situated in a comparatively thin zone
lying in the plane of the Milky-Way, while there is a zone
of nebulæ lying on each side of the stellar zone. He believes

that so much is certain with reference to the structure of our stellar universe: but he considers that we are as yet compara-

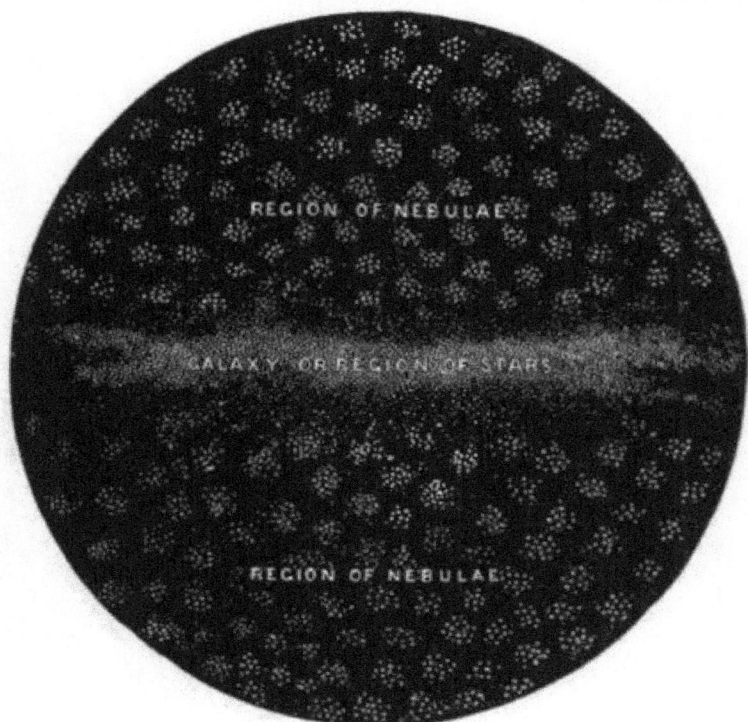

Fig. 460.

tively ignorant of the internal structure of either the stellar or the nebular zones. The structure of the stellar universe, according to this view, is shown in Fig. 460.

INDEX.

www.ingramcontent.com/pod-product-compliance
Lightning Source LLC
Chambersburg PA
CBHW031349290326
41932CB00044B/726